W9-BKA-789

RETIRE SECURE

for **Parents** *of a* **Child** *with a* **Disability**

James Lange
CPA/Attorney

Julieanne E. Steinbacher, Esq. CELA/LLM

Deborah L. McFadden,
Former U.S. Commissioner of Disabilities

Foreword by Burton Malkiel
Author, *A Random Walk Down Wall Street*

ISBN: 978-1-7354698-1-2

Copyright ©2024 James Lange

All rights reserved. No part of this publication may be reproduced, distributed, or transmitted in any form or by any means, including photocopying, recording, or other electronic or mechanical methods, without the prior written permission of the author.

Limit of Liability/Disclaimer of Warranty: James Lange, Lange Financial Group, LLC, Lange Legal Group, LLC, Lange Accounting Group, LLC and/or Lange Life Care, LLC do not have any affiliation with the funds mentioned or described in the book.

Material provided in this book is general in nature and does not, nor is it intended as a rendering of formal legal or investment advice. This book does not establish an attorney/client relationship. James Lange, Lange Financial Group, LLC, Lange Legal Group, LLC, Lange Accounting Group, LLC and/or Lange Life Care, LLC is not responsible for the results obtained from using the contents, nor any errors or omissions, nor does James Lange, Lange Financial Group, LLC, Lange Legal Group, LLC, Lange Accounting Group, LLC and/or Lange Life Care, LLC guarantee that all the information is current and accurate. Do not act upon information contained herein without a thorough evaluation of the facts relating to your specific circumstances and/or getting advice from the appropriate financial professional or team of professionals including an estate attorney.

Retire Secure for Parents of a Child with a Disability contains tax principles based on tax-law at the time of finishing the manuscript as well as the author's speculation on how some tax laws could change in the future. We went to press in October 2023 when 2024 information was not yet known. Tax laws will change, and the content of this book will become dated. Many of the principles will still apply, but specific numbers and charts, etc. will become outdated. In addition, some of the general recommendations might change as a result of future tax laws. Most likely, however, the principles will still apply. For example, if the maximum contribution to a Roth IRA or Roth 403(b) retirement plan is increased, the concept of maximize your Roth IRA and Roth retirement plan will still likely apply.

All investing involves risk, including the potential for loss of principal. There is never any guarantee extended that any investment plan or strategies discussed will be successful. Readers should consult with an attorney, CPA and/or financial advisor to get the best results. You should consult with a professional where appropriate. Neither the publisher nor the author nor Lange Financial Group, LLC, Lange Legal Group, LLC, Lange Accounting Group, LLC and/or Lange Life Care, LLC shall be liable for any loss of profit or any other commercial damages, including but not limited to special, incidental, consequential, or other damages. There is no solicitation being made for legal services by James Lange nor by Lange Legal Services, LLC.

Lange Accounting Group CPAs offer guidance on retirement plan distribution strategies, tax reduction, Roth IRA conversions, saving and spending strategies, optimized Social Security strategies and gifting plans. Asset location, asset allocation and low-cost enhanced index funds are provided by the investment firms with whom Lange Financial Group is affiliated. Life insurance can be offered by member of Lange Life Care for those interested. In each of these instances, these services are provided by employees in their capacity as CPAs or Registered Investment Advisors and are not legal services. The protection of the attorney-client relationship does not exist with respect to the accounting, insurance, and asset management services.

Cartoons by Randy Bish and Michael McParlane
Cover photo of Jim, Erica, and Cindy Lange by George Lange, George Lange Studio

Additional Disclaimer Regarding Lange Financial Group, LLC

Lange Financial Group, LLC is a registered investment advisory firm registered with the Commonwealth of Pennsylvania Department of banking, Harrisburg, Pennsylvania. In addition, the firm is registered as a registered investment advisory firm in the states of Arizona, Florida, New York, Ohio, Texas, and Virginia.

Lange Financial Group, LLC may not provide investment advisory services to any residents of states in which the firm does not maintain an investment advisory registration. This does not in any way imply that Lange Financial Group is failing to preserve its rights under the respective states' de minimus rule.

The presence of this book shall not in any direct or indirect fashion, be construed or interpreted to suggest that the firm is offering to sell or soliciting to provide investment advisory services to residents of any state or states in which the firm is not maintaining an investment advisory registration.

Again, Lange Financial Group preserves all rights under each state's de minimus rule but wishes to emphasize that it is not directly or indirectly soliciting investment advisory clients in states where it has no legal right to do so.

Praise for:

Retire Secure for Parents of a Child with a Disability

Jim's previous book, *Retire Secure for Professors and TIAA Participants*, published in October 2023, swiftly rose to #1 on Amazon in the categories of personal taxes and retirement planning. Within days it amassed 60 glowing reviews from grateful readers. This book adapts many of that book's acclaimed methods for accumulating and distributing retirement assets, estate planning, and multiple cutting-edge Roth IRA conversion strategies for parents of a child with a disability. Plus much more.

" As a world-champion wheelchair racer, I have made it my mission to advocate for children with a disability. *Retire Secure for Parents of a Child with a Disability should become required reading for all parents of children with disabilities.* It combines multiple strategies from three experts in the field (including my mother, Deborah McFadden). You couldn't find better coaches anywhere to help you provide for your child's long-term financial security. Take action. Win your race. And put your fears and anxieties on the sideline."

> — **Tatyana McFadden**,
> Winner of 20 Paralympic medals including eight gold medals
> and 24 World Major Marathon Wins

" Combining warmth and compassion with functional hard-headed advice, the dream team of Jim Lange, Deborah McFadden, and Julieanne Steinbacher have provided families of children with disabilities with the guidance they need to achieve financial security." (*From the Foreword*)

> — **Burton G. Malkiel**,
> Professor of Economics, **Princeton University** and Author,
> *A Random Walk Down Wall Street*, 13th ed., 2023

"More than three million children under the age of 18 in the United States have a disability. *Retire Secure for Parents of a Child with a Disability* provides a clear roadmap for their parents to ensure these children's financial futures."

> — **Jan Cullinane**,
> Author, *The New Retirement: The Ultimate Guide
> to the Rest of Your Life*, 3rd edition (Wiley 2022)

"The authors have been there and done that when it comes to serious financial planning for a disabled child. Their professional experience combined with personal experience with the subject can't be beat."

> — **James M. Dahle, MD**,
> Founder of *The White Coat Investor*

"As a consultant for families at **AgingParents.com**, I hear of the worries of older parents about their disabled adult children. There is significant fear that the disabled family member will be neglected or receive poor care after the parents pass. James Lange's book offers wise insight into how to do excellent estate planning to maximize a child's inheritance and pass on wealth without endangering the disabled person's access to public benefits. Lange's book eliminates dread and relieves the worries of countless older parents with adult children who need protection."

> — **Carolyn L. Rosenblatt**, RN, Attorney

"*Retire Secure for Parents of a Child with a Disability* combines the powerhouse strategies of three experts. It should be required reading for any parent who worries about the long-term financial security of their child with a disability. James Lange, CPA/Attorney specializes in cutting edge retirement and Roth IRA tax strategies. Julieanne Steinbacher, Esq., founding shareholder of an elder care and special needs law firm has worked on estate plans for hundreds of parents of children with disabilities. Deborah McFadden, who was instrumental in writing the Americans with Disabilities Act, is an expert on qualifying children for SSI and SSDI. The strategies in this book can help secure your child's financial future long after you're gone. Anxieties resolved; sleep restored."

> — **Dr. Linda Babcock**, James M. Walton
> Professor of Economics, Carnegie Mellon University,
> and Author, *Women Don't Ask* (Princeton University Press)

"Nationally recognized IRA expert Jim Lange, CPA/Attorney has harnessed his significant expertise and practical experience to develop cutting-edge retirement and estate planning recommendations for parents who have a child with a disability. It is personal to Jim. He and his wife have a daughter with a disability. Their fears for her long-term financial security drove him to find solutions. His family's story will resonate with other parents of children with disabilities. Never before have so many critical long-term planning strategies for parents of children with disabilities been presented and detailed in one place." (*From the Introduction*)

> — **Larry Swedroe**, Chief Research Officer, **Buckingham Strategic Wealth**
> and Prolific Financial Author

"*Retire Secure for Parents of a Child with a Disability* by James Lange with Julieanne Steinbacher and Deborah McFadden is an incredible resource with common sense information and insightful planning strategies that can easily be put into practice. Jim, Julie, and Deborah address the unique issues associated with planning for the future of a disabled adult with their three-step plan. Their wisdom is extraordinarily helpful and is a must for parents of a child with a disability."

> — **Robert S. Keebler,**
> CPA/PFS, MST, AEP (Distinguished), **Keebler & Associates, LLP**

Praise for:
Our Special Advisory Report for Parents of a Child with a Disability
https://DisabledChildPlanning.com

"Having a severely autistic child in our extended family, I personally know the frustrations, hopelessness, and depression you may be feeling. Here by noted experts on the subject is important accurate and objective information and more importantly insight, and wisdom."

> — **Steve Leimberg,**
> Co-Author of *Tools and Techniques for the Modern Family*

Other Books in the *Retire Secure* Series

"In *Retire Secure!*, CPA and estate planning attorney Jim Lange provides a road map for tax-efficient retirement and estate planning. This is an invaluable resource for investors and planners alike."

> — **Charles R. Schwab,**
> Chairman and Founder, The Charles Schwab Corporation

"Think of *Retire Secure!* As a GPS for your money. You may know where you are and where you want to go, but you don't know how to get there. Jim offers the best routes."

> — **Larry King,**
> (from the Foreword of *Retire Secure!*), **Larry King Now**

"*Retire Secure! Second Edition* covers two areas particularly well—Roth IRA conversions and estate planning for IRA owners."

> — **Jane Bryant Quinn**,
> *Newsweek* and **Bloomerg.com**

"The fear of running out of money has grown from a lingering, nagging concern to widespread dread. Readers need long-term effective tax-savvy strategies. I highly recommend that you read *Retire Secure!* "

> — **Ed Slott**,
> (from the Introduction to *Retire Secure!*), America's IRA Expert, Speaker, and Author of *Stay Rich for Life*

" Jim Lange's *Retire Secure for Professors and TIAA Participants* covers the practical aspects of investments that really matter to us: spending and saving, tax efficiency, charitable and family giving, and estate planning. Along the way he examines taxable and retirement accounts, insurance, and annuities, often using TIAA, CREF, and IRAs, that professors are already familiar with. Although there is no magic to investing, there are lots of things we can do to help meet our goals and make our retirement more secure."

> — **Roger G. Ibbotson**,
> Professor in Practice Emeritus, **Yale University** and Author of many books including *Stocks, Bonds, Bills and Inflation Yearbooks*

Table of Contents

Foreword

Retire Secure for Parents of a Child with a Disability
by Burton G. Malkiel*
Professor Emeritus of Economics, Princeton University

Combining warmth and compassion with functional hard-headed advice, the dream team of Jim Lange, Deborah McFadden, and Julieanne Steinbacher have provided families of children with disabilities with the guidance they need to achieve financial security.

Investment and tax *"experts"* have always been active in offering their services, but their advice has often been designed to maximize their fees rather than to optimize results for their clients. Conflicted and misleading information existed long before the Internet, but social media has vastly increased the scale, severity, and impact of misinformation as digital platforms have extended their reach and become more central to our lives.

Parents of a child with a disability often don't know where to turn to protect their child. But how does one find a trusted source? As a retired college professor, let me assure you that if you follow the sound advice provided by Jim Lange in this book, you will be sure to know that you are taking the right financial steps to increase your and your child's financial security. This book provides exactly the information you can trust.

In my own publications designed for a wide audience, I have tried to distill decades of historical evidence on financial markets to facilitate practical, evidence-based investment decisions. These include broad diversification to contain risk, strategies to minimize costs, and the use of index funds as the primary investment vehicles. Jim Lange builds on these investment concepts to provide serviceable strategies for optimal retirement planning and minimization of taxes. He and fellow author Julieanne Steinbacher also provide advice on the best way to pass wealth on to your disabled child in a tax-advantaged manner that preserves government benefits.

Deborah McFadden, former Commissioner of Disabilities, provides critical strategies to help you qualify your child for SSI and/or SSDI.

---

* Author of *A Random Walk Down Wall Street*, 13th Edition, 2023. *Note: prior editions sold 1.5 million copies.* Professor Emeritus of Economics, Princeton University.

Some of the most useful material in the book concerns Roth IRA conversions. I have not seen a better discussion of the advantages and potential pitfalls of converting your IRA into a Roth. In general, there can be enormous value in conversions for both retirement plan owners and their heirs, especially when you are leaving money to your child with a disability, but the book is very clear on the caution such decisions deserve.

There are many more gems in this book. Guidance is given on charitable giving, family gifting, life insurance, and estate planning strategies. The practical and tested advice that is offered will serve parents of a child with a disability extremely well. No one does it better and explains how to best provide for a child with a disability more clearly than Jim Lange, Deborah McFadden and Julieanne Steinbacher.

Introduction

Retire Secure for Parents of a Child with a Disability
by Larry Swedroe

Author, and Director of Research, Buckingham Strategic Wealth

Just imagine the relief you would feel if you were confident that you had a secure long-term financial plan for you and your child. You could knock out at least one huge area of anxiety. But as a person who believes in science, math, and peer-reviewed materials, where do you go to get information you know you can trust? This book offers parents of a child with a disability a roadmap to help secure both your and your child's financial security.

Jim Lange put together a dream team of authors in the disability area. Deborah McFadden is an expert in qualifying people with disabilities for SSI and SSDI. Qualifying a child for SSI or SSDI is like winning the golden ticket. Julieanne Steinbacher is an expert estate attorney who writes and practices in the disability community. Jim is the number-crunching CPA and attorney who figured out the optimal financial plan for his daughter who has a disability. The same action plan that Jim applied for his daughter will likely be applicable for your family.

1. Qualifying the child for SSI or SSDI

2. Getting the estate planning right

3. Getting IRA planning, including Roth IRA conversion planning, right. A bonus is getting other tax-free vehicles like an ABLE account right.

With the realization that there is such a huge need for this information and the stakes are so high, it became his mission to share his solution—and the wisdom of Deborah and Julieanne—with the entire community of parents of children with disabilities.

A good and trusted source is in your hands. Reading this book and acting on the recommendations has the potential to change your family's financial future. If you have doubts about the value of the information, or the credibility of the source, read the testimonials from some of the top trusted experts in the field.

One of Jim's strengths is describing the pros and cons of any strategy. Plus, Jim is a good storyteller, and it elevates this book's readability on topics that can seem a bit dry, but important.

The book is filled with examples illustrated through stories drawn from his experience, and the experiences of his co-authors. Readers will quickly identify elements that resonate with their own experiences and situations.

Jim has probably done more research—quantitative and qualitative—on Roth IRA conversions than the vast majority of professionals in the field. He was a Roth IRA expert with peer-reviewed articles and a dedicated Roth IRA book even before his daughter's disability was diagnosed. Jim's knowledge of Roth IRAs, a myriad of retirement plans, the SECURE Act, and beneficiary designations of retirement plans leads to groundbreaking advice and recommendations for families facing the exceptional challenges of providing for a child with a disability. Characteristically, Jim and his team of number-crunching CPAs run the numbers and show you how Roth IRA conversions can protect you, your spouse, and your child with a disability. Though Jim sees enormous value in Roth IRA conversions, he approaches them with the caution they deserve. They are only one part of the equation.

Julieanne has over 20 years of experience drafting special needs planning documents for families and administering estates. She is also the founder and president of Estate & Long-Term Care Planning, an organization that educates estate attorneys from across the nation in areas of law and best practices.

Deborah was instrumental in writing the Americans with Disabilities Act and was appointed by President George H.W. Bush as U.S. Commissioner of Disabilities, a position she held from 1989 through 1993. She is the mother of two USA Paralympic athletes. Tatyana is one of, if not the most honored and recognized track and marathon athletes with a disability in the world. Hannah, another of Deborah's daughters, is ranked third in the world in rock climbing for an athlete with a disability.

The authors' credentials speak volumes about their dedication and expertise.

There are many more important topics in this book—guidance on charitable giving, family gifting, life insurance, and more. All three authors put their clients' best interests first, and for someone looking for reputable advice and recommendations, look no further.

The practical advice in this book makes it required reading for parents of a child with a disability. Tens or hundreds of thousands of dollars or even over a million dollars could hang in the balance for you and your family. It would be wise for anyone who has a child with a disability to take the authors' recommendations to heart and, most importantly, to take action.

How to Read this Book

This book reflects my most heartfelt wishes that all parents and guardians of children with disabilities will learn about and use these strategies to dramatically improve the long-term financial security of themselves and their children.

Everyone who reads this book will be approaching this with different needs. While the ideas in the book build on and reinforce each other, each chapter can be read on its own. We don't expect or for that matter even recommend that you read every page of this book unless you have a serious sleep problem. Instead, we would encourage you to look at the detailed Table of Contents (TOC) and read the chapters or even portions of each chapter that grab your attention. We have spent many hours fine tuning the TOC, and we think you will find it an excellent starting point to search for a topic or topics of interest.

The key to getting value from this book is to scan the TOC.

Obviously, you will benefit greatly if you read all sections of the book that apply to your situation, and then, either on your own or with some help, act on some of the appropriate recommendations for you and your family.

Be warned, however, that many important decisions are multi-faceted and sometimes an incomplete reading or interpretation of a particular point may lead you to an action that you would not take with a full understanding of the topic.

The TOC does a great job of helping you find the information you want. We include many internal pointers to chapters that expand on a particular topic that we mention in passing so you can find all the information you need. That said, here are a few tips that could also save you time and reduce frustration.

Chapter 1: The Bedrock Principles of Retirement and Estate Planning presents an overview of important concepts and a summary of the best order to accumulate money for retirement and the best order to spend money once you are retired. This chapter summarizes much of the content in the book.

If you want to jump into the chapters that specifically address the special concerns of parents of children with disabilities, feel free to skip to the middle of this book, where you'll find:

Chapter 11: Three Critical Steps to Protect Your Child's Financial Security After You Are Gone...and More discusses the three steps Cindy and I have taken to ensure our daughter Erica will be $1.89 million better off than if we had not taken these pro-active steps. Here I cover the incredible benefits of maximizing your Roth retirement accounts so that your child will have plenty of money after you are gone.

Chapter 12: How to Win the Golden Ticket of SSI or SSDI Approval is written by Deborah McFadden, an internationally known expert in the disability arena. In this chapter, she reveals the steps she uses to quickly and reliably get young adults with disabilities approved for SSI and SSDI benefits. Winning this "Golden Ticket" opens the door for many benefits, including the ability to stretch payments from an Inherited IRA/Roth IRA over your child's lifetime. This "stretch" benefit—which is huge—is no longer available to most children who inherit a retirement account because of the horribly misnamed SECURE Act.

Chapter 13: Special Needs Trusts and Legal Considerations for Children with Disabilities is authored by me and Julieanne E. Steinbacher, an attorney with special expertise in estate planning and legal guidance for parents of children with disabilities. Here we explain what Special Needs Trusts are, and how they can be used to supplement income for your child without jeopardizing means-tested government benefits. Julieanne also discusses important considerations for planning for your child's care after your death.

Chapter 14: Tax-Free Savings Under the ABLE Act is co-authored by attorneys John Montoya and Julieanne E. Steinbacher and describes ABLE accounts and how they can be used as a savings vehicle for individuals with disabilities. You'll learn about eligibility requirements, what the funds can be used for, the limitations on annual contributions, and how best to coordinate an ABLE Account with a Special Needs Trust.

Chapters 11-14 will provide you with the framework of crucial strategies that will help you provide a more abundant and secure future for your child with a disability. But to fully execute these strategies, you'll also need to understand the basics of saving for your retirement, which are the topics of Chapters 1-10. The remainder of the book, Chapters 15-27, covers specialized topics related to retirement, such as estate planning, Roth conversions, smart ways to spend money in retirement, charitable giving, life insurance, inflation, and the financial benefits of getting married.

We highly recommend that as a minimum you read Chapters 1 and 11-14 in addition to any of the chapters that interest you.

Virtually every chapter contains proof that my recommendations have been mathematically tested and proven worthy. You may want to skip over portions of the proof and just read the advice. Sometimes, when I am looking for information or advice, I want to scream, "Don't tell me *why*, just tell me *what* to do." If you feel similarly, or you find yourself moving in that direction after realizing there is enormous support for virtually every recommendation I make, the book's sidebars and summaries at the end of the chapters will serve you well.

In addition, we have included many "war stories" to illustrate a concept. These are true stories that have been modified for confidentiality. We know some readers like reading the stories more than the text describing the concepts and the math because it is more interesting and fun. For many of us, reading these war stories is the best way to learn and remember some of the concepts. Others will prefer to skip the stories. We have tried to graphically distinguish the concepts and math from the stories to make it easier for you to read what you like.

In addition to the "war stories," I have tried to spice up the content by including occasional sarcastic comments, at least one witty quote per chapter, and perhaps the most fun, the cartoons. I hope you enjoy them.

I would also encourage you to note separately any thoughts or concepts that you think might be important to your own planning. Then, either on your own or with the help of the appropriate financial professional, take action to improve your and your family's financial position.

If you are a financial professional, I encourage you to make a list of all your clients who have children with disabilities, or for that matter all your clients who have substantial IRAs and retirement plans, even before you begin reading the book. As you read and reflect on the various strategies and hypothetical scenarios, you will likely get ideas for ways to personalize those strategies for specific clients. Then you can review the client files for the clients you identified during your reading to get an even better idea of whether those strategies might be beneficial for them. After that, you can schedule meetings with the clients for whom the strategies may be appropriate to discuss incorporating them into their retirement and estate plans.

I sincerely hope this book inspires you to take action on your retirement planning and that you will derive enormous benefits from this information. If you are interested in additional information, updates, and other valuable information, please go to **https://DisabledChildPlanning.com/freestuff**. If you're interested in the services of any of the authors, please see page xxxvii.

We hope you find value and take action to ensure you and your child has the financial resources he or she will need to live the best life possible!

Respectfully submitted,

James Lange
CPA/Attorney

Acknowledgments
By James Lange, CPA/Attorney

Although three authors, Deborah McFadden, Julieanne Steinbacher and Jim Lange are featured on the cover, the truth is that this book is the product of a monumental team effort. The authors and the readers who find value in these pages are indebted to a great team of the best CPAs, estate attorneys, and other professionals anyone could possibly hope to work with.

The starting point for my portion of this book was a book that I wrote and published this year, *Retire Secure for Professors and TIAA Participants*. That book is my magnum opus; by far the best and most comprehensive book I have ever written for *all* IRA and retirement plan owners—despite the title's specificity. But it could not fully address the issues and concerns facing another set of readers about whom I and my co-authors care deeply. In this book, we revisit much of that previously published content but we also zero in on the unique and challenging financial challenges facing families who have a child with a disability.

Included below are people that not only contributed to this book, but also contributed to *Retire Secure for Professors and TIAA Participants*.

The Team of CPA Contributors

Jennifer Hall, CPA, CMA, CFP, CRPC, helped by providing many important ideas as well as copy editing. Jen is a real tax nerd, she really cares, and loves helping parents of a child with a disability. She added a lot of ideas acquired through a lifetime in the field and her extensive financial education. She also updated many of the calculations that Steve Kohman made for prior editions of *Retire Secure!* as well as working on new calculations and figures. She is one of our full-time number crunching CPAs who works with parents of a child with a disability, and she was able to bring that experience to her recommendations.

Liz Farr, CPA and writer, made extremely valuable contributions and edits. It is rare to find a CPA who can understand these concepts, let alone write articulately about them. Liz updated many of the seven-year-old chapters of the third edition of *Retire Secure!* which was technically quite difficult. She also refocused a lot of the content of *Retire Secure for Professors and TIAA Participants* to this book.

Dominic Bonaccorsi, CPA wrote Chapter 22 and also reviewed the book for technical accuracy. He is another of our number crunching CPAs who works with parents of a child with a disability and was able to bring that experience to his contributions.

Steve Kohman, CPA, CSRP, CSEP and our veteran number cruncher wrote some of the Roth IRA conversion chapters and the qualified charitable distribution chapter. Steve has mentored and trained our in-house CPAs in the methods of our comprehensive quantitative analysis, which is among the reasons they are so qualified.

Shirl Trefelner, CPA, CSRP made major contributions to the quantitative analysis by preparing some of the original graphs and charts in earlier versions of *Retire Secure!*

The Team of Estate Planning Attorney Contributors

Matt Schwartz, Esq. worked through some of the fine legal points of the law with me and reviewed *Retire Secure for Professors and TIAA Participants* for technical accuracy.

John Montoya, Esq. helped by updating the Inherited IRA minimum distribution chapter (which was a bear) as well as researching and adding valuable contributions to the section on beneficiaries with a disability. He also made contributions to the chapter regarding the ABLE Act.

Karen Mathias, Esq. has provided excellent analysis on ways to optimize Social Security and on the advantages of combining Social Security strategies with Roth IRA conversions.

Megan Ingram, who works with Julie Steinbacher, made important contributions to some of the legal portions of this book.

The Rest of the Team

Cynthia Nelson, our senior editor for 26 years, is not only a great technical editor but she is also committed to clearly communicating the ideas, advice, and recommendations that come from our talented team. She strives to use language that is respectful to our readers. She also allows my unique personality (and humor, where appropriate) to express itself in my voice—sometimes even against her better judgment! The book is better organized and easier to read in large part to her valuable editing.

Sandy Proto, our Project Manager, runs the show. She was largely responsible for doing much of the behind-the-scenes work to make the book a success. There are few tasks Sandy can't take on: editing, organizing, prodding when progress stalls, and brainstorming solutions when challenges arise.

Erika Hubbard edited and contributed to the content of several sections of the book and has made major marketing contributions to all of my recent books.

Eric Emerson is not only our digital marketing expert extraordinaire but is a highly skilled marketer who has helped get the word out about both new books and many of my earlier books.

Chris Molé did the layout for this book. She did a great job on a tight timeline and was a joy to work with, making many last-minute changes without complaint.

Special thanks go to **Randy Bish** and **Michael McParlane** for the cartoons throughout the book.

Other team members, though not directly involved with the book, allowed me and other team members the luxury of working on the book, and frankly we would not have a company without them. Special thanks to **Mary Naeser,** our controller, **Erin Einwag,** our client coordinator, **Donna Master,** our bookkeeper, **Justin Pape,** our facilities coordinator, **Jeremy Bucklew,** one of our CPAs and **Alice Davis** for all your contributions.

Susan Abrams of **Abrams Design,** who has also been working with us for over 32 years, designed Jim's magnum opus, *Retire Secure for Professors and TIAA Participants,* including its cover. The layout of this book is based on her work. She also designed the charts and graphs in this book.

Finally, though many of the team members mentioned above have been with me for almost 20 years, **Sandy Proto,** Project Manager, and **Steve Kohman, CPA, CSRP, CSEP** have been working with me for close to 30 years.

To matters of the heart, a special thanks goes to my wife of 30 years and best friend, **Cindy Lange.** Cindy also spent roughly the last three months before going to press working nearly full time on edits and improvements to the book.

Special thanks also go my daughter, **Erica Lange.** Erica gave me permission to share that she has a disability and how we provided for her. She did this in the hope that this book will help readers better provide for their children with a disability. This book would never have happened without Cindy's and Erica's love and support.

Finally, a special thanks to one of, if not the most popular athlete in the world with a disability, **Tatyana McFadden.** Tatyana has contributed so much to the special needs community and has allowed us to share her story in this book. She is an inspiration to millions.

Thank you all.

Special Note from the Author Regarding Client Confidentiality

I am the son of a journalism professor who had high journalistic integrity. She was a great fan of Walter Cronkite and before that Ed Murrow. I would love to say that all the client stories I include in the book are completely accurate. Unfortunately, if I reported actual client situations, it would be a violation of confidentiality which I place even above journalistic integrity. Therefore, though the stories included were all inspired by actual events, I attempted to change the details enough to make them unidentifiable from the actual clients and events that inspired the stories.

Additional Free Video, Free Reports, and Information

We highly recommend you take advantage of our offers for the valuable resources listed below:

- The synopsis of the book
- The video, *Taming Parents Fears for their Child with a Disability* by James Lange
- Video footage or transcript of James Lange interviewing Jack Bogel and Burton Malkiel
- Other valuable reports and videos from James Lange, Julieanne Steinbacher and Deborah McFadden

To access your free information, please go to **https://DisabledChildPlanning.com/freestuff** and download any or all of the resources listed above.

For Synopsis, Videos & More

Quickly Locate Information in the Book about the Authors' Services

James Lange CPA/Attorney: If you are interested in working with Jim and his team for either a Financial Masterplan or a Financial Masterplan and an assets-under-management arrangement, please see page 449.

Julieanne Steinbacher, Esq., LLM: If you are interested in working with Julieanne for estate planning services (PA residents only) and/or appealing SSI and SSDI cases (anywhere in the country) please see page 459.

Deborah McFadden: If you are interested in receiving Deborah's help with applying for your child's SSI or SSDI benefits, please see page 465.

Are You Are Interested in Working with One or More of the Authors?

We anticipate a huge influx of work in response to our book. All three of us have a limited capacity for new clients. If you want to work with any of us, we recommend you contact us sooner rather than later. We all want to help and genuinely look forward to hearing from you.

SECURE Act 2.0

As we go to press, SECURE Act 2.0 has passed. The 90 provisions included in the bill provide incentives for both employees and employers.

In March, the House of Representatives passed a version of the bill, known as the SECURE Act 2.0. The Senate Finance Committee proposed a more expansive version later in 2022, known as the EARN Act. While neither bill passed, SECURE 2.0 reflects what was agreed to by both parties in December 2022.

The bi-partisan goal of the bill was to increase retirement savings through employer-sponsored plans and IRAs.

There are notable changes included in SECURE Act 2.0 which encompasses 4,100 pages. Below is a snapshot of the "key" highlights that may impact your future retirement. *Note:* We have not included all the provisions of the bill—rather, we only included those provisions that we feel will have the most impact on our clients and their future retirement. These changes will affect your overall retirement planning.

We were surprised the legislation did not include any provisions to eliminate back-door Roth conversions and mega back-door Roth conversions, nor did it place more restrictive limits on Roth contributions. Earlier in the year, we were led to believe these Roth conversion/contribution strategies would be restricted.

It is also important to note that many of the provisions outlined below will require the employer to make plan amendments and/or modify their procedures to accommodate these changes. Therefore, it may be a while before some of these changes are implemented. The effective dates of the provisions vary between the passage of the SECURE Act 2.0 up to year the 2028.

Please see the provisions below we thought were most important to our readers.

Employer Matching Contributions

Optional Roth Treatment vs. Pre-Tax Treatment—This is an important change and not thoroughly covered in this book. Effective in 2023, employers can now allow the employer match to go into a Roth account for 401(k)/403(b)/457(b) plans. The employee will be taxed on the contribution, and the match will be immediately vested. This is an optional provision, and the employer plan must be amended to allow these types of contributions.

Required Minimum Distributions (RMDs)

Child with a Disability—The SECURE Act eliminated the ability for most non-spousal beneficiaries to stretch an Inherited IRA or Inherited Roth IRA beyond ten years. This change does not impact Eligible Designated Beneficiaries or EDBs (which include people with a disability or chronic illness), who are permitted to stretch the Inherited IRA/Roth IRA over their own lifetime. SECURE Act 2.0 clarifies that beneficiaries who have already been qualified as disabled by the Social Security Administration will also qualify as an EDB for the purposes of the SECURE Act. So, if your child is already qualified to collect SSI or SSDI for a disability, you will not have to prove the disability again beyond the required periodic updates.

Increased Age for RMDs—Currently, the age for RMDs is 72 (previously, the RMD age was 70½ before the SECURE Act was passed). Now, beginning on January 1, 2023, the age is 73, and by year 2033, the RMD is increased to age 75. We will now have an extra three years for additional planning considerations, including accelerating more Roth conversions and/or smoothing out Roth conversions over a period of time to lower IRMAA charges, net investment income taxes, and possibly, capital gains tax brackets.

Surviving Spouse—In 2024, a surviving spouse inheriting a retirement account will be treated as the deceased account holder for RMD purposes. If the surviving spouse is younger than their deceased spouse, they may be able to delay RMDs.

RMDs on Roth 401(k)s Eliminated—While you do not have to take RMDs on a Roth IRA, before SECURE Act 2.0, you had to take an RMD on a Roth employer plan. With SECURE Act 2.0, you no longer must take an RMD beginning in the year 2024. Prior to SECURE Act 2.0, employees would roll their Roth 401(k) into a Roth IRA to avoid the RMD rules. With the passage of SECURE Act 2.0, they no longer must employ this strategy. By keeping their money in the 401(k)/403(b) Plan, the employee is provided with greater asset protection, as the employer sponsored plans are subject to ERISA rules and provide the best asset protection.

Increased Roth Contribution Opportunities

Roth SIMPLE and SEP IRAs—Roth contributions to SIMPLE and SEP IRAs are now permitted beginning in year 2023.

Catch-Up Contributions for High Income Earners—For employees earning $145,000 or more, their catch-up contributions will no longer be allowed to be tax-deferred. Instead, they will have to be in the form of Roth contributions. Initially when the Act was passed, employers were required to begin the Roth contributions in 2024. The transition period has been extended until 2026 to implement the change. This means these contributions will not be in the form of pre-tax dollars and will be subject to income taxes. *Note:* This does not affect catch-up contributions to IRAs (including SIMPLE IRAs). If the employer does not have a "Roth" feature in their employer-sponsored plan, then no employees will be permitted to make catch-up contributions.

Transfers from 529 Plans to Roth IRAs—Effective in 2024, a tax and penalty-free rollover from a 529 plan to Roth IRAs will be permitted under certain circumstances. Beneficiaries of 529 plans will be permitted to roll over up to $35,000 over the course of their lifetime from their 529 plan account in their name to their Roth IRA. The rollovers are subject to Roth IRA annual contributions limits, and the 529 plan account must have been established for more than 15 years. The rollover contribution from the 529 plan to the Roth IRA replaces the Roth IRA contribution. Any contributions made within the past five years, as well as the earnings on those contributions, are not eligible to be transferred into the Roth IRA. A great planning tool to note: as the rule is currently written, the beneficiary is not subject to any income limits to be eligible for the Roth rollover. The beneficiary must have earned income, however, but there is not an income ceiling. This new opportunity helps reduce the risk of having leftover funds in the 529 plan account.

Increase in Catch-Up Limits

The retirement plan contribution limit is increased for those age 50 or older. For 2023, the catch-up contribution limit amount is limited to $7,500 and is indexed for inflation.

SECURE Act 2.0 provides a second layer increase in the contribution amount for those age 60, 61, 62, or 63, effective starting in tax year 2025. The "second" catch-up limitation is $10,000 for 401(k)/403(b) plans, and $5,000 for SIMPLE plans. These limits are also subject to inflation adjustments. This provision will dovetail with the provision above for employees earning more than $145,000 wherein the catch-up contribution will need to be in the form of a Roth contribution beginning in year 2026, providing greater opportunity to contribute to their Roth 401(k)/403(b) account.

For participants of IRAs age 50 and older, the catch-up limit is $1,000. Under current law, the catch-up limit is not subject to increases for inflation. The current bill makes the IRA catch-up amount adjusted annually for inflation adjustments for the year 2024 and thereafter.

Modification of Age Requirement for Qualified ABLE Plans

Previously, the disabled person had to be disabled before age 26 to have an ABLE account established; starting in year 2026, the disability must have begun before age 46 to qualify for an ABLE account.

Disabled Beneficiaries and Special Needs Trusts

Charity as Remainder Beneficiary—Effective in 2023, a Special Needs Trust can now name a charity as the remainder beneficiary of the Special Needs Trust.

Penalty Reductions

RMD Penalty—The RMD penalty was 50% of what you should have withdrawn but did not prior to SECURE Act 2.0. Now, the penalty is reduced to 25% starting in 2023. Also, if you correct your distribution in a timely manner, the penalty is reduced to 10%.

Corrective Distributions of Excess IRA Contributions—No longer subject to the 10% excise penalty on excess contributions and the earnings on the contributions.

Statute of Limitations for Excise Tax on Excess Contributions and Accumulations—The statute of limitations for assessing the penalty for a missed or reduced RMD is three years. The statute of limitations for assessing the penalty for excess contributions is six years.

Penalty-free Distributions—Penalty-free distributions are permitted for "unforeseeable or immediate financial needs relating to necessary personal or family emergency expenses" up to $1,000. However, only one distribution may be made every three years or one per year if the distribution is repaid within three years. This provision is effective for distributions made in 2024 or later.

Withdrawals for Domestic Abuse—Effective after the passing of the SECURE Act 2.0 allows retirement plans to permit participants that self-certify that they have experienced domestic abuse to withdraw 50% of the account balance up to $10,000, indexed for inflation.

A distribution made under this section is not subject to the 10% excise penalty tax on early withdrawal distributions. Also, the participant has the opportunity to repay the withdrawn money over a period of three years and will be refunded the income taxes on the money that is repaid. This section is effective for distributions made in 2024.

Withdrawals for Terminal Illness—Effective after the passing of the SECURE Act 2.0, those individuals with a terminal illness will no longer be subject to the

10% early withdrawal penalty rules. The employee is considered terminally ill if they have been certified by a physician as having an illness or physical condition which can reasonably be expected to result in death within 84 months. The distributions can be repaid within three years.

Withdrawals for Qualified Federally Declared Disasters—One can withdraw up to $22,000 from their retirement plan penalty-free in the event of a federal disaster. Taxes on the withdrawal can be spread over three years. The money can also be repaid into the retirement plan account. This change is retroactive to 1/26/21.

Withdrawals to Purchase Long-Term Care Contracts—Effective beginning in 2026, one can withdraw the lesser of 10% of their vested account balance up to $2,500/year to pay for long-term care premiums without paying the 10% early withdrawal penalty. As of this writing, the provision is for the purchase of 'Traditional 'long-term care' contracts and not for a portion of the premium on a life insurance contract that includes a chronic care rider.

Age 50 Exception Expanded to Include Firefighters, Correction Officers, and Public Safety Workers with 25 or More Years of Service—Allows these employee groups to take penalty-free distributions at age 50.

Withdrawals for Hardship Distributions—Employers may rely on an employee certifying that the hardship distributions conditions have been met.

Mandatory Automatic Enrollment

Effective in 2025, new 401(k) and 403(b) plans must automatically enroll eligible employees. Automatic deferrals start between 3% and 10% of compensation, increasing by 1% per year, to a maximum of at least 10% (no more than 15% of compensation). *Note*: This provision does not apply to current 401(k) and 401(b) plans. Of course, the employee has the option to reduce the amount of the contribution or eliminate making contributions altogether.

Savers Credit—The Savers Credit is now a Savers Match into the retirement account vs. a deduction. It can be as much as a 50% match on the first $2,000 contributed. It is for low-income earners and begins in 2027.

Emergency Savings—Employers can add an emergency savings account that is a designated Roth account eligible to accept participant contributions beginning in 2024. Contributions are limited to $2,500/year and the first four withdrawals per year would be tax and penalty-free. Contributions may be eligible for an employer match as defined by the plan rules. The purpose of the emergency savings fund is to encourage employees to save for short-term and unexpected expenses.

Qualified Charitable Distributions (QCDs)—The previous limit for QCDs was $100,000 per IRA owner, but now with SECURE Act 2.0, they are indexed for inflation. In addition, you can make a one-time charitable distribution of $50,000 to a Charitable Remainder Trust (CRAT/CRUT) or a charitable gift annuity beginning in 2023 if you are age 70½ or older. This is an expansion of the type of charity that can receive a QCD.

Qualifying Longevity Annuity Contracts (QLACs)—Effective for contracts purchased or exchanged in 2023 or later, up to $200,000 can be placed into a QLAC. Previously, only 25% of the qualified plan up to $145,000 could be placed into a QLAC. Also, there is a 90-day "free look" period that may be offered.

Employer Matching of Student Loan Repayments—Effective in 2024, employers have the option to match student loan repayments as if the student loan repayments were employee deferrals. This applies to 401(k)s, 403(b)s, SIMPLE, and 457(b)s.

Improving Coverage for Part-Time Workers—Prior to SECURE Act 2.0, part-time workers needed to have at least 1,000 hours of service in a 12-month period or 500 service hours in a three consecutive year period to participate in the employer's qualified retirement plan. SECURE 2.0 reduces the three-year period to two years for plan years beginning in 2025.

De Minimus Incentives for Participation are Permitted—Employers may offer de minimus financial incentives to increase participation in retirement plans, such as gift cards. The financial incentives cannot be purchased with plan assets, however.

Creation of National Online Searchable Database—SECURE Act 2.0 creates a national database to assist employees to locate missing retirement plan assets. The database must be established within two years of passing the SECURE Act 2.0.

Preamble

To optimally care for a child with a disability, you generally have to get two major but connected things right.

1. You have to plan for your child with a disability.

2. You have to improve your own finances with a view toward providing for your child.

That said, many of the strategies that will be optimal for your child will also be optimal for you. This book provides recommendations in both areas: your financial future and your child's financial future.

Every parent wants to do every-thing possible to make sure their children have the best life possible, and when you have a child with a disability, the stakes are so much higher. Whether your child was born with a disability, or became disabled later in life, you have almost always put their needs first.

I know my wife Cindy and I did. From the time it became clear that our daughter Erica's health problems were signs of something more serious, we embarked on a crusade to find a diagnosis and any kind of treatment that would help Erica feel better. Admittedly, Cindy and I have had the luxury of adequate financial resources to fund that quest. I'm the founder of Lange Accounting Group and Lange Financial Group and Cindy is an electrical engineer.

But despite our relative financial comfort, we still experienced significant financial anxiety worrying about how Erica would manage her life and health after we were gone. As I'll explain in Chapter 11, Erica was ultimately diagnosed with dysautonomia, which means that her autonomic nervous system—which governs critical involuntary functions like breathing, heartrate, and digestion—doesn't function correctly. She has good days and bad days, but not enough good days that she will likely ever be able to work enough to fully support herself.

That fear meant that Cindy and I couldn't rest easy until we put in place a plan that would ensure Erica had more than enough money to allow her to live comfortably for the rest of her life. It took us quite a long time to devise our plan. We made mistakes along the way, and found incredible resources for great information and support, but a big key to that plan has been saving for our own retirement and optimizing options including Roth IRA conversions.

But throughout, we let math and science be our guide. Cindy is a worrier, but "running the numbers" really helped in two areas:

1. It showed how much we could spend and how to plan.

2. It helped us optimize our options.

We ran the numbers and devised strategies, including Roth conversions. (By the way, did you know if you die with certain types of 401(k) or 403(b)s your heirs may be eligible to make a conversion after you die? See *The Under-Publicized Inherited 401(k) Strategy for IRA Owners in a High Tax Bracket with a Disabled Child Who Will Be in a Low Tax Bracket* in Chapter 11.)

I want every parent struggling with the same issues to have the benefit of learning the best course of action based on math.

Better Financial Strategies = More Money and Less Taxes for Your Child After You Are Gone

Most of the recommendations below will not only help your child but will also help you.

That's right—optimizing our retirement options has been the key to making sure Erica will have adequate financial resources for the rest of her life. Retirement savings accounts offer tax advantages that no other kind of savings option offers. With a Traditional 401(k), 403(b) or IRA, you get a tax deduction now, and tax-deferred growth until you take the money out. If you invested those same funds with a regular after-tax investment account, you pay tax every year on the investment income you earn. Over time, those taxes seriously erode your investment gains.

As I demonstrate in Chapter 2, this tax-deferred growth could mean you would have as much as an extra $2.6 million more at age 88 than if you invested the same money outside of your retirement account. That extra cash in old age means you'll be able to leave much more money to your child after you're gone.

Roth IRAs and Roth 401(k)s and Roth conversions are usually even better. While you don't get a tax deduction when you contribute to a Roth account, those funds grow tax free for the rest of your life, and potentially to some extent for the rest of the life of your child with a disability. I'm a fan of Roth accounts, and by leveraging the tax-free growth in Roth accounts and taking the steps we detail in Chapter 11, our daughter will have an extra $1.8 million more over her lifetime in today's dollars—not counting government benefits—than if we had done nothing.

As I mentioned, many of the same steps that you should consider for yourself will ultimately benefit your child. Roth IRA conversions are a perfect example. Not only will we be better off by $491,829, our daughter will be $1,890,544 better off because we made a series of Roth conversions, coupled with the full stretch of the Inherited Roth IRA account because she is an eligible designated beneficiary (EDB) with a disability.

For many parents of a child with a disability, running the numbers may show that it is advisable to make either a large or more likely a series of Roth conversions. These conversions can enhance both your and your child's financial security.

Due to an exception in the SECURE Act, your child with a disability—who gets qualified as an EDB—will be able to "stretch" their Inherited IRA or Inherited Roth IRA over their lifetime. Again, this means doing what is likely best for you will be best for your child.

Stretching Inherited IRAs/Roth IRAs is not a new concept to me. This is based on a law that was passed in 1997 with a 1998 effective date. The peer reviewed article, that I wrote for *The Tax Adviser* at that time, pointed out the advantages of making a Roth IRA conversion and then ultimately having that Roth IRA go to your younger beneficiaries, allowing them to stretch the Roth IRA over their own lifetime. With the passage of the SECURE Act, most non-spousal heirs must withdraw the money from an Inherited IRA/Roth IRA within 10 years. But if your child qualifies as an EDB, that child is still permitted to take advantage of stretching the Inherited IRA/Roth IRA over their own lifetime. So, many of the numbers that I ran back in 1998 for a peer reviewed article for the AICPA, which won article of the year, still apply to beneficiaries with a disability (though obviously tax rates and other changes have to be considered). My point is this way of thinking has a significant peer reviewed analysis in it. In planning for a child with a disability, it is important to get the Inherited stretch IRA or better yet the Inherited stretch Roth IRA in place.

What is really cool is you can make a Roth conversion and though your child has to take ever increasing distributions from the Inherited Roth, it is all tax-free.

We also like parents to consider our "Who Gets What" strategy. Sometimes it makes sense for different beneficiaries to inherit different assets with tax minimization in mind. For example, it might make sense to leave your IRA or Roth IRA to a special needs trust for your child who has a disability and your after-tax dollars to your child without a disability.

To be fair, throughout this book there will be certain steps that we recommend that will be better for your child and will not directly benefit you. For example, buying a life insurance policy on both parents' lives isn't a direct benefit to you but might be a good strategy in your situation. In addition, it might make sense to make an even larger Roth IRA conversion than you would if you weren't concerned about providing for your child. Obviously, there will be some differences in your wills, trusts, and estate plan that might not be a direct benefit to you.

We could point out other exceptions to the general rule "more retirement savings = more money for your child after you are gone." But optimizing your own planning is a great starting point to best provide for your child.

I realize that this may seem impossible to some of you. How can I possibly put money away for such a seemingly selfish purpose as my own retirement when my child has such profound needs? Saving money in your retirement account, if you can swing it, is the most valuable asset you can leave to your child when you are gone.

A Note About the Language in This Book

We have tried to consistently adopt respectful language to describe a child with a disability. Some argue we should use special needs child. Others disagree. I personally don't like "disabled child," even though it is short, because that label puts more emphasis on the disability than the child who should be respected. We have tried to be consistent, but when space is at a premium, as in the naming of a supplemental website we created to help parents of children with disabilities plan for the future (**https://DisabledChildPlanning.com**), we have defaulted to concise language not people-first language.

1

The Bedrock Principles of Retirement and Estate Planning

"Anyone may arrange his affairs so that his taxes shall be as low as possible; he is not bound to choose that pattern which best pays the treasury. There is not even a patriotic duty to increase one's taxes."

— Judge Learned Hand

Our goal is to equip you with the best resource available to help you provide for yourself and your family.[1]

My daughter has dysautonomia and it is likely she will never be able to provide for herself. With the added knowledge of two other experts in the field, I figured out the appropriate long-term planning for her and she will be better off by $1.9 million in today's dollars. That does not include any government benefits she is eligible for. This book contains all the steps we took to provide for her as well as much more. If you skip ahead to Chapter 11, you'll learn more about what my wife and I did to make sure our daughter will be financially secure for the rest of her life.

The financial stakes for families who have a child with a disability are astronomically high. I have spent 35+ years helping IRA and retirement plan owners get the most out of what they've got. But frankly, if your children are healthy and capable of getting a job and supporting themselves, less than optimized estate planning has fewer dire consequences.

Let's assume you didn't optimize your accumulation, distribution, and Roth planning, so instead of being able to spend $150,000 per year, you could only spend $120,000 per year. Or, instead of leaving your children $1,000,000, you left them $400,000. Of course, that would be unfortunate and potentially could have been avoidable. But if your children can support themselves, and you could make do with $120,000, it wouldn't be tragic.

But, if your child or children can't support themselves, the cost of not optimizing your planning could easily mean the difference between your child being well provided for during their life versus running out of money and having to

---

1 There is no solicitation for legal services being made by me, James Lange, nor by Lange Legal Group, LLC.

be dependent on the pittance the government pays out, assuming they qualify.

This book comes on the heels of a 55-page special report and a one-page summary of highlights that I and my two co-authors, Deborah McFadden, and Julieanne E. Steinbacher, Esq., CELA, wrote and published. Both of those reports are available at no cost at **https://DisabledChildPlanning.com**.

But this book delves much deeper into the entire process of retirement planning for parents, and planning for families of children with disabilities.

I've tried keeping it entertaining with stories, quotes, and cartoons, but it is still a lot of information to digest. We cover core information that has appeared in our six previous editions in the *Retire Secure* series, as well as a treasure trove of unique information for parents of a child with a disability.

In recognition of the amount of material we cover, we provide an extremely detailed TOC so if there is a specific item you are looking for, please look there. If you scan the TOC, you will likely find something of great interest that you did not even realize you needed to know!

In this first chapter, we start with the critical core concepts which most taxpayers get wrong. Most of this chapter, or for that matter, most of this book, will be helpful for any IRA or retirement plan owner. This chapter is loaded with valuable information and worth your time and energy to read it. The concepts in this chapter are essential to *anyone* who wants a financially secure retirement. However, these core strategies are not enough when you have a child with a disability. The stakes are much higher for us. To fully protect our children, we will also need to implement additional strategies, which we cover in Chapters 11 through 14. But as we said in the Preamble "you have to put on your own oxygen mask first."

This book covers much of the same territory as my recently published **Retire Secure for Professors and TIAA Participants**, but this one also includes information specifically for families who have a child or children with a disability. While many of our strategies work to the advantage of all families planning for their retirement, the two books, though similar, are intended for different audiences.

One other note. We are very aware that we just can't spout advice without backing up our claims with proof. Much of the time that proof takes the form of graphs or charts that result from our mathematical analysis. Don't be alarmed. You don't need to follow our precise calculations or interpret all of our assumptions. The facts are there for anyone who wants to check our reasoning, but you should feel free to not go through the proof or entire sections that you just don't feel like reading.

So, with this introduction, I invite you to begin your journey to safeguard your own retirement, and the long-term health and well-being of your family.

Lifecycle Planning for a Child with a Disability

The most important steps to take to ensure your child's financial future is taken care of depend on the stage in your child's and the lifecycle that you are currently in. Laying the groundwork early and taking the right steps in the right order is absolutely critical. I've identified three separate lifecycle stages and the most important action steps to take in each. But don't worry, even if you are just now reading this information, and you're in the second—or even third—stage of the lifecycle, you can still make a big difference in your child's life by implementing as many of these strategies as you can now.

Stage One: Birth to 18 Years

Most likely, at some point between your child's birth and the time he or she turned 18, you became aware of your child's specific disability. Perhaps this was instantly obvious at birth or adoption, as was the case for my colleague Deborah McFadden's daughters Hannah and Tatyana, whose stories you'll read about in Chapter 12. Perhaps this was revealed over time, as my wife Cindy and I discovered with our daughter, Erica, whose disability emerged as she got older. Or perhaps your child suffered a devastating injury or illness that resulted in disability.

If you can start planning now, time is on your side.

At this early stage in your child's life, one of the most important things you can do is to start gathering as much documentation as you can regarding your child's disability, even if there is not an official diagnosis yet. This can be really important if you later want to obtain benefits for your child that require that the onset of the disability occurs before a certain age. These records may be from doctors, early intervention evaluators, and schools. These documents may be easily accessible via patient portals or other online sources, but you shouldn't delay in compiling them. Many people assume that providers will keep these records indefinitely, but most offices destroy records after a certain time.

Depending on your own financial situation, your child may be eligible for certain government benefits. In certain circumstances, your child may be eligible for Supplemental Security Income (SSI) benefits. SSI is essentially a poverty program with low limits on asset value and income. Before the child turns 18, they count the parents' assets and income, so it is highly unlikely you will be able to get your child qualified for SSI before the child turns eighteen.

That doesn't mean you shouldn't do anything. This is an important time to get your child qualified for Medicaid. Medicaid is administered by the states, and each state has its own program and its own qualifications. Some children may qualify based on income and asset limits, but some states include additional eligibility avenues. For example, Pennsylvania allows individuals under 18 to qualify for Medicaid if they have a disability that meets the Social Security childhood disability standards, and they do not count the parents' resources when the child qualifies based on a disability.

As a parent, you will be the one responsible for gathering the documentation of your child's disability and submitting the Medicaid or Medicare application. Medicaid is a joint state and federal program, while Medicare is a federal program. The Social Security office will not do this on your behalf. Qualification criteria and application procedures vary greatly across different states, so you will need to research the program in your state.

Later in this chapter I present a hierarchy of how to prioritize your retirement savings. However, unless you're broke, I implore you to get to at least the Roth layer. Chapter 3 explains the many advantages that Roth accounts have over Traditional retirement accounts. As will become clear when you read Chapter 11, where I explain the three-part plan my wife Cindy and I put in place to safeguard our daughter after we're gone, Roth accounts provide a potential opportunity for a lifetime tax-free stream of income for your child.

At the very least, you should be saving at least enough to take care of any employer match. If your employer's plan provides a Roth option for the employer match, this is most likely the option to choose. While it will cost you a bit more in terms of the taxes you pay now, the long-term benefits for your child will far outweigh that expense.

Alongside your Roth contributions, you should probably set up an ABLE account for your child with a disability and contribute to it on a regular basis. ABLE accounts are discussed in greater detail in Chapter 14. In brief, ABLE accounts allow persons who have been certified as disabled to accumulate up to $100,000 without jeopardizing eligibility for government benefit programs. The funds in an ABLE account can be used to pay for qualified disability expenses, a category that includes many of the daily living expenses your child will have. Read Chapter 14 to learn more about this valuable program.

At least a year before your child turns 18, you should begin the process of transition planning so that there are no gaps in benefits and no surprises. The most crucial step in transition planning is to get your estate plan done. Your estate plan should include a special needs trust for your child so your child can inherit money and retirement accounts without jeopardizing eligibility for government benefits. If you don't know if your child will qualify as disabled, discuss the implications of a toggle trust with your estate attorney who is knowledgeable in drafting documents when there is a child with a disability. Toggle trusts, which are described in Chapter 13, don't force you to guess what might be best for your child in the unknown future, but allow estates to be administered appropriately depending on the actual circumstances at the time of your death. Chapter 13 explains how special needs trusts work and the important role they play in estate planning when you have a child with a disability.

Be sure to update the beneficiary designations on all your retirement accounts with the appropriate language that refers to a testamentary trust inside your will or to a revocable trust created to receive all retirement plan distributions. If you don't update the beneficiary designations on every one of your retirement accounts, all this careful planning could be in jeopardy, and your child could end up broke and/or ineligible for government benefits.

Transition planning may also include preparing guardianship petitions and making any other plans and arrangements to ensure continuity of benefits once your child reaches adulthood. Don't wait until your child turns 18 to begin the planning discussion.

Stage Two: 18 Years to Parent's Retirement

As soon as your child turns 18, you'll want to start the process of assisting your child in applying for Supplemental Security Income (SSI) benefits. In Chapter 12, my colleague Deborah McFadden explains the process she uses to help young adults win the Golden Ticket of SSI approval. Winning this approval opens the door for many other benefits for your child, including getting college paid for and eligibility for many other support programs. Your child may not need all the benefits, but it's reassuring to know that these many programs are available in case he or she needs them later on. In most states, individuals who qualify for SSI will also qualify for Medicare.

If your child became disabled after he or she began working, your child may be eligible for Social Security Disability Insurance (SSDI) benefits on his or her own work record. As Chapter 12 explains, SSDI benefits tend to be higher than SSI benefits, and do not have the same strict means-testing requirements that can result in SSI benefits being reduced or completely cut. More often than not, at least in my experience, SSDI benefits for a child are based on the parent's work record, not the child's. For that reason, you must wait until the parent is eligible for Social Security. Once an individual has been covered by SSDI for 24 months, they will also be eligible for Medicare, which is administered at the federal level. (If your child is under the age of 20, Medicare is only available to them if they have end-stage renal disease or ALS.)

On an ongoing basis, you'll want to do regular reviews of your finances, your wills and trusts, and all of the other arrangements you have made to ensure your child is well taken care of after you are gone. You'll also want to be sure your own retirement savings are on track, and to keep contributing funds to your child's ABLE account.

Stage Three: Parent's Retirement and Beyond

When you or your spouse, or possibly both of you, are contemplating taking Social Security, you should at least consider switching your child's benefits from SSI to SSDI. As mentioned above, benefits under the SSDI program tend to be higher and do not have the same strict means-testing restrictions that SSI requires. Under current law, if the onset of your child's disability was before age 22, your child will be eligible for SSDI benefits based on the parent's work history. Here are the conditions for qualifying for SSDI under a parent's work record:

- The child must be age 18 or older with a disability that began prior to age 22.

- The parent must have worked enough to fully qualify for Social Security retirement benefits.

- The parent must be either deceased, permanently disabled, or currently receiving Social Security benefits.

The earliest you can apply for Social Security is at age 62, but the longer you wait before applying for benefits, the higher your monthly benefit. You'll get the maximum benefit at age 70, but in some circumstances, it may make sense to apply early. This is a situation where "running the numbers," as we call it in our accounting firm, can provide guidance on the best option for your family.

Please note that these are general guidelines only, but based on our experience this is the ideal timeline. Following this schedule can help optimize retirement savings so that no one runs out of money too early. Now that we've mapped out the most crucial steps at each stage of your child's lifecycle, let's delve into the details.

The Bedrock Principles of Retirement Planning

Please note while this chapter contains a critical overview of the bedrock principles of retirement and estate planning, this is a summary chapter of the entire book followed by more detailed chapters that delve into the topics of this summary chapter. This chapter contains our recommendations for the most tax-efficient manner to save for retirement as well as which dollars to spend first after you retire. We know most readers don't make it past the first chapter, so we included a lot of our gems in this chapter.

Pay Taxes Later—Except for Roths

Don't pay taxes now; pay taxes later, except for a Roth IRA and Roth conversions. These words, subject to exceptions, represent the *bedrock* principles of tax planning for accumulating and distributing wealth. It is critical in the accumulation stage when you are saving for retirement. It is essential in the distribution stage when you are withdrawing money from your portfolio after you retire. And in the estate-planning stage, it can dramatically improve the financial lives of your heirs.

The SECURE Act radically modified Required Minimum Distribution (RMD) rules for Inherited IRAs and other retirement accounts. The new rules force your heirs to pay taxes at a significantly accelerated rate (in contrast to the previous "stretch IRA" rules). In other words, the new rules require you to pay taxes sooner. That can be a major problem for parents of children with disabilities, but with proper timing and planning, children with disabilities are exempt from this requirement.

Like many parents, your IRAs and other retirement accounts likely hold the bulk of your wealth, so planning for the distribution of your retirement accounts, both while you are alive and after you are gone, is critically important.

I did say "Pay Taxes Later, except for a Roth IRA and Roth conversions." We devote three entire chapters to address Roth IRA conversions in this book. In addition, Roth IRA conversion strategies are mentioned many times throughout the book. It is one of the best defenses parents can use to combat the devastation of the SECURE Act. For more on this, please see Chapters 16, 17 and 18.

For even more information comparing Roth IRAs and Roth 401(k)s to Traditional retirement accounts, and the related issues of Roth IRA conversions, please go to **https://PayTaxesLater.com/Books/**. There, you can download a free copy of one of our best-selling books, *The Roth Revolution: Pay Taxes Once and Never Again*. If you are interested in Roth IRAs and Roth IRA conversions—and you probably should be—please read at least the Roth IRA chapters in this book. If you want to take it a step further, please read at least Chapter 1 of *The Roth Revolution*. You can also get a printed copy by requesting it from our office (contact information is included in the back of the book) or by purchasing a copy from Amazon.

In this chapter, I'll give you an overview of the principles of ensuring a secure retirement, which I will elaborate on in following chapters. For those of you who want to delve into more detail, you will find the full story in the other chapters throughout the book.

The Accumulation Years: Saving for Retirement While Working

First the conclusion, then the analysis.

Let's assume you are working and have a certain amount of money that you can afford to contribute for your retirement. What is the best hierarchy for contributing to the different types of retirement plans available to you?

Subject to exception:

1. Take advantage of any employer match.
2. Take advantage of a Health Savings Account, if available to you.
3. Contribute to Roth IRAs and Roth 401(k)s
4. Contribute to an ABLE account for your child.
5. Contribute to traditional retirement plans or IRAs.
6. Contribute to nondeductible IRAs or other nondeductible retirement plans.
7. Save money in a plain old after-tax brokerage account.

If you are thinking of putting away money now in a tax-free account for the benefit of your child who has a disability, then we recommend an ABLE account contribution. Please see Chapter 14. Be aware that contributions to ABLE accounts are a variation of a gift, not something for your retirement.

Make no bones about it: the cardinal rule of saving for retirement is taking advantage of employer-matching contributions to any retirement plan. Many employers offer a matching contribution, but some offer a percentage of your salary regardless of whether you contribute to the plan. So, if your employer has a retirement plan and an employer match is available to you, make sure you are (1) participating in that plan and (2) contributing at least enough to take full advantage of the match. It's like free money!

For example, many employers opt for a basic safe harbor match on their 401(k) plans. For these plans, employers match 100% of an employee's contribution, up to 3% of compensation, and 50% of the next 2%. You have to contribute to the plan to get the match, but if you contribute 3%, that's a *100% return on your investment in one day.* This doesn't include the enormous benefits of tax deferral.

The money in your retirement plan grows either tax-deferred, as in a Traditional IRA or 401(k), or tax-free in a Roth IRA or Roth 401(k). Many employers allow you to direct your own contributions to a Traditional or Roth account. Recent legislation allows employer matching contributions to go into either a Roth or a Traditional account if the plan permits this. Before this, and the more likely rules in your retirement plan, at least for now, are that the employee's share could be Roth or Traditional, but the employer share must be Traditional. Because this legislation was so recent, your plan will need to be updated to allow you the option for the employer's share to be either Roth or Traditional.

Health Savings Accounts

After taking advantage of your employer's matching contribution, and after contributing to an ABLE account for your child, the next thing you should consider is making contributions to a Health Savings Account (HSA). HSAs are only available to those who choose a health insurance plan with a high deductible. HSAs have more tax benefits than a Roth IRA or a Traditional IRA.

With an HSA you get a tax deduction for your contribution, the money grows tax-free, and the distribution is entirely tax-free, assuming you withdraw it to pay for qualified medical expenses. With a Roth IRA, you don't get a deduction up front. With a Traditional IRA, you don't enjoy tax-free treatment when you make a distribution.

With an HSA, there are no income-based contribution limits to qualify for the deduction. In addition, you don't have to wait until retirement or age 72 for tax-free and penalty-free withdrawals of contributions and earnings as long as the withdrawals are for qualified expenses.

A deduction for contributions to an HSA can reduce any type of taxable income, while deductions for contributions to a Traditional retirement plan require service-related income in order to receive a deduction. HSAs do not have any Required Minimum Distributions (RMDs) at a certain age as is required with Traditional retirement plans.

For those individuals 55 years and older, an additional $1,000 catch-up contribution is allowed per spouse. For 2024, the self-only coverage limit has been increased to $4,150 (increased from $3,850 in 2023) and $8,300 for family coverage (increased from $7,750). This means for those 55 years and older, a total of $10,300 will be able to be contributed in 2024. As of this writing, the catch-up contribution for both spouses cannot be contributed to the same HSA account. There is legislation pending to permit both spouses to contribute to the same HSA account, but it has not been passed. This means the other spouse's catch-up contribution needs to be contributed to a separate HSA account. Not all HSA owners realize both spouses can make their additional $1,000 catch-up contribution. They can. The catch-up contribution can't be to the same HSA account.

HSAs are the only area in the IRS tax code where you receive a deduction for a contribution and tax-free distributions for withdrawals. In addition, HSAs do not have a "use it or lose it" provision like flexible spending accounts, so they are a great way to sock away money for the increased medical expenses you will likely have in retirement.

Plus, under the current tax rules, there are no requirements to take the distribution in the year the qualified medical expense is incurred. This means you can save your receipts, allow your HSA account to grow, and take the distributions later tax-free. A solid tax strategy is to pay medical expenses from non-HSA funds, retain the expense documentation and defer taking the distribution until a time when you need to take a distribution. This strategy, however, assumes you can afford to pay the medical expenses from sources outside of your HSA. While keeping tax optimization in mind, it is advisable to spend the HSA before both spouses pass away since the HSA is subject to lump sum taxation when paid to a non-spousal beneficiary at death, even if the beneficiary has a disability.

Unfortunately, under current law, anyone on Medicare is not permitted to contribute to an HSA. There is a proposed bill to make HSA contributions available to those individuals covered under Medicare since senior citizens are the group of individuals with the highest medical expenses. I will not provide any further coverage regarding HSAs in this book, but since this section is on the optimal way to save for retirement, I would be remiss to not mention them.

After contributing enough to get the full match from your employer's retirement plan and to your HSA (if you have access to an HSA), the next priority during the accumulation stage (subject to exceptions determined by personal circumstances) is to direct maximum contributions to your Roth 401(k)s, and Roth IRAs through whichever provider your employer uses. Of course, with a plain old Roth IRA not associated with your employment, you have an enormous array of options.

If you happen to work for a state or local government, including in law enforcement, higher education, or as a civil servant, you may be eligible to also contribute to a 457(b) plan. If you're eligible to participate, consider contributing the maximum to the Roth account in your organization's 457(b) plan.

Many government employees are unaware that they may have access to a 457(b). Even some benefits administrators aren't aware employees often do have access to a 457(b) plan. You can often make 457(b) contributions in addition to a 403(b) contribution. That second contribution essentially allows you to double your retirement plan contributions if you can afford to put away that much into your retirement plan.

Please see the 457(b) section in Chapter 2 for important additional details about 457 plans.

Since combining a 457(b) plan with your Traditional retirement plan can double your retirement plan contributions, it will pay to find out if you have access to a 457(b) plan and consider whether you can afford additional contributions, even if it doesn't have a matching feature which it probably won't.

Finally, if you meet the income guidelines, contribute to a Roth IRA. If you don't meet the Roth income guidelines but you meet other requirements, contribute to a Traditional IRA, and use a technique called a "back-door Roth IRA" to immediately convert the Traditional IRA to a Roth. As we go to press, the back-door Roth IRA is still allowed, but we fear it will be eliminated sometime in the future. We cover the back-door Roth IRA conversion in Chapter 7.

Why Roth? Because the math proves that, subject to exception, you will have more purchasing power in the long run if you contribute to a Roth account than to a Traditional retirement account. Please see Chapter 3.

As we mentioned above, until recently, your employer's matching contributions had to go to the Traditional account in your retirement plan. Recent legislation gives employers the option to give you a choice of whether the employer's contribution of your retirement plan is directed to a Traditional or Roth retirement plan (of course if the employer Roth contribution was selected, it would be included in your taxable income). Your employer's plan will need to be amended to allow for both pre-tax Traditional and after-tax Roth options for employer matching contributions besides simply allowing a Roth option for employee contributions.

So, if you direct all of your own contributions to the Traditional account as well, every withdrawal that you take after you retire will be taxable. Most parents would be well served to have a diversity of Roth and Traditional accounts. I'll talk more about Roth IRA conversions in Chapters 7 and 16. Subject to exceptions, after the matching portion I generally recommend Roth IRAs.

If your employer doesn't offer a Roth account in their retirement plan offerings, and you don't qualify for a Roth IRA contribution because your income is too high, and you don't qualify for a back-door Roth IRA conversion, the next best option would be to save inside a Traditional 401(k) or an IRA. Even though it's not tax-free, it is still preferable to saving in a taxable brokerage account. I will cover this topic in greater depth in Chapter 2.

So, for the sake of simplicity, I offer this figure as proof of the value of saving in retirement accounts as opposed to a regular investment account (labeled after-tax funds). The figure shows the difference in savings over a lifetime.

In the following figure, two parents with the same tax rates, investments, etc. invest in their retirement differently. The parent represented in the solid black line took advantage of his employer's retirement, even disregarding the match. The parent represented in the dashed line invested the same amount of money in a regular investment account, and did not take advantage of his employer's retirement plan.

Figure 1.1

Tax-Deferred Savings Build Wealth*

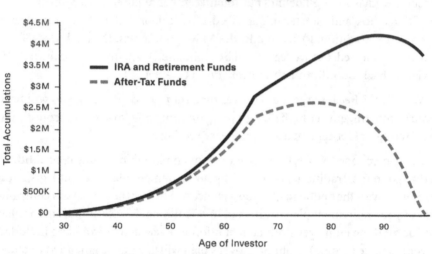

*Detailed assumptions can be found in the Appendix.

The parent who made Traditional (meaning, non-Roth) contributions to his employer's retirement plan enjoyed immediate tax savings and enjoyed tax-deferred growth during the accumulation years. That parent is represented by the solid black line. Ultimately, however, he had to pay taxes when he began taking distributions.

The parent who saved outside of his employer's retirement plan, didn't invest in a Roth, didn't get a tax break up front, and had to pay taxes on the interest, dividends, and realized capital gains every year. This parent is represented in the figure by the dashed line.

The parent who used his employer's plan had $1,118,724 more at age 80 than the parent who did not invest in his employer's plan, even though the amount of money he saved on a tax-adjusted basis was the same and there was no employer match. This figure reflects our basic premise that *paying taxes later* while you are in the accumulation stage means you can retire richer instead of "broker."

We have also analyzed the issue of saving in Roth 401(k)s and Roth IRAs versus Traditional 401(k)s and IRAs. Though the difference is not nearly as dramatic, subject to exceptions, workers contributing to Roth 401(k)s and Roth IRAs will usually be much better off in the long run than workers contributing to Traditional 401(k)s and IRAs. Please see Chapter 3.

Roth IRAs and Roth 401(k)s are wonderful because they can grow income tax-free for your life, your spouse's life, and for as many as 10 years after you and your spouse are gone. If your beneficiary qualifies under one of the exceptions, the Roth IRA to some extent can be invested tax-free for the life of your beneficiary. Of particular interest to parents of children with disabilities, beneficiaries with disabilities may still qualify for the ability to stretch payments over their entire life. See Chapter 11 for my story of how this will mean an additional $1.9 million for my daughter Erica over her life. Designated Roth accounts in a 401(k) or 403(b) plan are subject to the RMD rules for 2022 and 2023. However, for 2024 and later years, RMDs are no longer required from designated Roth accounts.

Having the ability to access tax-free money during your retirement years can provide useful options. But since the passage of the SECURE Act, there is an even greater incentive for parents of children with disabilities to contribute to Roth 401(k)s and Roth IRAs instead of Traditional 401(k)s and IRAs.

The SECURE Act mandates that, subject to exceptions, your retirement plans must be fully distributed within 10 years of your and your spouse's death. That could be brutal if all Inherited retirement money is subject to income tax. Your contributions to a Roth account and Roth conversions can provide you with much-needed flexibility during retirement and will be an even more valuable asset to leave behind. But under an important exception to the SECURE Act, beneficiaries who can be certified as "disabled or chronically ill" can stretch Inherited retirement plans and Inherited Roth IRAs for their life like under the pre 2020 rules. We discuss this exception in Chapter 10.

Planning for Retirement Before You Retire

Advance planning for retirement and for your estate is always a good idea. First, you must make sure you have sufficient resources to afford the life you want to live after you retire. Unfortunately, more than one client has come to see me after they signed their retirement papers, and they will not be able to confidently afford the life they pictured. Had they come to me beforehand, I would have either counseled them to plan on spending less in retirement or to keep working. Working part time rarely has anywhere near the financial impact of just working longer.

Second, whether you understand the nuances of all your options or not, making the wrong choices can negatively impact your financial position and that of your family.

We have seen many clients come through our doors over the years and for a multitude of reasons comment, "I wish I would have met you five years ago." Sometimes, it is extremely profitable to do appropriate planning while you are still working. You and your family might profit in ways you couldn't have imagined. And there may be advantages that are not available if you wait until after retirement.

I try to counsel all my clients to talk to me or one of the other CPAs on our team before announcing their retirement. I would offer the same advice to you. Please see someone you trust that can provide good advice before you announce your retirement or sign any retirement papers. The same holds true with phased retirement.

Roth IRA Conversions

Please see Chapters 16, 17, and 18 regarding Roth IRA and Roth 401(k) conversions. This is a critical topic for parents. This is also an area that most people fail to **optimize**, and the result is a dramatic and unnecessary tax burden for themselves and their families, and a huge missed opportunity if you have a child with a disability.

The Distribution Years: Spend the Right Money First When You Retire (Including a New Wrinkle in our Bedrock Principle)

Again, we start with the conclusion and then move to the explanation. Assume you are retired, are receiving some income that you must pay taxes on (like Social Security, RMDs, interest and dividends, and capital gains), and you also have investments in Traditional retirement plans, Roth retirement plans, and plain old after-tax dollars. Subject to exception, we recommend you spend money in the following order:

1. **Spend your income first.**
2. **Spend your after-tax dollars that don't have any or much appreciation.**
3. **Spend your highly appreciated after-tax dollars.**
4. **Spend your Traditional retirement assets like IRAs and 403(b)s.**
5. **Spend your Roth dollars last.**

The following figure supports the premise that, subject to exception, you should spend your after-tax dollars before your retirement plan or IRA dollars. Spending your Roth dollars last will not only be good for you but will help you provide for your child who has a disability.

Please look at the figure that follows. Both retirees start with the same amount of money in a regular brokerage account—which I refer to as after-tax dollars—and in their Traditional retirement plans which could be IRAs or 401(k)s. The figure below indicates, subject to exceptions, that most readers should spend their after-tax dollars first and then IRA and retirement plan dollars. The solid line shows what happens to the first retiree who spends after-tax dollars first and withdraws only the minimum from the IRA when required to (more on RMDs in the next section). *He paid taxes later.* The dashed line shows what happens to the second retiree who spends his IRA before his after-tax dollars. *He paid taxes now.*

The only difference between the dashed line and the solid line in this figure is that the first retiree retained more money in the tax-deferred IRA for a longer

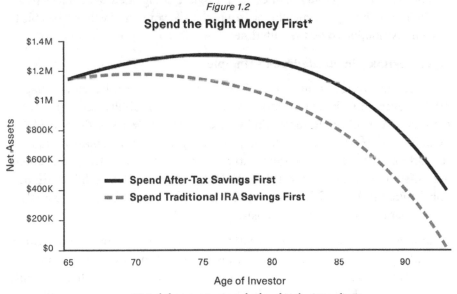

Figure 1.2
Spend the Right Money First*

Detailed assumptions can be found in the Appendix.

period. Even starting at age 65, the decision to defer income taxes for as long as possible gives the first retiree an extra $340,199 if he or his spouse lives to age 89. If one of them lives longer, paying taxes later will be even more valuable to them.

Subject to exception, I generally prefer that you not spend your Roth IRA dollars unless there is a good reason. The Roth IRA grows income tax-free for the rest of your life, your spouse's life and for 10 years after you and your spouse are gone. That 10 years is extended to your child's lifetime if your child has a disability and is recognized as an Eligible Designated Beneficiary. In addition, there is no RMD for you or your spouse with a Roth IRA.

So, in general, the last dollars you want to spend are your Roth IRA dollars. Of course, there may be time when it makes sense to spend your Roth dollars before other retirement plan dollars if it keeps you in a lower tax bracket because the alternative would be making taxable withdrawals that would push you into a higher tax bracket.

That said, subject to exceptions, you and your spouse will realize a benefit by deferring the income taxes due on your retirement plans for as long as possible and generally hold off on spending your Roth IRA. And with the SECURE Act now part of the law, your children, and grandchildren (subject to some important exceptions, which I will cover in Chapter 10) will have to pay income taxes on the Inherited Traditional IRA within 10 years of your death. One of those important exceptions is if your child qualifies as an Eligible Designated Beneficiary based on their disability or chronic illness, in which case, your child will still be able to stretch distributions over their lifetime.

A New Wrinkle in our Bedrock Principle

Since the passage of the SECURE Act, which will be explained in Chapter 10, however, and when your end beneficiary has a disability, adhering to the pay-taxes-later rule in the distribution stage might not always be the best advice. With income tax rates likely on the rise, for some parents it might make more sense to plan for a transition from the taxable world (most IRAs, 401(k)s retirement assets, etc.) to the tax-free world (Roth IRAs, 529 plans, HSAs, life insurance, your children's ABLE accounts, etc.). To get the best result, it is best to analyze each situation on a case-by-case basis.

In short, the SECURE Act dramatically accelerates the taxes on your retirement plan after your death. For your children, losing the lifetime stretch on an Inherited retirement account can carry a huge tax burden, unless you ensure that your child qualifies as "disabled or chronically ill" according to the IRS rules. I will cover this idea more in Chapter 10.

One reasonable strategy for some parents with significant IRAs and retirement plans who will not likely spend all their money is to make taxable withdrawals from the retirement plan and/or IRA, pay the tax, and then gift the net proceeds. The gift could be invested in something that grows tax-free like a 529 plan, HSA plan, your children's ABLE account or Roth IRA (if earned income is present), life insurance, etc. That serves the purpose of getting some money out of your estate and allows tax-free growth for your children.

As a result, for many parents, an earlier transition from the taxable world to the tax-free world might work better than the standard rule of "pay taxes later." We call this strategy transferring assets from the taxable world to the tax-free world. We cover this strategy in greater detail in Chapter 3.

Required Minimum Distributions (RMDs) Explained

You may already know that the SECURE Act raised the age at which you are required to take mandatory distributions from your Traditional retirement accounts to 72 (technically April 1 of the year after you turn age 72). And you may know that the SECURE Act 2.0, passed in December 2022, raised the age again. Anyone born in 1949 or earlier is stuck with the old law and had to start RMDs at 70 ½. If you were born in 1950 and turned 72 in 2022, your RMDs start at age 72. Those born between 1951 and 1959 can wait until age 73, and anyone born in 1960 or later starts at age 75. For the sake of convenience, I'll be using 73 as the starting date for RMDs but be aware that you may be starting later—or you may have already started.

In simple terms, your RMD is the minimum amount you must withdraw from your retirement account each year. That income will be added to your taxable income unless it was contributed on an after-tax basis or if the qualified withdrawals are tax-free, as in the case of the Roth IRA or Roth 401(k). Beginning at age 73 (or whatever age you need to start your RMDs), you must withdraw your RMD by December 31 of every year. Roth IRA accounts are excluded from this requirement; they do not require withdrawals until after the death of the Roth IRA owner and his or her spouse.

If you decide to defer your initial RMD to April 1 of the year following the year you reach age 73, you will be required to take two RMDs in that year. For example, if you reach age 73 in November 2024 and decide to take your RMD on March 15, 2025, you will still need to take another RMD before December 31, 2025, to meet your 2025 RMD requirement. This means you will receive two RMDs in the 2025 year. This is where additional planning can make a big difference in how much tax you will pay. If you are planning on retiring, depending upon the amount of the RMD, you may be better off taking the RMD in the year in which you turn 73, even though you will have taxable wages, instead of taking two RMDs the following year.

Your RMD is calculated by dividing the year-end balance of your IRA or retirement account by a distribution period (or factor) found in IRS Publication

590. Table III (also called the Uniform Lifetime Table) applies if you are married and your spouse is NOT more than 10 years younger than you, or if your spouse is not the sole beneficiary of your IRA, or if you are unmarried.

Table I would only be used to calculate your RMDs if you inherited an IRA from someone other than your spouse prior to January 1, 2020. Table I is also used when a spousal beneficiary elects to defer distributions until the original owner would have turned 73, or whenever the original owner would be required to begin taking distributions. If you are married and your spouse is more than 10 years younger than you and the sole beneficiary of your IRA, you would use Table II: Joint Life and Last Survivor Expectancy.

Most of you will probably use Table III. Effective 2022, the Table III distribution period (or factor or divisor) for your first RMD at age 73 is 26.5. (That is a change from the old law but isn't part of the SECURE Act).

It doesn't matter if you're in perfect health and that both of your parents lived to be 100. Table III is based on the government's estimate of the joint life expectancy of the IRA owner, and someone deemed not more than 10 years younger than the IRA owner.

The following is an oversimplification and isn't technically accurate, but it is easy to remember. If you're 73, the government assumes under the new life expectancy factors that you will live for roughly 17 more years and then tacks on another 10 years to determine the Lifetime Table life expectancy factor. So, let's look at how your first RMD will be calculated.

Start by looking at how much money you had in your retirement plans as of December 31 of the previous year. To keep the math simple, I'm going to assume that you had exactly $1 million. To calculate your first year's RMD, divide the $1 million by the factor in Table III that matches your age. For this example, I will assume the IRA owner is 73, so the factor is 26.5. Dividing $1 million by 26.5 equals $37,736. That's how much you must withdraw from your IRA. It will count towards your taxable income.

Here's another way of looking at it. Your first RMD at age 73 will be a little less than 4% because the 26.5 divisor is a little larger than 25. If the factor were 25, it would be 4% exactly. And as you age, the distribution period that you must divide into your IRA balance gets smaller, which means you are required to take out even larger RMDs. If you have $1 million in your IRA at age 90, your divisor is only 12.2, which will cause an RMD of $81,967. Many of our clients have a lot more than a million dollars in their retirement accounts, which really equates to massive future taxation, both while they are alive and while they are gone.

These forced withdrawals cause headaches for many retirees, not just because they are taxable distributions but because they have an impact on your entire tax return. The distributions can throw you into a higher tax bracket, increase the percentage of taxable Social Security benefits, raise your Medicare B and D premiums, and trigger the Net Investment Income ('NII') tax of 3.8% on investment income. But, notwithstanding the problems you face when you are forced to withdraw money from your retirement plans, the advantages of years of tax deferral usually far outweigh the disadvantages of not saving money in the tax-deferred environment.

Please note that Table II, used if your spouse is more than 10 years younger than you, gives you a much higher divisor resulting in a lower RMD and a lower tax. Additional details about these rules and a description of how your RMD is calculated based on your life expectancy factor can be found in IRS Publication 590-B, available online at **https://www.irs.gov/pub/irs-pdf/p590b.pdf**.

When mandatory distributions are added to wage income and Social Security benefits, it is not uncommon for us to see the taxable income jump up one full bracket and sometimes two. If you don't need the income to live on, most people are much better off deferring withdrawals from Traditional retirement plans for as long as they can. I'll dive into more details about RMDs in Chapter 6.

What if You Work Beyond Age 73?

If you are still working full-time at age 73 (and potentially beyond) you will not have to take RMDs from retirement accounts sponsored by your *current* employer. Traditional IRAs and 401(k)s from *prior* employers do have mandatory RMD requirements at age 73 whether you are working or not, so that may invoke additional planning.

What is 'Retired' for the Purpose of Delaying Your RMD?

Over the years, our accounting office has received the question, 'What if I continue to work part-time after I retire? Can I still defer taking my RMD because technically I'm still working?'

This is an interesting question and unfortunately sounding like an attorney (again) the answer is it depends. Each employer negotiates its own contract with its retirement plan provider so some workplaces may have more restrictive rules.

We recommend you contact your employer's HR Department <u>and</u> pension plan provider directly about your specific situation as this is a complex area and some of the information is unclear and you may not receive the correct advice.

The IRS does not define how many hours are considered 'still working' for the RMD exception. As long as your workplace considers you as an employee and you are *eligible* to participate in the employer plan and you remain employed *after* December 31, meaning January 1st, you MAY qualify for the still-working exception.

An important distinction to know: even if you work through the end of the year and retire on December 31, you are required to take your RMD by April 1 of the following year even though you were working through December 31. In addition, you would need to be employed by your current employer into the next year to possibly qualify for this exception (meaning, receive a W-2 the following year for *hours worked* in the following year). If you defer receiving your accrued sick pay or vacation pay into the following year, this will not qualify for *hours worked*. We are referring to *earned income* that is reported on a W-2 or possibly a 1099 form from the same workplace you are retiring from.

The rules are designed so you cannot 'retire' on a certain date, take distributions from your 401(k) plan, and then decide to work part-time and say, by the way, I'm working now and am no longer required to take my RMD. There is a lot of complexity in the rules surrounding this exception, so we caution you to plan carefully as there can be some unique tax planning opportunities and blunders if not handled correctly.

You can get even more bang for your tax-deferred buck by rolling any IRAs that you may have accumulated over the course of your career into your current work plan, assuming your employer permits it. That way, you can avoid taking RMDs on your old retirement plan or IRA money, too. However, check with your employer's HR department and pension plan provider BEFORE you do this to make sure this is allowed in your employer's plan.

If you decide to employ this strategy, we strongly recommend a 'trustee-to-trustee' transfer of the IRA monies into your current work plan since there are limitations on the number of rollover transfers permitted in a given year.

Once you do stop working, subject to exception, you should limit your taxable withdrawals to the RMD. The exception is when you are trying to reduce what will become an Inherited IRA because you know that your kids are going to get clobbered with taxes after you die. That is a possibility that our CPAs evaluate for all our clients, especially since the SECURE Act eliminated the stretch IRA (although, the stretch option remains for EDBs). That is the exception we discussed above that we call transferring money from the tax-deferred environment to the tax-free environment.

Now that your children who do not qualify as "disabled or chronically ill" are required to distribute their entire Inherited IRA within 10 years of your death, it may make more sense for you to pay tax on the withdrawals. *But paying taxes sooner rather than later is still the exception, not the rule.* You must consider which of your children will inherit your IRA and whether they will qualify as an EDB. An analysis of your future tax bracket(s) and state of residence as well as those of your children also becomes a consideration. I will cover more about evaluating those factors in Chapter 10.

Another exception to the "pay taxes later" maxim is that it sometimes makes sense to distribute IRAs before other funds when you can take advantage of an income tax bracket that is temporarily lower than normal. When I run into that situation, I also think about Roth IRA conversions—especially now for years 2023-2025. The Tax Cut and Jobs Act of 2017 (TCJA) reduced income tax brackets *temporarily* and that can make Roth IRA conversions much more favorable for more people, at least until the rates go up in 2026, as scheduled by this law.

Comparing Current and Future Tax Brackets

In 2017, the 25% income tax bracket topped out at $153,100 for a married couple. In 2023, the 24% tax bracket tops out at $364,200. To oversimplify, income tax rates for most taxpayers were higher in 2017 than they are now, and for a large number of higher-earning families tax rates were *much* higher in 2017 than they are now. This means that many individuals who looked into Roth conversions in the past and found that they would not be cost-effective may find that that is no longer true. Because of the "sunset" provisions of the 2017 TCJA, these reduced tax rates are scheduled to revert to the higher 2017 rates (plus inflation) starting in 2026. Please see the following chart.

As we go to press, the 2024 updated tax brackets were not available. We will be posting the updated numbers on our website at **https://DisabledChildPlanning. com/UpdatedRules**.

Still, you might be thinking, "What are you talking about, Jim? My income isn't anywhere near $364,200 now that I am retired." Maybe so, but if your normal taxable income is $100,000, that means you can now either withdraw more from your retirement plans (or better yet, make a Roth IRA conversion of up to $264,200 or make an ABLE account contribution) and still be in the 24% tax bracket assuming you aren't taking additional Medicare premiums and other issues into account. Please see Chapter 17.

In 2017, that same withdrawal would have put you in the 33% bracket. So, before

Compare Tax Rates for 2017 and 2023

2017 Married Filing Jointly			2023 Married Filing Jointly		
$ 0 – 18,650	x	10%	$ 0 – 22,000	x	10%
18,651 – 75,900	x	15%	22,001 – 89,450	x	12%
75,901 – 153,100	x	25%	89,451 – 190,750	x	22%
153,101 – 233,350	x	28%	190,751 – 364,200	x	24%
233,351 – 416,700	x	33%	364,201 – 462,500	x	32%
416,701 – 470,700	x	35%	462,501 – 693,750	x	35%
470,701 *and above*	x	39.6%	693,751 *and above*	x	37%

Notes: Make Roth conversions at 24% now. Otherwise, you might pay 28% or 33% on RMDs later.

you say that taking more than your RMD from your IRA (or, better yet, making a series of Roth IRA conversions) isn't for you, please be open-minded and examine the data. (In God We Trust, all others bring data.) And if taxes go up in the long run, Roth IRA conversions will be even more profitable for you and your family.

One very valuable service that our CPAs provide for our assets-under-management (AUM) clients[2] is our annual running of the numbers. "Running the numbers" is our shorthand affectionate term for preparing a detailed quantitative analysis of a client's finances to optimize financial decisions. We test the tax implications of a variety of different scenarios based on varying assumptions. For example, we were relatively sure that the SECURE Act (or something like it) was coming, which would likely include accelerating income taxes on Inherited IRAs, so we included those assumptions in many of the different scenarios in our projections even before the SECURE Act passed. Correctly foreseeing the likely changes in the law led us to recommend more and bigger Roth IRA conversions which in hindsight worked out extremely well. Then, those numbers become the basis for a Financial Masterplan. Please see the back of the book for more details.

Many financial professionals who neither "run the numbers" nor understand

---

2 Lange Financial Group, LLC is a registered investment advisory firm registered with the Commonwealth of Pennsylvania Department of banking, Harrisburg, Pennsylvania. In addition, the firm is registered as a registered investment advisory firm in the states of Arizona, Florida, New York, Ohio, Texas, and Virginia. Lange Financial Group LLC may not provide investment advisory services to any residents of states in which the firm does not maintain an investment advisory registration. This does not in any way imply that we are failing to preserve our rights under the respective states' de minimus rule. The presence of this book shall not in any direct or indirect fashion, be construed or interpreted to suggest that the firm is offering to sell or soliciting to provide investment advisory services to residents of any state or states in which the firm is not maintaining an investment advisory registration. Again, we preserve all rights under each state's *de minimus* rule, but we wish to emphasize that we are not directly or indirectly soliciting investment advisory clients in states where we have no legal right to do so.

critical concepts assume that it does not make sense for retired individuals to make Roth IRA conversions. But after we "ran their numbers," we found ourselves recommending that many 72- and 73-year-old+ clients continue executing Roth conversions—even though they were already taking RMDs and receiving Social Security benefits. And if you are not yet retired, many employers now allow you to execute Roth conversions inside your 401(k) plan, assuming the plan document allows in-service conversions.

This is not a "one-size-fits-all" proposition, because every taxpayer has unique circumstances. That said, patterns do emerge. It is an interesting idea to consider making Roth conversions or utilizing the transfer from the taxable to the tax-free environment while you are in the 22% tax bracket that will push you into the 24% bracket if you project that your future RMDs will be taxed at 24% or a higher tax rate.

Three Reasons Your Taxes Will Likely Increase

The recommendations our CPAs make to our clients that are based on tax rates increasing are based on three factors we think are likely to occur. First, our current low tax rates are set to expire at the end of 2025, and unless Congress votes to extend them, tax rates will automatically go up. This isn't even to mention the fiscal problems the United States has. The money needed to pay even the interest on our debt must come from somewhere. In the past, that issue has been partially solved by inflation, which allows the government to pay off debt in dollars that have less purchasing power. In an exclusive interview that I had with Burton Malkiel, he predicted there will be long-term inflation for just this reason.

Second, we also know that your RMD will increase as you age, which will increase your taxable income, your tax rate, and thus, your taxes.

Finally, for couples currently filing income tax returns using the 'married filing jointly' status, there is an additional future tax increase to take into consideration. Eventually one of you will die. Excepting the year of death, the surviving spouse, whose taxable income will likely be similar to what it was in the years preceding their husband or wife's death, will have to file their taxes using the 'single' status which subjects them to much higher rates than they had been paying while their spouse was alive. So, for many couples making a series of strategic Roth conversions before these likely tax raises occur could be extremely valuable to your surviving spouse and to your heirs, down the road.

Please note that if you engage Lange Accounting Group, LLC for our Financial Masterplan service or receive Financial Masterplan services as part of our assets-under-management arrangement with Lange Financial Group, LLC, these services are provided by employees in their capacity as CPAs and are not legal services. The protection of the attorney-client relationship does not exist with respect to these accounting and asset management services.

The point is that just because you are taking minimum distributions and Social Security, don't assume you aren't a suitable candidate for Roth IRA conversions.

These are areas where it really pays to do a Financial Masterplan including "running the numbers". Please see the back of the book if you would be interested in working with us.

Important Point About Required Minimum Distributions and Annuities

If you own annuities inside of your retirement plans (or qualified annuities), you need to be aware of one specific feature that can affect your RMD. Specifically, if you have elected to take a lifetime income from your annuity (also called annuitizing), then the money in that annuity is exempt from the balances you must include when calculating your RMD since you are withdrawing income from your annuity. And if you have a non-qualified annuity (also called a personal or after-tax annuity), you are not required to take a minimum distribution from it at all. But these are just two more reasons why there is no "one-size-fits-all" answer when it comes to determining the best spending strategies for retirees.

As with the old law, you will always be allowed to take out more than the minimum, at least with your IRA. If, however, you can afford to limit your distributions to the minimum, there are significant financial advantages in doing so. Limiting distributions to the minimum defers taxes on the IRA for the longest time available and, subject to exceptions, confers the greatest financial benefits.

The SECURE Act 2.0 defers the time you are required to take your first minimum distribution until age 73 or 75, depending on when you were born. For many people, this will allow additional time for your assets to grow tax-deferred and will likely allow an additional two years during which Roth IRA conversions will be beneficial to you and your family.

On the other hand, many retirees are far more frugal in their spending than they need to be. I would hate to hear you were reducing your spending because you didn't want to withdraw more than the RMD even though you could otherwise afford to spend more. Likewise, if the choice is spending more money or making a Roth IRA conversion, most of the time, I will recommend spending more money.

I remember one client saying he had to cut back on his spending and his charitable contributions because he was planning on paying the taxes on a large Roth IRA conversion that year. No. No. No. The point of the Roth conversions is to enhance the quality of your life, not restrict it.

Though I practically begged him not to cut back on his spending, he did indeed cut back on his spending, depriving himself and his family of certain pleasures they could have enjoyed.

Then, he died. The difference between what he actually spent and what he could have comfortably spent in the big picture was fairly meaningless. His widow, who was left with way more money than she will ever need, referred to her wealth as "numbers in a bank."

So, now that we have an overview of some of the basics of saving and spending retirement assets, let's look at some specific planning issues that all parents need to consider. Please read on.

KEY IDEAS

- Subject to exception, follow the recommended accumulation and distribution strategies and order of saving and spending as suggested in this chapter.

- Pay taxes later, except for Roth.

- Take advantage of any employer match.

- Take advantage of a Health Savings Account, if available to you.

- Contribute to Roth IRAs and Roth 401(k)s

- Contribute to an ABLE account for your child.

- Contribute to traditional retirement plans or IRAs.

- Contribute to nondeductible IRAs or other nondeductible retirement plans.

- Save money in a plain old after-tax brokerage account. • Subject to exception, spend your after-tax dollars before your retirement money.

- Most parents of a child with a disability should try to limit withdrawals from retirement accounts to the minimum required by law (RMD).

Key Ideas continue on the following page.

KEY IDEAS
(continued)

- Spend your Roth accounts last, especially if you have a child with a disability.

- Get your child with a disability or chronic illness qualified for SSI or SSDI and for Medicare.

- Set up a special needs trust for your child with a disability or chronic illness and update beneficiary designations of your retirement plans.

2

The Accumulation Years: Fund Retirement Plans to the Maximum

"The most powerful force in the universe is compound interest."
—Albert Einstein

Please note there is some repetition of Chapter 1 in Chapter 2. This chapter provides additional proof for the recommendations made in Chapter 1. In addition, this chapter explores some of the exceptions to our general rule.

We repeat what we said in Chapter 1 in terms of the best order to accumulate money for retirement. Let's assume you have a certain amount of money that you can afford to contribute for your retirement. What is the best order of the different types of retirement plans that you should consider contributing to?

Subject to exception:

1. Take advantage of any employer match.
2. Take advantage of a Health Savings Account (HSAs), if available to you.
3. Contribute to Roth IRAs, subject to exception based on tax brackets.
4. Consider an ABLE contribution for the benefit of your child with a disability.
5. Contribute to Traditional retirement plans or IRAs.
6. Contribute to nondeductible IRAs or nondeductible contributions to a retirement plan.
7. Save money in a plain old after-tax brokerage account.

Why Contributing the Maximum to a Retirement Plan Is So Important

A trusted client of mine recently referred to me as her "guardian angel." At first, I was totally taken aback—no one had ever called me a guardian angel before. She continued, "Thirty years ago you advised me to put the maximum into my retirement plan. I didn't know if it was a good idea or not, but I trusted you and did what you recommended. Now I have a million dollars in my retirement plan. What should I do now?"

Another client recently reminded me of a similar recommendation I made many years ago. He was basically retired from his university but was teaching one course and was paid with a W-2. I recommended that he should maximize his retirement plan contributions even though his net check was close to zero.

These comments compelled me to complete a comprehensive analysis of why it was such good advice to maximize your retirement plan. I wanted to be able to persuasively convince anyone who harbored the least little doubt about the advantages of saving money in a retirement plan over saving money outside of a retirement plan. Also, I didn't think this was a concept I could prove with words. It had to be proven by math and a mini "running the numbers" comparison.

I set out to evaluate the outcomes of two different scenarios. For this example, we do not consider the employer match:

You earn the money, you pay the tax, you invest the money you earned, and you pay tax on the dividends, interest, and capital gains.

You earn the money and then invest money in your retirement plan, and you get a tax deduction. The money grows tax-deferred, and you don't pay taxes on that money until you take it out.

So, which is better: saving inside the retirement plan or outside the retirement plan? The answer: it is better to save within the retirement plan. Why? This isn't a touchy-feely issue. It comes down to numbers. Let's take a deeper look into the scenario I briefly presented in Chapter 1.

···································· **MINI CASE STUDY 2.1** ····································

The Clear Advantage of Pre-Tax IRA and Retirement Plan Savings

Mr. Pay Taxes Later and Mr. Pay Taxes Now are neighbors. From the outside, you wouldn't be able to tell them apart: they own the same type of car; their salaries are the same; and they are in the same tax bracket. Their savings have the same investment rate of return, and they even save the same percentage of their gross wages every year.

They have one big difference. Mr. Pay Taxes Later invests as much as he can afford in his tax-deferred retirement plan—his Traditional 401(k)—even though his employer does not match his contributions. Mr. Pay Taxes Now feels that putting money in a retirement account makes it "not really his money" as he puts it. He doesn't want to have to pay taxes to take out his own money or put up with other restrictions that limit his access to "his money." Thus, he contributes nothing to his retirement account at work but invests his savings in an account outside of his retirement plan. Mr. Pay Taxes Now invests the old-fashioned way: earn the money, pay the tax, invest the money, and pay the tax on the income that the invested money generates (dividends, capital gains, etc.).

Both men begin investing at age 30.

- In 2022, they each started saving $8,000 per year, indexed for inflation.

- Mr. Pay Taxes Later has his entire $8,000 withheld from his paycheck and deposited to his tax-deferred 401(k). (The analysis would be conceptually identical if he contributed the money to a Traditional deductible IRA.)

- Mr. Pay Taxes Now chooses not to have any retirement funds withheld but rather to be paid in full. He pays income taxes on his full wages—which includes the $8,000 he chose not to contribute to his retirement plan. After the 24 percent income tax is paid, he has only 76 percent of the $8,000, or $6,080, left to invest.

Now look at Figure 2.1. Mr. Pay Taxes Later's investment is represented by the solid line, and Mr. Pay Taxes Now's by the dashed line. Look at the dramatic difference in the accumulations over time.

Now, to be fair, Mr. Pay Taxes Later will have to pay taxes eventually. When he is retired, for every dollar he wants to withdraw, he must take out $1.32. He pockets the dollar and pays $0.32 in taxes (24 percent of $1.32). If Mr. Pay Taxes

Figure 2.1

**Retirement Plans and Tax-Deferred Savings *vs.*
After-Tax Savings Accounts***

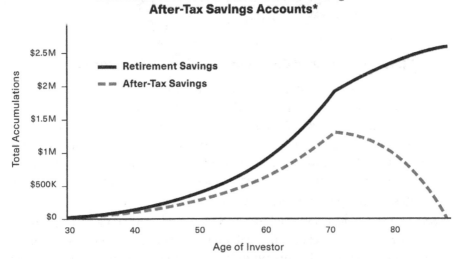

Age of Investor

Detailed assumptions can be found in the Appendix.

Now withdraws a dollar, subject to some capital gains taxes, it's all his, just as he wanted. At age 88, however, Mr. Pay Taxes Now has depleted his funds entirely whereas Mr. Pay Taxes Later has $2,606,774 left in his retirement plan.

Given reasonable assumptions and all things being equal, following the adage, "Don't pay taxes now—pay taxes later" can be worth over $2 million over your lifetime.

After spending your life working hard, paying the mortgage, paying the bills, raising a family, and paying for braces, putting your kids through college, etc. you may never have expected to have such a substantial IRA or retirement plan and be so well off in retirement. For many of my clients, it seems like a fantasy. But it isn't a fantasy, and you need to think about the best ways to manage that money.

Make Those Nonmatched Contributions to Retirement Plans

What conclusion can we draw from Mini Case Study 2.1? Don't pay taxes now—pay taxes later. Even if your employer does not offer the additional advantage of matching contributions, you should contribute the maximum to your retirement plan, assuming you can afford it. Money contributed to a retirement plan, whether a 401(k), 403(b), SEP, SIMPLE, 457, deductible IRA, or another type of retirement plan, is a pre-tax investment that grows tax deferred. There are no federal income taxes on the wages contributed.

Some taxpayers view contributions as tax-deductible. Others say those contributions aren't taxable. Whichever way you look at it, you are getting a tax break for the amount of the contribution multiplied by the tax rate for your tax bracket.

> **All things being equal, following the adage,**
> ***"Don't pay taxes now — pay taxes later"* can be worth**
> **over $2 million over your lifetime.**

Furthermore, once the contribution is made, you do not pay income taxes on the interest, dividends, and appreciation *until you take a distribution* (i.e., withdrawal) from the retirement plan. In other words, you pay taxes later.

By not paying taxes up-front on the wages invested in your retirement plan, you reap the harvest of compounding interest, dividends, and capital gains on the money that would have gone to paying taxes—both on the amount contributed, and on the growth, had the money been invested outside of the retirement plan.

In the real world, not only is there a tax advantage to saving in a retirement plan but doing so builds in the discipline of contributing to your retirement plan with every paycheck. The example above assumes that if you are not putting the money in your retirement plan, you are saving and investing an amount equal to what your retirement contribution would have been. But can you trust yourself to be a disciplined saver? Will the temptation to put off saving for retirement until the next paycheck undermine your resolve? Even if you do put it in savings, knowing you have unrestricted access to the money, can you be confident that you would never invade that fund until you retire?

In my accounting practice, the clients who usually have the most money saved at retirement are the ones who religiously contributed to a retirement plan over the course of their long careers.

The idea of paying taxes later and contributing the maximum to your retirement plan(s) is something that I have preached in my practice for over 35 years. Many of my long-standing clients took my advice 20 or 30 years ago—even if they didn't completely understand why—and now they are thanking me.

The Employer Matching Retirement Plan

"Money won is twice as sweet as money earned."

—Paul Newman, *The Color of Money*

With all due respect, broadly speaking, you must be pretty "simple" (that's a nice word for "stupid") not to take advantage of a retirement plan where the employer makes a matching contribution.

In my practice, the clients who usually have the most money saved at retirement are the ones who religiously contributed to a retirement plan over the course of their long careers.

The Cardinal Rule of Saving for Retirement

If your employer offers a retirement plan matching contribution, the cardinal rule is: contribute **at least** the amount the employer is willing to match—even if it is only a percentage of your contribution and not a dollar-for-dollar match. Imagine depositing $1,000 of your money in a bank, but instead of getting a crummy toaster, you receive an extra $1,000 to go along with your deposit. To add to the fun, imagine getting a tax deduction for your deposit and not having to pay taxes on your gift. Furthermore, both your $1,000 and the gift of $1,000 grow (hopefully), and you don't have to pay income tax on the interest, dividends, capital gains, or the appreciation until you withdraw the money.

When you withdraw the money, you will have to pay taxes, but you will have gained interest, dividends, and appreciation in the meantime. That is what employer-matching contributions to retirement plans are all about. If the employer matches the employee contribution on a dollar-for-dollar basis, it is the same as a *100 percent return on the investment in one day* (assuming no early withdrawal penalties apply, and the matched funds are fully vested).

Over the years, I have heard a lot of excuses for not taking advantage of an employer-matching plan. With few exceptions, all those reasons come down to two words: *ignorance* and *neglect*. If you didn't know that before, you know it now. If you are not currently taking advantage of your employer-matching plan, run—don't walk—to your plan administrator and begin the paperwork to take advantage of the employer match. Matching contributions are most commonly found within 401(k), 403(b), and 457 plans. Many eligible 403(b) plan participants also may have access to a 457 plan. You can, in effect, enjoy double the ability to tax-defer earnings through participation in both the 403(b) and 457 plans. Even if your employer is only willing to make a partial match up to a cap, you should still take advantage of this opportunity. For example, a fairly common retirement plan agreement may provide that the employer contributes 50 cents for every dollar up to the first 6 percent of salary that you contribute. Keep in mind: This is free money! Again, this isn't touchy-feely stuff. It is backed by hard numbers.

Many eligible 403(b) plan participants also may have access to a 457 plan. You can, in effect, enjoy double the ability to tax-defer earnings through participation in both the 403(b) and 457 plans.

···························· **MINI CASE STUDY 2.2** ····························

Running the Numbers for Employer-Matched Retirement Plans

Scenario 1

- Bill earns $75,000 per year and is subject to a flat 24 percent federal income tax (for simplicity, I ignore other taxes and assume a flat federal income tax: 24% x $75,000 = $18,000 tax).
- He spends $50,000 per year.
- He doesn't use his retirement plan at work, so he has $7,000 available to invest: ($75,000 income—[$18,000 tax and $50,000 spending] = $7,000 available cash).

Scenario 2

Bob also earns $75,000 per year, has the same tax rate, and spends the same amount. But Bob's uncle was a very wise man—he bought the original **Retire Secure!** After reading the original version of this chapter, he advised all of his nieces and nephews to be sure to contribute the maximum amounts to their retirement accounts that their future employers were willing to match. Bob took his uncle's counsel to heart, so he contributes $8,000 to his retirement account and his employer matches his contribution 100 percent. Thus $16,000 goes into his retirement account. Bob's contribution is higher than Bill's because Bob is investing not only his employee contribution but his employer is matching his contribution, so Bob is investing more than double the amount of money than Bill on a tax-deferred basis. Bob is still able to spend the same $50,000 a year that Bill is spending.

Under current tax laws, Bob will not have to pay federal income tax on his retirement plan contribution or on the amount his employer is willing to match, until the money is withdrawn from the plan. By using his employer's retirement plan, Bob's picture changes for the better as follows:

- Bob pays tax on only $67,000.
    ($75,000 income—$8,000 tax-deferred)
    (24% x $67,000 = $16,080 tax)
- He now has $58,920 ($75,000 income—$16,080 taxes).
- He makes his plan contribution of $8,000, leaving him with $50,920 outside the plan.
- His employer matches the $8,000 (also tax-deferred).
- He now has $16,000 in his retirement plan (growing tax-deferred).
- He spends $50,000 per year.
- He is left with $920 in cash.

Which scenario strikes you as more favorable: Scenario 2, with $16,000 in a retirement plan and $920 in cash, or Scenario 1, with no retirement plan and $7,000 in cash? The extreme cynic can figure out situations when a little extra cash and no retirement plan would be preferable, but the rest of us will take advantage of any employer-matching retirement plan.

Please keep in mind that the money in the retirement plan will continue to grow, and you will not have to pay income taxes on the earnings, dividends, interest, or accumulations until you (or your heirs) withdraw the money. But, even without weighing in the advantages of the long-term deferral, at the end of the first year, assuming the employer-matched funds are fully vested, the comparative values of these two scenarios are measured by after-tax purchasing power as follows:

	Scenario 1	Scenario 2
After-tax cash available	$ 7,000	$ 920
Retirement plan balance	0	$ 16,000
Tax on retirement plan balance	0	($ 3,840)
Early withdrawal penalty	0	($ 1,600)
Total Purchasing Power	**$ 7,000**	**$ 11,480**

Even if Bob has a financial emergency and must withdraw money from his 401(k) prior to age 59½, resulting in tax and an early withdrawal penalty, and even if he doesn't qualify for any of the exceptions, he still has $4,480 more than Bill, who saved his money in an after-tax account. And if Bob is older than 59½ when he needs to make the withdrawal, the penalty doesn't apply, and the difference is even greater. Obviously, it is better to take advantage of the retirement plan and the employer's matching contributions.

Figure 2.2 demonstrates that the long-term advantages of the employer match are even more dramatic using the same basic facts and circumstances as in Mini Case Study 2.1 but adding in a 100 percent employer match of annual contributions. Figure 2.2 compares stubborn Bill who refuses to use the retirement plan versus prudent Bob who contributes to his retirement plan.

Using slightly higher spending assumptions than Mini Case Study 2.1, to be consistent with taking a RMD (please see Chapter 6), Bill runs out of money at age 84 instead of at age 88 as in Mini Case Study 2.1. However, Bob's matched retirement savings plan has $5,446,284 remaining when he is 84 instead of zero. And despite the large distributions being made after age 84, prudent Bob's savings are still growing when he reaches 94. The obvious conclusion again is, if you are not already taking advantage of this, run—don't walk—to your plan administrator and begin the paperwork to take advantage of the employer match.

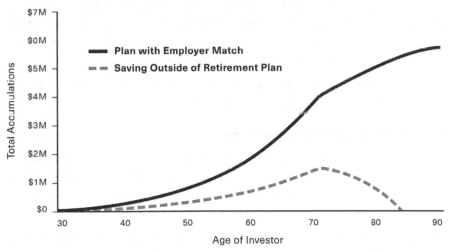

Figure 2.2

**Retirement Assets Plus an Employer Match *vs.*
After-Tax Accumulations***

Detailed assumptions can be found in the Appendix.

Occasionally, clients moan that they literally can't afford to make the contribution, even though their employer is willing to match it. I am not sympathetic. I would rather see you borrow the money to make matching contributions. Beg, borrow, or steal to find the money to contribute to an employer-matching plan.

Taking Advantage of the Employer's Match for Your Children Through Gifting

There is an interesting application of this idea if you have a child who is working, and you want to see that child's retirement plan grow, but your child claims he or she isn't making enough to contribute to his or her retirement plan, even though the company offers a matching contribution. You may want to consider making a gift to your child in the amount that your child would be out-of-pocket, if they contributed an amount that would be matched. Your child can then maintain their spending levels, which are probably way too high by your standards for someone in your child's position. Then, they could use the money you give them to maximize the matching portion of their retirement plan at work. Let's assume a 100% match of $5,000. Your child puts $5,000 into their Roth 401(k), and the employer matches the $5,000 in the Traditional 401(k). In effect, your $5,000 gift conferred $10,000 of value (and much more if you consider the future tax benefits) for a cost of $5,000.

Alternatively, your child could use the money and put it in a regular pre-tax 401(k), not a Roth 401(k). Here are the numbers for that transaction. Let's say your child's employer matches 100 percent, up to $5,000, and your child is in the 22% tax bracket. If you make a gift of $3,900 ($5,000 - $1,100 tax), your child should now have enough cash to make a $5,000 retirement plan contribution and would end up with $10,000 in his or her retirement account. That is an example of a leveraged gift. Lots of bang for your gifted buck!

Of course, if you want to provide for your child with a disability, then the gift should be to an ABLE account. Please see Chapter 14.

Two Categories of Retirement Plans

Before I get into the details, let me offer a big picture comment. Many parents can make bigger contributions than they are actually making even though they can afford it. That is still true even if they have read a prior version of this section but for some reason still didn't take the advice offered here.

Generally, all retirement plans in the workplace fall into two categories: *Defined Contribution Plans* and *Defined Benefit Plans.* Depending on the options available in your state and at your employer, you may be able to choose either a Defined Contribution Plan or a Defined Benefit Plan. While many employers offer a Defined Contribution Plan, not all offer a Defined Benefit Plan.

Defined Contribution Plans

Defined contribution plans are relatively easy to understand, and usually offer a wide variety of tax-favored investment options. In a defined contribution plan, each individual employee has an account that can be funded by either the employee or the employer, or both.

Employers frequently say that the employee's contributions are tax-deductible, which is not technically correct. The employee's taxable income is reduced by the amount that they contribute to the plan, which means that employees who do not have enough deductions to itemize at tax time, will still realize a tax benefit from contributing to the plan. At retirement or termination of employment, subject to a few minor exceptions, the money in a defined contribution plan sponsored by the employer represents the funds available to the employee that can be rolled into his or her own IRA.

In a defined contribution plan, the employee bears the investment risks. In other words, if the market suffers a downturn, so does the value of your investments. Conversely, if the market does well, you are rewarded with a higher balance. The plan illustrated in Figures 1.1 and 1.2 is an example of a defined contribution plan.

Most employers are now offering Roth account options within their defined contribution plans. More information on the advantages of each option is covered in Chapter 4. If offered, the employee can direct all of their contributions to the Roth account or split them between the Roth and Traditional accounts. The Roth accounts are excellent options that provide tax-free growth within defined contribution plans. But unlike employee contributions to Traditional accounts, Roth contributions do not reduce taxable income.

In addition, as of this writing, recent legislation allows employer matching contributions to be added to the employee's Roth account. However, because this is a very new option, plans must be amended to include the Roth option for employer matching contributions. Check with your benefits administrator to find out if this has been done. Most likely, at least as we go to press, it has not.

Common Defined Contribution Plans

Please note as we go into design for this book, the numbers that follow are accurate. But the proposed regulations would increase these amounts so literally by the time this book goes to press, there could be higher limits. That said, the concepts won't change.

401(k) Plan: This plan can accept both employee and employer tax-deferred contributions. The contributions to the plan and the earnings are not federally taxable until they are withdrawn.

Employee contributions to 401(k)s are usually determined as a percentage of salary or wages and are limited to a prescribed amount. In 2023, for taxpayers under age 50, that limit is $22,500. For taxpayers aged 50 and older, the IRS permits additional "catch-up contributions" of $7,500 for a total of $30,000. Beginning in year 2025, as part of SECURE Act 2.0, the maximum catch-up contribution for taxpayers who are age 60-63 during the tax year will be able to contribute the greater of $10,000 or 150% of the catch-up contribution limit. These limits are increased for inflation and as mentioned above will likely be higher by the time you read this book.

The company—that is, the employer—is responsible for providing the employee with investment choices, typically six to ten choices in either one or two families of mutual funds. Some large employers offering 401(k) plans also allow their employees to purchase individual stock shares in their plans. Fortunately, after the spectacular collapse of Enron, companies are no longer permitted to *require* that their employees own company stock inside their retirement plans.

The employer is also responsible for setting the basic rules of the plan—for example, whether they will offer a matching contribution, or if they will permit loans against the plan. They are also responsible for choosing the investments that are made available to the employee, and for plan administration. The employee is responsible for choosing his or her own investments from the options made available by the employer. 401(k) plans are typically found in for-profit entities.

403(b) Plan: This plan is similar to a 401(k) plan but is commonly used by certain charitable organizations and public educational institutions, such as universities, colleges, and hospitals. Like a 401(k), the maximum contribution is limited in 2023 to $22,500 for employees under age 50, or $30,000 for those over age 50. 403(b) plans also have a special "15 years of service" catch-up provision— so even if you're not age 50 or older, you may be able to contribute more than $22,500 to your plan.

One big difference between a 401(k) plan and a 403(b) plan is that, for non-church employees, 403(b) plans can only invest in annuities and mutual funds.

457 Plan: After the Economic Growth and Tax Relief Reconciliation Act of 2001 (EGTRRA), 457 plans have become more similar to 401(k) plans. They are commonly used by state and local governmental employers and certain tax-exempt organizations. Typical 457 employees are police officers, firefighters, teachers, and other municipal workers.

An interesting side note is that many eligible 457 plan participants don't realize they are eligible to make a 457 plan contribution. They may have a 403(b) plan and don't know they can "double" their tax-deferred earnings through participating in both a 403(b) and a 457 plan. A perfect candidate for using both plans would be a married employee whose spouse has income, and their combined income is more than sufficient for their needs. If they have enough income and if they are age 50 or older in 2023, the employee could contribute a maximum of $22,500 to his or her 403(b), $22,500 to a 457 plan, and make an additional catch-up contribution of $7,500. By doing so, the couple could reduce their taxable income by $52,500. Some 457 plans provide a "catch-up" provision for employees who are within three years of normal retirement age, which allows them to contribute even more.

Like other retirement plans, you can't have a Roth 457 unless the plan allows for Roth contributions. Hopefully, that same plan would allow in-plan rollovers to designated Roth accounts.

A question came up in our accounting office, can a state university employee contribute to a Roth account within a 457(b) plan? One CPA thought 'no,' you can only contribute to a pre-tax Traditional account. Another CPA professional said, 'yes' you can contribute to a Roth. What is the correct answer? Well, despite not being attorneys, after doing the appropriate research, the consensus among the CPAs was "it depends."

Governmental 457(b) plans allow employee contributions to a Roth account, provided the plan document permits Roth contributions. The rules do not allow Roth contributions to 457(b) plans sponsored by *non-profit* organizations. But what if you work for a state university? This is where it gets interesting. Some state universities have adopted the *governmental* 457(b) plan over the *non-profit* 457(b) plan. The professors who work for a state university who have a *governmental* 457(b) plan can contribute to a Roth (for example, University of Michigan, Ohio State University, and University of Pittsburgh).

Bottom line, if you are employed by a state university, you will need to check with your Human Resources Department to see if your employee contributions can go towards a Roth account but more importantly whether your institution allows any 457 contributions.

Note, there is an annual maximum of the amount that can be placed into a defined contribution plan in a given year, which includes the total of your employee elective deferrals to the 403(b) plan and 457(b) plan, and any matching contributions made by the university to your 403(b) plan. The maximum amount for 2023 is $66,000 plus a catch-up contribution of $7,500 if age 50 or older, for a total annual contribution limit of $73,500 or 100% of compensation (whichever is lower). The annual contribution limit usually increases annually.

401(a) Plan: These are also known as money-purchase retirement savings plans and are most commonly offered by government agencies, educational institutions, and not-for-profit organizations. They are highly customizable by the employer, so you may find vastly differing options at different organizations, and even different options offered to different subsets of employees. Many 401(a)s are structured to offer employees an incentive to stay at the organization. They may be funded with dollar-, or percentage-based contributions from the employer, the employee, or both. Employers may match a fixed percentage of employee contributions, or they may make fixed dollar or percentage contributions. Employee participation may be mandatory. The combined limit for employee and employer contributions for 2023 is $66,000, or up to the employee's compensation. The contribution limits for 401(a) plans are computed separately from the limits for 457 plans and 403(b) plans, so if you and your employer contribute the maximum, you could theoretically get up to a maximum of $66,000 between all three of these defined contribution plans or $73,500 if over age 50.

SEP: SEP is an acronym for Simplified Employee Pension. These plans are commonly used by employers with very few employees, and self-employed individuals. Under a SEP, an employer makes contributions to IRAs, which are not taxable for federal income tax purposes, on behalf of employees. Contribution limits are higher with SEPs than with IRAs. Maximum allowable contributions equal 25 percent of the employee's compensation, up to $66,000 in 2023. If considering a SEP, you must be careful to look at how *compensation* is defined. After you go through the technical hoops, the contribution actually works out to be about 20 percent of what most self-employed people think is compensation. Beginning in year 2023, a taxpayer can elect to have their SEP contributions be in the form of a Roth contribution. Prior to 2023, the contributions could only be Traditional pre-tax contributions.

SIMPLE: SIMPLE is an acronym for a Savings Incentive Match Plan for Employees. They provide an attractive defined-contribution plan option for small companies that do not sponsor a retirement plan, or self-employed individuals. The maximum allowable contribution ($15,500 in 2023) is lower than that of a SEP, and the employer is required to make either a two percent (2%) non-elective contribution for each eligible employee, or a three percent (3%) matching contribution for all participating employees. These plans also allow additional "catch-up" contributions to be made by employees over age 50 in the amount of $3,500 for 2023. As with the SEP IRA described above, effective in 2023, a taxpayer's contributions can now be contributed as a Roth contribution after an election has been made. Prior to 2023, the contributions could only be Traditional pre-tax contributions.

SEP, SIMPLEs, and One Person 401(k)

Of the three options, we generally prefer a one-person 401(k) a.k.a. Solo-K, a.k.a. Super-K.

Solo-K or One-Person 401(k): The Solo-K is commonly used by self-employed individuals (with no employees) who want to contribute the most money possible to their own retirement plan. The business owner who has this kind of plan wears two hats—he can contribute to his personal 401(k) as an employee, and then make an additional contribution as the employer. Employee contributions are limited to $22,500 in 2023 ($30,000 if age 50 or over), or up to 100% of compensation if earnings are lower than $22,500. As the employer, the business owner can also make an additional maximum contribution equaling 25 percent of his or her annual compensation. (As with a SEP plan, be careful to define compensation accurately.) Between the employee and employer contributions, a business owner could contribute $66,000 in 2023 ($73,500 if they are age 50 or older) to their own retirement plan.

For an example of the power of the Solo-K and a calculation, please see Judy's example in Mini Case Study 2.3. These Solo-K plans can also be set up to contain a Roth savings option. This is also the type of plan I usually prefer for the new self-employed retiree that has some type of consulting or other income.

There is a little known but enormously effective strategy, especially advantageous if you have a child with a disability. Consider planning for your heirs to make Inherited Roth IRA conversion possibilities with an Inherited 401(k). This posthumous conversion is not available for an Inherited IRA—only an Inherited 401(k). Please see Chapter 11.

Payroll Deduction IRA: This is a relatively newer savings option created in 2013, and it works for businesses of any size. It is probably the simplest and least expensive retirement plan option available to employers, but the contribution limits are low. The employee is responsible for opening an IRA account (either a Traditional or Roth) with any financial institution that offers one. The employer is then responsible for deducting IRA contributions from the employee's pay and depositing the funds into the employee's IRA account. The employer is not permitted to make matching contributions.

The 2023 contribution limit for this type of account is $6,500, with an additional catch-up contribution of $1,000 allowed for employees aged 50 and over. If you think this sounds a lot like a regular IRA, you're right; the major difference is that the payroll deduction by the employer forces the employee to contribute to his or her account.

Deferral Contribution Limits Compared

As a result of a series of tax law changes starting with the Economic Growth and Tax Relief Reconciliation Act of 2001 (EGTRRA), the new deferral contribution limits for employees and owners of many of these individual and defined-contribution plans have grown substantially more generous. The government now allows us to put more money in our retirement plans and provides greater tax benefits. I recommend that we take the government up on its offer to fund our own retirement plans to the extent we can afford it.

The maximum deferral contribution limits for 2023 are shown in the chart below. (The maximum contributions for individuals younger than age 50 appear in the first line and the maximum contributions for those age 50 and older are in the second line and in italics.) As we go to press, the updated deferral contribution limits for 2024 were not available. We will be posting the updated numbers on our website at **https://DisabledChildPlanning.com/UpdatedRates**.

Please remember that, with the exception of the Roth accounts discussed more fully in Chapter 3, every one of the retirement plans listed above works basically the same way. Subject to limitations, your taxable income is reduced by the amount you contribute to your plan. Your employer's contribution is not subject to federal income taxes when it is made, nor is your deferral contribution. You pay no federal income tax until you take a withdrawal from the plan, and your money can only be withdrawn according to specific rules and regulations. Ultimately, the distributions are taxed at ordinary income tax rates. These plans offer tax-deferred growth because as the assets appreciate, taxes on the dividends, interest, and capital gains are deferred—or delayed—until there is a withdrawal or a distribution.

There are important potential tax considerations depending on which state you live in and which state you retire to, and sometimes you should take appropriate action before you even pack up your belongings and move. For example, one client of mine who lived in Washington State was planning to move to California. Because California taxes IRA distributions and Roth conversions, we had him make a series of Roth IRA conversions before he moved. The conversions we recommended were even higher than we normally would have recommended had we not taken into account his pending move. He didn't have to pay Washington

Maximum Deferral Contribution Limits for 2020-2023

	2020	2021	2022	2023
SIMPLE Plans [a]	$13,500	$13,500	$14,000	$15,500
50 and older	*$16,500*	*$16,500*	*$17,500*	*$19,000*
401(k), 403(b), 457 [b]	$19,500	$19,500	$20,500	$22,500
50 and older	*$26,000*	*$26,000*	*$27,000*	*$30,000*
401(a) [c]	$57,000	$58,000	$61,000	$66,000
Roth 401(k) + Roth 403(b)	$19,500	$19,500	$20,500	$22,500
50 and older	*$26,000*	*$26,000*	*$27,000*	*$30,000*
SEP [d, e]	$57,000	$58,000	$61,000	$66,000
50 and older	*$57,000*	*$58,000*	*$61,000*	*$66,000*
Solo-K [One-Person 401(k)] [d, e]	$57,000	$58,000	$61,000	$66,000
50 and older	*$63,500*	*$64,500*	*$67,500*	*$73,500*
Traditional and Roth IRA	$6,000	$6,000	$6,000	$6,500
50 and older	*$7,000*	*$7,000*	*$7,000*	*$7,500*
Payroll Deduction IRA	$6,000	$6,000	$6,000	$6,500
50 and older	*$7,000*	*$7,000*	*$7,000*	*$7,500*

[a] SIMPLE plans are for enterprises with 100 or fewer eligible workers.

[b] 403(b) plans are for nonprofits; 457 plans are for governments and nonprofits. In the last three years before retirement, workers in 457 plans can save double the "under age 50" contribution limit.

[c] The limits for 401(a) plan are for combined employer and employee contributions. There are no catch-up contributions for ages 50 and older.

[d] Overall, plan limits for business owners include total of all contributions by the employer (self owned business), employee (self), and any forfeitures. SEP plans do not permit catch-up contributions.

[e] Plus amounts for inflation-related adjustments.

tax on the Roth conversion. After he moved to California he could have tax-free distributions of his Roth IRA not only for federal purposes, but for California purposes also. When he dies and leaves his Roth IRA to his spouse and then their son who lives in California, neither his wife nor his son will ever have to pay California taxes on the Roth IRA or Inherited Roth IRA. If he leaves the money to a child with a disability (if qualified), that child could "stretch" the Inherited Roth IRA over their lifetime.

It is important to know that states tax retirement plans differently. Some states, such as Pennsylvania, do not give employees a tax deduction for their retirement plan contributions but they don't tax retirement plan distributions.

So, Pennsylvania becomes a less desirable state to work in, but a more desirable state to retire to.

California, on the other hand, does give employees a tax deduction for their retirement plan contributions, but California taxes IRA and retirement plan distributions, which presumably over time would mean more revenue for the state because the distributions would include appreciation.

A bad scenario for tax purposes would be to live and work in Pennsylvania, not get a tax break for your retirement plan contributions and IRAs, and then retire to California where your IRA and retirement plan distributions would be taxed. That is exactly what one of my tax-savvy clients did. His justification was he wanted to live in California more than he wanted to save taxes in retirement.

A better plan would be to work in California, get the tax break for your retirement plan and IRA contributions, and then retire to Pennsylvania, with no state taxes on retirement plan distributions. You could also retire to a state that doesn't have an income tax, like Texas or Florida. The problem with retiring to Texas isn't Texas taxes. The problem is you have to live in Texas.

Kidding aside, don't let the tail wag the dog. Usually, it is best to live and work where you want and retire to where you want. But sometimes, you can do some tax planning. Sometimes, if it is close, like you spent 175 days in a no or low-tax state, maybe spend an extra week and become a resident of that state. Though time spent is only one test of being a resident. There are other factors to consider when determining residency and we suggest you consult with a tax advisor before making the determination.

Timing and Vesting of Defined Contribution Plans

It is important to understand when employers are required to make their deposits to your retirement plan, and when your interest in the plan becomes vested.

First, your employer is not allowed to hang on to the money they deduct from your paycheck indefinitely. Department of Labor rules require that your employer deposit your contributions to your retirement plan "as soon as possible, but no later than the fifteenth business day of the following month." There are more restrictive rules in place for employers having fewer than 100 plan participants—these employers are required to deposit your contributions within seven business days.

Note, however, that the rules are different for the employer contribution; employers must make their contributions to an employee's retirement plan by the due date of the employer's federal tax return (including extensions). As a result, if your employer is on a calendar year-end, you might not see the matching portion of your 401(k) until well after year-end. Other employers match immediately when a contribution is made.

Also, just because the money is credited to your account doesn't necessarily mean it is all yours immediately. The portion you contribute will always be yours, and if you quit tomorrow, your contribution remains your money. The employer's contribution might only become available to you after working a certain number of years—once you have put in your time. Your employer may refer to this as being "vested" in the plan. A common vesting schedule is 20 percent per year that an employee remains with the company until five years have passed. At that point, the employee is 100 percent vested. This is called graded vesting. Other plans allow no vesting until the employee has worked for a certain number of years. Then, when he or she reaches that threshold, there is a 100 percent vesting in the employer's contributions. This is called cliff vesting and cannot be any longer than three years.

A Quick Note about Retirement Plan Loans

Loans against IRAs and IRA-based plans (SEPs and SIMPLEs) are prohibited by law, but loans are permitted against 401(k), 403(b), 457(b), profit sharing and money purchase plans. Some employers offering these types of defined contribution plans allow their employees to take loans against their retirement accounts. Federal tax laws specify that, if loans are permitted, the amount can't be more than 50% of the participant's vested account balance, up to a maximum of $50,000. Federal laws also specify that the loan must be repaid within five years unless the proceeds were used to buy your primary residence.

Remember, the employer is responsible for setting the rules of their own plan, so some employers might only permit loans in the event of financial hardship, and some might not permit them at all. If loans are permitted, the employee must sign a written loan agreement that specifies the repayment schedule. Most employers require that the loan be repaid through payroll deductions.

If someone needs a loan, many people prefer to take one against their retirement plan because the interest rates are generally lower than what they can get from a bank, and they pay that interest back to themselves. There are some negatives with this strategy that you need to be aware of though. The money taken out of the plan is no longer earning an investment rate of return and, even if the loan is repaid with interest, the interest rate will likely not be as high as the investment rate of return that would have been earned if the money had remained in the account. Because most employers require repayment via payroll deduction, many employees can't afford to continue their 401(k) contributions while they are repaying their loan—which affects their ability to reach their long-term retirement goals. And if your employer offers a matching contribution, you lose their matching contribution (which I call free money) during the time you are not contributing to the plan. In some plans, when you take out a loan, you are prohibited from making employee contributions to the plan for one year. This rule is specific to the employer's plan document and not an IRS rule.

While these might seem like relatively minor points, I think you will really regret taking a loan from your retirement plan if you are separated from service before it is repaid. If you lose your job for any reason, you are generally obligated to repay the full balance remaining on the loan, within 60 days. What do you think the chances are of a bank giving you another loan to repay your retirement plan loan, when you are unemployed? If you are unable to repay it, then your employer is required to treat the loan as a distribution, and you will receive a 1099-R that you will have to include on your tax return the following year. In addition to having to pay taxes on the unpaid balance of the loan, you may also owe a 10 percent penalty if you are under the age of 59½. And while you might not plan on leaving your job, that decision could be made for you by a change in your employer's priorities. Then, you are left with a tax problem that you didn't see coming when you were filling out your paperwork for your loan.

We have seen people that had to file for bankruptcy because they couldn't pay the massive taxes on the distributions from their IRA or retirement plan.

To add to their misery, their IRA or retirement plan, which is now reduced, was one of the assets that would have been protected from creditors in a bankruptcy.

Defined Benefit Plans

With a defined benefit plan, the employer contributes money according to a formula described in the company plan to provide a promised monthly benefit to the employee at retirement. Many people refer to these types of plans as "my pension." While most commonly offered by federal, state, and local governments, there are a few private employers who still offer them.

If your employer offers a choice between a defined benefit and a defined contribution plan, think carefully before making your choice. This is a situation where "running the numbers" can help you see the financial implications of your decision.

Defined benefit plans were far more common 30 years ago than they are today. For people with defined benefit plans, there are few opportunities to make strategic decisions during the working years to increase retirement benefits. It might be possible to increase the retirement benefit by deferring salary or bonuses into the final years or working overtime to increase the calculation wage base. These opportunities, however, depend on the plan's formula, and they are often inflexible and insignificant.

At retirement, the employee is often given a wide range of choices of how to collect his or her pension. Distribution options generally involve receiving a certain amount of money every month for the rest of one's life. Receiving regular payments for a specified period, usually a lifetime, is called an annuity. (Please don't confuse this type of annuity with a tax-deferred annuity or a 403(b) plan, which is also often called an annuity.) The annuity period often runs for your lifetime and that of your spouse. Or it might be defined with a guaranteed period for successor beneficiaries; maybe it is guaranteed for the life of the longest living spouse, or perhaps for a 10-year term regardless of when you die, or your spouse dies.

Guaranteeing Income for Life

Employees who have defined benefit plans have some very important options to consider at the time of retirement. For example, let's assume that you are in good health and want the highest monthly income for the rest of your life. That often seems like the best option. However, choosing this option means that, if you die first, your surviving spouse is out of luck because your monthly pension payments stop at your death. More times than not, if we need to protect the income for both spouses' lives, I will recommend a reduced pension but with a 100% guarantee for the surviving spouse.

Sometimes pension plan owners take my usual advice and choose a lower monthly payment because it will last through their life and their spouse's life. Sometimes the owner will take a large annual payment and his or her surviving spouse will receive a fraction, perhaps half or two-thirds throughout his or her life. But there is another option to consider. One of the options frequently pushed by insurance agents is to buy a one-life (not two-life) annuity and use some of the extra income to purchase life insurance on the owner's life. Should the owner die, the life insurance death benefit can go toward the surviving spouse's support. When you look at the numbers, as we have, this usually isn't the best strategy if you still have the option to choose a pension benefit that protects your spouse after your death.

You can see that there are many important decisions to be made at your retirement. In these situations, "running the numbers," that is, comparing different potential scenarios, can provide guidance towards making a decision that is right for your family. And if you have already retired and made an irrevocable choice, it might not be too late to improve your situation. For example, if you already decided to take the highest pension without a survivorship feature, it might not be too late to get insurance, if you are still insurable. In other words, if you are retired and, after reading this book, are now concerned that by taking a one-life annuity with the highest monthly payment you did not sufficiently provide for your surviving spouse, you might want to consider purchasing life insurance. In many, if not most situations, it is often simplest and best to choose a two-life option ensuring full income to you and your spouse. But these questions are so complex that I strongly encourage you to consult with a CPA or other retirement planning specialist, who can objectively "run the numbers." That way, you can make a decision with full knowledge and understanding of the alternatives available for your family.

Risk of Default

One other issue to consider—although hard to quantify and anticipate—is state retirement systems failing to make their promised payments. The number of announcements about reduced payments and no payments has reached crisis proportions and is getting worse. Retirees in many states and industries have suffered serious reductions in their pension income, and many people who are not yet retired have been notified that their plans have been frozen, meaning that they will get the benefit accrued up to the frozen date, but no additional credit for more years of service or increases in pay. The Pension Benefit Guaranty Corporation is a federal agency that administers the pensions of companies that cannot meet their obligations to their employees, but even they are stretched to the limit because of the sheer number of pension plans that are inadequately funded. If you are a participant in such a plan, you might want to consider establishing a defined contribution account in addition to this plan, to supplement your retirement income.

Failing pension plans may soon be the cause of another financial crisis in this country. As if the inadequate funding (formally known as the "stated deficit") isn't enough to scare the daylights out of many pension plan participants, what about the understated liability? Many defined benefit plans use interest rate assumptions of 7 percent or higher, which is not realistic. If a plan is currently paying out to pensioners, as most are, it is extremely imprudent for the plan assets to be invested aggressively. A safer strategy would be to invest the plan assets in a mix of stocks and bonds. So, let's assume that the plan has 50 percent of its assets in stocks, and 50 percent in bonds. If stocks pay 7 percent over the long term and bonds pay 2 percent over the long term, the plan as a whole won't earn a 7 percent rate of return. It will earn an average rate of return of 4.5 percent. There are also costs associated with pension plan administration—maybe 0.5 percent to 1 percent—that have to be considered as well. The solution, unfortunately, is not to try and earn a higher rate of return by investing all of the plan assets in stocks. Pension plan owners, especially government agencies, must bite the bullet and contribute more to the pension plan. And when they don't have the money in their budget to do so, they make the plan deficit disappear (on paper, anyway) by increasing the assumed rate of return.

I believe the problem of underfunded pension plans is going to blow up on us and, to a large extent, it already has. As part of the American Rescue Plan Act of 2021, the Pension Benefit Guaranty Corporation ("PBGC") created a Special Financial Assistance ("SFA") Program to address the immediate financial crisis of underfunded pension plans. The program will provide an estimated $94 billion in assistance to more than 200 eligible plans that are severely underfunded. For example, according to Joel Anderson in an article published by gobankingrates. com dated May 10, 2022, New Jersey has $254.4 billion in unfunded pensions. That is up 29% since 2019 despite the good market at that time.

My brother, like thousands of others who worked for a university or entity in Oregon that had a state pension plan, had his pension payments reduced significantly and he didn't get a lot of notice. Perhaps this will put you on notice and you might want to access the viability of the pension plan in your state or company before relying on a 100% payment.

Cash Balance Plan

A relatively new and unique version of a defined benefit plan is known as a *cash balance plan*. Technically, this is a defined benefit plan, but it has features similar to a defined contribution plan. Though on the rise, this type of plan is not common. Each employee is given an account to which the employer provides contributions or pay credits, which may be a percentage of pay and an interest credit on the balance in the account. The account's investment earnings to be credited are usually defined by the plan, and the employer bears all downside risk for actual investment earnings shortfalls. The increase in popularity of cash balance plans has been spurred by the increased number of small business owners who are getting closer to retirement age.

Most cash balance plans are established for the primary benefit of the owner(s) of the company, so contributions from the company for the owners are usually very large with a smaller contribution provided to employees. In our accounting practice, we see Cash Balance plans for physician or dental practices where the owner professional is looking to retire in a few years and wants to significantly increase their retirement plan balances and receive a corresponding tax deduction not only for the contributions to the employee accounts but also to the owner's account.

How Many Plans Are Available to You?

There is a good possibility that you have the opportunity to invest more money in your retirement plan or plans than you realize. For many readers who are still working, applying the lessons of this Mini Case Study could save you thousands of dollars a year. If you have access to more than one retirement plan, this mini case study might be one of the most important sections of the book.

·· **MINI CASE STUDY 2.3** ··

Contributing the Maximum to Multiple Retirement Plans[1]

Tom and his wife, Judy, both 55, want to make the maximum retirement plan contributions allowable. Tom earns $61,000 per year as a professor at a university that has both a 403(b) plan and a Section 457 plan. Judy is self-employed, has no employees, and shows a profit after expenses on her Schedule C, Form U.S. 1040, of $80,000 per year. Tom and Judy have a 16-year-old computer-whiz child, Bill, who works weekends and summers doing computer programming for Judy's company. Bill is a legitimate subcontractor, not an employee of Judy's company. Judy pays Bill $40,000 per year. What is the maximum that Tom and Judy and Bill can contribute to their retirement plans for calendar year 2023?

Tom: *Calculating Maximum Contributions to Multiple Plans*

Under the 2001 EGTRRA, Tom could contribute $30,000 to his 403(b) plan in 2023 ($22,500 normal limit plus another $7,500 because he is over 50). Under a special rule specifically relating to 457 plans, he could also contribute another $22,500 to his 457 plan in 2023. He is also eligible to contribute $7,500 to a Roth IRA ($6,500 per year limit plus $1,000 because he is over age 50). (Roth IRAs are discussed in more detail in Chapter 3.) Please note the new law allows contributions to all three plans—something not previously permitted. Ultimately, Tom was able to contribute nearly all of his income to retirement plans. Now, for most people, this isn't realistic, but here, we're just looking at the maximum that this family *could* contribute, disregarding any other financial

---

1   We have used 2023 amounts for this example. The retirement plan contribution limits for future years are likely to be even higher. The current year contribution limits are available on our website at **https://PayTaxesLater.com**. You can also receive these updates as soon as they happen, by signing up for our free e-mail newsletter.

> **If you have access to more than one retirement plan,
> this Mini Case Study might be one of the most important
> sections of the book.**

needs. The maximum contribution between the three plans is the lesser of the deferral limits established under the tax rules for that plan type for the year or 100% of your eligible compensation defined by the plan's terms. The total combined contributions cannot exceed the lesser of the annual maximum amount established by the IRS ($73,500 in 2023) or a taxpayer's earned income ($61,000 for Tom in the case study above).

Judy: *Calculating Maximum Contribution to a Solo-K*

The following example is a little complicated but offers many readers with self-employment income an opportunity to contribute more money to their retirement plan than they are contributing right now.

After rejecting a more complicated and more expensive defined benefit plan, Judy chooses the one-person 401(k) plan, or the Solo-K plan. Judy could contribute as much as $44,870 into her personal 401(k) plan. This plan for self-employed taxpayers has the equivalent of an employee and employer share. The first component is the 401(k) elective employee deferral amount that is limited to $30,000 in 2023 (the same limits as Tom's 403(b) plan). Most Solo-Ks are set up so that you can deduct this portion on your tax return and have it taxed like a regular 401(k). If you want this portion to enjoy the tax-free benefits of a Roth IRA, which we generally recommend, you can set up a Roth Solo-K, and elect to put this $30,000 into the Roth Solo-K. So, she has options—Traditional Solo-K or Roth Solo-K. Please see Chapter 4 for a detailed comparison of a Roth 401(k) vs. a Traditional 401(k).

The second component is a $14,870 discretionary profit-sharing, or employer's contribution. As of 2023, the employer portion can be made to either a Roth account or a Traditional account, assuming the employer's plan allows that option. Most plans, as we go to press, do not allow the employer's portion to go into a Roth. To arrive at the $14,870, Judy's net self-employed income of $80,000 must be reduced by half of her computed self-employment tax, which is $80,000 x 92.35% x 15.3% = $11,304 x 50%, or $5,652. Then that amount is subtracted from her net income, $80,000 ($80,000—$5,652 = $74,348). The $74,348 is multiplied by the 20% contribution rate limit (for self-employed individuals, and equal to 25 percent of earnings net of the contribution itself) to yield the maximum profit-sharing contribution amount of $14,870. (If Judy's income had been higher, the total of both the employer and employee contributions to her Solo-K could be as high as $73,500 in 2023. The maximum contribution allowed to the plan is $66,000 and she can also make a $7,500 catch-up contribution.)

Judy also can make an additional $7,500 contribution to her Roth IRA including the catch-up contribution since she is over age 50. *Note: if Judy's self-employment income is an eligible small business, the qualified business income deduction ("QBID") would need to be subtracted from the Solo-K employer contribution computation. Since this calculation is beyond the scope of this chapter, we have not included the QBID deduction in the calculation.*

Bill: *For Parents Who Are Considering Funding Retirement Plans for Their Children*

Although Bill is young, if he can afford it, he should use his $40,000 income to begin making contributions to his retirement plan. In a simple calculation, Bill will owe approximately $6,120 of self-employment tax, half of which is deductible, so his net earned income for the purposes of retirement plan contributions is $36,940.

Bill could open a SIMPLE plan and contribute $15,500, plus a three percent (3%) SIMPLE matching contribution, which would be $1,108 (3% of $40,000 x .9235). The net earned income less these amounts is $17,272 which is enough to fully fund his Roth IRA with $6,500. If he already spent some of his income, his parents could gift him the money.

The tax-free benefit of the Roth IRA and the tax-deferred benefit of the SIMPLE plan are so important to a child during his or her lifetime that some parents who have sufficient money are willing to fund their child's retirement plan. This is a wonderful idea. However, in order to contribute to a retirement plan or IRA, the child must have *earned* income. Some parents will be tempted to create a sham business for their child or even put their child on the payroll as a sham transaction. I do not recommend this approach. I advocate that the child does legitimate work, complying with all child labor laws. All retirement plan contributions should stem from legitimate work or businesses, and if based on self-employed earnings, be a real business. (I had to say that in case the IRS reads this. In all seriousness, however, there are also non-financial benefits in having a child do legitimate work to receive money.)

I have seen parents paying infants to model, characterizing the payment to the infant as self-employment income and making a retirement plan contribution for the infant. I think that goes too far. Any situation where a child younger than 11 years old receives employment compensation is highly suspect. Even at age 11, legitimate compensation should not be too high.

Let's assume that Tom, Judy, and Bill max out their retirement plan contributions. Even though Tom and Judy earned only $141,000 and Bill earned only $40,000, the family could contribute nearly $135,478 into their retirement plans and Roth IRAs. For subsequent years, or maybe even this year, the contribution limits are likely to be even more generous. I am assuming, of course, the family could afford these contributions. Even if they can't and have substantial after-tax funds held in a brokerage account, they should still consider these higher retirement plan contributions and use money from their brokerage account for living expenses. Is this a great country or what?

This example intentionally exaggerates the family's likely contributions. The point is to show the maximum contribution limits and the variety of plan options available. In this particular case, Tom and Judy and Bill may choose not to maximize their contributions because they may not receive any income tax benefits beyond a certain level of contribution. It is worthwhile, however, to review this case study to help with choosing and implementing a new plan.

Minimize Your Life Insurance Costs to Maximize Your Retirement Contributions: The Ladder Approach

Many old classic whole life insurance agents are going to hate me (many already do) for writing this section of this chapter. Many of our younger clients complain that they face a choice between fully funding their retirement plan contributions or paying for enough life insurance to adequately protect their families (among other competing costs). Even though some organizations are more generous in the amount of life insurance they provide to employees, and even though many can often purchase additional optional coverage at a discount, this may not be enough to fully protect their family especially if there is a child with a disability in the family.

I am extremely leery of whole life, especially for young parents.

Term insurance is almost always a better solution for individuals who want to make sure of a guaranteed and needed sufficient death benefit at a relatively low cost.

The objective of term life insurance is to protect a family from the financial devastation that can ensue from the untimely death of a primary bread winner(s). It is also important to insure the value of the services of a stay-at-home parent, which can be especially important when you have a child with a disability. It is critically important insurance, but it is also to your advantage to try to get the appropriate level of coverage for the most reasonable price. The following section, though by no means complete, presents my favorite idea for many young families to protect themselves in the event of an early, unexpected death, but to do so relatively cheaply. I am working from the premise that I do not like to see people underinsured, but I also want everyone to be thinking ahead to retirement and if the parents need to provide long-term for a child with a disability.

One of the most common mistakes my younger clients make is not having sufficient term insurance. Most healthy young people survive until retirement age and paying for term insurance is not something anyone really wants to do. In my experience as an estate planning attorney, or for that matter in virtually any large estate planning practice, we see young healthy people who died much too early. In my experience, it is rarely the result of a catastrophic car or plane accident, but more frequently because of the sudden onset of cancer or some other fatal disease.

Most people, however, also have this vague sense that the responsible thing to do is to purchase insurance to protect their families. Some people seek out an insurance provider and initiate a policy; others do something when a life insurance professional approaches them. In either case they usually end up with some kind of policy. The key is to find a policy that balances adequate insurance and minimum premiums. I don't like to see people, especially younger people who are working on a limited budget, pay high life insurance premiums.

The best way to start thinking about how much life insurance you need is to consider "How much income will your survivors require to live comfortably?" Let's say that after some analysis, you decide that an appropriate income is $60,000 per year in today's dollars. Please note I would not derive this number as a multiple of current salary; it should be based purely on projected need.

I am not going to delve into the intricacies of calculating a safe withdrawal rate—that is to say, how much as a percentage of principal you can withdraw and have the money last for a lifetime—but I would say for young people with a long-life expectancy, four percent (4%) would probably be on the high side for a safe withdrawal rate. This means if there is no other source of income, to achieve that income requirement of $60,000 a year, an individual will need at least $1,500,000 of life insurance ($60,000/4% = $1,500,000).

First, I hope I didn't just bum you out and make you realize you are vastly underinsured because $60,000 of income doesn't sound that high, and you don't have anywhere near $1,500,000 of insurance. Admittedly, whatever resources you have can be used to reduce the need for life insurance. If both spouses work, the income of the survivor can certainly be factored in. If you have significant investments or savings, they can also be used to reduce the need for insurance.

Many insurance professionals make a convincing case for permanent insurance, which is a type of policy that ultimately has cash value. There is a payout when you die, or sometimes upon reaching a certain age. Term insurance, on the other hand, at least the way I use it, will likely not pay out if you survive to a normal life expectancy. It is designed to protect your heirs if you don't live to a normal life expectancy.

Permanent insurance is expensive, so many families who like the idea that there will always be a payout in the future go ahead and buy permanent insurance. They are usually woefully unprotected at the insurance premium levels they can afford. Term insurance is less expensive, so when cost is an issue—which it nearly always is for younger families—I recommend considering laddered term insurance to help keep premiums more affordable but to also provide you with sufficient protection. Even though you give up a permanent benefit, I would rather see the money going toward sufficient term insurance, so the surviving spouse and other family members are protected rather than having a permanent policy but with an insufficient amount of coverage.

What is the "Ladder Approach?" Let's assume that you do projections and determine that you will have sufficient money to retire at age 60 (assuming you are age 30 now). You might logically think "Okay, I need a 30-year level term policy (premiums are guaranteed never to go up) for $1,500,000."

If you work and save for ten years, you may only need $1,000,000 at that point in time. Perhaps in the ten years beyond that, your need may drop to $500,000. I am trying to keep it simple to make a point. The point is as you age, your insurance needs will change, usually getting smaller, and thinking within this more flexible framework offers some new options.

Since I am being frugal with your insurance budget, consider the following set of policies, assuming the above situation.

- Get a 30-year term policy for $500,000 coverage
- Get a 20-year term policy for $500,000 coverage
- Get a 10-year term policy for $500,000 coverage

If you die between the date the policy is issued and year ten, your heirs get $1,500,000, which is what we determined was the needed amount. At the end of ten years, the first policy ends, and you will only have $1,000,000 of coverage. That is okay. By this point you should have $500,000 in retirement plans and savings. In addition, the need for insurance will be down a little bit because your heirs will have a shorter life expectancy.

After 20 years, the second policy ends, and you will only have $500,000 of coverage remaining. That is okay because by this time you should have $1,000,000 of retirement and savings, and your need will only be $500,000. At the end of 30 years, you will have no coverage, but again, that is okay because hopefully by then you will have accrued sufficient resources for your surviving spouse.

Of course, in the above example, I have kept things really simple. I have not included relevant factors like inflation, children's true needs, timing of education needs, the ability of the surviving spouse to work, and so forth.

But you get the idea. We have helped a number of our clients reach their goal of adequate coverage through this laddered system. Frequently, a 30-year level term policy costs more than individuals might want to pay or can afford, so they compromise by not getting the insurance coverage they really need. I would prefer to see you get the coverage you need by using some variation of the laddered approach that I have suggested. Remember, the goal is sufficient coverage for a reasonable cost. That said, my recommendation for many younger clients is to have most of your coverage through term insurance, but also consider adding a small permanent policy to the mix.

In all fairness, I didn't invent this layered approach. I learned it from Tom Hall, an excellent broker I work with in Pittsburgh. This brings up another point. After you decide to get the insurance you need, I recommend purchasing your insurance through an ethical insurance broker (someone who can purchase insurance from many different companies). In our experience, working with a broker is the way to get the best policies at the best rates.[2]

Consider Conversion Options Before You Buy Term Life Insurance

Also, when considering term insurance, a key consideration should be the policy's conversion features. Conversion features provide additional flexibility in case your insurance needs change in the future. Suppose you become uninsurable due to health issues, or you decide you need coverage for a longer period. Without conversion options, you might have to buy a new policy with a higher premium because you're older and likely have medical issues or—worst case scenario—those options may be unavailable.

Conversion options allow you to convert to an insurance company's 'permanent' product without medical underwriting at the same rate class as you were originally

---

2   Life insurance can be offered by a member of Lange Life Care for those interested. These are not legal services. The protection of an attorney-client relationship does not exist with respect to these insurance services. There is no solicitation being made for legal services by James Lange nor by Lange Legal Group, LLC.

approved. Most insurance companies have an expensive conversion feature, but some insurance companies offer conversions to any product available in their portfolio at the time of conversion. Having the option to convert to the lowest cost product available can be a game changer as we get older and medical issues begin to arise. Also, if you should become uninsurable and you have a good conversion option, you may have the ability to sell your policy. Please refer to Chapter 26 where we include Exit Strategies for your life insurance policy in the event you do not want to pay the premiums anymore.

Let's look at an example. One of our clients had a ten-year term policy that was expiring when he turned age 64. He was originally approved at the best rate class (preferred plus) and became uninsurable. He had a valuable conversion option that allowed him to convert to the lowest cost permanent product in the insurance company's portfolio. He decided to convert his original $1 million term policy to a $1 million permanent policy without any medical underwriting. Not only did he have a greatly reduced life expectancy, but he was also able to obtain a valuable asset at a reduced rate to protect his family. It also included a chronic care provision which he did not previously have with his term policy. It was a wonderful investment and offered additional protection for the future needs of his spouse and family.

Consideration of a permanent life insurance policy with a chronic care rider and/or a second-to-die policy may make sense when planning long term for a child with a disability.

Please see Chapter 13, *Special Needs Trusts and Legal Considerations for Children with Disabilities* for protecting your child with a disability with a special needs trust funded with life insurance. For more information on how to get the best deal on life insurance, and how to use life insurance as a tool to protect your family and your child with a disability after you die, be sure to read Chapter 26, *Life Insurance as an Estate Planning Tool.*

What If You Think You Can't Afford to Make the Maximum Contributions?

What if you think you can't save more than the minimum amount in your retirement plan to get your employer match? The truth is you may very well be able to afford to save, but you don't realize it. That's right. I am going to present a rationale to persuade you to contribute more than you think you can afford.

Let's assume you have been limiting your own contributions to the amount that your employer is willing to match and yet you barely have enough money to get by week to week. Does it still make sense to make nonmatched contributions assuming you do not want to reduce your spending? Maybe.

If you have substantial savings, and if maximizing your retirement plan contributions causes your net payroll check to be insufficient to meet your expenses, I still recommend maximizing retirement plan contributions. The shortfall for your living expenses from making increased pre-tax retirement plan contributions should be withdrawn from your savings (money that has already been taxed). Over time this process, that is, saving the most in a retirement plan and funding the shortfall by making after-tax withdrawals from the after-tax account, transfers money from the after-tax environment to the pre-tax environment. Ultimately, it results in more money for you and your heirs. For your child who has a disability, once approved as an eligible designated beneficiary, they will be able to stretch your retirement plan over their lifetime.

A final point worth mentioning is that you should consider your personal tax bracket when making contributions to your retirement plan. Your tax bracket will likely change over the course of your lifetime because of your marital status, and changes in your income and likely changes in the tax law. While I still want you to contribute the maximum you possibly can to your retirement plan, in some instances it may make more sense to contribute to the Traditional account rather than the Roth account, and vice versa. These strategies are covered in detail in Chapter 4.

Keep in mind that the contribution amounts to retirement plans will likely go up every year. However, the concepts and the advice will be the same, which will usually be to max out your Roth first and Traditional for the rest.

KEY IDEAS

- You should contribute the maximum you can afford to all the retirement plans to which you have access in the order recommended above.

- Don't neglect life insurance during your accumulation years. Using a laddered approach can be an affordable way to protect your family as your retirement savings accumulate. Purchasing a permanent life insurance policy may be necessary for the long-term planning of your child with a disability.

Key Ideas continue on the following page.

KEY IDEAS
(continued)

- Conversion privileges may be a future game changer when securing term life insurance. The lowest price is not the sole consideration when purchasing term life insurance products.

3

Traditional IRAs versus Roth IRAs

"Saving is a very fine thing. Especially when your parents have done it for you."

—Winston Churchill

For many people, the primary vehicle for retirement savings will be in an employer-sponsored retirement plan such as a 401(k) plan, and I'll discuss those plans at length in the next chapter. But some of you may have spouses or partners whose only option for accumulating retirement assets is with an IRA. Or you may have IRA accounts funded by rollovers from retirement plans from other institutions. Or perhaps you've contributed enough to your employer's retirement plan and HSA to get the full employer match, and you want to explore IRA options. Or you've retired, or even if you are still working, and have a side business as a self-employed speaker/writer/consultant and you want options for continuing to accumulate your savings.

What is the Difference Between an IRA and a Roth IRA?

Prior to the SECURE Act, individuals could not contribute to Individual Retirement Accounts (IRAs) past age 70½. After passing the SECURE Act, effective in the year 2020, individuals of any age can contribute to an IRA. The only requirement is the contribution cannot exceed the smaller of earned income or the IRA contribution limit.

There are two major types of IRAs, the Traditional and the Roth. Traditional IRAs were created in 1974 as an incentive for taxpayers to begin saving for their retirement. Owners of Traditional IRAs enjoy tax-deferred growth on their investment, but the contributions and earnings are taxed at the federal level when a qualified withdrawal is made. IRA owners can also take a tax deduction for their contributions if they meet either of these two requirements:

- They (and their spouse, if married) do not have a retirement plan at work.

- They earn less income than the Adjusted Gross Income (AGI) limit for deducting IRA contributions. (Please see discussion regarding Traditional IRA eligibility rules.)

If IRA owners have income above the limit for which they are permitted to deduct the contribution, they may still contribute to an IRA, but without the benefit of a tax deduction. These are commonly referred to as *nondeductible IRA contributions*.

With the exception of the Roth IRA (discussed below) and the Defined Benefit Plan, all the other retirement plans mentioned in Chapter 2 can usually be rolled into an IRA, income tax-free, at retirement or service termination.

Roth IRAs were first established by the Taxpayer Relief Act of 1997. The main characteristic of the Roth IRA is that the investment grows tax-free and is not taxed when qualified withdrawals are made. However, unlike the Traditional IRA, there is no income tax deduction up front. The Roth IRA income limit on contributions is much higher than the Traditional deductible IRA income limit on contributions. This allows many higher income earners who are not eligible for a deductible IRA to participate in a Roth IRA.

I was a big fan of Roth IRAs even before they became law. I wrote the first peer-reviewed article on Roth IRAs and Roth IRA conversions that was published in *The Tax Adviser* in 1998. At the time, few understood how fabulous the Roth plans could be. I am still advocating IRA owners strongly consider Roth IRAs and Roth IRA conversions in many situations.

Here is a comparison of the differences between Roth and Traditional IRAs:

Contribution Limits for Both Roth and Traditional IRAs

The permitted contribution amounts are the same for both Roth IRAs and Traditional IRAs. Note that the *total* permitted contribution amount applies both to IRAs and Roth IRAs, which means that for 2023, you can only contribute a total of $6,500 ($7,500 if you are 50 or older) to IRAs and Roth IRAs. Unlike the contribution limits for most employer-sponsored qualified retirement plans, the maximum contribution limits for Traditional and Roth IRAs remained the same until 2023. The total IRA and/or Roth IRA contributions cannot exceed your *earned* income, and, as with Traditional IRAs, a married individual filing a joint return may make a Roth IRA contribution for the nonworking spouse by

> The essence of a Roth IRA is that you pay tax on the seed *(the contribution)*, but you can reap the harvest tax-free *(the distribution)*. With a Traditional IRA, you deduct the seed, but pay tax on the harvest.

treating his or her compensation as his or her spouse's. The contribution limits for 2019 through 2023 are shown in Figure 3.1 below.

Sharp-eyed readers may notice that, while the IRS found it necessary to adjust the maximum contribution limits for most employer-sponsored qualified retirement plans for inflation in 2022 and three years prior, they left the maximum contribution limits for Traditional and Roth IRAs unchanged until 2023. Previous to 2019, the contribution limit of $5,500 remained the same from 2013 through 2018, with the catch-up contribution limit remaining at $1,000 for those over age 50.

Figure 3.1

IRA Contribution Limits for 2019 through 2023

	Roth IRA	Traditional IRA
Investment	Grows tax-free	Grows tax-deferred
Withdrawals *(qualified)*	Tax-free	Taxed as ordinary income
Contributions	Income level	Income level
Income Limits	Affects ability to contribute	Affects deductibility of contribution
Contribution Limits	Same as IRA	Same as Roth IRA
Required Distributions	Not if you are the original owner	Yes

Contribution Limits for Individuals 50 and Older

Year	Annual IRA *and* Roth IRA	Catch-Up Contribution Limits
2019	$6,000	$1,000
2020	$6,000	$1,000
2021	$6,000	$1,000
2022	$6,000	$1,000
2023	$6,500	$1,000

Traditional IRA Eligibility Rules

1. All taxpayers who have earned income are allowed to contribute to a Traditional IRA without regard to income level.

2. If neither you nor your spouse participates in an employee-sponsored retirement plan, you both can deduct the full amount of your Traditional IRA contributions.

3. If you are covered by a retirement plan at work, there are AGI limits for allowing full deductions, partial deductions, and limits above which no deductions are permitted. They are shown in Figure 3.2 below.

A spousal contribution can be made for a nonworking spouse if the other spouse has earned income, and a joint tax return is filed. A spousal IRA has been around for decades, but as of 2013, it has a new name: the Kay Bailey Hutchison Spousal IRA. And while the dollar amounts for contributions were increased for inflation, the basic rules for spousal IRAs are still the same. IRA contributions for both spouses are still limited by the amount of income earned by the working spouse. If the working spouse earns $8,000, then the maximum that can be contributed to both IRAs combined, is $8,000. Please note "contribution amounts" and "deduction amounts" are two different things. If the working spouse is not covered under a retirement plan at work, the non-working spouse's IRA contribution (maximum of $6,500 - $7,500 if over age 50 – in 2023) is fully deductible. If the working spouse is covered under a retirement plan at work, the nonworking spouse can still contribute the same amount, but the tax deduction may be limited, as shown in Figure 3.3.

4. If you have too much income to deduct your Traditional IRA contribution, you can still make a nondeductible IRA contribution if you are eligible. You won't get the income tax deduction up front, but you will still gain the advantage of the tax-deferred growth in the account.

Roth IRA Eligibility Rules

1. As with a Traditional IRA, an individual can contribute to a Roth IRA after reaching age 70½ as long as he or she has earned income. Earned income includes wages, commissions, self-employment income, and other amounts received for personal services, as well as long-term disability benefits received prior to normal retirement age, taxable alimony, and separate maintenance payments received under a decree of divorce or separate maintenance.

2. Individuals must meet the income tests, which exclude higher income taxpayers from contributing to Roth IRAs. (See Figure 3.4 below.)

3. A married individual filing a joint return may make a Roth IRA contribution for the nonworking spouse by treating his or her compensation as his or her

Figure 3.2

2022 and 2023 AGI Limitations for Deducting a Traditional IRA if You are Covered by a Retirement Plan at Work

Year	Fully Deductible	Partially Deductible	Not Deductible
Single & Head of Household			
2022	$ 68,000 *or less*	$ 68,001 - $ 77,999	$ 78,000+
2023	$ 73,000 *or less*	$ 73,001 - $ 82,999	$ 83,000+
Married Filing Jointly			
2022	$109,000 *or less*	$109,001 - $128,999	$129,000+
2023	$116,000 *or less*	$116,001 - $135,999	$136,000+
Married Filing Separately			
2022	N/A	*Less than* $10,000	$ 10,000+
2023	N/A	*Less than* $10,000	$ 10,000+

Figure 3.3

2022 and 2023 AGI Limitations for Deducting a Traditional IRA if You are NOT Covered by a Retirement Plan at Work

Year	Fully Deductible	Partially Deductible	Not Deductible
Single & Head of Household			
2022	No Income Limit	–	–
2023	No Income Limit	–	–
Married Filing Jointly or Separately *(Spouse Does Not Have a Plan at Work)*			
2022	No Income Limit	–	–
2023	No Income Limit	–	–
Married Filing Jointly or Separately *(Spouse Does Have a Plan at Work)*			
2022	$204,000 *or less*	$204,001 - $213,999	$214,000+
2023	$218,000 *or less*	$ 218,001 - $227,999	$228,000+
Married Filing Separately *(Spouse Does Have a Plan at Work)*			
2022	–	*Less than* $10,000	–
2023	–	*Less than* $10,000	–

spouse's but must exclude any of his or her own IRA contributions from the income treated as his or her spouse's. (For example, in 2023, if you are not yet age 50 and make $8,000, you can contribute $6,500 to your Roth, but only $1,500 to your spouse's Roth.) Total contributions cannot exceed your income.

Figure 3.4

2022 and 2023 Income Eligibility Rules for Roth IRAs

Year	Full Contribution	Reduced Contribution	No Contribution
Single & Head of Household			
2022	*Up to* $129,000	$129,001 - $143,999	$144,000+
2023	*Up to* $138,000	$138,001 - $152,999	$153,000+
Married Filing Jointly			
2022	*Up to* $204,000	$204,001 - $213,999	$214,000+
2023	*Up to* $218,000	$218,001 - $227,999	$228,000+

Advanced Distribution Rules for Traditional IRAs

1. Traditional IRA withdrawals are generally taxable at the federal level, but not necessarily at the state level. If you make nondeductible contributions to your IRA, you will have *basis* (in other words, money that you put into the account, that you already paid tax on, and on which the IRS can't tax you again). If all of your IRA contributions were tax deductible, you have no basis in the account. It is important to know if you have non-deductible contributions (otherwise known as "basis") in your nondeductible IRA, because you don't want to pay more taxes on your IRA withdrawal than required.

   The burden of proving that a portion of the withdrawal is not taxable falls on you, so I hope you filed a Form 8606 to keep track of the basis in your IRA. This form should be filed every year as an attachment to your tax return once you have any basis in your IRA. When a withdrawal is made from an IRA with basis, a calculation is made to determine what percentage of the money in the account is your contribution, and what percentage reflects earnings on your contributions.

   Let's say your non-deductible contributions were $20,000 and the value of your IRA at year-end after taking a $10,000 withdrawal is $90,000. In this case, 20 percent of the withdrawal is considered a return of your own money and is not taxable. The remaining $8,000 is taxable. (My book, **The Roth Revolution**, covers in detail a great technique for converting after-tax or nondeductible IRAs or after-tax dollars inside a Traditional 401(k) to Roth IRAs without paying any tax. Please visit **https://PayTaxesLater. com**, for more information about that book.) An example of this strategy is also presented in Chapter 7.

2. All Traditional IRA withdrawals prior to age 59½ are subject to an additional 10 percent penalty (for amounts exceeding basis) unless the withdrawal falls under one of the following exemptions:

   - They are made to a beneficiary (or the individual's estate) on or after the individual's death.
   - They are attributable to the individual with a total or permanent disability.
   - They were used for qualified first-time home purchase expenses.
   - The distributions are not more than your qualified higher education expenses.
   - They were used for qualified medical expenses that exceed 7.5 percent of AGI.
   - The distributions are not more than the cost of your medical insurance due to a period of unemployment.
   - They are part of substantially equal periodic payments over the life of the participant—that is, distributions qualifying under Section 72(t) (which we do not cover in this book) for exemption from the premature distribution penalty.
   - They are due to an IRS levy on the account.
   - The distribution is a qualified reservist distribution.
   - The distribution is a coronavirus-related distribution from January 1, 2020 to December 30, 2020, up to an aggregate limit of $100,000. The CARES Act allows you to spread out your taxes for the withdrawal over three years (2020-2022). If you repay some or all of the distribution back into your IRA, the IRS considers that amount a 'rollover' and not subject to income tax.

With the passing of SECURE Act 2.0, new exceptions were added for penalty-free distributions:

   - Qualified Disaster Recovery Distributions are retroactively permanently reinstated to disasters occurring on or after January 26, 2021. If a distribution is made within 180 days of the disaster occurring, up to $22,000 for expenses related to a federally declared disaster can be spread equally over three years beginning with the year of distribution unless the person elects to report the full amount in the year of distribution. The taxpayer may also repay the distributions back within 3 years of the time the distribution is received.

- Effective in 2023, a distribution taken by someone with a terminal illness that will cause death within seven years as certified by a physician qualifies.

- Effective in 2024, a distribution taken by a victim of domestic abuse (physical, psychological, sexual, emotional, or economic abuse) during the preceding one-year period can be eligible for penalty relief up to the lesser of $10,000 (indexed for inflation) or 50% of the account value.

- Effective in 2024, up to $1,000 per calendar year can be distributed for personal or family emergency expenses to meet unforeseeable or immediate financial needs. No further emergency distributions are permitted during the three-year repayment period unless the funds are repaid or new contributions are at least equal to the distribution.

- Effective in 2026, withdrawals for Qualified Long-Term Care Distributions of up to the lesser of 10% of an individual's vested balance or $2,500 (adjusted for inflation) can be taken annually to pay for long-term care insurance.

3. All Traditional IRAs are subject to RMDs after age 72, 73 or 75, depending on the year of your birth. If you were born in 1950, your RMDs began at age 72. If you were born between 1951 and 1959, your RMDs start at age 73. For those born in 1960 or later, RMDs don't start until age 75.

Distribution Rules for Roth IRAs

1. In order to take completely tax-free (or qualified) withdrawals from a Roth IRA that has grown in value, five years must have elapsed since opening the account. There is a separate five-year holding period for each Roth IRA conversion as well (conversions are discussed in more detail in Chapter 16). Do you want the practical wisdom regarding the 5-year rule? In the vast majority of cases, it isn't relevant. Roth IRAs and Roth IRA conversions are long-term strategies, and it almost always makes the most sense to keep them for longer than five years. That said, I get asked about the 5-year rule a lot.

Distributions must be made on or after age 59½, unless one of the following special circumstances applies:

- A distribution is made to your beneficiary (or your estate) on or after your death.

- A distribution is attributable to your disability.

- A distribution is made for a qualified first-time home purchase expense up to $10,000 (lifetime maximum).

2. This restriction also applies to the beneficiary of a Roth IRA whose owner dies before the five-year period has ended. The beneficiary may withdraw funds tax-free as long as they do not exceed the contribution amount, but he or she must wait until the five-year period has passed before being able to enjoy tax-free withdrawal of the Roth IRAs earnings.

3. Withdrawals prior to age 59½ may be taken without tax or penalties to the extent of previous annual contributions.

4. Withdrawals in excess of previous contributions made before the five-year holding period is met are taxable, but penalty-free under the following circumstances:

- For qualified college expenses for yourself, spouse, child or grandchild.

- For qualified unreimbursed medical expenses that exceed 7.5 percent of AGI.

- For health insurance premiums or unreimbursed medical expenses paid for certain unemployed individuals.

- If withdrawals are part of substantially equal periodic payments over the life of the participant.

- If the distribution is part of an IRS levy.

- You are the beneficiary of a deceased IRA owner.

- If you withdraw up to $5,000 in the year after the birth or adoption of your child.

The withdrawal was made when you were a reservist.

All other withdrawals prior to age 59½ that are in excess of previous contributions are taxable and subject to a 10 percent penalty.

5. Roth IRA amounts are not subject to RMDs during the original owner's lifetime.

Furthermore, a Roth IRA owner can designate his or her spouse as the beneficiary who, upon the Roth IRA owner's death, would have the option of postponing RMDs until the second death. After the surviving spouse's death, the subsequent beneficiary (usually a child) would be required to take nontaxable minimum distributions of the Inherited Roth IRA over 10-years in accordance with the new rules in the SECURE Act. According to the IRS' most current proposed regulations (which codify how the IRS plans to interpret the SECURE Act), distributions do not need to be taken every year, but all of the Roth IRA money must be distributed by year 10. (Please see Chapter 10 for distribution rules for Inherited IRAs and Inherited Roth IRAs.) If the beneficiary has a disability or chronic illness and qualifies as an eligible designated beneficiary (please also see Chapter 11 and 12), then the child can stretch the Inherited Roth IRA over their lifetime like the pre-2020 rules. Because of this exception to the new distribution requirements for Inherited retirement plans, Roth IRAs are an ideal asset to leave to your child with a disability or chronic illness if they qualify as an eligible designated beneficiary.

The five-year holding requirement for Roth IRAs is intended to promote long-term savings. The five-year clock starts ticking on January 1 of the tax year associated with the first contribution or conversion, which actually results in making the five-year waiting period less than five years. The period begins on the first day of the tax year for which a contribution is made. If you open a Roth IRA account for the 2023 tax year by making a contribution on April 15, 2024 (the last day you can make your Roth IRA contributions for 2023), the five-year period is from January 1, 2023, to December 31, 2027. To achieve the same five-year period, start date when opening a Roth IRA account using a Roth IRA conversion, you must make the conversion by December 31, 2023 (the last day you can make your Roth IRA conversions for 2023). Pursuant to these Roth IRA rules, if you suddenly need the money the day after or at any time after you make the contribution, you can take out the amount you contributed, free of tax. Any interest or gains, however, have to remain in the account for five years, in order to become tax free. Note, however, that the IRS has a process called "ordering rules" that determine if there is tax due on your distribution. Distributions are ordered as follows:

- your contributions,
- conversion and rollover contributions, on a first-in, first out basis (generally, taken from the earliest year first), and
- earnings on contributions.

Assume you converted $80,000 from a Traditional IRA to a Roth IRA in 2019, and that $20,000 of that amount was your basis. At the time of the conversion, you

> **Wealthy clients and readers raise a lot of questions about the five-year holding period. In most cases, it is best not even to consider the five-year rule because the likely investment period of a Roth IRA is likely not only greater than 5 years, but likely your entire life and beyond.**

would have included $60,000 in your taxable income. In 2020, you made a $7,000 contribution to the Roth IRA. In 2023, at age 60, you take a $9,000 distribution from the Roth IRA. How much of your distribution is taxable? Well, our accounting office can always figure it out for you, but if you'd rather do it yourself, use the above "ordering" rules.

The money you contributed is considered first. You contributed $7,000, so $7,000 of the $9,000 is not taxable. The next $2,000 isn't taxable either, because that was part of your conversion, and it was taxed in 2019. There is no early withdrawal penalty because you are over 59½. But suppose that your Roth IRA has grown to $150,000 and you want to withdraw everything so that you can buy a second home. Following the same rules, the $7,000 you contributed is not taxable, and the $80,000 conversion amount is not taxable. The gain of $63,000 is taxable because a second home is not a qualified exception to the five-year holding period rule. You should wait until 2024 to withdraw the final $63,000 because it will not be taxable then since you held the money in the account for five years.

Wealthy clients and readers raise a lot of questions about the five-year holding period. What I really want to do when I hear that question is yell, "Why do you care?" It is extremely unlikely that anyone would need to spend all of their money at one time. Let's face it, if you did, you'd be broke, and the five-year holding period on the Roth account would be the least of your worries. Realistically, most people will spend their retirement savings over a period of many years. And the people who have a Roth IRA as part of their retirement accumulations generally have at least some after-tax money and some Traditional IRA or retirement plan funds—at least, this would be my advice. But because the Roth IRA is the last money I want people to spend, it should not matter that there is a five-year waiting period to achieve tax-free growth. The Roth's advantages almost always more than make up for any lack of liquidity resulting from the five-year rule.

Advantages and Disadvantages of Roth IRAs

The principal advantages:

- With limited exceptions, they grow income-tax free.

- More liberal contribution rules are in place. Taxpayers may also elect to convert all or part of their Traditional IRAs to Roth accounts, by paying the taxes at the time of the conversion. The future growth on the converted amount is tax-free.

- They are not subject to the RMD rules mandating withdrawals beginning at age 72, 73 or 75. As of this writing, you are not required to take distributions during your lifetime. (You may choose to, but you don't have to). If you die and leave your Roth IRA to your spouse, your spouse will not have to take RMDs either.

- If needed, all of your after-tax annual contributions are always eligible for withdrawal at any time without tax consequences.

- If you have earned income after your RMDs begin at age 72, 73, or 75, you can keep contributing money to your Roth IRA (and so can your spouse, based on your income).

- In cases where maximum retirement contributions are made and there are also after-tax savings, forgoing a tax deduction helps to lower the amount of after-tax savings while putting more value in the tax-free environment. Keep in mind that after-tax savings have inefficient tax consequences on their investment returns.

- The long-term advantage of the Roth IRA is that, in many cases, your heirs receive a 10-year stretch on the income earned on the Roth IRA. The 10-year limit does not apply to spouses or other eligible designated beneficiaries (EDBs), including children with disabilities and deemed EDBs.

The principal disadvantages:

- You do not receive a tax deduction when you make a contribution. You will then have less money to invest in after-tax funds or to spend. But remember, after-tax funds are not tax efficient due to income taxes. And if you simply spend the tax savings, the Roth alternative will look even better because it forces you to save and build a more valuable IRA.

- If you drop into a lower tax bracket once you begin taking your IRA distributions, you may sometimes do better with a Traditional IRA. In this case, the tax savings from the deductible contribution would exceed the taxes paid upon withdrawal. This disadvantage can often be offset by a longer period of tax-free growth.

- The Roth IRA account may go down in value. In that case, if the decline becomes large enough, you would have been better off with a deductible IRA because at least you would have received a tax deduction on your contributions. As always, I recommend that you use prudent investment strategies so that the possibility of losses in your Roth account are minimized.

- If Congress ever eliminates the income tax in favor of a sales tax or value-added tax, you will have given up your tax deduction on the Traditional IRA. And since the distribution will be tax-free anyway, in retrospect, the choice of a Roth IRA would have been a mistake. This situation is similar to the extreme example of having lower tax brackets in retirement.

People who have earned income, and who are ineligible to make Traditional deductible IRA contributions because their income is above the limits, can still make contributions to an IRA, but *without* the tax deduction. These nondeductible IRAs are also available for people who are above the income limits to make Roth IRA contributions.

Nondeductible IRAs

If your income is below the threshold and you are eligible to make Roth IRA contributions, it is important to understand that the Roth is always a much better choice than the *nondeductible* IRA. Remember, you don't get a tax deduction for either, but all the money in the Roth IRA will be tax-free when the money is withdrawn. In contrast, the growth in the nondeductible IRA will be taxable. Roth IRAs can provide a much better result over the long term. Many people make the mistake of contributing to a nondeductible IRA instead of a Roth IRA when they have a choice. Although the mistake can be mitigated if caught in time, this mistake results in future taxes that could have been avoided.

Nondeductible IRA contributions that provide tax-deferred growth, however, are still of great benefit for many high-income people who do not qualify for Roth IRA and deductible IRA contributions. Better yet, as of this writing, high income individuals are still eligible to convert their nondeductible IRA accounts into Roth IRAs with little or no tax cost. A recent IRS ruling also permits individuals who have both deductible and non-deductible contributions in their retirement plans, to split the plan assets. This means that the pre-tax portion of the plan can now be rolled into a Traditional IRA, and the after-tax portion can be rolled into a Roth IRA—effectively allowing a tax-free Roth IRA conversion. (See Chapter 16

> The Roth is always a much better choice than the
> nondeductible IRA. Remember, you don't get a tax
> deduction for either, but all the money in the Roth IRA
> will be tax-free when the money is withdrawn, but the
> growth in the nondeductible IRA will be taxable.

and 17 for more information on Roth IRA conversions.) This is an opportunity knocking, given a little forethought.

What Makes a Roth IRA So Great When Compared with a Traditional IRA?

The advantages of compounding interest on both tax-deferred investments and on tax-free investments far outweigh paying yearly taxes on the capital gains, dividends, and interest of after-tax investments. As you saw in Chapter 2, you are generally better off putting more money in tax-deferred and tax-free accounts than in less efficient after-tax investments. Remember that with regular after-tax investments, you must pay income taxes on annual dividends, interest, and, if you make a sale, on capital gains.

The advantage the Roth IRA holds over a Traditional IRA builds significantly over time because of the increase in the purchasing power of the account. Let's assume you make a $6,500 Roth IRA contribution (not including the $1,000 catch-up contribution if over age 50). The purchasing power of your Roth IRA will increase by $6,500, and that money will grow income tax-free. On the other hand, let's assume you contribute $6,500 to a deductible Traditional IRA and you are in the 24 percent tax bracket. In that case, you will receive a tax deduction of $6,500 and get a $1,560 tax break (24% X $6,500). This $1,560 in tax savings is not in a tax-free or tax-deferred investment. Even if you resist the temptation to spend your tax savings on a nice vacation and put the money into an investment account instead, you will be taxed each year on realized interest, dividends, and capital gains. *This is inefficient investment growth.* The $6,500 of total dollars added to the Traditional IRA offers only $4,940 of purchasing power ($6,500 total dollars less $1,560 that represents your tax savings). The $1,560 of tax savings equates to $1,560 of purchasing power, so the purchasing power for both the Roth IRA and the Traditional IRA are identical in the beginning. However, in future years, the growth on the $6,500 of purchasing power in the Roth IRA will be completely

> **One of the few things in life better than tax-deferred compounding is tax-free compounding.**

tax free. The growth in the Traditional IRA is only tax-deferred, and the $1,560 you invested from your tax savings, is taxable every year.

One of the few things in life better than tax-deferred compounding is tax-free compounding. If your income is not over the limit and you can afford to do so after making your employer-matched contribution and the appropriate nonmatched contributions to your retirement plan, I generally recommend making additional annual contributions to a Roth IRA. Although you don't get an income tax deduction for your contribution to a Roth IRA, as you might with a Traditional IRA, the tax savings you realize from a Traditional IRA contribution are neither tax-free nor tax deferred. When you make a withdrawal from your Traditional IRA, the distribution is taxable. But when you (or your heirs) make a qualified withdrawal from a Roth IRA, the distribution is income-tax free.

Should I Contribute to a Traditional Deductible IRA or a Roth IRA?

As stated earlier, a Roth versus a nondeductible IRA is a no-brainer: if given the choice, always go for the Roth. But for those individuals with a choice between a Roth IRA (or work retirement plan) and a fully deductible IRA (or work retirement plan), how should you save? The conclusion is, in *most* cases, the Roth IRA is superior to the deductible IRA (and nonmatched retirement plan contributions like 401(k)s).

To determine whether a Roth IRA would be better than a Traditional IRA, you must take into account:

- The value of the tax-free growth of the Roth versus the tax-deferred growth of the Traditional IRA including the future tax effects of withdrawals.

- The tax deduction you lost by contributing to a Roth IRA rather than to a fully deductible IRA.

- The growth, net of taxes, on savings from the tax deduction from choosing a deductible Traditional IRA.

In most circumstances, the Roth IRA is significantly more favorable than a regular IRA. (A number of years ago, I published an article in *The Tax Adviser*, a publication of the American Institute of Certified Public Accountants, which

> The conclusion is, in most cases, the Roth IRA is superior
> to the deductible IRA and nonmatched retirement plan
> contributions like 401(k)s.

offered the mathematical proof that the Roth IRA was often a more favorable investment than a regular IRA.) The Jobs and Growth Tax Relief Reconciliation Act of 2003 (JGTRRA) and subsequent tax legislation changed tax rates for all brackets and reduced tax rates for dividends and capital gains.

After these tax laws changed, I incorporated the changes into the analysis of the Roth versus the Traditional IRA. The Roth was still preferable in most situations, although the advantage of the Roth was not quite as great as before JGTRRA. However, our country is currently facing unprecedented financial challenges, and I would be surprised to hear that our government intends to reduce our tax rates any time soon. And, if the tax rates on dividends and capital gains, or even the ordinary tax rates increase, the Roth's advantage will be even greater.

Figure 3.5 shows the value to the owner of contributing to a Roth IRA versus a regular deductible IRA measured in purchasing power.

The amounts reflected in the figure show that saving in the Roth IRA is more favorable than saving in the Traditional IRA, even if the contributions are made

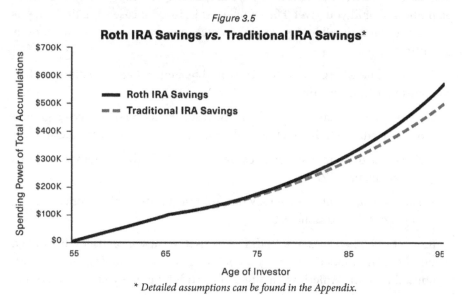

Figure 3.5

Roth IRA Savings *vs.* Traditional IRA Savings*

Age of Investor

* Detailed assumptions can be found in the Appendix.

for a relatively small number of years. If tax rates become higher in the future, or if a higher rate of return is achieved, the overall Roth IRA advantage will be larger. Given a long-time horizon (such as when monies are passed to succeeding generations), the Roth IRA advantage becomes even bigger. The spending power of these methods at selected times is shown in Figure 3.6 below.

Figure 3.6
Total Spending Power of Traditional *vs.* Roth IRA

End of Year Age	Traditional IRA	Roth IRA
55	$ 7,207	$ 7,210
65	$ 118,688	$ 119,948
75	$ 208,237	$ 214,809
85	$ 359,336	$ 384,694
95	$ 607,278	$ 688,931

Figure 3.6 may seem to show that there is not a significant difference between the two, but keep in mind that this illustration was purposely created using a very limited (11-year) contribution period and very conservative (6%) rate of return. In short, it demonstrates that, even with minimal contributions, shorter time frames and very conservative rates of return, the Roth IRA will still provide more purchasing power than a Traditional IRA.

The Effect of Lower Tax Brackets in Retirement

I will usually recommend the Traditional IRA over a Roth IRA if you will drop to a lower tax bracket after retiring and have a relatively short investment time horizon. Under those circumstances, the value of a Traditional deductible IRA could exceed the benefits of the Roth IRA. It will be to your advantage to take the higher tax deduction for your contribution and then, upon retirement, withdraw that money at the lower tax rate.

I usually will recommend the Traditional IRA or 401(k) over a Roth IRA or Roth 401(k) when you will drop to a lower tax bracket after retiring and have a relatively short investment time horizon.

For example, if you are in the 24 percent tax bracket when you are working, and you make a $6,500 tax-deductible IRA contribution, you save $1,560 in federal income taxes. Then, when you retire, your tax bracket drops to 12 percent. Let's assume that the Traditional IRA had no investment growth—not an unrealistic assumption for a taxpayer who chooses to invest his IRA in a certificate of deposit. If he makes a withdrawal of $6,500 from the Traditional IRA, he will pay only $780 in tax—for a savings of $780.

> $ 1,440   Initial Tax Savings from IRA Contribution
> - 720   *Tax Due on IRA Withdrawal*
>
> ---
>
> **$ 720   Final Tax Savings**

With that caveat, however, my analysis shows that the Roth can become more favorable when a longer investment period is considered. The tax-bracket advantage diminishes over time. So, I ran the analysis again, starting with the same assumptions as in the previous example, except that, beginning at age 66, the ordinary income tax bracket is reduced from 24 to 12 percent.

The spending power of these methods at selected times is shown in Figure 3.7 below. You can see that, under this particular set of circumstances, the Traditional IRA would be more beneficial to you during your lifetime. Note, however, that the Roth offers more spending power from age 100 on. Of course, most people will not survive until 100, but we show the analysis to point out that even facing a reduced tax bracket, the Roth IRA will become more valuable with time—an advantage for your heirs.

Figure 3.7

Total Spending Power of Reduced Tax Bracket in Retirement

End of Year Age	Traditional IRA	Roth IRA
55	$ 6,692	$ 6,695
65	$ 99,438	$ 100,235
(Lower Tax Bracket)		
75	$ 193,216	$ 179,506
85	$ 336,783	$ 321,468
95	$ 577,168	$ 575,700
100	$ 751,200	$ 770,416
105	$ 974,773	$1,030,990

If you anticipate that your retirement tax bracket will always remain lower than your current tax rate and that your IRA will be depleted during your lifetime, I will usually recommend that you use a Traditional deductible IRA over the Roth IRA. Unfortunately, once the RMD rules take effect at age 72, 73, or 75 for tax-deferred IRAs and retirement plans, many individuals find that they are required to withdraw so much money from their IRAs, that their tax rate is just as high as their pre-retirement tax rate. And, when their RMDs are added to their Social Security income, some taxpayers find themselves in a higher tax bracket than when they were working. For these people, a Roth IRA contribution is usually preferable to a Traditional IRA.

These numbers demonstrate that even with a significant tax-bracket disadvantage, the Roth IRA can become preferable with a long enough time horizon. Furthermore, when you consider the additional estate planning advantages, the relative worth of the Roth IRA becomes more significant. (Please see Chapter 16 for a more detailed discussion of making a Roth conversion in a higher tax bracket when you will likely be in a lower tax bracket after retirement.)

Please also note that Roths are usually preferred even more if your end beneficiary is a child with a disability who is able to qualify as an Eligible Designated Beneficiary. The ability for the child to stretch the tax-free distributions of the Inherited Roth IRA over their lifetime is extremely valuable. In addition, distributions from your Inherited Roth IRA are tax-free which means the distributions should not impact any federal or state government assistance programs.

Comments on Your Actual Tax Brackets: A Subtle Point for the Advanced Reader

The above analyses reflect simple assumptions of 24 percent income tax savings on your deductible IRA or retirement plan contributions. This is in essence the cost of the Roth IRA or Roth 401(k)/Roth 403(b) in the comparisons above. However, the U.S. tax code has several complications that create actual incremental tax brackets that are much higher than the tax brackets listed on the federal tax tables based on your taxable income. These items must be considered in the context of measuring the advantages of Roth IRAs to deductible IRA contributions.

These tax code complications can have extreme effects on the actual tax bracket for some people, most notably retirees with Social Security income, significant capital gain income, and less frequently with the increase in the standard deduction included in the Tax Cut and Jobs Act, and itemized deductions that involve medical expenses.

Careful tax planning is so important. There are many things in the tax code that result in a different actual tax bracket than the IRS tables would indicate. Before finalizing Roth contribution or conversion decisions, it is best to run the numbers or see a competent tax advisor to determine the actual effects.

When we analyze Roth IRA advantages and disadvantages for our clients (when compared to deductible contributions), we keep referring to the marginal tax rates to help us decide if the conversion makes sense in the long term. For most people, the current actual marginal tax rate is not hard to determine and is similar to what the IRS tables would indicate. Therefore, we will continue to use simply calculated tax bracket rates in our analyses of Roth accounts. But please keep in mind that it is prudent to calculate the actual current year tax cost of the Roth.

The fact that individuals can continue to contribute to a Roth IRA if they continue working past age 72, 73 or 75 is a great opportunity to continue saving, especially since more and more people continue to earn income well after the Traditional age of retirement. The no-RMDs rule for Roths gives rise to significant estate planning opportunities to stretch savings for those willing to leave the money in the tax-free account for a long time. Depending on the lifespan of the beneficiary, and whether the beneficiary is an eligible designated beneficiary (e.g., spouse, child deemed disabled by the government, etc.), the funds can grow tax-free to their great advantage.

KEY IDEAS

- The Roth IRA is always preferable to a nondeductible Traditional IRA and is usually better than a deductible Traditional IRA contribution.

- For Roth IRAs, no taxes are due upon the eventual distribution.

- No distributions from Roth IRAs are required during the owner's or the owner's spouse's lifetime.

- Withdrawals from Roth IRAs prior to age 59½ are free from tax and penalties to the extent of previous contributions.

- Inherited Roth IRAs are particularly beneficial for beneficiaries with a disability and if you have a child with a disability, that would be a strong argument to prefer Roth to Traditional IRAs.

4

Traditional 401(k)s *vs.* Roth 401(k)s

"The question isn't at what age I want to retire,
it's at what income."

— George Foreman

At the risk of sounding like a broken record, I'll repeat what I think is mission critical when you have a child with a disability. Please consider putting at least a portion of your retirement savings in a Roth account. This is one of the most important strategies you can put in place to improve the financial security of your child with a disability. The Roth strategy and other plans my wife and I implemented will mean an extra $1.9 million over our daughter's lifetime, as we explain in Chapter 11. The Roth conversions alone will be worth $1.3 million, and the 'stretch' feature on the Roth conversions will mean an extra $386,300. Chapters 9 and 10 explain why Roth accounts have become so valuable for providing financial resources for a child with a disability after you are gone. If your employer offers a Roth option, it is most likely prudent to utilize the Roth option. Of course, there will be situations when a Roth is not warranted for either the parent or the child. But, because of the tax-free stretch over the lifetime of a beneficiary with a disability (if qualified), the Roth will often make sense for the family when it would not make sense if the only consideration was the parents themselves.

The ideas in this chapter comparing Traditional 401(k)s with Roth 401(k)s are pretty much equally applicable to comparing Traditional 403(b)s to Roth 403(b)s. Conceptually, they are similar to comparing Traditional IRAs to Roth IRAs.

What Are Roth 401(k)s?

Many—but not all—employers offer a Roth option inside their retirement plans. If this option is available to you, I highly recommend you take advantage of it (of course, there are always exceptions). In Chapter 2, we touched on some of the basic differences between Traditional and Roth 401(k)s. The Roth 401(k) combines the features of a Traditional 401(k) with a Roth IRA. Employees are permitted to deposit part or all of their own contribution, which is the amount deducted from their paychecks, as a contribution to a Roth account and the contribution will be taxed. The laws governing retirement plan contributions, however, require that employees always have the option to defer money into the Traditional deductible account when the Roth account is offered as an option. No one is forced to use the Roth account if they prefer to take the tax deduction.

Unlike Traditional contributions to a 401(k) plan, employee contributions to a Roth 401(k) account do not receive a federal tax deduction. But the growth on these contributions will not be subject to taxes when money is withdrawn, because the Roth account grows tax-free. In short, if you have two options for your retirement plan, one a Traditional account and the other a Roth account, with the same amount of money in each, the Roth account, over time, will be of greater value since the income taxes imposed on withdrawals from the Traditional 401(k) greatly reduce its overall value. By this, I do not mean to imply that the Roth retirement plans are better than theTraditional plans for everyone, but they are for many. The choice is similar to deciding whether to make a Roth IRA contribution or a *deductible* contribution to a Traditional IRA as discussed in Chapter 3.

However, I must point out, that if you have a child with a disability, the opportunity for many decades of compounded tax-free growth in a Roth account becomes even more valuable when your child is named as beneficiary of your retirement account. As we explain in Chapter 10, your child may qualify for tax-free distributions from Inherited Roth accounts for their entire lifetime, an option no longer available to most heirs since the SECURE Act was passed in 2019.

Roth retirement plans were first offered in 2006, but under temporary rules. Many employers did not add the Roth feature to their existing plans because of the additional paperwork, plan amendments, reporting, and recordkeeping involved. Since then, the law has become permanent, and more organizations are now offering Roth 401(k) features. These significant additions to the retirement planning landscape offer many more parents an extraordinary opportunity to expand, and, in many cases, to begin saving for retirement in the Roth environment where their investment grows *tax-free*. Coupled with the increased contribution limits for the Traditional 401(k) plans, employees and even self-employed individuals will be able to establish and grow their tax-free retirement savings at a rate greater than ever before.

How Do Roth 401(k) Accounts Differ from a Roth IRA?

One of the most significant advantages of the Roth 401(k), and the one that distinguishes it from a Roth IRA, is that Roth 401(k) plans are now available to a much larger group of people. Roth IRA contributions are only available to taxpayers who fall within certain Modified Adjusted Gross Income (MAGI) ranges. The 2023 income limit for Roth IRA contributions for married couples

> **Unlike Traditional contributions to a 401(k) plan, employee contributions to a Roth 401(k) account do not receive a federal tax deduction. But the growth on these contributions will not be subject to taxes when money is withdrawn, because the Roth account grows tax-free.**

filing jointly is $228,000 and for single individuals and heads of household, less than $153,000. If your income exceeds these limits, you are not permitted to contribute to a Roth IRA. High income earners might get around that limitation through a backdoor Roth IRA. But even then, we are talking about a contribution of $7,500 per year in a Roth IRA for a taxpayer aged 50 or over versus $30,000 for a Roth 401(k). The restrictive MAGI limitations do not apply to Roth 401(k) plans, providing higher income individuals and couples easy access into the tax-free Roth environment.

With the passage of SECURE Act 2.0 in December 2022, more options have been provided to contribute more money into the Roth 401(k). Effective with the enactment, employers are permitted to deposit the matching and/or nonelective contributions to an employee's Roth 401(k) and 403(b) plans. Of course, the employee is required to pay income tax on the matching and/or nonelective contributions in the year of contribution and the employer contributions cannot be subject to any vesting schedule. As of this writing, the plan administrators, payroll software programs, and the IRS are all having a difficult time implementing this change. It is fair to say, while the option is available in 2023, it may take some time to see this important provision in practice.

Another provision contained in SECURE Act 2.0 is higher wage earners are *required* to use the Roth option for any catch-up contributions beginning in 2024. Higher wage earners are defined as an employee earning $145,000 or more in the preceding calendar year. In September 2023, the IRS announced they are permitting a two-year transition period to implement the provision until 2026 for the same reasons noted above. It is an administrative nightmare! As we go to press, it is unclear how the provision will affect self-employed individuals whose income is higher than $145,000 if they would be required to make their catch-up contribution in the form of a Roth.

For 2025, a special catch-up contribution has been included as part of SECURE Act 2.0 allowing individuals between the ages of 60-63 to increase their catch-up contribution limit to the greater of $10,000 or 150% of the standard catch-up contribution limit (indexed for inflation).

As you would expect, I would highly recommend you consider all of the above options to increase the amount of money you can contribute to your Roth. This is especially important as you plan for the future needs of your child with a disability or chronic illness.

This increased accessibility is really important. Roth IRAs have always appeared to be ideal savings vehicles for wealthier individuals, but up until January 1, 2006, or more recently if their employers just began offering the 401(k) option, wealthier individuals had been precluded from establishing Roth accounts due to the income limits. The "rothification" opportunities offered through SECURE Act 2.0 really helps wealthier individuals to be able to save more money in a Roth so I greatly encourage you to take advantage of it.

In Chapter 3 we demonstrated the Roth IRA's great advantages as part of a long-term retirement and estate plan. And wealthier individuals can generally afford to let money sit in a Roth account and gather tax-free growth. The longer the funds are kept in the tax-free Roth environment, the greater the advantage to both the Roth IRA owner and his or her heirs. And when that heir is a child with a disability, the tax-free growth has the potential to extend for that heir's lifetime.

Advantages and Disadvantages of Roth 401(k) Contributions

The Roth 401(k) plan option offers advantages and disadvantages similar to those of Roth IRAs discussed in Chapter 3, but they are worth repeating and expanding upon here:

Advantages of the Roth Plans

1. By choosing the Roth, you pay the taxes up front on your contributions. (Can we say this often enough?) While you might have taken the tax savings from your Traditional plan contribution and invested the money in after-tax investments, over time, you will receive greater value from the tax-free growth.

2. If your tax bracket in retirement stays the same as it was when you contributed to the plan, you will be better off (assuming the Roth account grows, and possibly even if it goes down in value somewhat).

3. If your tax bracket in retirement is higher than when you contributed to the plan, you will be much better off. (Please note that we will look more closely at the effect of higher and lower tax brackets in retirement later.) There are many reasons why you could move into a higher tax bracket after you retire.

The longer the funds are kept in the tax-free Roth environment, the greater the advantage to both the Roth IRA owner and his or her heirs.

Here are a few examples:

a. The federal government will decide to raise tax rates (highly likely).

b. You need to increase your income with taxable withdrawals from your Traditional IRA plan, perhaps because you have medical expenses that were not covered by insurance.

c. You own or inherit income-producing property or investments that begin to give you taxable income.

d. You own annuities or have other lucrative employer or state pension plans that begin paying you income because of Required Minimum Distributions (RMDs).

e. The combination of your pension, Social Security, and RMDs are higher than your former taxable income from wages.

4. While you are alive, there are no RMDs from the Roth IRA accounts. Beginning in 2024, under the SECURE Act 2.0, Roth 401(k)s will no longer be subject to RMDs either. Prior to the passage of the 2022 SECURE Act 2.0, many investors sidestepped this requirement by rolling their Roth 401(k) into a Roth IRA upon retirement. Traditional 401(k)s have RMDs beginning at age 73 or 75 for retirees, depending upon when you were born. The Roth option provides a much better long-term, tax-advantaged savings horizon, as shown in Chapter 3.

5. Your heirs will benefit from ten years of tax-free growth if the Roth is left in your estate. Whatever advantage you achieved with the Roth can be magnified by your heirs over their lifetimes. If they qualify for one of the exceptions, tax-free growth will to some extent continue for the rest of their lives. As we'll cover in more detail in Chapter 10, one of those exceptions is for persons who can be certified by the government as "disabled or chronically ill."

6. The Roth provides greater value for the same number of dollars in retirement savings. This may lower federal estate and state inheritance taxes in an estate with the same after-tax spending power.

7. If you are in a lower tax bracket now, or even if you have no taxable income (possibly because of credits and deductions), contributing to the Roth plan instead of the Traditional plan will not cost you a significant amount now, but it will have enormous benefits later.

8. If you were previously unable to consider Roth IRAs because your income exceeded the income caps, contingent on your employer's retirement plan options, you may now be eligible to consider Roth 401(k) accounts.

9. If you need to spend a large amount of your retirement savings all at once, withdrawals from a Traditional plan would increase your marginal income tax rate. The Roth has a significant advantage in these high spending situations. Because Roth withdrawals are tax-free, they do not affect your marginal tax rate.

10. Having a pool of both Traditional plan money (funded by the employer contributions and taxable upon withdrawal) and Roth plan money (funded by the employee and if you make the election, by your employer, and tax-free to withdraw) to choose from, can provide you an opportunity for effective tax planning in retirement. With both types of plans, you could invest in the Traditional 401(k) portion in high income years and invest in the Roth 401(k) in lower income years when you are in a reduced tax bracket.

11. Simply put, however, the tax-free growth in the Roth will give both you and your heirs purchasing power.

Disadvantages of the Roth Plans

1. You are close to retiring and your income will be lower after you retire than while you are working. That is the most likely exception where you would be better off with a Traditional contribution rather than a Roth contribution.

2. Your paycheck contributions into the Roth 401(k) are not tax deductible, as is a Traditional 401(k) contribution. You will get smaller net paychecks if you contribute the same amount to a Roth account, rather than a Traditional account, because of increased federal income tax withholding. Losing the tax-deferred status means that by the time you file your tax return, you will have less cash in the bank, that is, in your after-tax investments. (Keep in mind, however, when compared to tax-deferred or tax-free retirement savings accounts, after-tax investments are the least efficient savings tool.)

3. The retirement investments may go down in value. Retirement assets may be subject to market fluctuations. If the decline becomes large enough, it is possible that you would have been better off in a Traditional tax-deferred plan, because, at the very least, you would have received a tax deduction on your contributions.

4. If Congress ever eliminates the income tax in favor of a sales tax or value-added tax, you will have already paid your income taxes. However, it seems unlikely that such a system would be adopted without grandfathering the rules for plans in place to prevent such inequities.

5. If your tax bracket in retirement drops, and you withdraw funds from your retirement assets before sufficient tax-free growth, the taxes you save on your Roth 401(k) plan withdrawals are less than the taxes you would have saved using a Traditional plan. This can be the case if you earn an unusually high amount of money in one year, maybe from consulting fees, that puts you in a very high tax bracket, but ultimately you do not end up with such a high income after retirement. If that were the case, a better approach might be to use the Traditional account for deferrals in that year or other years where your income is unusually large. (Please note that later we will look more closely at the effect of lower tax brackets in retirement.)

6. This is a hard one to quantify, but many retirement plan owners, including my wife and I, are extremely reluctant to spend our Roth. Even though we have a seven-figure Roth, psychologically we are treating it as sacred and consider it part of our daughter's inheritance. You'll learn more about that in Chapter 11, and how the actions we've taken have virtually eliminated our worries about whether our daughter, who has a disability, will have enough money to support a healthy lifestyle after we're gone. We have gone through spending contortions, even borrowing money, so we don't touch that Roth. This is not unusual. If instead of making Roth conversions we had Traditional IRAs, we likely would have spent the after-tax dollars that we used to convert to the Roth IRAs to pay certain expenses. My wife has a large Roth, but it doesn't feel liquid.

I have many clients who could afford to spend a lot more money than they do and having large Roth accounts that they are reluctant to spend compounds the problem.

Availability of the Roth 401(k)

Employers who now offer a 401(k) plan may choose to expand their retirement plan options to include the Roth 401(k), but they are not required to do so. Some organizations were early adopters; others may take more time to incorporate the new plans into their offerings; still others may never offer them.

Under the recently passed SECURE Act 2.0, employers can offer the option for the employer match portion of 401(k) contributions to be added to a Roth account beginning in 2023. Because this is a recent change, your employer's plan will need to be amended to allow this option. If this option is selected, the employer match will be added to your taxable income.

Contribution Limits for Roth and Traditional 401(k)s

For 2023, the Traditional and Roth 401(k) employee contribution limits are $22,500 per year, or $30,000 if you are age 50 or older). Employer matching contributions don't affect this limit. If you participate in both a 401(k) plan and a 403(b) plan, this limit applies to all your contributions to both plans.

In 2023, a 50-year-old employee cannot make a $30,000 contribution to a Traditional 401(k) account and a $30,000 contribution to a Roth 401(k) account; the contributions to both accounts combined cannot exceed $30,000. The Roth 401(k) contributions will be treated like a Roth IRA for tax purposes.

Beginning in 2025, employees who are ages 60-63 will be allowed to make increased catch-up contributions to their employer's retirement plans. These specific employees can make an additional contribution of $10,000 or 150% of the regular catch-up contribution amount, whichever is greater. The current catch-up contribution amount is $7,500, which means that, as the law currently stands, employees who will be between ages 60 and 63 in 2025 will be able to contribute an additional $11,250 ($7,500 x 150% = $11,250) on top of their regular employee contribution.

However, high-wage earners may face a different kind of hurdle for catch-up contributions starting in 2026. Employees who earn over $145,000 will only be able to make catch-up contributions to Roth 401(k) accounts starting in 2026. The original date for this provision was 2024, but because of the administrative complications, the IRS has delayed the required implementation date until 2026. Employers can adopt the change as early as 2024 if they are able to do so. This

> **Employers who now offer a 401(k) plan may choose to expand their retirement plan options to include the Roth 401(k), but they are not required to do so.**

means their catch-up contributions will no longer be tax-deferred and will not be deductible from taxable wages. This also means that the employer plan must have a Roth option. If the employer-sponsored plan does not have a Roth option, and if there are employees over age 50 who are also earning over $145,000, then no employees—regardless of income—will be allowed to make catch-up contributions. This odd provision makes it imperative that employees encourage their employers to include the Roth option in employer-sponsored retirement plans.

Perhaps an example of a Traditional vs. Roth contribution would help.

························· **MINI CASE STUDY 4.1** ·························

Contributing to a Traditional 401(k) vs. a Roth 401(k)— Lower Income Tax Bracket

Joe, a prudent 55-year-old civil engineer, participates in his company's 401(k) plan. He has dutifully contributed the maximum allowable contribution to his 401(k) plan since he started working. This means he is also taking full advantage of the employer match, which is a generous 6% of his salary. Until his employer adopted the new Roth 401(k) option, his expectation was to continue contributing the maximum into his Traditional 401(k) for 2023 and beyond.

Now Joe has a choice. In 2023, he can either continue making his regular deductible 401(k) contribution ($30,000); he could elect to make a $30,000 contribution to the new Roth 401(k); or he could split his $30,000 contribution between the regular 401(k) portion and the Roth 401(k) portion of the plan. His employer also amended the company retirement plan to allow employer matching contributions to go into either a Traditional tax-deferred account or a Roth account.

When Joe decides what options to choose for his 401(k), he needs to consider the fundamental difference in the way a Traditional 401(k) is taxed and the way a new Roth 401(k) is taxed. With the Traditional 401(k), Joe gets an income tax deduction for his contribution. Employer match contributions to Traditional 401(k) accounts are not included in Joe's taxable income. After Joe retires, however, and takes a distribution from his Traditional retirement plan, he will have to pay income taxes on that distribution. If Joe contributes to the Roth 401(k), he will not get a tax deduction for making the contribution, but the money will grow income-tax free. Similarly, employer matching contributions to Roth accounts are included in Joe's taxable income and he will pay tax on that money if he chooses to send the company match to a Roth account.

When Joe takes a distribution from his Roth retirement account, he will not have to pay income taxes, provided other technical requirements are met. These other requirements are usually easy to meet and include such things as waiting until age 59½ before making retirement account withdrawals and waiting at least five years from the time the account is opened before the first withdrawal.

Because Joe has some after-tax savings already and does not really need more income tax deductions, he is advised to contribute to the Roth 401(k). Assuming Joe takes my advice and switches his annual contributions and his employer's match to the Roth 401(k), he will have four components to his employer's retirement plan. He will have the employer's matching contributions in his Traditional account, plus the interest, dividends, and appreciation on those contributions, to the extent that he is vested in the plan. He will have his own (the employee's) Traditional portion of the plan, which consists of all of his contributions to date plus the interest, dividends, and appreciation on those contributions. Then, starting in 202, he will have a Roth portion for his Roth contributions and a Roth portion for his employer's Roth matching contributions.

If Joe is married and filing a joint tax return and his 2023 adjusted gross income is less than $228,000, he may have already been making contributions to a Roth IRA outside of his employer's retirement plan. In 2023, he will be able to make the maximum Roth IRA contribution of $7,500 ($6,500 for people under age 50) to the plan. And remember that Joe can contribute the maximum ($30,000) to his Roth 401(k), plus the maximum ($7,500) to his Roth IRA, assuming that his income is below the exclusion limits. As long as Joe is working, the Roth 401(k) through his employer will remain separate from any Roth IRA he may have outside of his employer's plan.

If his 2023 adjusted gross income was more than $218,000, he would not have been allowed to contribute to a Roth IRA (the income phase-out range is between $218,000 and $228,000). What is much different for Joe is that the amount of money he will be allowed to contribute into the income tax-free world of the Roth will see a dramatic increase, because there is no income limit for employees who want to contribute to a Roth 401(k) plan at work.

....

Choosing Between the Roth and Traditional 401(k)

Many clients come to us wondering whether they would be better off making contributions to a Roth account or to a Traditional retirement account. If the choice is between using a Roth IRA versus a nondeductible Traditional IRA, it is pretty easy to make the case for the Roth. However, because of the nature of the Roth's advantages and disadvantages, which are contingent on your current and future income tax brackets, there is no one size fits all answer if the choice is between a Traditional deductible IRA and a Roth. So, I have formulated some

The following analysis is equally important for individuals considering a Roth IRA conversion. I do not repeat this analysis in Chapter 16, but people who are considering a Roth IRA conversion, or interested in learning more about them, should read this material with the Roth conversion in mind.

different scenarios showing how the Roth accounts become advantageous for some people and a bad idea for others.

Setting the Stage

Assume that we have a software engineer named Gary who is 55 years old, and who is able to contribute $30,000 to his 401(k) plan for eleven years, until he retires at age 66. His employer offers a Roth account in their 401(k), and Gary wants to know if he should direct his contributions and his employer's matching contributions to the Roth, if available, or the Traditional side of the plan. Our number crunching CPAs ran the numbers using the following assumptions:

1. Gary earns a conservative rate of return of 6 percent annually on all of his accounts.

2. Gary knows that he will save a significant amount in taxes if his contributions are made to the tax-deductible Traditional account. Gary is more disciplined than most savers. He is willing to take all of the money that he saved on taxes and contribute it to an after-tax brokerage account environment.

3. In this scenario, Gary's income tax rates are as follows:

   a. 24 percent ordinary incremental tax rate during his working years.

   b. 24 percent ordinary incremental tax rate during his retirement years.

   c. Capital gains tax rates are 15 percent.

4. Gary is planning to take his RMDs from his Traditional 401(k) account beginning at age 75. He will pay ordinary income taxes on the distributions and will use the rest of the money to pay his living expenses. He will take tax-free spending withdrawals in the same amount from his Roth account.

5. The calculated income tax rate on all growth of the after-tax account averages 18 percent. (24% is the marginal tax rate, not the actual tax rate.)

6. At the end of each year, we measure the spending power for each scenario. To measure the spending power of pre-tax Traditional 401(k) plan balances, an allowance is made for income taxes. The tax rate of this allowance or liquidation rate is, initially, 24 percent, comparable to the ordinary tax rate.

Now we are able to run the numbers and see the resulting spending power of the remaining assets as shown in Figure 4.1.

Calculating the Results

Figure 4.1 shows that there is an increasing advantage from investing in the Roth 401(k) instead of the Traditional 401(k) plan. Although it's difficult to see, the advantage begins in the first year. At Gary's retirement age of 66, the advantage has grown to $6,652, or 1.58 percent. By age 75, after RMDs have begun, the advantage is 4.10 percent; by age 85, it is 9.45 percent; and by age 95, it is a 21.71 percent advantage resulting in an additional $169,962 for the Roth owner.

Figure 4.1

Roth 401(k) Savings *vs.* Traditional 401(k) Savings – Lower Income Tax Bracket

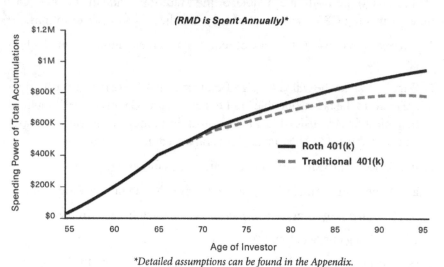

Detailed assumptions can be found in the Appendix.

For an individual whose circumstances match the assumptions above, the cumulative advantage over the 40-year projection period should provide the incentive to use the Roth rather than the Traditional 401(k). And if a rate of return greater than six percent is assumed, the advantage to the Roth owner increases significantly. In addition, if there is a tax increase, the Roth would be of even greater advantage.

Under current rules, if Gary should pass away and leave his Roth account to his surviving spouse, she will not have to take RMDs from the account over her lifetime. If he leaves the Roth account to someone other than his spouse, perhaps a child, the SECURE Act requires that the entire account balance be distributed within 10 years, subject to exceptions (e.g., your child with a disability deemed to be an eligible designated beneficiary would be able to stretch the account over his lifetime). The rules regarding RMDs are discussed in detail in Chapter 6, but for now it's important to know that RMDs force money out of a tax-deferred or tax-free environment, into a taxable environment. And remember Mr. Pay Taxes Now and Mr. Pay Taxes Later from Chapter 2? Mr. Pay Taxes Later was the clear winner.

If you're trying to figure out the most opportune strategies for naming beneficiaries of your IRAs, you should refer to Chapter 9 for an in-depth discussion on the subject, but here is a simplified explanation of the inheritance rules for a spouse:

- If you leave behind a Traditional IRA, your spouse can treat the IRA as his or her own and ultimately take RMDs based on his or her own life expectancy (technically the life expectancy of her and someone deemed ten years younger than her). Your spouse can also elect to take distributions over your life expectancy and start distributions at the time that you would be starting to take RMDs.

- If you leave behind a Roth, your spouse is never required to take RMDs.

With the confiscatory SECURE Act, the rules have changed drastically—and not for the better—if your beneficiary is not your spouse or does not qualify for an exception (e.g., a beneficiary deemed eligible by nature of his disability or chronic illness). We'll cover those changes in Chapter 10. In fact, the new rules for Inherited IRAs under the SECURE Act could provide an additional incentive

Even though we are not talking about Roth IRA conversions at this point in the book, the reasoning that goes into deciding to put money in a Roth 401 (k) versus a Traditional 401 (k) is conceptually similar to the reasoning that goes into deciding to make a Roth IRA conversion. So, although you may be retired, the following analysis is relevant for retirees thinking about a Roth IRA conversion.

for committed couples who have not legally married to do so. We'll take a deeper look at the financial reasons that committed couples might want to marry for the money in Chapter 25.

Additional Advantages for Higher Income Taxpayers

One great feature of the new Roth options for 401(k) plans is that it allows higher income taxpayers to save money in the Roth environment. How does the advantage change in their situation? Figure 4.2 uses the same assumptions as Figure 4.1; except that Gary's ordinary income tax rate has been increased to the current maximum of 37 percent, including the liquidation tax rate used for measurement.

In Figure 4.2, we discover that the Roth 401(k) advantage for a higher income taxpayer is greater than for the lower income taxpayer in the 24 percent tax bracket (Figure 4.2). The advantage has now become a higher 29.41 percent, or $308,766, after 40 years. Why such a large difference? There are several reasons why this happened, and they relate to the ever-changing tax laws. First, the maximum federal income tax rate was increased from 37 percent to 39.6 percent. Second, there were several new taxes imposed on higher income taxpayers. Higher earners (in 2023, single individuals whose adjusted gross income exceeds $200,000 or married taxpayers filing jointly whose income exceeds $250,000) are now subject

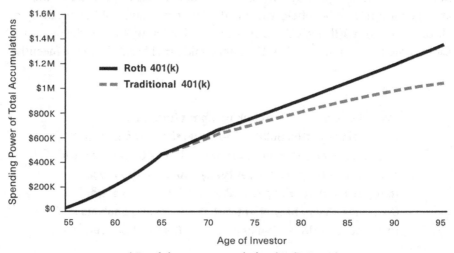

Figure 4.2

Roth 401(k) Savings *vs.* Traditional 401(k) Savings RMD is Spent Annually—Higher Income Tax Bracket*

* Detailed assumptions can be found in the Appendix.

to the Net Investment Income Tax, which adds on an additional 3.8 percent tax to certain investment income earned outside of the Roth account. Higher income earners are also subject to an additional 0.9% Medicare tax on all wages in excess of $200,000 for individual taxpayers and $250,000 for married taxpayers. These and other factors all combine to make the Roth an even more attractive option for higher income taxpayers than in prior years.

And guess what? The higher income taxpayer is less likely to spend the Roth investments, thus making the long-term benefits more achievable. The bottom line is that the Roth 401(k) is dollar for dollar more valuable for the higher income retirement plan owner than a middle-income retirement plan owner. The counter argument is that the amount of savings to middle income taxpayers, though smaller, is more meaningful in terms of the impact on their lives.

The Roth savings options can change people's lives for the better. Subject to a few exceptions discussed above, if you have access to a Roth option in your employer's retirement plan, I highly recommend that you take advantage of it, and if you can afford it, contribute the maximum allowed. Also, please keep in mind that this analysis is also quite valuable for someone interested in Roth IRA conversions because there are a lot of similarities in the calculations and the sensitivity of tax brackets.

Making It Happen

Notice, however, there is a caveat. I said, "If you have access." Though Congress has made Roth 401(k)s available for employers to use, that doesn't mean your employer has adopted these features or has made plans to do so. If your employer does not provide options for a Roth 401(k) and you like to waste time attempting to argue with your human resources department who is responsible for those decisions, you can gently (or not so gently depending on your personality) suggest that your employer include a Roth 401(k) option in its retirement plans and allow you to participate.

> The Roth savings options can change people's lives for the better. Subject to the exceptions discussed in this chapter and in other parts of the book, if you have access to a Roth option in your retirement plan at work, I highly recommend you take advantage of it, and if you can afford it, contribute the maximum allowed.

KEY IDEAS

- Roth 401(k) plan options offer more people a powerful entrée into the world of tax-free wealth accumulation.

- Roth 401(k) plans are most valuable over the long term for high income participants.

- Saving at least a part of your retirement funds in a Roth account can be one of the best things you can do for yourself and your family.

- Even in situations where Roth conversions would not be warranted if the only consideration was maximizing wealth for the parents, a Roth is often the best strategy when a child with a disability or a trust for that child is the retirement account beneficiary.

5

Optimal Spending Strategies for Retirees

"I am having an out-of-money experience."

— Author Unknown

First, subject to exceptions, this is the best order to spend your money after you retire.

1. Spend your existing income first, which includes things like any pension, interest, dividends, Social Security, RMDs, and any self-employment income because you have to pay tax on that money anyway.

2. Spend after-tax dollars that are not in an IRA or a Roth IRA, and that don't have any or much appreciation.

3. Spend highly appreciated after-tax dollars that do incur a capital gain.

4. Spend your Traditional retirement assets like IRAs and 401(k)s.

5. Spend your Roth IRA and Roth 401(k) dollars last.

Of course, there will be exceptions based on individual tax brackets, and on individual and family situations, and one big exception that is covered in Chapter 16, transferring your money from taxable to tax-free, but that is primarily for higher net worth individuals. But, subject to those exceptions, this is generally the best order for spending to minimize taxes.

This and the following chapters have a nitty gritty analysis of how we reached the above conclusion to determine the optimal spending order when you need to take money from your portfolio to meet your living expenses. We also examine the exceptions which are important, particularly for high income and high net worth individuals.

Which Assets Should I Spend First?

Recent changes in tax laws that affect capital gains and tax brackets, and new taxes aimed specifically at high income individuals have made it increasingly difficult to simplify spending strategies for retirees. Under the old laws, it was much easier and generally more accurate to recommend spending after-tax dollars first, then IRA dollars, and Roth dollars last. Even under the old laws, that wasn't always accurate for everyone, but unfortunately this basic guideline is no longer accurate for an ever-growing number of taxpayers.

Sometimes it is the best course of action, but sometimes it now makes sense to spend Roth IRA dollars before Traditional IRA dollars in order to stay in a lower tax bracket. In addition, the Tax Cuts and Jobs Act (TCJA) of 2017 added the extra wrinkle of establishing temporary tax rate cuts which will expire in 2026 unless they are extended. So, your long-term strategy should likely incorporate an eventual tax hike from today's relatively low rates. Plus, as I'll discuss in greater detail in Chapter 10, the SECURE Act drastically accelerates taxes on Inherited IRAs and retirement plans for most beneficiaries. Heirs which have been deemed to have a disability or be chronically ill are not subject to this acceleration and may continue to stretch the Inherited retirement assets over their lifetime. This may change the kinds of assets you are planning to leave to each of your children and grandchildren. In addition, we now must consider the SECURE Act 2.0 which was recently passed as law.

In order to get the best answer for your specific situation, you could have a qualified advisor or CPA "run the numbers" for you. Or you might prefer to do the calculations yourself if you like to pack your own parachute. (That was too broad. Certain things, like drafting wills and trusts really should be handled by a competent expert. Other things, like working out the best spending order for retirement assets, while tricky, may not be out of reach for quantitative individuals who have a lot of time and like the challenge of figuring this stuff out.) However, it would not be helpful for me to tell you that it is best to run the numbers, and not give you general guidelines which illustrate the points I'm talking about. Therefore, please understand that the information presented in this chapter is just that—general guidelines—that may not produce the optimal result for your own situation.

Finally, perhaps the most important exception to our recommended spending order involves shifting taxable assets to tax-free assets. Please see Chapter 16, *Roth IRA Conversions Before and After the SECURE Act*.

At retirement an individual moves into distribution mode—that is to say, he or she begins to spend retirement savings. This is *not* to say that accumulation stops. Income and appreciation on the investments, Social Security funds, and any pension plan proceeds might still be exceeding your expenses. In fact, most of my retired clients have more money now than they did when they initially retired.

You may be fortunate enough to find that your Social Security, pension, Required Minimum Distributions (RMD) from your IRA (if any) and from

In general, it is preferable to spend principal from your after-tax investments rather than taking taxable distributions from your IRA and/or retirement plan.

your 401(k) accounts, and dividends and interest on your after-tax investments provide enough funds for your living expenses. Let's assume, however, that isn't the case, and you need to either tap into your after-tax funds (you might think of that as your "nest egg") or make additional taxable withdrawals from your IRA or retirement account to make ends meet.

I've been in business for over thirty years. Most of my clients actually listen to me, but I always have a few who don't. Instead of following my recommendations, they choose to spend their IRAs first. It drives me crazy. When I used to prepare taxes, when the exception applied even less frequently, I used to see clients spending the wrong money first.

With this one particular accounting client, every year, when I delivered his tax return, while I was still preparing tax returns, I would include a personal note saying, "I really hate to see you pay income taxes on this." I would also call him. He said his stockbroker wanted to maintain a balance between his IRA and after-tax dollars. Now, I'm all for an appropriate and well-balanced portfolio. I agree that you don't want to have all your eggs in one basket. But I'm not into this allocation between IRA and non-IRA dollars at the expense of considerable extra taxes right now. If you're older than 59½, you don't have to worry about maintaining the liquidity of your after-tax dollars because you can take money out of an IRA whenever you want without a penalty. I would much rather that, subject to some exceptions. Most taxpayers follow my "pay taxes later" rule.

Mini Case Study 5.1 and Figure 5.1 provide a comparison of the benefits of spending after-tax savings before pre-tax accumulations. Please note that the calculations below reflect the tax rates and the tax law in effect for 2022. While tax rates have changed, and the starting age for taking RMDs is later, the overall analysis will not change.

······································ **MINI CASE STUDY 5.1** ··
Spend Your After-Tax Money First

Both Mr. Pay Taxes Now and Mr. Pay Taxes Later started from an identical position in 2022. They are both 65 years old and both have $300,000 in after-tax funds and $1,100,000 in retirement funds. They both receive $25,000 per year in Social Security income. They want to spend $86,000 per year, after paying income taxes. Their investment return is 6.5 percent and the rate of inflation on expenses is 3.5 percent. Income tax assumptions include ordinary income and capital gains tax rates established by the Tax Cuts and Jobs Act of 2017 and subsequent tax laws. State income taxes are ignored.

Mr. Pay Taxes Now does not spend any of his after-tax funds until all the retirement funds are depleted. By spending his retirement funds first, he triggers income taxes on the withdrawals, reducing the tax-deferral period, and his balance goes down. He also subjects a larger share of his after-tax funds to income taxes on the dividends, interest, and potential capital gains. All income taxes due on the retirement funds and the after-tax funds cause a greater amount to be withdrawn from his retirement account. In 25 years, by paying taxes prematurely, he has sacrificed a fortune in tax-deferred growth. Shortly after his 89th birthday, Mr. Pay Taxes Now is out of money.

Mr. Pay Taxes Later first uses his after-tax funds to meet expenses. Only when the after-tax funds are depleted are withdrawals made from the retirement accounts. He fully uses the tax-deferred features of the IRA. Mr. Pay Taxes Later has over $350,000 on his 89th birthday. Both he and Mr. Pay Taxes Now enjoyed an identical lifestyle, investments, and so forth, but there is a significant difference in the amount each has remaining at their age 89. Mr. Pay Taxes Now is broke, and Mr. Pay Taxes Later has enough funds to support himself for an additional 3 years. In states such as Pennsylvania that do not tax retirement

Figure 5.1

Benefits of Spending After-Tax Savings Before Traditional Retirement Plans*

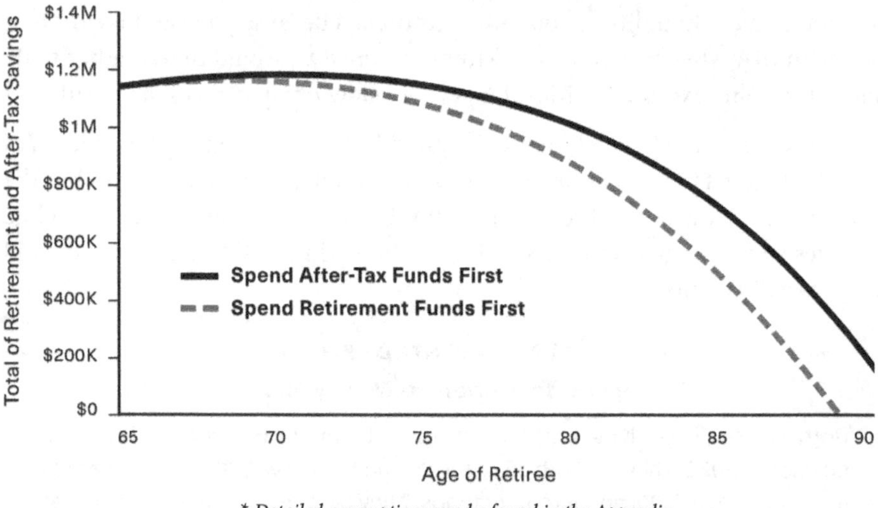

* Detailed assumptions can be found in the Appendix.

income but do tax after-tax investment income, the benefit of spending the after-tax money first is even greater. The conclusion would most likely be the same for any reasonable set of assumptions in terms of how much money each individual has, and what rate of return you want to assume. The principle stands: don't pay taxes now—pay taxes later even after you retire.

The Big Picture

Once the after-tax money is spent, there is no longer a one size fits all answer as to whether it is more advantageous to spend Traditional IRA or Roth IRA money. In later stages of spending and under certain other circumstances, it does not hold true that no Roth dollars should be spent while Traditional IRA dollars remain. If you live long enough to fully deplete your Traditional IRAs and are left with only Roth dollars and little taxable income other than Social Security, you will likely be in the zero percent tax bracket. From that point on, you will be missing out on what could have been tax-free Traditional IRA withdrawals. Before the Traditional IRA is all gone, it makes sense to spend a combination of Traditional and Roth IRA dollars so that zero percent tax brackets never get wasted.

In 2023, a married couple filing a 2023 tax return jointly could withdraw up to $27,700 ($30,700 if both spouses are age 65 >) from their Traditional IRA and, if they have no other taxable income, would pay zero tax on the withdrawal! Also, there are strategic times when spending Roth dollars can save more in taxes than the 12 percent tax bracket you expect to be in. Your actual taxes on incremental additional IRA withdrawals may be 27 percent or more because of the phase-in rules on the taxability of Social Security and the addition of the new Net Investment Tax. There may be other situations where spending some Roth dollars before Traditional IRA dollars could benefit you in retirement.

Keep in mind also that the current low rates are scheduled to go up in 2026, due to the sunset provisions of the 2017 Tax Cut and Jobs Act at which point we will go back to the 2017 rates (plus inflation). So, it may be wise to spend more Traditional IRA and 401(k) dollars now, and more Roth dollars later if and when the rates go up. As I said, it is more difficult now to make blanket recommendations for spending order. A case-by-case analysis is needed.

························ **MINI CASE STUDY 5.2** ························
Capital Gains May Affect Spending Order

What follows is a detailed mathematical analysis regarding whether it is a good idea to spend highly appreciated dollars that will incur a capital gain or spend IRA dollars. We try to be even handed and use a "running the numbers approach" to produce recommendations. The problem in real life, however, is that the highly appreciated assets often comprise a large percentage of the portfolio. Furthermore, frequently those assets have been good performers in the past and clients often have strong emotional ties to the stock, especially if it is the stock of their former employer. Though hard to quantify, there is significant value that might even exceed any tax disadvantage in reducing your exposure to any concentrated positions in stocks or funds, even if you have to incur a capital gain.

One of the primary reasons people think it may be better not to spend the after-tax money first is because of capital gains. Changes to the capital gains tax rules in 2012 make this an issue for far fewer people than in the past. Capital gains tax rates now vary depending on whether the gains are short-term or long-term, and they no longer apply *at all* to taxpayers whose taxable income falls in the 10 percent or 12 percent marginal tax bracket. Yes, you read that right. If you are in the 10 percent or 12 percent tax bracket, your capital gain is not subject to federal tax unless your capital gain pushes you above the 12 percent bracket.

In the following example, we are using the tax brackets and tax rates in effect for 2022. While the exact numbers will be different for subsequent years, the basic conclusions remain the same.

Example:

You are married and your joint taxable income before any capital gains is $60,000 which places you in the 12% marginal bracket. (For 2022 the married filing jointly (MFJ) top ordinary income level at 12% is $83,550, and for incomes below $83,350, the capital gains tax rate is 0%.) You incur a $23,350 long-term capital gain. There is not any capital gains tax on that realized capital gain.

High income taxpayers who fall into the 35 percent tax bracket are subject to a 20 percent capital gains tax plus the 3.8% Net Investment Tax for a total of 23.8 percent tax. Taxpayers whose income falls into a bracket higher than 12 percent but less than 35 percent are subject to a 15 percent capital gains rate and possibly the 3.8% net investment income tax. Let's assume that the after-tax assets in the previous example have a zero-cost basis, and that the entire $300,000 will now be taxed as capital gains. Is that a problem? The answer is, not necessarily.

Mr. Pay Taxes Later is a single man in Figure 5.1, so let's assume he's single here too. If he liquidated 100 percent of his after-tax stock account all at once, he would have a $300,000 capital gain. That's nowhere near enough to put him into the highest income and capital gains tax brackets, but 85 percent of his Social Security is now taxed. The tax he owes on just his Social Security and the capital gain is $40,824. It doesn't stop there, though. He also has to pay Net Investment Tax of $4,608. Since he has such a high income this year, Mr. Pay Taxes Later is going to have to pay the IRS $45,432 on April 15th.

If Mr. Pay Taxes Later had talked to us or another firm that actually does advance planning to help clients reduce their tax bill before liquidating all of his stock, we would have told him that he could save a lot of money in taxes by liquidating only as much as he needs to meet his expenses each year. Let's assume that he cashed in only $69,000 of his stock each year. This is approximately the amount he has to withdraw if he needs $86,000 to live on after he pays his taxes. 85 percent of his Social Security will still be taxed, but he's in a lower tax bracket because his total income is significantly lower. His income is so much lower, in fact, that he does not have to pay the additional Net Investment Tax at all. This year, he will owe the IRS only $6,174. If he liquidates the $300,000 stock account at an equal rate over four years ($75,000 each year), the tax savings compared to liquidating it all at once are significant ($17,136 in savings)!

The really surprising news, though, comes if we make Mr. Pay Taxes Later a married man. We're going to assume that he has a wife who is his age, and that she collects the same amount of Social Security that he does. In this scenario, they will have more to spend ($90,000) by liquidating less (only $40,000) of the after-tax stock account each year. When he was a single man, he had to liquidate $69,000 each year in order to be able to spend $86,000. How on earth is that possible?

One obvious reason is that his wife is receiving her own Social Security benefits (I used $25,000 for purposes of this illustration), and they can use that money toward their spending needs. The not so-obvious reason lies in their tax return. Their standard deduction is double that of a single person, which reduces their taxable income. Because their taxable income is lower, only 48 percent (as compared to 85 percent) of their Social Security benefits are taxed. Their taxable income for the year is only $37,950 (as compared to $77,300 when he was single), and because of the favorable capital gains rates, they pay nothing—yes, zero—in federal income tax. In this scenario, Mr. Pay Taxes Later liquidated $40,000 of after-tax stock with a zero-cost basis, paid almost nothing in tax, and still has more spending money than he needs! They have $50,000 in Social Security benefits and $40,000 in proceeds from the sale of the stock, which leaves them with $90,000 and nothing owed to the IRS!

Let's even go so far as to consider what happens if the married Mr. Pay Taxes Later decides to listen to his buddy, Mr. Pay Taxes Now, instead of me. Accordingly, he withdraws the additional money he needs from his retirement plan instead of his after-tax account. He didn't know that the money he takes from his retirement plan is subject to ordinary income tax rates. If he withdraws just enough to meet his living expenses, $36,000, from his retirement plan instead of his after-tax account, he will owe the IRS $3,255 on April 15. If he had cashed in his after-tax stock that had a cost basis of zero and the income was from a $36,000 capital gain, he would have owed the IRS nothing. Zero. Nada. Unfortunately, he doesn't have enough money to pay the tax bill, because his Social Security and the $36,000 retirement plan withdrawal were just enough to cover his normal monthly expenses. That means that he must withdraw even more from his retirement plan to pay the tax, which is going to increase his tax bill next year. The amount he needs to withdraw to cover his spending needs in addition to the tax due on his retirement plan distribution is $40,000, which increases the tax amount due to $4,143. And as you can imagine, paying all of these unnecessary taxes will cause him to burn through his retirement plan very quickly. For higher income taxpayers, the outlook for very high taxes is even gloomier, because they are in higher income tax brackets and are potentially subject to the additional Net Investment Income Taxes as well.

When considering spending in retirement, there are many factors that need to be taken into consideration in order to make sure that there are no unpleasant surprises by the time April 15th rolls around. This is one area where it is well worth your time and money to consult with an accountant who is highly skilled in tax planning. It is a specialty in my accounting practice, and it allows us to make recommendations concerning Roth IRA conversions to our clients with confidence. But above all, I hope I have made it very clear that the old assumption that you can never cash in highly appreciated investments without getting hit with a huge tax bill is simply not true.

Consider, though, which may be of interest to readers who have more than enough income from other sources, and who expect to have money in their estates to leave to their children. The 'step-up in basis rule' states that, if property is inherited, it assumes a basis equivalent to its fair market value at the date of the decedent's death. It is referred to as a 'step-up' because frequently the fair market value of the property at the date of death is much greater than the decedent's basis—which was the cost when it was first acquired. If you have $100,000 of Google stock for which you paid $10,000, your basis is $10,000. If you sold the stock, you would have to report a $90,000 capital gain. If instead of selling it before you die, you die owning the stock and leave the stock to a child, though, his basis in the stock would be $100,000 because that was the value at the time of your death.

So, if you are preparing an estate plan assuming that your life expectancy is short, it may be advantageous for you to not spend highly appreciated after-tax investments before your retirement funds. If you anticipate being in a situation like this, either on your own or with a qualified advisor, run some numbers. Most of the numbers we have run indicate that unless you are going to die in a few years, you are usually better off spending your after-tax dollars first, even if you will incur capital gains tax and give up your step-up in basis.

On the other hand, it is possible, even likely, the step up in basis rules will be repealed in the near future.

Another factor to consider when deciding which assets to leave to your children and grandchildren is the impact of the SECURE Act on Inherited IRAs and retirement accounts. As I'll cover in more detail in later chapters, the SECURE Act will cause a massive income tax acceleration for beneficiaries of retirement accounts. Under the old law, beneficiaries could stretch distributions of retirement account assets over their lifetimes, which allowed those assets to continue to appreciate, and to spread the tax bite over years. But now, beneficiaries have no choice but to take full distribution of those accounts within ten years, unless they qualify for an exception. Fortunately, one of those exceptions is for beneficiaries who qualify as eligible designated beneficiaries because of their disability or chronic illness, so your child may still be eligible to stretch distributions from Inherited retirement accounts over his or her lifetime. If this is the case, and your child will be able to take advantage of the lifetime stretch, leaving them your retirement account makes enormous financial sense.

If your children do not qualify for the stretch, then this change may make it even more beneficial to spend your retirement accounts and to leave your highly appreciated after-tax investments to your children. Your children will be able to take advantage of the step-up in basis and will have money that they can access according to their timetables. You can potentially spare them the pain of the huge tax bills they would incur if their inheritance had fewer high-dollar IRAs and other retirement accounts, which would have to be distributed—and taxed—in ten years. Later in this book, I will cover strategies to minimize the tax bite. As with all my recommendations, you have to run the numbers to see what the best spending strategy is for your unique situation.

·· **MINI CASE STUDY 5.3** ··

Which Accounts Should I Save For My Children?

Phyllis Planner is 65 years old and widowed (though the conclusion would be basically the same for a married taxpayer). She is thinking ahead. She wants her money to provide her with a comfortable standard of living, and she also wants to leave some money to her three children. How should Phyllis evaluate which pool of money to spend first and which to save for as long as possible?

There are four general categories of money to support her retirement. They are ranked in order of how I recommend Phyllis spend her money, exhausting each asset category before breaking into the next asset category.

1. After-Tax Assets Generated by Income Sources:
    *   Pension distributions
    *   Dividends, interest, and capital gains
    *   Social Security

Of course, when Phyllis is 73 or 75, depending on the year of her birth, under the current rules, she will be required to take minimum distributions from her IRA. Since she will have to pay income taxes on the distributions, the proceeds that remain after she pays taxes on the IRA distributions could also be spent before any of the following assets or sources of income.

2. After-Tax Assets (investments that are not part of a qualified pre-tax retirement plan that would generate income subject to taxes annually):
    *   Investments that will either sell at a loss or break-even
    *   Then, more highly appreciated investments

3. IRA and Retirement Plan Assets (assets subject to ordinary income tax):
    *   IRA, 403(b), 401(k), and so forth, dollars over and above Required Minimum Distributions

4. Roth IRA:
    *   Roth IRA dollars

The assets in the income category should be spent first since she has to pay tax on that money anyway. But let's assume that Phyllis' Social Security, and the pension, dividends, and interest are not sufficient to meet her spending needs. Then the question becomes, "Which pool of money should be spent next?" If we keep in mind the premise of "don't pay taxes now—pay taxes later," the answer is obvious: the after-tax dollars. If we spend our after-tax dollars, except to the extent that a capital gain is triggered on a sale, those dollars will not be subject to income taxes and the money in the IRA can keep growing tax deferred. Then, when Phyllis has exhausted her after-tax funds, she can delve into her IRA or pre-tax funds.

Whenever you make a withdrawal from a Traditional IRA or from another non-Roth retirement account, you are going to have to pay income taxes. To get an equivalent amount of spending money from the IRA assets and the after-tax assets, you have to take the taxes into consideration. Assuming that you are in a 24 percent tax bracket, you need $1.32 from the IRA assets to get $1.00 of spending money ($1.00 cash + $0.32 to pay the taxes). (We get $0.32 cents because $1.32 x 24 percent = .32.) On the other hand, the after-tax money is withdrawn tax-free, so to get $1.00, you withdraw $1.00 unless capital gains tax applies. Even if you are subject to capital gains tax, the rate is 15 percent for taxpayers who are in the 24 percent tax bracket. You are still ahead by 17 cents for every dollar you withdraw.

Finally, when Phyllis exhausts her IRA and pre-tax funds, she spends her Roth IRA. Why should she spend her Traditional IRA before her Roth IRA? If tax-deferred growth is a good thing, then tax-free growth is even better. By spending taxable IRA money before Roth IRA money, she increases the time that the Roth IRA will provide income tax-free growth.

....

If your plan is to leave money to your heirs, their tax situations should be considered as well. If you have heirs who have tax deferral/avoidance as a goal and their tax bracket is the same as yours or higher, then the Roth assets are the best assets for them to inherit. The opposite conclusion may be reached if you have other heirs who plan on spending the money soon after they inherit it and are in a lower tax bracket. If that is the case, you could be better off spending the Roth IRA yourself. The facts of each case should be considered. Please see the discussion of "Who Gets What?" in Chapter 19.

································· **MINI CASE STUDY 5.4** ·································

Using Tax Planning to Determine
the Best Spending Order

One possible exception to spending after-tax dollars first is to make small IRA withdrawals, or small Roth IRA conversions if your current tax bracket is lower than your future tax bracket will be once you retire. This strategy saves some taxes since you are getting some money out of your IRA before you must take Required Minimum Distributions (RMD), which will be taxed at your higher post-retirement rate. If you withdraw just enough to take you to the top of your current (low) tax bracket, then you get that money out at a lower tax rate without pushing yourself into a higher tax bracket. But first, let me clarify a common misunderstanding about taxes and tax brackets.

What many people don't understand is that tax brackets are tiered. A married couple who is filing their joint tax return in 2024 (for their 2023 taxes), and who has taxable income up to $22,000 is taxed at 10 percent. If they earn more than that, then the next tier of their income is taxed at the next bracket (income from $22,000 to $89,450 is taxed at 12 percent for married filing jointly), and so on. Some people are deathly afraid of getting one more dollar. They think, "Oh no! If I get one more dollar, I'm going to be thrown into the 24 percent tax bracket, and my taxes are going to explode." But that's not right. What happens is that *the one additional dollar* will be in the 24 percent bracket. This is illustrated in Figure 5.1 which shows the tax brackets for returns filed for the tax year 2023. You can see that a taxpayer, who falls into the maximum tax bracket of 37 percent, does not actually lose 37 percent of his income to taxes.

Let's look at a hypothetical example. Though Joe and Sally Retiree, aged 65, have an estate of $1.5 million, their taxable income is only $30,000. (Taxable

> Determining a strategy for the distribution years is where the rubber meets the road. I've had clients who, after meeting with me or reading my materials, realize they made costly mistakes along the way. That's water under the bridge. If that's you, that's par for the course. Just do the best you can with your starting point now. Most of us are in "clean up mode" meaning mistakes were made in the past and we are planning to do the best we can with whatever we have now, no matter how we got to where we are now.

income is arrived at after subtracting itemized or the standard deduction.) Right now, they are in the 12 percent tax bracket, but when Joe reaches age 73, his minimum distribution will push his income well into the 22 percent tax bracket. Joe decides to make voluntary withdrawals from his IRA every year until he reaches his RMD date as follows. Please note that depending on your year of birth, under SECURE Act 2.0 your RMD date could be age 75. Please see Chapter 6, **Required Minimum Distributions**.

The top income limit of the 12 percent bracket for married filing jointly (using 2023 tables) is $89,450. Joe and Sally already have $30,000 in taxable income before any IRA withdrawal. If Joe makes a voluntary $59,450 IRA withdrawal now, assuming no additional tax on Social Security, Medicare Part B, etc. he still pays tax on the withdrawal at the same 12 percent rate as the rest of his income. If he waits until age 73, when he is required to make a withdrawal, much of the later distributions will be taxed at 22 percent.

Figure 5.2
Tax Brackets for Use in Filing 2023 Returns in 2024

Married Filing Jointly and Surviving Spouses		
Taxable Income is between:		**The Tax is:**
$ 0 – 22,000	10% of taxable income	
$ 22,001 – 89,450	$ 2,200 + 12% of the excess over	$ 22,000
$ 89,451 – 190,750	$ 10,294 + 22% of the excess over	$ 89,450
$ 190,751 – 364,200	$ 32,580 + 24% of the excess over	$ 190,750
$ 364,201 – 462,500	$ 74,208 + 32% of the excess over	$ 364,200
$ 462,501 – 693,750	$ 105,664 + 35% of the excess over	$ 462,500
$ more than 693,751	$ 186,601.50 + 37% of the excess over	$ 693,750

Single		
Taxable Income is between:		**The Tax is:**
$ 0 – 11,000	10% of taxable income	
$ 11,001 – 44,725	$ 1,100 + 12% of the excess over	$ 11,001
$ 44,726 – 95,375	$ 5,147 + 22% of the excess over	$ 44,725
$ 95,376 – 182,100	$ 16,290 + 24% of the excess over	$ 95,375
$ 182,101 – 231,250	$ 37,104 + 32% of the excess over	$ 182,100
$ 231,251 – 578,125	$ 52,832 + 35% of the excess over	$ 231,250
more than $ 578,125	$ 174,238.50 + 37% of the excess over	$ 578,125

Depending on the circumstances, it might be a reasonable strategy for him to begin distributions before he turns age 73. Calculations reveal that the higher distribution yields a slight long-term advantage, although not as much as you might think because of the simultaneous loss of some tax deferral.

For many clients, particularly frugal clients, I would prefer a variation of this strategy that provides better long-term benefits. Instead of making an IRA withdrawal of $59,450, paying tax on the funds, and then being left with after-tax dollars that will generate taxable income, I would recommend Joe make a $59,450 Roth IRA conversion.

Many clients will resist this advice, but I urge you to at least consider it. My wife and I have made Roth IRA conversions well into the six figures of our own money, paid an enormous tax bill, and I still recommend that clients take advantage of the lower tax bracket this way. This advice is perfectly consistent with Jonathan Clements' article in **The Wall Street Journal**, in which Jonathan quoted me giving this identical analysis. We will cover the reasons to consider Roth IRA conversions in more detail in Chapter 16. For now, suffice it to say that I am a big fan of Roth IRA conversions, especially if you have a child with a disability.

If Joe doesn't want to make a Roth IRA conversion, he should at least consider taking IRA distributions even before he is required to, based on his tax bracket. Please note that adding income in the form of extra IRA distributions and/or Roth IRA conversions may have an impact on the taxability of Social Security benefits, Medicare premium surcharges, capital gains, and net investment income taxes (refer back to "Comments on Your Actual Tax Brackets" in Chapter 2), which should be worked into the numbers for the amount to withdraw or convert.

KEY IDEAS

- Subject to exception, spend after-tax dollars before IRA or Roth dollars.

- Leave money in tax deferred and tax-free environments as long as possible.

- Determining the best spending strategy depends on your individual situation.

Key Ideas continue on the following page.

KEY IDEAS
(continued)

- Sometimes the strategy of shifting from the taxable environment to the tax-free environment will change the optimal spending order.

- Future changes in tax rates may make it more beneficial to spend funds from Traditional IRA and 401(k) accounts now while tax rates are low.

- The SECURE Act will have a big impact on how Inherited IRA and retirement plan assets are taxed. If your child qualifies as an eligible designated beneficiary because of their disability or chronic illness, they will still be eligible to stretch distributions from Inherited retirement accounts over his or her lifetime.

- Determining which assets to leave to your children requires consideration of their financial situations and their income levels, which will determine the magnitude of any tax burden they face from Inherited assets. Because of the opportunity to stretch retirement assets, their disability status is also a key aspect to consider.

6

Required Minimum Distribution Rules

"There was a time when a fool and his money were soon parted,
but now it happens to everybody."

— Adlai Stevenson

Eventually Everyone Must Draw from Retirement Savings

Even if you stick to the game plan to spend your income and after-tax dollars first, eventually, by law, you will have to withdraw funds from your Traditional IRA or other type of plan. This is also true, subject to exceptions, of most qualified retirement plans. Since these distributions are typically taxable, if you don't need the money, you will likely only want to withdraw the smallest amounts you can. These distributions are known as Required Minimum Distributions (RMDs). Roth IRAs are currently exempt from this requirement.

At some point in your 70s, you will need to take your first RMD. According to the newly passed SECURE Act 2.0, the age for taking RMDs depends on the year of your birth.

- If you were born before 1950, you were required to take RMDs when you turned age 70 ½.

- If you were born in 1950, you were required to take RMDs at age 72.

- If you were born between 1951 and 1959, you will start taking RMDs at age 73.

- If you were born in 1960 or later, your RMDs will start at age 75.

You must take your first RMD by April 1 of the year after you reach the age your RMDs begin. The key word here is minimum. Keeping in mind the "don't pay taxes now—pay taxes later" rule of thumb. Subject to important exceptions, I want you to continue to maintain the highest balance in your IRA. If you take an RMD the year you turn 72—or whatever age your RMDs begin at—and a distribution the following year, you may remain in a lower tax bracket which would be advantageous. You can always take out more if you need it.

For the sake of convenience, throughout this chapter, I'll use age 73 for the age

> Eventually, by law, you will have to withdraw funds from your Traditional IRA or other type of plan. This is also true, subject to exceptions, of most qualified retirement plans. Since these distributions are typically taxable, if you don't need the money, you will likely only want to withdraw the smallest amounts you can.

that your RMDs begin, but as you read the rest of this chapter, keep the adjusted ages shown above for starting RMDs in mind.

During the financial crisis of 2009 and in response to the Covid-19 pandemic during 2020, the federal government temporarily suspended the RMD rules. The reasoning was that older retirees shouldn't be forced to sell their investments when the value of the investments is low.

That reasoning didn't make sense to me because investors have always been allowed to take their RMD in stock instead of cash, if they prefer—it's called an in-kind distribution. So, if the investments in your IRA have decreased in value, you can have the investment shares transferred directly to a non-IRA account and leave them alone until they increase in value again. You still have to pay tax on the amount of the transfer, but the only reason you would be forced to sell when the value is low would be if you did not have a lot of cash on hand and you needed to sell some of the securities to pay the tax on the RMD or to meet living expenses.

Another point to consider is that, while the IRS requires that you calculate the RMD for every IRA account that you own, you are not required to withdraw a minimum distribution amount from every IRA you own. You can add up all of your RMDs and take the total amount from one account, preferably from one that has not gone down in value. Hopefully, being aware of these little-known rules will help you avoid having to take a loss on your investments if you need to take a RMD when the markets are down.

On the other hand, taking smaller distributions from one IRA and larger ones from a different IRA could lead to attention by either the organization investing the money or the IRS. Personally, I would rather not deal with a pain in the butt problem than save a few dollars, but potentially you could save more than a few dollars and maybe you don't mind dealing with notices and issues because you love getting the last drop out of the tax code.

Calculating Your RMD After Age 73

Currently, RMDs are calculated by taking your projected distribution period, based on your age and the age of a beneficiary deemed to be no less than 10 years younger than you, and dividing that factor into the balance of your IRA or qualified plan as of December 31 of the prior year. Bear in mind that your projected life expectancy factor or the projected distribution period is not based on your personal eating and exercise habits or even your genetic history! It is an actuarial calculation from the IRS determined solely by age. Many large financial institutions offer tools on their websites that automatically calculate RMDs. If you would like to do the math yourself, the IRS's Supplement to the Publication 590 contains worksheets that you can use to work through the calculation, as well as the tables that you will need to use to find your RMD factor. For those who would just like a quick glance, the tables are published in the appendix at the end of this book.

The IRS provides three life expectancy tables in Publication 590-B. After more than 20 years, these tables were updated in February 2022, to a new version to be used for distributions made in calendar year 2022 and beyond. The most frequently used table is Table III, not Table I. I present them here in reverse order.

1. **Table III: Uniform Lifetime Table** (for use by unmarried IRA owners and married owners whose spouses are not more than 10 years younger). This table is available in the appendix of this book.

2. **Table II: Joint Life and Last Survivor Expectancy Table** (for IRA owners with spouses 10 or more years younger). This is not covered in the appendix of this book because it is too long. See IRS Publication 590.

3. **Table I: Single Life Expectancy Table** (for IRA beneficiaries of deceased IRA owners a.k.a "Inherited IRAs"). This table is available in the appendix of this book.

Table III: Uniform Lifetime Table for IRA Owners

Generally speaking, most IRA owners will use Table III. In effect, the age-dependent projected distribution periods in Table III are based on the joint life expectancy projections of an IRA owner and a hypothetical beneficiary not more than 10 years younger. Using a joint life expectancy is advantageous because the longer joint-life expectancy factor reduces the annual RMD. But rather than using the actual life expectancy of the beneficiary for the calculations, the IRS simplifies the terms. Table III deems all beneficiaries—from children to grandmothers—to have a life expectancy 10 years longer than that of the owner.

At age 73, the projected distribution period is 26.5 years (roughly the single life expectancy from Table I plus 10 years, although you must refer to the tables for the precise factor). If you are already receiving RMDs (born before July 1, 1949), your distribution that was required to be paid by December 31, 2022, will be based on the new factors effective January 1, 2022.

·· **MINI CASE STUDY 6.1** ···
RMD Calculation for IRA Owners

Bob turns 77 in 2023. As of December 31, 2022, he has two IRAs that are each worth $500,000. He names his son, Phillip, as the beneficiary for one IRA and his 74-year-old wife, Mary, for the other. To calculate his 2023 RMD for the IRA with his wife as beneficiary, he takes the life expectancy at his age 77 from Table III, 22.9, and divides that into his balance, $500,000, to arrive at $21,834. He uses the same table and the same factor to arrive at the same RMD from the IRA that has his son as the beneficiary. When Bob dies, the amounts that his wife and son will be required to take from the IRAs they inherited from him will be different. I'll go into more detail about that later in this chapter.

··· **MINI CASE STUDY 6.2** ···
RMD Calculation with IRA Owner and Spouse
More Than Ten Years Younger

Bob will have to use a different calculation for the RMD for the IRA with his wife as the beneficiary if Mary is only 65 years old. According to Table II, Bob's and Mary's joint life expectancy factor based on the ages they will be on their birthdays in 2023 is 24.3. Bob calculates his RMD by dividing 24.3 into his balance of $500,000 to arrive at $20,576. Bob's RMD for the account with his wife as the beneficiary is lower than for the account with his son as the beneficiary because Bob and his wife were permitted to use their actual *joint* life expectancy factor for his calculation.

We will cover more about IRA beneficiaries in Chapter 9. For now, please look at the table on the preceding page to see how the age of his spouse affects Bob's RMD.

··

Table II: Joint Life and Last Survivor Expectancy Table for IRA Owners with Spouses Ten or More Years Younger

Because nothing that the government does is ever without complications, there is an exception for married individuals when the IRA owner is 10 or more years older than his or her spouse. Those individuals are permitted to use their actual joint life expectancy factor, which will result in smaller RMDs.

Figure 6.1

| IRS Table III | | | | IRS Table II | | | |
| Spouse Who is *Not* 10 Years Younger (or Child) as Beneficiary | | | | Spouse Who is 10 Years Younger as Beneficiary | | | |
Bob's Age	IRA Balance ($)	Factor	RMD	Bob's Age	IRA Balance ($)	Factor	RMD
77	500,000	22.9	21,834	77	500,000	24.3	20,576
78	478,166	22.0	21,735	78	479,424	23.4	20,488
79	456,431	21.1	21,632	79	458,936	22.5	20,397
80	434,799	20.2	21,525	80	438,539	21.6	20,303
81	413,275	19.4	21,303	81	418,236	20.7	21,303
82	391,972	18.5	21,188	82	398,031	19.9	20,205
83	370,784	17.7	20,948	83	378,030	19.0	20,002
84	349,836	16.8	20,824	84	358,133	18.2	19,896
85	329,012	16.0	20,563	85	338,456	17.4	19,678
86	308,449	15.2	20,293	86	319,004	16.5	19,451
87	288,156	14.4	20,011	87	299,671	15.7	19,334
88	268,145	13.7	19,573	88	280,583	14.9	18,831
89	248,573	12.9	19,269	89	261,752	14.2	18,433
90	229,304	12.2	18,795	90	243,319	13.4	18,158

Table I: Single Life Expectancy Table for IRA Beneficiaries

When a spouse dies before receiving their RMDs at age 73, the younger spousal beneficiary of the IRA has two options. He or she can roll the Inherited IRA into his or her own IRA and begin RMDs when he or she reaches age 73. Or he or she can decline to treat the IRA as his or her own and simply defer distributions until the year that the original IRA owner would have attained age 73. At that point, he or she would begin distributions based on his or her Table I life expectancy factor. This is an extremely important decision that you will have to make if your spouse predeceases you, and the advantages and disadvantages of each option are covered in detail in Chapter 9.

Non-spouse beneficiaries (there are some exceptions) of Inherited IRAs have no options. And, under the SECURE Act, effective January 1, 2020, a radically different law governs Inherited IRAs and retirement plans from what we had in the past. Now, subject to exceptions, the beneficiary of a Traditional IRA inherited after 2019 must withdraw and pay taxes on that Inherited IRA by the end of the

10th year after the IRA owner's death. Also, most beneficiaries who inherited the IRA from someone who had already begun receiving their own RMDs will be required to continue taking annual distributions until the Inherited IRA is fully distributed (required by the end of year 10).

The exceptions to the ten-year rule, in addition to your spouse mentioned above, include eligible designated beneficiaries: people deemed "disabled or chronically ill", , the IRA owner's children younger than age 21, and beneficiaries who are not more than 10 years younger than the IRA owner. These non-spouse exceptions (or beneficiaries inheriting prior to 2020) are not subject to the 10-year rule and must begin to take distributions based on their own life expectancy (as projected in Table I) as of the year following the year of the IRA owner's death. For each subsequent year, the non-spouse beneficiary subtracts one (1) from his original factor, because his life expectancy is diminished by one year for every year he survives. This is frequently referred to as the "minus one method."

Calculating Your Life Expectancy after the Initial Year

It is interesting to note that Table I life expectancies are reduced by one full year as each year passes. Tables II and III, however, reduce the life expectancy of the IRA owner by less than one year. This is analogous to the old double recalculation method. (Readers who remember those rules get bonus points). The idea is that as we age, our life expectancy declines, but it does not decline by an entire year.

So, if you are a surviving spouse who inherits an IRA, but you don't treat the Inherited IRA as your own IRA, your life expectancy is recalculated each year based on the life expectancies shown in Table I (the full year decline).

When you die, your non-spouse heirs must use your life expectancy at the time of your death, reduced by one for each subsequent year, for their RMD calculation. For a discussion on whether a spouse should treat an IRA as his or her own IRA, refer to Chapter 10.

With the new Single Life Tables taking effect as of January 1, 2022, there is a transition rule for Inherited IRA beneficiaries to reset the life expectancy calculation in line with the new tables. This redetermination requires the beneficiary to go back to the year after the year of the IRA owner's death and find the beneficiary's single life expectancy factor as of his/her age in that year under the new tables. Subsequently, one year will be deducted from the new life expectancy for each year since the first distribution year to arrive at the new factor for the relevant post-2021 year.

Here's an example of how that works. In 2019, Gina inherited an IRA from her father when she was 33. From the old Single Life Table, her life expectancy was 50.4. She used that as a denominator to calculate her RMD for 2020. For 2021, using the "minus one method," she used 49.4 (50.4 -1). With the new Single Life Table, her life expectancy at age 33—her age when she inherited the IRA—has increased to 52.5. To calculate her RMD for 2022, she takes her new initial factor of 52.5 and reduces it by the two calendar years since 2020 (2021 and 2022) to get a new factor of 50.5. Remember, in the example above, Gina inherited the IRA from her father under the pre-SECURE Act rules where a non-spouse beneficiary could still stretch an Inherited IRA over their lifetime. For deaths after 2019, the 10-year rule applies unless the beneficiary is an eligible designated beneficiary (EDB).

Timing Your First Required Distribution

If you were born between 1951 and 1959, then your first distribution will be required in the year that you turn age 73, though you have the option to take it as late as April 1 of the following year. For example, retirement plan owners born in 1951 will have to take one distribution in 2024 and one in 2025, or two distributions in 2025 if they don't take a distribution in 2024. If you don't take a distribution in 2024, the first distribution in 2025 will have to be taken prior to April 1, 2025 (in effect, for what should have been taken in 2024), and the second distribution will have to be taken by December 31, 2025. Annual minimum distributions would continue for the rest of the participant's life.

So, if you have a choice regarding when and how to take your first distributions, should you take one distribution per year, or should you wait and take two the following year? That decision might rest on the implications for your tax bracket. If you take a minimum distribution the year that you turn age 73 and one distribution the following year, you may remain in a lower tax bracket, which would be advantageous. Taking two distributions in one year, though, could push you into a higher tax bracket and possibly accelerate the phase-out of certain tax credits or deductions. If that is the case, you will likely be better off violating our "Pay Taxes Later" rule by taking one distribution and paying some tax before you have to. On the other hand, if you will remain in the same tax bracket even with two distributions, then it makes no difference if you wait until you are required to begin distributions. This allows you to take advantage of the additional period of tax-deferred growth.

In the example above, for participants born in 1951, the first RMD can be taken either by the end of 2024 or by April 1, 2025 at the very latest. Unless the participant needs the money or is pursuing the early distribution of an IRA because of a lower income tax bracket or estate plan strategy, he or she is better off leaving the money in the IRA and taking the first RMD in 2025. However, this means that there will be two RMDs in 2025, which may result in an unexpected increase in taxes.

There can be a significant planning opportunity when deciding the year to take your initial RMD, especially if you have taxable wages from your current employer to consider. Our advice is to either actually make the calculations yourself or consult with the appropriate financial professional, even your tax preparer before making the decision as to which year to take your initial RMD in order to 'smooth out' the taxable income and 'manage' the tax brackets when possible.

Failing to take a minimum distribution when required, however, or not taking a large enough minimum distribution has very expensive consequences. Until the SECURE Act 2.0 passed at the end of 2022, the IRS charged a 50 percent excise tax on the amount that was not distributed as required. Effective for 2023 and future years, this penalty will drop to 25%. If you fix this error promptly, the penalty will be "only" 10%. So, if you were required to take a $10,000 minimum distribution in 2022 and didn't do so, you would have owed $5,000 in excise tax. If you missed that $10,000 RMD in 2023, you would owe excise tax of $2,500. If you correct the error and take that missed 2023 distribution by the end of 2026—or prior to getting a notice by the IRS of a missed distribution – the excise tax penalty drops to $1,000. And that's in addition to the normal income tax you will owe on the distribution, as well as general penalties for underpayment of tax.

Special Rule for Qualified Plan Owners Who Are Still Working Past Age 73

RMD rules apply to Traditional IRAs (not Roth IRAs) and qualified plans [401(k)s, 403(b)s, Roth 401(k)s, and Roth 403(b)s, etc.]. However, the rules governing 401(k)s and 403(b)s are slightly different than for IRAs.

- If you are still working after age 73, the IRS does not require you to take a distribution from the retirement plan connected to your current job as long as you do not own more than five percent of the company. Remember, though, that your employer is responsible for setting the rules for your plan. Even though the IRS doesn't require you to take a distribution, your employer might.

- If you have a plan such as a 401(k) associated with a job from which you have retired, the IRS says you will have to take your initial RMD by April 1st of the year following the year in which you reach age 73. Some employers allow you to keep your retirement plan with them when you start to take withdrawals, and some employers require that you roll the account into an IRA before you start to take withdrawals.

- If you have two or more retirement plans associated with jobs from which you have retired, the IRS requires that each plan calculate a minimum distribution for you when you reach age 73. This is different from their rules for calculating RMDs on IRAs, which allow you to add up the values of all of your IRAs, calculate the RMD, and then take the full distribution from one account. This can be a very important consideration for people whose old plans happen to include stock in the company they worked for, because the RMD requirement might cause you to have to sell stock when the value is low. As long as you have enough other assets to pay the tax on the RMD, though, you can take your company stock as an "in-kind" distribution and keep it in a brokerage account until the time that it increases in value again. The one exception to this rule is for 403(b) plan owners. The IRS allows participants in 403(b) plans to add up the values of all their accounts, calculate the RMD, and then take the full distribution from one account. For individuals such as retired university professors who have multiple 403(b) plans, this makes the paperwork much simpler to deal with at year end.

- If you had a 401(k) plan from a former job and rolled that 401(k) plan into a plan associated with the job at which you are still working, then you will have to check with the plan administrator of your current plan to see whether you will be forced to take RMDs upon attaining age 73 from the portion of that 401(k) plan that is attributable to your former employment. PLR 200453015, published in January 2005, states that the IRS permits deferral of the RMDs on all of the funds in the new employer's account including the rollover contributions from the former employer until April 1st of the year after the employee retires from the new employer. You must, however, make sure that your employer's plan will allow you to do what the IRS will allow you to do.

·· **MINI CASE STUDY 6.3** ··
RMD If Stlil Working Past Age 73

Joan continues to work although she is older than 73. She was born in 1951, so will need to start taking RMDs in 2024 or, at the latest, by April 1, 2025. She has a total of $1 million in her 401(k) plans: $500,000 associated with her current job and $500,000 from a previous job. She has never consolidated the two plans. Her new plan includes both her and her employer's most recent contributions.

By April 1 of the year after she turns age 73, she will be required to take minimum distributions from the $500,000 associated with the job she left, but not from the account that is still active due to her employment. Whether she could take the money from the 401(k) from the job she retired from, roll it into her current plan (by trustee-to-trustee transfer), and avoid an RMD is not clear. The IRS will allow it, but her current employer may not. If your employer does permit it, this may be an incentive for someone still working after age 73 to consider rolling money out of their IRA and into a retirement plan at work. This will eliminate the RMD from the former employer's plan. Usually, I prefer money going the other way, which is from 401(k) to IRA, or my current preferred strategy, from a work 401(k) or IRA to a one-person 401(k) plan that you control

I have a client who became really excited about the prospect of avoiding his minimum distribution. He wanted to start his own retirement plan (actually a one-person 401(k) based on his small self-employment income). Then he wanted to roll his IRA into a one-person 401(k) and suspend his RMDs on his IRA. It was a good thought, but with a fatal flaw. He is more than a five percent owner of his consulting business, and the rule about deferring the RMD after age 73 if you are still working does not apply to individuals with a five percent or greater ownership in the company.

Special Rules for 403(b) Participants for Pre-1987 Retirement Plan Funds

Participants in 403(b) plans are subject to some special rules that do not apply to participants in other types of plans. Both employee and employer contributions to a 403(b) plan made before January 1, 1987, are not subject to RMDs until age 75. As a result, the balance that was in your 403(b) as of December 31, 1986, is not subject to RMDs until you reach age 75, not age 70½ or 72 or 73, even if you have retired. If you fall into this special category of 403(b) account holders, you should consult with your organization's benefits office to determine the balance in the account as of December 31, 1986. Surprisingly, many institutions do a good job of tracking that balance. If your 403(b) plan included pre-1987 contributions and you roll it into an IRA, the "grandfathered" status of those contributions is lost, and you will be required to take minimum distributions on them at age 73. Contributions made on January 1, 1987, and later are subject to RMDs at age 73. Note, however, that the growth and appreciation on pre-1987 dollars are not grandfathered and are treated like a regular 403(b).

On the other hand, when you actually calculate the tax advantage of keeping the funds in the 403(b) to defer a portion of the minimum distribution, it is relatively small. If you think you could get even a slight investment advantage by doing a trustee-to-trustee transfer from your 403(b) to an IRA to gain additional investment options, it would still be worthwhile.

Retired public safety officers, including law enforcement and firefighters, have a special exception to the distribution rules. They can receive a distribution of up to $3,000 completely tax-free from their 403(b), as long as the proceeds are used to directly pay for accident, health or long-term care insurance.

A Possible Compromise for Those Who Don't Need Income and Are Charitably Inclined

Although there is no way to avoid taking RMDs from Traditional (not Roth) IRAs, there is an option available to those individuals who do not need that income for living expenses, and who are inclined to donate to charity. The Pension Protection Act of 2006 created something called a Qualified Charitable Distribution, which allows IRA owners to specify that a payment of up to $100,000 from their RMDs be sent directly to a **qualified** charity upon reaching age 70½.

Here is how it works. IRA owners electing this option are still required to take their RMD, but the amount of the distribution is sent directly to the **qualified** charity and can be excluded from their gross income. For individuals who are charitably inclined, this can make a lot more sense than having the RMD sent to them, and then issuing a separate check to the charity, particularly if the taxpayer doesn't itemize deductions. (The Tax Cuts and Jobs Act of 2017 made it more difficult for many Americans to itemize their charitable contributions.) So, if you don't itemize, the charitable contribution isn't tax deductible, and the IRA distribution is taxable. With a Qualified Charitable Distribution (QCD), you still can't deduct the charitable donation, but at least you're not taxed on the IRA distribution. In essence, you are making charitable contributions on a "pre-tax" basis vs. an "after-tax" basis. In addition, there are many potential tax benefits from reducing your adjusted gross income using a QCD:

- Less of your Social Security income may become taxable.
- The phase-out of medical expenses you claim as itemized deductions is reduced.
- The phase-out of total itemized deductions is reduced.
- The Net Investment Income tax surcharges can be reduced.
- You may avoid future increases in your Medicare premiums.
- Your Alternative Minimum Tax may be reduced.

QCDs were originally supposed to be effective only in 2006 and 2007, but over the years Congress extended them on a temporary basis and finally made them permanent as part of the Consolidated Appropriations Act of 2016. It is worth pointing out that the while the SECURE Act 2.0 increased the RMD age to 73 or 75, the qualifying age for a QCD remains at age 70½. However, there is one major drawback: all of your post-70½ deductible IRA contributions must be tracked against your QCDs and your otherwise tax-free QCD will be reduced by your contribution amount.

Another change with SECURE Act 2.0, allows some IRA owners to make a one-time QCD to a split-interest entity such as a charitable gift annuity or a charitable remainder trust (discussed further in Chapter 20). If both spouses are receiving annual RMDs, they can each make QCDs of up to $100,000 annually (adjusted for inflation beginning in 2024).

Qualified Charitable Distributions have three criteria that you must be aware of:

1. You have to make sure that the charitable organization is a *qualified* charity. A qualified charity for QCDs is one that has a valid 501(c)(3) tax-exempt status. Donor-advised funds and private foundations do not qualify. While many donor-advised funds such as Fidelity or Vanguard Charitable Giving accounts may qualify as 501(c)(3) charities, they cannot be used for QCDs. There are some very good causes that I personally donate to, but they do not meet the definition of a qualified charity. As such, I cannot deduct those contributions, nor could I send them a QCD. The organization will be able to tell you if they're tax-exempt or not, or, if you want to be 100 percent sure, you can search on the IRS.gov website.

2. You have to be at least age 70½ to make a QCD.

3. QCDs are only available for IRAs, or inactive SEPs and inactive SIMPLE plans. QCDs from an employer-sponsored retirement plan are currently not permitted.

Please see Chapter 20 for a dedicated chapter on QCDs written by Steve Kohman, CPA.

> **If you don't need the cash, I recommend scheduling your distribution for Thanksgiving or early December.**

When Should You Schedule Taking Your RMD?

Theoretically, you should take your RMD on December 31st to delay as long as possible withdrawing money from the tax-favored environment. In the real world, however, it is difficult to get any work done with financial firms in December and trying to comply with a deadline between Christmas and the last day of the year is a total nightmare. Remember, if you miss taking a withdrawal by year-end, you face the 25 percent penalty for failing to take your RMD—an expensive penalty. If you don't need the cash, I recommend scheduling your distribution for Thanksgiving or early December. If you need the RMD for your spending needs, it may be best to schedule 12 equal monthly distributions throughout the year.

If you don't need the cash, I recommend scheduling your distribution for Thanksgiving or early December.

Schedule your IRA distribution
for Thanksgiving

How to Get Your Interest-Free Loan from the IRS

I do not understand why anyone would have extra tax taken out of their paycheck to ensure that they get a big refund. Why on earth would you give the IRS an interest-free loan? It should be the other way around! Would you like to get an interest-free loan from the IRS? One way to do so is to take your RMD in December and have federal income tax withheld from it, rather than paying quarterly estimated taxes on your retirement income throughout the year. From the IRS's perspective, tax that is withheld is treated as if it has been withheld at an even rate throughout the year as opposed to being treated like a single estimated tax payment you made late in the year—so you won't get penalized for paying all of the tax due in December.

How to Avoid Paying Tax Estimates and Float the IRS at the Same Time

Here's an even better idea for those of you who hate paying estimated taxes and who love getting an interest free loan from the IRS. If you are currently paying quarterly estimated taxes on your non-IRA income, you can forgo your estimates completely and instead ask your IRA custodian to do up to a 100 percent tax withholding on the RMD you take at the end of the year.

Let's say that you have been paying estimates of $1,500 each quarter, and you've been told that you will have to take a RMD of $6,000 this year. In December, you can instruct your IRA custodian to withhold federal income tax from your RMD at a rate of 100 percent and have them send the entire $6,000 directly to the IRS. This strategy allows you to earn interest on the money you are required to take from your IRA for as long as possible, and also allows you to earn the interest on the estimated tax payments that you were going to send to the IRS. The best part is that, under current rules, as long as the amount of taxes withheld from your RMD is sufficient to cover the amount of tax you owe for the entire year, there is no penalty for paying 100 percent of your tax liability in December! I can't understand why so few people use this strategy.

KEY IDEAS

- Subject to the transferring from the taxable environment to the tax-free environment and other exceptions, keep your RMD to the required minimum. Do not take out more money than you need so that you keep the balance in your tax-deferred accounts as large as possible.

- If you turn 70 after July 1, 2019, you don't need to start taking your RMD until you turn 72, 73, or even 75, depending on the year of your birth.

  – Born before 1950, RMDs start at age 70 ½

  – Born in 1950, RMDs start at age 72

  – Born between 1951 and 1959, RMDs start at age 73

  – Born in 1960 or later, RMDs start at age 75

Key Ideas continue on the following page.

KEY IDEAS
(continued)

- If you don't need the cash, make a habit of taking your RMD at Thanksgiving or in early December.

- If you're paying quarterly estimated taxes, consider having your IRA custodian withhold the full amount of your annual estimates from your RMD. Ideally, if you don't need the money earlier, have the distribution and the federal withholding later in the year. This is not only an interest-free loan from the IRS and avoids late payment penalties, but it is easier than sending in quarterly estimated taxes.

7

Should You Transfer Your 401(k) to an IRA at Retirement?

(Rollovers vs. Trustee-to-Trustee Transfers and Other Strategies)

"They say it is better to be poor and happy than rich and miserable, but how about a compromise like moderately rich and just moody?"

— Diana, Princess of Wales

When someone retires or is "service terminated," the big question is: *"What should I do now?"*

Without getting into specific investment ideas, let's consider whether it makes sense for you to keep your money in your existing retirement plan, transfer it to an IRA, take a lump-sum distribution, or make a trustee-to-trustee transfer into your new one-person 401(k) plan. In this chapter, we'll be looking in detail at your retirement asset distribution options. Contingent on the specifics of any given retirement plan, the basic options are as follows:

1. Transfer the money into a separate IRA.

2. Leave the money in your current plan.

3. Annuitize the balance *(for more information on annuitizing, see Chapter 8).*

4. Use some combination of options 1 and 2 (often my favorite choice).

5. Take a lump-sum distribution.

6. Transfer money to a one-person 401(k) plan.

An Important Consideration Before You Do Anything

The first question you should ask yourself before making any transfers is whether you have any after-tax dollars in your retirement plan. These dollars would likely be the result of contributing more than you were allowed to deduct in your retirement plan, but you did it anyway in order to get deferred earnings.

If you have after-tax dollars in your retirement plan and don't think carefully, you could end up transferring them to an IRA or doing something else. You already paid tax on these dollars, but that fact could easily get lost if you move them with the rest of your pre-tax dollars to an IRA. The result is overpaying on taxes when you start taking distributions from your IRA. You may potentially be missing a significant opportunity to do a tax-free Roth conversion. Please see Chapters 16 and 1 7, where I talk about Roth conversions after the SECURE Act without having to pay any taxes if you have after-tax dollars in your IRA or retirement plan and about the possible impacts that Roth conversions can have on Medicare premiums.

Rolling Over to an IRA

Retirees often talk about rolling over to an IRA or rolling money out of a retirement plan and into an IRA. Technically, we should use the term *transfer* simply because the IRS makes a significant distinction between the mechanics and regulations of a rollover versus a trustee-to-trustee transfer. The trustee-to-trustee transfer is simpler, and what I usually recommend. I'll explain the distinctions between rollovers and transfers later in this chapter. (In keeping with common usage, when referring to a transfer, I will use the terms *rollover* and *transfer* interchangeably throughout this book, but please understand that what I am referring to is following the technical procedures of a trustee-to-trustee transfer.) (See the section in this chapter called *The Mechanics of IRA Rollovers and Trustee-to-Trustee Transfers.*)

Though there are a few downsides, transferring retirement plan accumulations into an IRA or your own one-person 401(k) via a trustee-to-trustee transfer is usually the best option. As with most decisions, there are advantages and disadvantages.

> **Retirees often talk about rolling over to an IRA or rolling money out of a retirement plan and into an IRA. Technically, we should use the term trustee-to-trustee transfer simply because the IRS makes a significant distinction between the mechanics and regulations of a rollover versus a trustee-to-trustee transfer. In addition to using the term trustee-to-trustee transfer, we should actually employ the mechanics of a trustee-to-trustee transfer as opposed to an IRA rollover.**

Tax Advantages of Transferring Your Company 401(k) into an IRA

Proper planning requires taking the appropriate steps while you are alive and having in place the appropriate procedures after you and your spouse have died. Prior to the SECURE Act, with a bit of planning, your heirs could stretch taxable distributions from an Inherited IRA and certain retirement plans for decades. But, as we'll describe fully in Chapter 10, unless the beneficiary of your IRA is your spouse or qualifies for an exception, the SECURE Act will force your heir to completely drain that account within 10 years of your and your spouse's death, drastically accelerating the income taxes due on those funds. One exception is if the beneficiary is disabled or chronically ill. In Chapter 11, I'll explain the steps my wife Cindy and I took to ensure that our daughter, who has a disability, will have plenty of money after we are gone.

On top of that, if your employer's retirement plan document stipulates the wrong provisions, even the measly 10-year stretch may be replaced by a screaming income tax disaster. Your heirs could be in for a tax nightmare if you never transferred your company 401(k) retirement plan to an IRA or a Solo 401(k). Different rules apply if a spouse inherits a 401(k) versus someone other than your spouse—say, a child—so it is important to understand how your decisions can affect the outcome.

The old Westinghouse 401(k) plan in Pittsburgh forced non-spousal beneficiaries to withdraw their Inherited 401(k) and pay taxes on the withdrawal much faster than the IRS would have required if the retirement plan owner had done a trustee-to-trustee transfer to an IRA and the beneficiary could have "stretched" the Inherited IRA.

The old engineers didn't like transferring out of their plan because it had a high guaranteed income investment. Their compromise position was since the income acceleration provision didn't apply to the surviving spouse, they left the money in the plan at work until the first spouse died. Then, they made the trustee-to-trustee transfer to an IRA.

Some employees prefer to keep their retirement plan balance where it is rather than transferring it to an IRA, especially if their plan offers favorable fixed-income investments. Unfortunately, many employees fail to realize that the specific plan rules that govern their company retirement plan take precedence over the IRS distribution rules for Inherited IRAs or retirement plans.

The distribution rules that come into play when a retirement plan participant dies are found in a plan document created by the employer that few employees or advisors ever bother to read. You would like to think that, since employers participate in the plans they offer to their employees, they would design the rules of the plan to be as beneficial as possible. Unfortunately, that is not necessarily the case. Most people wouldn't even think that the rules that their employers set could affect their estate distribution after their death, but, since the plan rules always take precedence over the IRS rules, it is possible that your employer's decisions could haunt your beneficiaries long after your death. Here's how it works.

IRS Options for a Spouse Inheriting a 401(k) or Other Retirement Plan

The IRS provides three options if you inherit your spouse's 401(k) or retirement plan.

1. **The first option** is to leave the money in the plan. You have to change the name on the account, but sometimes there are advantages to keeping it where it is. For instance, even if you are not yet age 59½, you can take withdrawals and not have to pay the 10 percent penalty. You might also like the investment choices that the plan has. If you elect this option, though, you cannot change the beneficiary designations that were chosen by your spouse. They would continue to apply after your death. If your spouse was already taking Required Minimum Distributions, you will have to continue taking distributions. If your spouse had not started taking distributions, you will have to start taking distributions in the year that the original account owner would have been required to start taking their Required Minimum Distributions. In either case, you can calculate the distributions based on your own life expectancy.

2. **The second option** is to roll the money over into an Inherited IRA. You would be required to take (at least) the Required Minimum Distributions (RMD) based on your own life expectancy. Withdrawals would not be subject to the 10 percent penalty even if you are not yet age 59½, and you can name your own beneficiaries. I have never recommended this option in practice, but I include it because if the surviving spouse is younger than 59½ there may be situations when it makes sense.

3. **The third option** is to roll the 401(k) into your own IRA. This is the best option if you don't need the income, because you will not be required to take distributions until you reach age 73, or the age when your RMDs begin. You can also name your own beneficiaries with this option.

4. **Beginning in 2024, a fourth option** has been added as part of SECURE Act 2.0. A spouse will be able to elect to be treated as the "deceased" spouse. By making this special election, RMDs for the surviving spouse will be delayed until the deceased IRA owner would have reached the age when RMDs

begin. Once RMDs are required, the surviving spouse will calculate RMDs using the Uniform Lifetime Table used by account owners (Table III), rather than the Single Lifetime Table that applies to beneficiaries (Table I). Also, if the surviving spouse dies before their RMDs begin, the beneficiaries of the surviving spouse will be treated as though they were the original beneficiaries of the account (unlike the first option presented above). This means any EDBs would have the ability to stretch distributions over their life expectancy instead of the 10-year rule that would apply. This is especially important if you have a child with a disability or chronic illness. Once the election has been made, however, the election cannot be revoked without consent. To give you an example let's say Bob, a 401(k) participant is age 67 and his wife, Barb, is age 75. Bob dies and Barb is the spouse-beneficiary. Barb is already required to take her RMDs from her IRA. Under this new fourth scenario, Barb could make an election to step in the shoes of Bob and delay her RMDs until Bob's age of 72 (5 years later). Plus, once Barb begins taking RMDs 5 years later, the RMDs would be calculated based upon Bob's younger age and would be smaller than if the RMD was calculated on Barb's age.

As I've touched on previously, and as I'll explain in further detail in Chapter 10, the SECURE Act radically changed the rules for non-spouse beneficiaries.

The SECURE Act eliminated the options for most non-spouse beneficiaries to stretch RMDs over their lifetimes. Unless the beneficiary qualifies under one of the limited exceptions, all money must be withdrawn from the plan within ten years, a drastic acceleration of income and taxes. Technically, it must be withdrawn in the year of the tenth anniversary of death, but for simplicity, I will just refer to this date as ten years after the death of the IRA or retirement plan owner. Retirement plan sponsors can also add their own requirements, which may require plan assets to be fully withdrawn shortly after the death of the original owner.

But at the very least, non-spouse beneficiaries of any retirement plan, whether it's an IRA, a 401(k), or a 403(b), will have to withdraw the entire balance within ten years, if not sooner, unless the beneficiary is an EDB.

Let's assume you inherit a $1 million 401(k), and the plan requires that you withdraw all of the money within 10 years. Many 401(k)s previously required non-spouse beneficiaries to remove 100 percent of the proceeds of the plan within one year after the death of the owner, which meant that the beneficiaries had to pay tax on the entire plan balance. In prior years, those kinds of rules provided an enormous incentive to roll the money into an IRA rather than keeping it in a 401(k). Employers are no longer permitted to require that beneficiaries withdraw the money from the plan within one year. Even though the SECURE Act drastically limits the ability of non-spouse beneficiaries to defer distributions—and thus taxes—over their lifetimes, at least the limited 10-year rule allows impacted beneficiaries some ability to defer taxes. I'll discuss the implications of the SECURE Act on your family and your estate planning in detail in Chapter 10.

Reasons to Transfer an old 401(k) to an IRA or to a One-Person 401(k)

One of the most compelling reasons to transfer money out of a 401(k) retirement plan and into an IRA is the opportunity to take advantage of the universe of investment choices offered by IRAs. The challenge facing most IRA owners is choosing among the thousands of available investments such as index funds, mutual funds, stocks, bonds, etc. Leaving the money in the company plan will often limit your options to those your employer makes available to you. The argument for greater investment choices becomes even more critical if your plan does not offer good investment choices.

A second reason to consider moving an old 401(k) is that, nowadays, most people don't stay employed with one company for their entire career. Most people have several—even many—employers over the course of their careers. This might lead to the existence of several 401(k) or other retirement plans, all of which are likely to have different rules. It is possible to put different beneficiaries on different accounts which could lead to unintended and/or unfair allocations at death.

If you have a good plan where you work, you can ask your plan administrator if the plan accepts rollover contributions. If so, you can transfer your old 401(k) into your current 401(k). If not, you can roll your old 401(k) into an IRA.

Some financial writers, like Jonathan Clements of *The Wall Street Journal*, feel that naive retirement plan owners are likely to be the victims of unscrupulous financial advisors. The argument goes that if you stay in your 401(k) plan, you will avoid some of these unscrupulous advisors. I hate it when I see an "advisor" who has convinced their client to transfer their 401(k) to an IRA and then invests that money in products (which pay the advisor a high commission) and/or charges high fees to the client.

Advantages of Retaining a 401(k) Rather than Rolling It into an IRA

1. *Deferred Required Minimum Distributions:* Special rules allow employees to defer taking their RMDs from their company retirement plans until they retire, even after they turn age 73. For example, let's assume you are such an employee, aged 73, and still working. Half of your retirement assets are in a 401(k) at the company where you currently work. The other half is in an IRA, which came from a rollover from a previous employer. There is no RMD requirement from your current employer's plan, as long as you continue to work there. You must take your annual RMD from your Traditional IRA, even though you are still working. If your employer allows you to transfer your IRA into your 401(k), then you don't have to take an RMD on your money in the 401(k) including the money you just rolled into the 401(k). If you just left your money in an IRA, you would have had to take RMDs on the IRA. The exception to this rule is if you own 5% or more of the company you're working for, in which case, you will need to take RMDs.

2. *Superior credit protection:* Many ERISA (Employee Retirement Income Security Act of 1974) type plans enjoy federal protection against creditors and bankruptcy that IRAs do not enjoy. This means that if you file for bankruptcy or if you owe money to creditors, no one can touch the funds in an employer-sponsored retirement plan such as a 403(b) or 401(k). IRAs do not have federal protection, except in the case of bankruptcy. The Bankruptcy Abuse Prevention Act of 2005, signed in April 2005 by President Bush includes an exemption for contributory IRAs and Roth IRAs. At the time we went to press, the exemption was $1,512,350. The exemption amount is increased as needed for inflation every three years. It was last updated on April 1, 2022, so this exemption amount will be in effect until at least April 1, 2025. Fortunately, any rollovers from employer-sponsored retirement plans to IRAs as well as

SEP or SIMPLE IRAs are fully protected from bankruptcy, regardless of the account's value. The balances in these accounts do not count towards the $1,512,350 limit that protects contributory and Roth IRAs from bankruptcy.

Outside of bankruptcy, Traditional contributory IRAs and Roth IRAs only have creditor protection under state law. Rollover IRAs from ERISA plans also lose their federal creditor protection outside of bankruptcy and are only protected to the extent that state law allows.

There is one exception to the rule that protects contributory and Roth IRAs from bankruptcy. In 2014, the U.S. Supreme Court determined that *Inherited* IRAs and retirement plans are not subject to this exemption, and therefore are not protected from creditor claims in bankruptcy cases. Because there are two different types of creditor protection (federal and state), I usually advise owners of large IRAs to keep their rollover IRA in a separate account from their contributory IRA. IRAs usually have state law protections, but over time, even these state law protections have diminished.

For the vast majority of participants, a good umbrella insurance policy providing coverage of at least $1 million (to protect against unexpected liabilities) is a cheaper and easier solution than keeping funds in a 401(k) or 403(b), which might have better creditor protection, as the IRA does not offer any creditor protection.

For those who may have personal liability issues, such as emergency room doctors or surgeons, the superior credit protection provided by the 401(k) or 403(b) may be more important than the investment and estate planning advantages of the IRA. For example, I recently worked with a physician who decided to keep his money in his existing 403(b) plan when it would have given him more investment options to roll the plan balance into an IRA. For the physician, the additional protection of keeping his money in his 403(b) plan from work intact was more important than the investment flexibility of an IRA.

Recent case law has held that one-person 401(k) plans are not ERISA plans, so they are not federally protected against bankruptcy claims any better than an IRA. Depending on the state you live in, though, your state laws may provide creditor protection to your personal 401(k) that is somewhat superior to that of an IRA.

3. *Borrowing privileges:* The 401(k) plan may have provisions that allow you to borrow against the plan. I talked about the dangers of 401(k) loans in Chapter 2, but there can be situations when it may be handy to borrow money from

For the vast majority of participants, a good umbrella insurance policy providing coverage of at least $1 million (to protect against unexpected liabilities) is a cheaper and easier solution than keeping funds in a 401(k) or 403(b), which might have better creditor protection, as the IRA does not offer any creditor protection.

a 401(k) plan. Borrowing from an IRA is not permitted, with one caveat. The IRS does permit you to *withdraw* funds from an IRA and, as long as the funds are re-deposited within 60 days, there is no tax consequence. This is not a loan. If you do not redeposit the funds within 60 days, the distribution is fully taxable, and penalties apply if you are younger than age 59½.

4. *Roth IRA conversion possibility for non-spouse beneficiary:* This is a sleeper advantage of keeping money in a 401(k) or opening your own 401(k) that I have never seen anyone execute in practice, with the exception of clients in our accounting firm. Notice 2008 – 30 from the IRS provides a unique opportunity for a non-spouse beneficiary to do a Roth IRA conversion of an Inherited 401(k) plan. Non-spouse beneficiaries of Inherited IRAs are not allowed to do an Inherited Roth IRA conversion of an Inherited IRA. This ability for non-spouse beneficiaries of qualified plans to convert is an additional reason to retain assets in a qualified plan.

This could be a huge opportunity if you are in a higher income tax bracket than your beneficiaries. That is, die with your 401(k) and have one or more of your beneficiaries make a conversion from an Inherited 401(k) to an Inherited Roth IRA. Please note the plan document, which describes the rules of the plan, must allow this Inherited 401(k) to Inherited Roth IRA transfer as well as the custodian of the 401(k) plan.

Further discussion on this strategic concept is discussed later in Chapter 11 when the beneficiary is a disabled or chronically ill beneficiary when this strategy can be enormously favorable, even sometimes measuring in additional tax savings of tens, sometimes hundreds of thousands of dollars.

One caution is that it sounds tempting to start a small consulting business and establish a solo 401(k) plan, roll your IRA into that 401(k), and instruct your heirs to make a Roth conversion of that plan on your death. As I spell out in Chapter 11, Inherited Roth accounts can make a tremendous difference

> Notice 2008–30 from the IRS provides a unique
> opportunity for a non-spouse beneficiary to do a Roth
> IRA conversion of an Inherited 401(k) plan. Non-spouse
> beneficiaries of Inherited IRAs are not allowed to do an
> Inherited Roth IRA.

in lifetime financial resources for your child with a disability. I like that idea, but fear that it may be stricken due to the step transaction doctrine.

The step transaction doctrine says you can't do in two steps what you aren't allowed to do in one step. If you legitimately have money in a 401(k) or 403(b) and die with it, the IRS will allow your child to convert the Inherited retirement plan to a Roth, assuming the plan allows it. However, only a spousal beneficiary is allowed to make a Roth conversion of an Inherited IRA. So, if you have an IRA, transfer it to a 401(k) or 403(b) and then try to have your non-spouse heirs make a Roth conversion of the Inherited 401(k) or 403(b), you are trying to do in two steps what you aren't allowed to do in one step.

5. *Direct Roth IRA conversion from 401(k) plans:* It used to be that you had to transfer your 401(k) balance into a Traditional IRA before you could convert that Traditional IRA to a Roth IRA. Under current laws, it is possible to transfer your 401(k) account directly to a Roth IRA, eliminating the need for the extra step. But the good news doesn't stop there. For years, taxpayers who had after-tax contributions in their 401(k) accounts tried to roll those directly into their Roth IRA too. The IRS rules weren't clear, and the process was complicated. Many 401(k) plan sponsors simply issued one check for the amount in the Traditional account, and another check for the amount in the after-tax account and passed the responsibility for the legality of the rollover on to the new custodian. Some taxpayers were audited because of the transaction, and some weren't.

In September of 2014, the IRS issued Notice 2014-54 that formally permits what taxpayers have been trying to do all along. If you have after-tax contributions in your 401(k), you can now directly roll those contributions in to a Roth IRA, tax-free. Please don't miss this opportunity if this applies to you.

Music to the Ears of a CD Investor

I bet all you CD investors are tired of hearing everyone talk about the benefits of a well-balanced portfolio, aren't you? You don't want to hear that inflation will

> **Also, many retirees are unaware that most banks permit annual RMDs to be taken from CDs without breaking the CD or incurring any penalty or loss of earnings.**

eat at the purchasing power of your CD investments. You just want some good advice on how to manage your CDs. Okay. Fair enough. This is for you.

Maybe you just don't want to be in the market no matter what all the financial advisors say. Many people feel this way in light of the recent market volatility. If you feel this way, you will be happy to know that the FDIC insurance for CDs has been increased from $100,000 per person to $250,000 per person. Those seeking additional security can add a transfer on death designation to the CDs adding $250,000 of FDIC insurance protection per beneficiary named on the transfer on death designation.

Conservative retirees are also attracted by the offers made by some banks to allow seniors to upgrade their CDs annually to a higher interest rate and for a longer term. When the maximum term, typically 10 years, is reached, the annual upgrade in rates is still permissible, but you have to ask for it. Conservative investors should also be aware of the one-rollover-per-year rule, which restricts IRA owners from transferring their IRAs from one bank to another, to take advantage of higher CD rates. This type of transfer is only permitted once per 12-month period. Choosing CDs with a term of 5 to 10 years should alleviate some of the worry about market ups and downs but is certainly not advisable when interest rates are low.

Also, many retirees are unaware that most banks permit annual RMDs to be taken from CDs without breaking the CD or incurring any penalty or loss of earnings. But don't just arbitrarily roll over a sizeable portion of your 401(k) into CDs that you buy from your current bank. It would be better to get quotes from at least three or four banks. Share the quotes with the bank manager you really want to do business with and ask him/her for their best and final rates.

My Somewhat Unique Recommendation: The One-Person 401(k) Plan

Throughout this chapter and in other parts of this book, I have mentioned the possibility of creating a one-person 401(k) plan and using that as your primary retirement plan vehicle in the same way that many people now use IRAs. The difficult part of using this strategy is that you need self-employment income to open your own one-person 401(k) plan. Many retirees, by definition, don't have self-employment income. If that is your case, the best solution might be to roll the money into an IRA or if your retirement funds are in an IRA now, to leave them there.

If possible, it would be better if you could get some self-employment income. Do some consulting, work on a project, do something where you earn some income and based on that self-employment income, set up a one-person 401(k) plan. You will have control of the plan, and you can do a trustee-to-trustee transfer of all your retirement plans to this one-person 401(k) plan.

If you are retired and still have money in your former employer's 401(k) plan, subject to exceptions mentioned in this chapter, I would consider rolling at least a portion, if not all, of your existing 401(k) plan from your former job into your new one-person 401(k) plan. This offers the following benefits:

- extremely flexible investment choices.

- your beneficiaries would still be able to make a Roth IRA conversion of the Inherited 401(k). (See Chapter 11.)

- expanded Roth IRA conversion possibilities (new).

- depending on the state you live in, you may have better protection from creditors than with a Traditional IRA.

Having a lot of money in a company 401(k) or even a Traditional IRA is not bad, but, having it in a one-person 401(k) plan that is completely under your control is, for many retirees, a better strategy. If you don't have any self-employment income and have no realistic way of getting self-employment income, the classic trustee-to-trustee transfer to an IRA will usually be best with at least the majority of your retirement assets.

However, to be fair (as mentioned above), there are some advantages to leaving your workplace 401(k) plan where it is and not rolling the money into an IRA or one-person 401(k).

A Quick Note About the Aggregation Rules

Under the old Section 408(d)(2) IRA aggregation rules (also called the pro-rata rule), a retirement plan participant who wanted to transfer the balance of his plan, including the basis from after-tax contributions, to a Traditional IRA was not permitted to isolate the after-tax contributions and convert that money to a Roth IRA, and then transfer the balance of the account to a self-employed retirement plan or a qualified retirement plan with another employer without first considering the balances of his other existing IRAs.

It was unbelievably complicated, so I want to give you some historical perspective. Think of all of your retirement assets as being different pots of money. In the past, first, you would have needed to determine the value of all of your after-tax contributions to your IRA and retirement plan. Second, you would have needed to add up the value of all of your Traditional IRA accounts—Roth IRAs are not included. Finally, you needed to figure out the ratio of the after-tax contributions to the Traditional IRA accounts. That ratio was the percentage of your Roth IRA conversion that was not taxed. Let's look at an example.

Assume you had a $1,000,000 IRA with no basis and had an old $300,000 401(k) with basis of $50,000 from your after-tax contributions. You wanted to convert the $50,000 to a Roth IRA. Under the IRA aggregation rules, if you wanted to convert the $50,000 of after-tax contributions in your 401(k) to a Roth IRA, you would have had to previously convert the entire balance of the other Traditional IRAs as well as the $300,000 401(k). This would have caused a whopping income tax bill in the neighborhood of $437,500 ($1,250,000 total taxable conversion amount with taxes at 35 percent) to get the $50,000 of after-tax contributions into a Roth IRA. That would likely be a far too high Roth conversion than is appropriate.

Many retirees tried to circumvent the aggregation rules by taking advantage of a special rule that allowed them to roll the pre-tax contributions in their 401(k) directly to an IRA and take the after-tax contributions back. The plan administrator would issue two checks for the distributions, and the idea was that the pre-tax contributions would be rolled into an IRA, and the after-tax contributions would be deposited into a brokerage account where they would presumably earn taxable interest and dividends. What actually happened was that retirees would roll the pre-tax contributions directly to an IRA and then try to roll the after-tax contributions directly to a Roth IRA—in effect, giving themselves a tax-free Roth IRA conversion.

How to Successfully Convert your Non-deductible IRAs and After-Tax Dollars in Retirement Plans Without Having to Pay Any Taxes (Sometimes)

Of course, the IRS fought this strategy for years and said that the pro-rata rule which they considered the standard rule should still apply to those transfers. In October of 2014, though, the IRS finally gave up and issued a clarification stating that the after-tax amounts can, assuming certain requirements are met, be rolled directly into a Roth IRA (IRS Notice 2014-54).

The next couple of paragraphs are tough to understand, but there may be an opportunity here. This ruling gives high-income taxpayers an unprecedented opportunity to save money which ultimately can end up in a Roth environment.

In the past, there was a smaller incentive for them to contribute to the after-tax account in their 401(k)s, and their contributions to the pre-tax accounts were limited ($22,500 in 2023, or $30,000 if they were age 50 or older.) Assuming that their plans allow it, they can now contribute the maximum to their pre-tax account and the maximum to their after-tax account inside the retirement plan (in 2023, the total contribution limit is $66,000 or 100 percent of compensation below $66,000 or $73,500 if age 50 or older). Thanks to this new ruling, they now can roll the after-tax contributions into a Roth IRA at retirement.

Let's have an example with numbers to show how this works.

The Mega-Back Door Roth

Anna earns $100,000 from her employer. In 2023, she contributes the maximum $22,500 to her 401(k) plan, and her employer matches that, up to 6% of her salary, and adds $6,000 to her 401(k) account. Let's assume that Anna has elected that her employer match be added to Anna's pre-tax contributions. Now Anna has $28,500 in her 401(k) account. If Anna's retirement plan permits, she could contribute an additional $37,500 to her after-tax 401(k) account via a payroll deduction to get to the maximum of $66,000. Now, if Anna's 401(k) plan allows her to make in-service withdrawals from her account while she's still employed as well as allowing after-tax contributions, she can immediately convert her $37,500 of after tax-funds from her 401(k) and roll them into a Roth IRA before the after-tax contributions generate returns that would be taxable during a rollover. This is what's known as a mega-backdoor Roth, a fantastic method of quickly building up a large Roth IRA balance.

If your plan does not permit in-service withdrawals or additional contributions to the after-tax contribution inside the retirement plan, you can still do a mega-backdoor Roth after you leave your current employer, but you will most likely owe taxes on any investment earnings during the rollover. Remember, you cannot make the after-tax contributions required for a mega backdoor Roth until you've reached your 401(k) employee contribution limit of $22,500 in 2023 if under age 50 or $30,000 if over age 50. This means, the maximum amount of after-tax dollars that can be converted through the mega back-door Roth conversion is $43,500 in 2023 if age 50 or older since you must contribute the maximum employee contribution limit of $30,000 first.

It is important to know the pro-rata rules still apply to partial withdrawals. Let's say that you have a $1,000,000 401(k) that is still with your former employer and $200,000 of that is your after-tax contributions. You are reading this section and you want to convert the $200,000 to a Roth IRA. If you request a distribution

> **In October of 2014, though, the IRS finally gave up and issued a clarification stating that the after-tax amounts can, assuming certain requirements are met, be rolled directly into a Roth IRA (IRS Notice 2014-54).**

of only $200,000, then $160,000 will be considered pre-tax contributions and $40,000 will be considered after-tax contributions, because the pro-rata rules apply. If you want to move the entire $200,000 to a Roth IRA, then you have to take the entire $1,000,000 out of the plan. If you transfer $800,000 to a Traditional IRA and $200,000 to a Roth IRA, the transfer to the Roth IRA will be tax-free.

Roth Conversions Without Taxes

It is possible under certain conditions to make a Roth IRA conversion without having to pay any taxes. You can do this if you meet certain requirements and have after-tax dollars inside your retirement plan. In practice, taking an asset that is growing tax-deferred and turning it into an asset that is growing tax-free—without paying any tax on the transaction—almost seems too good to be true. But, given the right conditions, you can do it.

Let's assume you have some after-tax and pre-tax money in your IRA. First, let's start with what you are not allowed to do that I bet you want to do. Let's assume you have some after-tax IRA money that you could convert to a Roth IRA for free—but you also have some pre-tax IRA money that you would have to pay tax on if you converted that money. I bet you would like to convert only the after-tax portion of your IRA to a Roth IRA, not paying the tax, and then be left with a Roth IRA and a Traditional IRA and go your merry way.

The problem is that you are not allowed to do that. You must combine all your IRAs (including SEP and SIMPLE IRAs) and take them all into account when making a Roth IRA conversion because you are subject to the proration rules as outlined above.

No matter how many IRA accounts you may have, the Tax Code considers all your IRA money to be in 'one pot.' Any already taxed money in the IRA environment is your basis, regardless of which specific IRA account contains the after-tax money. For every dollar removed from the IRA environment, the ratio of your total after-tax IRA basis to your total tax-deferred IRAs (year-end values plus the conversion amounts) determines the proportion of the distribution that is taxed.

So, can we get around the aggregation rules? Fortunately, as of this writing there is a way.

There has been legislation proposed that would eliminate conversions of retirement accounts with 'basis' in them. While it ultimately didn't pass on its most recent journey through Congress, we are expecting future conversions of 'basis' in retirement accounts to be minimized for certain high-income levels and/or eliminated, so we wanted to include this important content in the event it is still available to you when you are reading this book.

I've written and hosted many webinars regarding this unintended loophole for many years. And now, the IRS has caught on, and legislation to disallow tax-free conversions of basis in IRAs has been proposed but has not yet garnered enough support to become law. As of the writing of this book, you are still permitted to make Roth conversions of your after-tax basis if done properly. Let's hope you are able to take advantage of the loophole and if they close it later on, you will be 'grandfathered' because you took advantage of it while it was still allowed.

I will be referencing a 401(k) plan, but the same concept works for 403(b) plans and many other types of retirement plans. The assumptions are you are still working and participate in an employer 401(k) plan and your 401(k) plan accepts IRA rollovers (that is to say, you can roll your IRAs into your 401(k)), and your 401(k) plan states that it will **not** accept after tax-dollars in your IRA for the rollover, as it will only accept the Traditional or pre-tax dollars in your IRA.

You can also do this plan after you "retire" from your regular job if you have consulting income, as the consulting income will then give you the capability of setting up your own one person 401(k) discussed above and below.

You then initiate a 'trustee-to-trustee' transfer of **only** the pre-tax dollars in your IRA to your 401(k) or one person 401(k) plan. The most crucial part of this transaction is that you do a 'trustee-to-trustee' transfer and not a direct rollover, as you are only permitted one direct rollover every 365 days. If you have multiple IRAs with pre-tax dollars and after-tax dollars and you do a direct rollover vs. a trustee-to-trustee transfer, you will blow the tax-free Roth conversion.

An Example of a Tax-Free Roth Conversion

Let's look at a client example of a tax-free Roth conversion that was completed by one of our clients based upon our recommendation. Our client who was age 50 had a total of seven IRAs including SEP, SIMPLE and regular IRAs, including both after-tax and pre-tax monies for a total combined IRA balance of $1.7 million. Of the $1.7 million, there was $150,000 in after-tax contributions. Since he was still working and had a 401(k) plan that accepted IRA rollovers of pre-tax contributions only, he requested 'trustee-to-trustee' transfers of the pre-tax dollars only from all of the IRA accounts into his employer's 401(k) plan. By doing so, this left only the after-tax monies in his IRAs, and he was able to do a tax-free Roth conversion of $150,000. The increase in the overall net asset values at age 100, using a 6.5% rate of return was $364,600, with his Roth IRA accounts increasing by approximately $819,000! Is this a great country or what?

Here is a PowerPoint slide that I have used to demonstrate this strategy in presentations for 20 years or more. The employer qualified plan also includes a one person 401(k) where you are the employer! The Traditional IRA money goes after-tax dollars inside the IRA become a Roth IRA. All without having to pay Uncle Sam a nickel.

To be fair, I have to mention the potential disadvantage of this plan. If you prefer to make your own investments, or you have a money manager who you think can outperform the 401(k), you are giving up control. After the transaction, that $1,550,000 will be held in your 401(k) plan at work. Presumably, your 401(k) will offer you a number of options but you will not have the entire universe of possibilities that you would if the money were in an IRA. At some point after the conversion, however, you could consider rolling money from your 401(k) back into an IRA.

What if you are retired? Is there a loophole for you? Maybe. What you would need to do is to establish your own solo 401(k) plan. The biggest problem you are likely to face in setting up your own solo 401(k) plan is that you need to have earned income. If you are completely retired and will never have earned income again, this entire plan won't work. But if you are doing some consulting work for

Figure 7.1

Slick Idea to Bypass the Allocation of Basis on IRA to Roth IRA Conversions

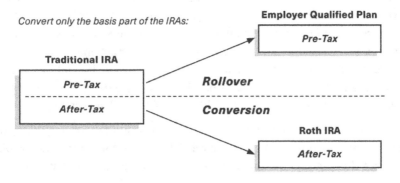

your former employer on a contract basis or you can develop any earned income, you can establish your own Solo 401(k) plan.

It is important that you are paid as an independent contractor and not a W-2 employee, most likely filing a Schedule C with your Form 1040. If you had your own Solo 401(k) plan, then you could execute the same strategy as shown in the previous section. Our client was able to roll the pre-tax dollars into his 401(k) plan at work and isolate the after-tax dollars in his IRA, avoid the proration and aggregation rules and make the Roth IRA conversion for free.

Actually, a slew of Westinghouse retirees utilized this strategy. I gave a talk every year to this group and after a few did it, some clients and frankly some non-clients did it and many followed. There are few things in life a Westinghouse retiree likes better than making a Roth IRA conversion without paying the taxes. They also like to talk about it. It's like finding a great bargain or better yet something you really want, and you find out you can get it for free.

Fair warning: The rules on this topic are very complicated. If you have any basis from after-tax contributions in your qualified plan account, you should consult with an expert advisor who can review your situation prior to completing a rollover to an IRA. Alternately, you could study the rules in depth, make certain there are no mechanical screw-ups, and try doing it on your own. Some of the Westinghouse retirees did do it on their own. But then again, many people would rather have a root canal than pay an advisor. I don't hear about the ones who tried it and screwed it up. They don't talk about it when they screw it up.

Combining Distribution Options

Frequently, sometimes due to my advice, my clients decide to leave the fixed-income component of their retirement plan in their 403(b) plans because of the favorable rate of return. Incidentally, I agree with that reasoning. Some of them will choose to transfer variable income component balances to an IRA because of the diversity of investment options. Finally, some participants will annuitize part of their plan to guarantee a set amount of income regardless of how long they live. Although not all plans offer an option to annuitize, it is still beneficial for retirees to consider splitting their retirement accumulations between their 401(k) plans or 403(b) plans and their IRAs in situations where there are investment and/or tax reasons to maintain a separate IRA and 401(k) or 403(b) plan account.

Many of my Westinghouse retiree clients follow a similar strategy. They opt to keep the fixed-income portion of their 401(k) plan in the Westinghouse plan and transfer the remaining funds into an IRA. Although not all plans offer the annuitization option, it is still beneficial for retirees to consider splitting their retirement accumulations between their 401(k) plans and their IRAs in situations where there are investment and/or tax reasons to maintain a separate IRA and 401(k) plan account.

Lump-Sum Distribution

First, let's get the terminology straight. When I refer to the *lump-sum distribution,* I am referring to the special tax treatment afforded retirees when they withdraw their entire account and pay income tax on the entire amount. Ouch!

Many retirees say they "took the lump sum," but what they really mean is that they chose *not* to annuitize their retirement plan accumulations—that is, not to accept regular monthly payments for the rest of their lives. (For more information on annuitizing, see Chapter 8.) What actually happened was that they rolled or transferred the money into an IRA or left the money in the existing retirement plan. Few retirees actually elect the special tax treatment per Internal Revenue Code (IRC) Section 402(d), which is the proper meaning of *taking a lump-sum distribution.*

So why is a lump-sum distribution significant? The advantage of a lump-sum distribution is that it qualifies for a special tax calculation. The tax calculation is called 10-year averaging, and it is available only to individuals born before 1936. The essence of the 10-year averaging calculation is that you may withdraw your entire retirement plan balance and pay income taxes on it immediately but at a reduced income tax rate. In addition, a capital gains tax rate is applied to the amount attributable to pre-1974 contributions to the plan. This amount will often be less than the ordinary income tax that would otherwise be due.

A lump-sum distribution is only permitted when the employee reaches age 59½, is separated from service, or dies. If the owner is self-employed and becomes totally or permanently disabled, they may also take a lump-sum distribution. Lump-sum distributions must be made within a 12-month period from the triggering event for the distribution (i.e., death, attainment of age 59½, separation from service), subject to certain exceptions, to qualify as a lump-sum distribution.

Ten-Year Averaging is a Hellish Calculation

Do you qualify? Should you do it?

The answer in both cases is usually no. I will spare you the details. Even assuming you are willing to jump through enough hoops to qualify, for most employees, it will result in a needless acceleration of income taxes, though admittedly at a lower-than-normal rate.

In practice, I have never recommended a 10-year averaging plan, instead preferring to take advantage of the net unrealized appreciation (NUA) provisions when available and roll the rest into an IRA. The NUA provisions apply to retirement plans that include appreciated employer securities. If this applies to you, see Chapter 9 in the third edition of the original *Retire Secure!* which can be accessed at **https://PayTaxesLater.com/Books/**.

My reason for not getting too excited about the 10-year averaging is not the restrictions, but the fact that you must come up with money to pay the taxes now. Remember the bedrock principle: **Pay taxes later—except for Roths**. Nonetheless, asking your financial professional to run the numbers for you is a prudent approach.

The general idea behind the lump-sum distribution is that if you successfully jump through a series of hoops, the IRS will discount your taxes. That said, even at a reduced tax rate, it would require some very compelling arguments backed by serious number crunching to persuade me that accelerating taxes is a good idea—especially if large sums of money are involved, which is often the case.

In theory, I can picture the lump-sum distribution (LSD) being useful in three situations.

You have a phenomenal use for the money. Some retirees, who have pensions in addition to a 401(k), have taken an LSD (let me reiterate LSD= lump sum distribution!) and used the money to speculate in real estate. They paid the reduced tax on the LSD and used the remaining proceeds as a down payment on commercial real estate. If the rent covered the mortgage, the idea was that the building appreciation would be on the entire purchase price of the real estate and not the amount invested (the down payment). During the boom real estate

@mwarlene

markets of past years, that strategy actually worked for a number of taxpayers. Unfortunately, it also lead to unrealistic expectations for the next generation of would-be landlords. During the best of times, that strategy was too aggressive for me, and in today's environment, I would not even think about it.

I could picture considering the LSD if the retirement plan owner was rich and either terminally ill or extremely old and if the value of the total estate was well more than the estate tax exemption equivalent amount ($12.92 million in 2023). In that case, they might want to consider the LSD to avoid the combined income and estate taxes on the IRA that heirs would pay after their death. If the alternative would be dying with the retirement plan and having distributions made by heirs subjected to the SECURE Act, an LSD might be a way of getting the money out at a cheaper tax rate.

Other professionals certainly disagree with me. My natural bias is toward keeping retirement assets in IRAs or retirement plans rather than withdrawing the money and paying the tax earlier than necessary, except if you are making a Roth conversion or paying the taxes and gifting the net proceeds to be invested tax-free by your heirs. If there is a good reason to make early IRA or retirement plan withdrawals, then the LSD becomes attractive. I just hate paying taxes up-front.

There could be times when the LSD may be a good choice, but I suggest that you approach it with a predisposition against the LSD and make a qualified financial professional prove to you with hard numbers that it would be a good thing to do in your specific situation. If you take that approach, you will likely be safe from making a bad decision.

Deciding on a good strategy for handling your retirement assets is an area where a good financial advisor can provide enormous value, particularly if he or she is a CPA-number runner. Getting good advice at this point can have a significant impact on your future.

The Mechanics of IRA Rollovers and Trustee-to-Trustee Transfers

Let's assume the goal is to move your retirement plan funds from one retirement plan either to another retirement plan, an IRA, or your new one-person 401(k) plan (what I generally recommend). Most people call this kind of transfer a rollover. But, particularly if you are a do-it-yourselfer, you need to be aware that the IRS makes a significant distinction between the mechanics and regulations of a rollover versus a trustee-to-trustee transfer.

Individuals planning to move money from a 401(k) retirement plan (or similar plan) to an IRA generally will want to conduct a trustee-to-trustee transfer. Why is the trustee-to-trustee transfer generally preferable in this situation? To find out we'll need to dig into the rules governing rollovers.

IRC Section 402 states that retirement plan distributions are not taxed if rolled over to a retirement plan or an IRA, *provided you comply with the rules.* Technically, a rollover is a distribution from one retirement plan, or IRA, to the owner, which he or she then moves into the new retirement plan. But if you affect a transfer of funds through a rollover, you have to worry about complying with the following rules:

- The 60-day rule
- The 20 percent withholding-tax rule
- The one-rollover-every-12-months rule

The best way to avoid the problems of the 60-day rule, the 20 percent withholding-tax rule, and the one-rollover-per-12-months rule is to complete a trustee-to-trustee transfer of a retirement plan to an IRA. In a trustee-to-trustee transfer you never touch the actual money. It is an electronic blip; a few pieces of paper (not green) and/or some digital data pass from one financial institution to another. Some institutions make the check payable to the new trustee but send it to the participant who is then responsible for forwarding the check to the new trustee. Although this is a permissible method of completing a trustee-to-trustee transfer, please speak to a qualified advisor and the plan administrator before completing a trustee-to-trustee transfer under these circumstances.

The following three sections provide a short description of the problems you may encounter if you do not do a trustee-to-trustee transfer. If the merit of doing the trustee-to-trustee transfer rather than a rollover is established in your mind, you may safely skip the next three sections and jump to *What You May Roll Over and What You May Not.*

(You can likely skip the next three sections if you plan to do a trustee-to-trustee transfer.)

Avoiding the 20 Percent Withholding-Tax Rule

When someone elects to roll over a 401(k) or other retirement plan to an IRA without using a trustee-to-trustee transfer, the transferring company must withhold 20 percent of the amount rolled over and send it to the federal government as an estimate of what you will owe on April 15th. (If you live in a state that taxes retirement income, they might also be required to withhold state income tax.) This could be a nightmare if your intent was to roll over the entire amount.

This withholding trap has caught many unwary 401(k) owners off guard. Since your former employer is required to withhold 20 percent, the only way you will not have to pay any income taxes on the rollover is for you to come up with an amount equivalent to that 20 percent from sources outside the 401(k). If you don't have the 20 percent amount to restore to your retirement plan, you'll have even more headaches because you will have to pay income taxes on the rollover to the extent that the 20 percent withholding is insufficient to cover the tax that you owe based on your final situation at year end.

The good news? The best way to avoid the 20 percent withholding-tax rule is simple: do a trustee-to-trustee transfer.

Note: The 20 percent withholding-tax rule does not apply when transferring one IRA to another.

The 60-Day Rule

Let's assume you can get around the 20 percent withholding problem. Another problem remains. You must comply with the 60-day rule. You must restore the funds to another retirement plan or an IRA within 60 days of receiving the distribution. Otherwise, income taxes must be paid on the entire amount; furthermore, if you are 59½ or younger, you may have the added 10 percent premature distribution penalty—a nightmare.

Are there exceptions? A few—but basically, you don't want to go there. If you are planning to do a rollover as opposed to a trustee-to-trustee transfer, you must get the money back in a retirement plan or IRA within 60 days.

Most of the reasons the IRS will accept as excuses for not doing so are so terrible that you would never want to plan for any of them to happen. If you do miss the 60-day rule accidentally, then you can start looking at the reasons the IRS will waive the rule, but don't expect to automatically obtain relief.

In practice, people who want to do a rollover rather than a trustee-to-trustee transfer may be looking to use their IRA or qualified retirement plan as the source of a short-term loan. Technically speaking, loans are not permitted against IRAs, and while qualified plans may provide for loans, the amount that can be borrowed is determined by the plan and the total loan amount that any plan may provide is capped at 50% of your vested balance up to $50,000 (whichever is less). One exception to this limit is if the vested account balance is less than $10,000, the 401(k) participant can borrow up to $10,000 subject to the plan rules. However, some people who think they are clever might choose to withdraw their IRA or retirement plan and attempt to repay the money within the 60-day window. That might work, but it is risky at best.

The classic reason for trying to finesse the system is to use the money for some type of real estate transaction. However, that is what bridge loans at the bank are for. If avoiding those fees is so critical, and you are confident that there will be no hang-ups with the sale or purchase of whatever the money is needed for, good luck. But if the deal goes sour because of some unforeseeable event, don't expect the IRS to have any sympathy.

Perhaps the Horse's Ass Award goes to the guy who wants to take advantage of some type of financial tip on an investment that isn't listed on one of the popular exchanges. He is told he can double his money in a month. The Horse's Ass has no other funds to invest except his IRA or retirement plan. He goes to his retirement plan, withdraws funds in order to procure his unofficial loan, invests in his sure winner, and plans to restore the retirement plan before 60 days pass. The sure winner implodes, and the Horse's Ass has not only lost money on his investment, but he will have to pay income taxes on money he doesn't have anymore. The $3,000-per-year loss limitation on deducting the capital loss will virtually make the tax benefits of the loss meaningless, and the income tax he must pay on the retirement plan withdrawal will be draconian.

If the hot tip were a stock or mutual fund that is traded over any of the recognized stock exchanges, he would have been better off rolling the money into an IRA and purchasing the security in his IRA account. That way, when the account gets clobbered at least he will not face the tax liability in addition to the loss.

The One-Rollover-Per-12-Months Rule

An individual is allowed only one rollover per any 12-month period, but the number of trustee-to-trustee transfers anyone can make is unlimited. If you have different IRAs or different retirement plans, you may have one rollover per separate IRA or separate retirement plan.

Also, the one-rollover-every-12-months rule applies only to IRAs. For example, a reader who initiates a direct rollover from a 401(k) to an IRA on January 2, 2015, can roll over to another IRA on January 15, 2015, if he or she so desires. This move is permissible because the first distribution was not from an IRA.

Again, life is complicated enough. Do a trustee-to-trustee transfer, and don't worry about this rule, the 60-day rule, or the 20 percent withholding-tax rule.

What You May Roll Over and What You May Not

Under the new expanded portability rules, my general rule of thumb is that an individual can roll anything into anything. Of course, that is a slight exaggeration. Still, the general idea now is that, if the paperwork is done correctly, funds can

Still, the general idea now is that, if the paperwork is done correctly, funds can go from one pre-tax plan to another without taxation, though some restrictions may apply.

go from one pre-tax plan to another without taxation, though some restrictions may apply.

Most of the recommended rollovers—or, to be more technically correct, trustee-to-trustee transfers—will be from taxable retirement plans to IRAs. For example, a retired or service terminated employee owning a fully taxable account, such as a 401(k), a 403(b), a 457 plan, a SEP, a Keogh, and so on, will usually be well served to institute a trustee-to-trustee transfer to an IRA. The employee is allowed to transfer from account to account if he or she likes. For example, if you leave your job and move to a new company, you might think it's a good idea to consolidate your old 401(k) with your new company's 401(k). You can, but it may not be in your best interests. I generally prefer that you transfer the old 401(k) into a separate IRA or your own one-person 401(k) and then start new contributions in the 401(k), which will eventually leave you with balances in an IRA, or your own 401(k) and a 401(k) from work.

There will be times when it might be advisable to go backwards. For instance, if a working or self-employed IRA owner wanted to use retirement funds to purchase life insurance, he or she might take his or her IRA (through which he or she is not allowed to purchase life insurance), transfer it into a different qualified plan, and then purchase his or her insurance inside the qualified plan. Caution is advised, however, for retirement plan owners who want to purchase life insurance inside a retirement plan. We do not cover that interesting but risky strategy in this book.

In summary, you cannot do the following:

- Transfer or roll over the Required Minimum Distributions (RMD) from a retirement plan or an IRA into another retirement plan. You must pay tax on that money. (But I liked that you may have at least at one time thought you had a great idea.)
  - Make a Roth IRA conversion from your RMD.
  - Open a Roth IRA with your RMD.
  - Transfer or roll over Inherited IRA distributions.

  – Make a Roth IRA conversion from your Inherited IRA.

  – Transfer or roll over Section 72(t) payments (a series of substantially equal payments distributed from a qualified plan for the life of the employee or the joint lives of the employee and his designated beneficiary that qualifies for an exception from the 10 percent penalty otherwise imposed on 72(t) payments).

Inexact Language on a Beneficiary Form Can Spell Disaster

If you do decide to roll your 401(k) into an IRA or transfer your IRA to a new custodian, you will have to fill out new beneficiary forms. Most people take this step for granted, but I have to caution you about it because sloppy titling could ruin the entire stretch IRA concept for your non-spouse beneficiaries. I discuss this in detail in Chapter 9, but for now, it is important to know that the deceased IRA owner's name must remain on the account.

·· **MINI CASE STUDY 7.1** ··
The Difference Between Proper and
Sloppy Language on a Beneficiary Form

Grandpa and Grandma both name a well-drafted trust for their grandchild, Junior, in the beneficiary designations of their respective IRAs. They both die during the same year. Due to a quirk in estate administration, Detailed Danny becomes the administrator for Grandpa's IRA, and Sloppy Susan becomes the administrator for Grandma's IRA. Detailed Danny, when transferring the Inherited IRA to the trust for Junior, follows the advice of Grandpa's financial planner and titles the account "Grandpa's IRA (deceased, December 2022) Trust for Benefit of Junior." Junior, being only 21 years old at Grandpa's death, is able to stretch payments from Grandpa's IRA for 10 years. Even when Junior is 31 years old and takes his final distribution, the account still has Grandpa's name. Because the Inherited IRA makes a tremendous difference in Junior's life and since his financial security as a young adult is assured, he often thinks of Grandpa's thoughtfulness and also appreciates Detailed Danny's care in handling the Inherited IRA.

Sloppy Susan, when doing similar work for Grandma's IRA, titles the account "Trust for Junior." The trust is audited, and the IRS requires the trust to pay income tax on the entire balance, which could lead to a five-year income tax acceleration instead of a ten-year acceleration. If the beneficiary meets one of the exceptions to the ten-year acceleration, then the mistake could amount to even more significant dollars as the lifetime stretch feature would be lost. This is critical when planning for a child with a disability or chronic illness.

··

Ensure your executor or administrator knows how to title the Inherited IRA correctly. If you are a financial planner, I hope I have made a compelling case for the correct titling of an Inherited IRA. If you are in charge of internal office procedures at a financial institution, create a policy that ensures that all Inherited IRAs retain the name of the deceased IRA owner; you will avoid costly mistakes for many beneficiaries.

Also, please don't assume that your financial professional, whether a CPA, financial planner or (with all due respect) an attorney, will know about proper titling and act accordingly.

Sloppy titling could accelerate the taxes on the Inherited IRA even faster than the dreaded SECURE Act for non-spouse beneficiaries of an IRA. It is imperative that the deceased IRA owner's name remain on the account.

Other Titling Notes

If there are multiple beneficiaries (as is typical with accounts left to "children equally"), the accounts should be split into separate Inherited IRA accounts after death. Please note that under the new rules, each minor child will be forced to take RMDs from the Inherited IRA until age 21 and then drain the balance within ten years. But, if one of the beneficiaries qualifies for one of the exceptions, that money could be taxed over his or her life expectancy. In addition, although the deceased IRA owner's name will remain on the account, the Social Security number of the beneficiary should be used.

KEY IDEAS

- Before you transfer any retirement plan assets to an IRA, check to see if there are any after-tax dollars or net unrealized appreciation for money in your plan. Converting those after-tax dollars to a Roth IRA will prevent you from paying taxes on the same dollars twice. Be aware of any pro-rata limitations when making Roth IRA conversions with after-tax dollars.

- Look into the ability to make a mega back-door Roth conversion if your institution allows you to make after-tax contributions to your retirement plan and immediate in-service distributions.

Key Ideas continue on the following page.

KEY IDEAS
(continued)

- For many individuals approaching retirement, initiating a trustee-to-trustee transfer of a qualified retirement plan to an IRA or a one-person 401(k) is a good decision.

- In certain circumstances, a retiree will be well-served by retaining at least a portion of his or her retirement plan in the original employer's plan.

- People who continue to work after age 73 may be able to defer their RMDs until they actually retire. Check with your plan documents to see if this is permitted.

- If you have self-employment income, moving your retirement plan assets into a solo 401(k) plan can provide many advantages, including flexible investment options, options for Roth conversions, and, depending on state law, you may have additional creditor protection.

- Weigh your decision carefully and look at all circumstances of your situation, including your estate plans.

- If you decide to move your 401(k) assets to an IRA or to a solo 401(k) plan, the easiest—and less prone to error—method is to conduct a trustee-to-trustee transfer. With a trustee-to-trustee transfer, you avoid the 60-day rule, the 20 percent withholding rule, and the one-rollover-per-year rule.

- Deciding how to manage your retirement assets at the time you retire is important and deserves your full attention.

- Inherited retirement plan assets must be clearly titled with the original owner's name, the word "inherited," and the beneficiary's name. Failing to do so may result in accelerated distribution—and taxation—of the entire balance within 5 years of death instead of ten or, if the beneficiary qualifies for one of the exceptions, over the beneficiary's life.

8

Annuitizing Your Retirement Accumulations—Does It Make Sense for You?

"I advise you to go on living solely to enrage those who are paying your annuities."

—Voltaire

Before I get into the meat of the chapter, I must get some definitions and terminology out of the way. We do include a glossary of terms in the book, but many readers probably skipped over it, and in this chapter, it is imperative for the reader to understand the terminology.

Please note we are not talking about investments that are called variable annuities, fixed index annuities, equity index annuities, or commercial annuities. If someone is trying to sell you one of these annuities, hang on to your wallet. Though I am sure there are a lot of annuity salespeople who would disagree with me, I think of these types of annuities as having high costs and not a great investment for most people. For me to sell or recommend one of these types of commercial annuities to anyone, I would have to move to the dark side. To be fair, however, these types of commercial annuities are not in my world, and they might be better than I think for some investors.

But that doesn't mean that if you already bought one you should dump it. Many times, the products have a high fee but offer downside protection. The costs are front-loaded, and my advice to people who have them is usually to hold on to them until at least they are past the penalty period for early distributions. If you find yourself with an annuity that's not suited for you, you may be able

> For me to sell or recommend one of these types of commercial annuities to anyone, I would have to move to the dark side.

to exchange that annuity or life insurance for a more suitable annuity. I explain how to do that in Chapter 9 of my previous book, *Retire Secure for Professors and TIAA Participants,* in the section on *Purchasing Deferred Annuities with Existing Annuities and Life Insurance.*

But I digress....

What is an Annuity?

An annuity is an investment vehicle (financial product) offered by a life insurance company. Annuitizing your retirement plan accumulations or after-tax money means exchanging your lump-sum savings for a stream of income that lasts for a specified period of years or the remainder of your life or your and your spouse's life. Annuities can be fixed (meaning that they pay a set interest rate and are guaranteed to never go down in value) or variable (meaning they will fluctuate in value depending on the chosen investments).

In simple terms, if you annuitize your retirement plan accumulations or after-tax money, you convert your investments into an income stream. You surrender all or a portion of your money to purchase regular, recurring payments for a defined period of time. The most common period to receive these recurring payments is the rest of your life or, if you are married, the rest of your and your spouse's lives.

Readers who can't stand the roller coaster ride of the stock market may derive some comfort from annuitizing a portion of their retirement savings, providing a monthly income to last their entire lifetime. But that sense of security can also impose limitations on access to your money. Finding the appropriate balance and the factors you should consider in your situation is what this chapter explores.

Annuity Basics

If you own a pre-tax annuity in your retirement plan, you will pay tax on the entire withdrawal unless you have basis in that annuity. (Basis represents the after-tax balance in your account. If you made non-deductible contributions to your IRA or retirement plan, the amount of your contributions equals your basis, and this money is not subject to tax upon distribution. In other words, it is the money you contributed to your IRA or retirement plan on an "after-tax" basis wherein you did not receive a "tax deduction" for the contributions.) If you never spend the money and pass it on to your heirs, they will have to pay taxes on their inherited retirement funds. If you leave your annuity, IRA, 401(k), etc., to a registered charity, it will pass tax-free because charities are tax-exempt.

If you own a Roth annuity in your retirement plan, you will generally pay no tax on your withdrawals, nor will your heirs. Donating a Roth annuity to charity

> **Choosing to annuitize your retirement plan is essentially the same as what someone covered under many State Employees' Retirement System (SERS) is forced to do in their defined-benefit plan. That is, you get regular guaranteed payments, usually for your life and/or your spouse's life, as opposed to having access to a large chunk of money.**

is almost always a bad idea unless you are leaving everything to charity. Whether it is a Roth or a Traditional (pre-tax) annuity makes no difference to them—taxes are a non-issue. It makes a big difference to your heirs.

You may also have contributed to annuities outside of your retirement plan, which the IRS refers to as non-qualified annuities. If you annuitize a non-qualified annuity, it is only partially taxable because some of it is considered a return of your own money, money you already paid taxes on.

Immediate Annuities

While annuities are most commonly associated with retirement, purchasing an immediate annuity that is not part of a retirement plan is also possible. For example, if you receive an inheritance, purchasing an immediate annuity with money that has already been taxed would allow you to receive a steady income stream for the rest of your life and, if you choose, your spouse's life.

I am going to focus on retirement annuities, specifically annuities purchased inside a qualified retirement plan. But much of this discussion will also apply to non-qualified immediate annuities. The primary difference is the income tax treatment of the annuity payments. The payments received from Traditional pre-tax retirement plan annuities are fully taxable, while payments from qualified or non-qualified immediate annuities purchased with after-tax dollars are only partially taxable because the money used to buy the annuity has already been taxed, and each payment represents a return of capital (nontaxable) and interest (taxable).

Longevity Annuities and Qualified Longevity Annuity Contracts (QLACs)

These are another flavor of annuities. Basically, the way they work is you buy one now, but you receive nothing immediately other than a guarantee that if you live long enough, you'll receive monthly or annual benefits. If your greatest fear is that you'll run out of money before you die, these can be a solution. That said, to the best of my knowledge, no client of mine has bought one, and I don't even know anyone who ever bought one.

If your priority is to provide for your child with a disability, longevity annuities are not generally a great choice. The chief benefit of a longevity annuity is to ensure that you'll have a guaranteed source of income in your later years. However, as I've discussed elsewhere in this book, there are many other options that do not force you to commit a substantial chunk of your retirement savings to a future stream of income that you may not live long enough to receive and that will also provide financial security for your child with a disability. But if you're curious, we have an entire chapter in our previous book, *Retire Secure for Professors and TIAA Participants,* dedicated to longevity annuities and QLACs.[1]

Payment Schedules for Annuitization

The terms and duration of the annuity payments depend on what your annuity company offers and the choices you make. Possible options include receiving payments for:

- the remainder of your life
- the remainder of your and your spouse's life
- a fixed number of years
- one of the plans above with an additional provision to extend benefits to your heirs, for example, your children, including a disabled child

There are many variations in payment schedules, including various guarantee periods. For example, one option might be payments for life with 10 years of payments guaranteed. In that case, if you die within 10 years of annuitizing, the remaining payments within the 10-year period are paid to your heirs. Sometimes, you can choose a higher payment while you and your spouse are both alive and a lower payment after your death, such as a 100% benefit initially and a 50% or 60% benefit for the surviving spouse. Since I like to provide for both spouses, I usually prefer a 100% benefit for the surviving spouse, even though it means a lower payment during the owner's lifetime.

Remember, unless you pick a payment option that includes a survivorship or guarantee option, there will be no money left to pass on to your heirs. On the other hand, if you live a long time, you will get a guaranteed income for as long

1   Life insurance can be offered by a member of Lange Life Care, LLC for those interested. These are not legal services. The protection of an attorney-client relationship does not exist with respect to insurance services. There is no solicitation being made for legal services by James Lange nor by Lange Legal Group, LLC.

as you live. So, if you live longer than projected (an actuarial calculation, not a guess based on your health), you are the big winner. It is important to remember that once you choose your annuity payout option, that option is irrevocable. You cannot change the payout later down the road.

Are Annuities the Best Choice for Parents of Disabled Children?

As I'll discuss below, annuities are often a great choice if you are primarily worried about having a guaranteed income stream during your life and the life of your spouse and you don't care about leaving something for your heirs. Unless you select an option that extends benefits to your child, your child will be out of luck after you are gone.

Also, if your child has qualified for SSI or is on Medicaid, naming your child as beneficiary of an annuity could jeopardize their eligibility for those benefits. You can avoid this by creating a Special Needs Trust (SNT) to name as beneficiary of the annuity. If you choose the SNT route, be sure to read Chapter 13, where we discuss the special requirements that such a trust must adhere to so as not to jeopardize your child's eligibility for government benefits. Also, be sure to read Chapter 12, where my colleague Deborah McFadden discusses the many benefits of getting your child qualified for SSI or SSDI and the method she uses to help young adults with disabilities qualify quickly and easily for the Golden Ticket of SSI or SSDI.

Every family is unique, so there may well be circumstances where annuitizing your retirement funds is the best way to ensure the financial security of the entire family. However, I have not recommended this route for my clients who are chiefly concerned about the financial security of their children, and it is not the route that my wife and I have chosen to ensure the financial security of our daughter who has a disability after we are gone. When our number-crunching CPAs run the numbers, we generally find that clients get more—sometimes much, much more—bang for their buck with a series of Roth conversions. Be sure to read Chapter 11 to find out what we have done that will ensure our daughter Erica has the resources she will need to live a full life.

Once you annuitize your funds, there's no going back. It's therefore critical that you understand all of your options and the consequences of your decision before you sign on the dotted line.

Annuitizing for the Life of Your Child with a Disability

There is a reasonable argument that if your child has a disability and a normal or even longer than normal life expectancy, you could consider purchasing an annuity on his or her life. A trustee could also do this after you are gone. Many children with a disability may have a reduced life expectancy, which would argue against purchasing an annuity on their life. But, for a child with normal or above normal life expectancy, the idea is that if costs can reasonably be estimated and the goal is for the child to never run out of money, purchasing a lifetime annuity on the child's life might be a reasonable idea. Just like it could guarantee you a floor income based on your life, it could offer a floor income based on your child's life.

This also might be appropriate when there just isn't enough money to justify a trust's formation and continuing costs. Let's assume the child is on SSDI, so there are no income or asset limitations. Let's also assume the child could take care of his own money. Annuitizing could be a simple way of handling a small estate. For example, if the entire estate is $200,000, the cost of creating and maintaining a Special Needs Trust might be so high that an annuity might become a reasonable choice. I have used annuities for spendthrift children where there wasn't a lot of money and nobody wanted to be the trustee.

That said, I have never seen anyone buy an annuity for the life of their disabled child.

What is the Best Deal?

Which is the better deal? It depends. An ideal candidate for annuitization is a healthy, single person with a long life expectancy who doesn't care about leaving any money behind. If you are married without heirs, a joint life annuity that will last throughout your and your spouse's lifetimes is often the best choice for at least a portion, if not a major portion, of your retirement assets.

Those are both more clear-cut situations. Even forgetting the "break-even analysis" that I will present later, most of the recommendations I have made for married clients who choose to annuitize at least a portion of their retirement assets is to take a 100% joint annuity that guarantees an income stream as long as one person in the couple survives. This is also consistent with what most clients want.

I can't tell you how many times I've had married clients say this—or something similar—to me: "Our first goal is to make sure we are financially comfortable for both of our lives and for the survivor of the two of us to remain comfortable for the rest of their life." A 100% joint life annuity goes a long way toward meeting that goal. Along with receiving their Social Security checks, the annuity enables them to count on a guaranteed amount of income every month.

If circumstances indicate a reduced life expectancy for one partner, a single-life annuity option might make sense. Even then, I would only recommend this if there were sufficient funds to provide for a survivor on the chance that the healthier spouse dies prematurely.

One way to protect a survivor if you take a single-life annuity is to purchase a separate life insurance policy—an approach advocated by many insurance salespeople. Most of the numbers we run, however, have shown that a two-life annuity often gives a better result than a single-life annuity with additional life insurance—assuming that both spouses have a reasonable life expectancy.

While guaranteeing a "base" income seems desirable, few investors want to (or should) annuitize 100% of their retirement assets. Striving for a balance is essential. Annuitizing a portion of a retirement plan ensures that a portion of your money will last at least as long as you do. Annuitizing too much of your retirement money could lead to a lack of flexibility and liquidity that you might later regret.

Most insurance companies will calculate your annuity payment according to a life expectancy table based on your age and sex, their experience with participants who have annuitized, and expected future interest rates. Please note that if you had reason to believe you would not live to your actuarial life expectancy determined by a measurement of the general population that chooses to annuitize, you should not likely annuitize. On the other hand, if you were in excellent health and had significant longevity in your family, you would be more likely to annuitize. Your actual physical condition does not generally enter the insurance company's calculation of your payment. Sometimes, if you prove to the insurance company you have a short life expectancy, they may increase the annuity payment.

This contrasts with the process of buying life insurance. When you buy life insurance, you want the life insurance company to recognize how healthy you are so that they give you the best possible rate for the coverage. With an immediate annuity, you want the life insurance company to project that you have a much-reduced life expectancy. If they don't expect you to live long, the amount you receive in each payment will be higher. It's a question of odds, and you want them in your favor! If you live a long life after annuitizing, preferably well past your actuarial life expectancy, the better it will work out for you and your family—however, they, too, are aware of those parameters.

I do not recommend annuitizing if you have a reduced life expectancy. Usually, the annuity company or retirement plan does not give sufficient weight to the applicant's health for me to recommend an annuity for someone with a dramatically reduced life expectancy. An insurance company may consider these factors, but not to the extent that they give you what I would consider a reasonable increase in payments. If I had a significantly reduced life expectancy and needed funds,

I would likely look at viatical settlement, but that is something we only briefly touch upon in Chapter 26 regarding life insurance.

I think the psychological reassurance that you will never run out of an income is a good thing, even if you don't like the idea that you could have premature deaths and money is lost. Get over it. It is cheap insurance. Don't think like an actuary. Think like an economist.

Inflation Protected Annuities—A Solution to Rising Costs?

As this book is being written, the US has been in an inflationary period. Inflation is the bane of those on a fixed income, which makes annuities less appealing. What happens if costs skyrocket even more in the future, and your annuity payments no longer cover your living expenses? Annuity sellers also offer options that may apply the annual increases to the Consumer Price Increase to future annuity payments, thus hedging against inflation.

The problem with this is that those future increases in payments come at a cost to you. Choosing the inflation-adjusted option results in smaller initial payments— sometimes as much as 25% lower. If your retirement plan offers this option, make sure you carefully analyze the future projected payouts and compare them to the fixed payment option. Depending on your situation, you may actually come out ahead with the fixed option. Beware of the gargantuan expenses of "commercial annuities," which may completely eliminate any advantages from this option.

How Much to Annuitize?

As parents, we want to make sure our children are provided for, especially when there is a child with a disability or chronic illness involved. Assuming you have set in place a financial plan that will provide your child with a disability ample funds to live a great life after you are gone, it may make sense for you to consider your own financial plan and annuitize enough so that when added to your Social Security, the basic needs of shelter, food, and necessities are provided for so you don't need to worry about your financial future. You want to be sure that not only are the needs of your disabled child met, but your needs are also met—as the airlines always reinforce, "you're putting your own oxygen mask on first". An example follows.

Let's say that the guaranteed annual income that would cover you and your spouse's basic necessities is $80,000 (in today's dollars). You and your spouse receive $40,000 and $20,000 in annual Social Security benefits, respectively. But we can only count $40,000 toward your total *guaranteed* annual Social Security benefit (because one spouse will eventually die, and the survivor will then receive the higher of the two Social Security benefit amounts.)

That leaves you and your spouse needing another $40,000 per year, which, for the purposes of this example, you'll get by annuitizing a portion of your retirement plan assets. Assuming you are both 70 years old, you would have to annuitize roughly $600,000 to receive that additional $40,000 annually.

Now, in effect, you and your spouse have income insurance for life, and hopefully, without the gargantuan expenses of the "commercial annuities," which are appropriately looked down on by sophisticated investors. Hopefully, at least one of you lives long enough to break even on where you would have been in cumulative payments if you had left that $600,000 in your retirement plan.

However, Larry Kotlikoff says that's the wrong way to think about it. As Kotlikoff, a professor of economics at Boston University, sees it, you're essentially buying "longevity insurance," which he believes is the best way to avoid running out of money. Larry says, "Don't think like an actuary on this issue. Think like an economist." If you're more worried about not living long enough to break even, that's "thinking like an actuary." But by including longevity insurance in your long-term planning, you're thinking like an economist.[2]

If you die early and don't break even, it won't make any difference to you because you will be dead. Dead people don't have financial problems.

Annuitizing: A Conservative Strategy?

One view holds that annuitizing over a lifetime or joint lifetimes is a practical, conservative strategy because it ensures you will not outlive your money. You lose access to the lump sum of money immediately after you annuitize, and the lifetime-based payments stop after your death, unless you choose a survivorship option or a guaranteed number of years options. But, in either case, the payments will not run out in your lifetime, no matter how long you live.

Annuitizing a large amount of money is sometimes an emotionally challenging choice to make. It feels like you are giving it all away even though you are actually ensuring a secure source of lifetime income. One solution to the fear of annuitizing is to annuitize only a portion of your available funds. Annuitizing a portion of your assets is probably sound for many situations. Jonathan Clements, a great financial writer and defender of the consumer, wrote the following in one of his columns for *The Wall Street Journal* where he quoted me.

----

2   For anyone interested, Larry is also the author of a wonderful book regarding Social Security called *Get What's Yours*. Of course, I still like my book on Social Security where I also cover the synergy between delaying your Social Security and making Roth IRA conversions. Please go to **https://PayTaxesLater.com/Books/** for a free digital copy of my book.

"I often suggest that income-hungry retirees take maybe a quarter of their nest egg and use it to purchase an immediate fixed annuity, thus buying a lifetime stream of income. But if you really want to generate a lot of income and you think you will live to a ripe old age, here is an even better strategy. Buy that immediate annuity—but wait until age 75, so you get a generous income stream based on your shorter life expectancy."

Some people do not like the idea of annuitizing because they are afraid that, if they die early, the money they paid into the account will be lost—it wouldn't matter to them, but it would be bad for any heirs. So be sure to choose a payout method that guarantees that your heirs will receive some of the capital you invested if you die early.

For example, one option would be to choose payments for life with a guaranteed 10-year payout to your heirs if you die prematurely. Sometimes, the annuity contract will specify that a large portion of the original cost will be returned to the family if the owner dies early. Asking for these types of guarantees is common, but they come at a cost—the amount you receive monthly will be reduced. Alternatively, you might want to consider forgoing the extra expense of an annuity guarantee feature in exchange for a higher monthly income. My personal preference is to keep it simple: when you annuitize your retirement accumulations, make it for your life or the lives of both you and your spouse.

The common advice among financial planners and attorneys is, "Don't sell a client an immediate annuity without a guaranteed feature because if the client dies early, the heirs might sue you or at least give you plenty of grief." From a financial planner or insurance agent's viewpoint, that is probably good advice. For the client, however, it may not be the best advice.

One idea I have expressed before is to annuitize enough so that, in combination with Social Security, your "base expenses" like shelter, food, and transportation are covered no matter what the market does.

> **If you die early and don't break even, it won't make any difference to you because you will be dead. Dead people don't have financial problems.**

RMD If Still Working Past Age 72

Jim and Mary Davies are both age 67 and plan on working until age 70 when they will also claim their Social Security benefits. They will receive an estimated combined $64,000 in annual payments from Social Security. They have a daughter Mandy, age 43, who has a disability and is currently receiving SSI. When the Davies begin taking Social Security, Mandy will also receive a bump in benefits and an end to means-testing if she switches from SSI to SSDI. Because they took to heart the ideas covered later in this book, they have $1,000,000 saved in Roth IRA accounts, which they are reserving for Mandy's needs. They also have $1,000,000 in Traditional IRAs and 401(k)s through their employers. According to the year of their births, they will need to start taking RMDs from their Traditional retirement accounts at age 73.

Their basic expenses are $85,000 per year. Mary, who worked as an economist, wants to run the numbers and see if annuitizing part of their Traditional accounts would make financial sense. They would like to annuitize enough of their Traditional retirement accounts to cover the shortfall so that they have no worries about keeping a roof over their head, food on the table, and all their bills paid. Any extra income from their retirement distributions will be earmarked for travel or will be saved for future needs. Whatever is left in their Traditional accounts will be inherited by Mandy.

One option—among many—they are considering is to each annuitize $150,000 of their balances, beginning at age 70, and with full benefits paid to the survivor upon the death of the first spouse. The example below shows what would happen if they both invested $150,000 in a fixed annuity:

	Monthly Payment	Paid Annually
Fixed payments for Jim	$ 998	$12,168*
Fixed payments for Mary	$ 998	$12,168*
Combined payments	$1,996	$24,336

*Calculated with an online annuity calculator.

They are considering retiring before age 73 when they must start taking Required Minimum Distributions from their retirement assets, so for the first few years of their retirement, their income will consist of their Social Security benefit and their annuity income. Then, at age 73, they will begin taking their RMDs. The portion of their retirement accounts that they annuitize is not included in the calculation of their RMDs.

The table below shows that by annuitizing $300,000 of their retirement account balances, Jim and Mary will have adequate funds for the rest of their lives. The first column shows the income generated by the remaining $700,000 in their retirement accounts, assuming a 6% rate of return. Starting at age 73, they will begin taking their RMDs, based on a percentage that comes from IRS life expectancy tables and increases each year, gradually depleting their Traditional account balances. If they both live to age 95, their RMD will be $28,127. If we assume that the Social Security benefits will include an estimated annual cost-of-living-adjustment of 3.0% and that annual expenses will increase by 3.5% with inflation, even at age 90, the Davies' income will still exceed their expenses.

AGE	RMD	ANNUITY	SSA INCOME	TOTAL INCOME	EXPENSES	SAVINGS	TOTAL ANNUITY PAID
70	$-	$24,336	$64,000	$88,336	$(85,000)	$3,336	$24,336
71	$-	$24,336	$65,920	$90,256	$(87,975)	$5,617	$48,672
72	$-	$24,336	$67,898	$92,234	$(91,054)	$6,796	$73,008
73	$29,680	$24,336	$69,935	$123,951	$(94,241)	$36,506	$97,344
74	$32,695	$24,336	$72,033	$129,063	$(97,539)	$68,030	$121,680
75	$34,718	$24,336	$74,194	$133,247	$(100,953)	$100,323	$146,016
80	$38,324	$24,336	$86,011	$155,620	$(119,901)	$258,650	$267,696
85	$36,613	$24,336	$99,710	$168,140	$(142,405)	$371,843	$389,376
90	$33,465	$24,336	$115,591	$181,391	$(169,132)	$422,792	$511,056
95	$28,127	$24,336	$134,002	$194,141	$(200,876)	$390,464	$632,736

The column labeled **Savings** shows the *cumulative* excess that the Davies will have. This shows they will have a nice cushion that can be used to fund travel and entertainment and to spend on the causes they care most about. The final column shows the cumulative annuity payments they receive. By age 85, they will break even on the amount they annuitized and will have received back their initial annuity investment in benefits. Because they both chose full survivor benefits, this income stream will continue as long as at least one remains alive. If at least one of them lives to age 95, the Davies will receive a 211% return on their investment of $300,000 in their annuities.

So, how do they lose with this strategy? They both die young. But, again, to quote Larry Kotlikoff, dead people don't have financial problems. Think like an economist, not like an actuary.

Now, to be fair, I picked the facts and made close to the ideal couple to annuitize. The big thing with the Davies is they also have Roth IRA accounts with substantial balances, which will be inherited by their daughter Mandy. I also said they were in excellent health which would favor longer life expectancies. In the real world, there will likely be more heirs, competing demands, the income from annuitizing might come too soon, or a myriad of other problems. But it makes sense for more parents to consider utilizing annuities as an income strategy than currently do so.

Based on this very simple projection, the Davies are reassured that it appears they will not outlive their assets and that they will have an ample excess of funds that they can use for travel and to live perhaps a bit better than they do now. This example, of course, is a simplification and ignores their other financial assets— which, with an economist in the family—they certainly have in abundance. Including all their other assets would make this too complicated. This projection aimed to see if annuitizing a portion of their Traditional retirement accounts combined with Social Security would generate enough income for them to live on without dipping into their other investments, especially their Roth accounts.

It also ignores the impact of income taxes. Still, as a first estimate of their finances, this scenario puts their minds at ease that they will have plenty of money to fund their retirement without dipping into the accounts they have earmarked for Mandy after they are gone.

Annuitizing Retirement Accumulations

Retired parents must take RMDs from their retirement plans once they reach age 73, or their required beginning age under current law. Instead of taking these payments based on the annual value and life expectancy factors, they can choose to annuitize the balance. This way, they no longer must worry about managing the money and what happens if the balance dwindles or becomes depleted. The risk and responsibility are transferred to the insurance company that provides the annuity. In many situations, annuitizing at least a portion of the retirement assets is a good choice. In the late 1990s, and even more lately, when the market was up and you could smell confidence in the air, annuitizing was frowned upon.

If you are reading this book, you have likely lived through some turbulent financial times. There is a lot to be afraid of these days: Heightened fears of global warming, economic disruption, economic downturns, the recent Russian assault on Ukraine, the enormous problems in the U.S. political system, the failure of major financial institutions, terrorism, federal deficits, stock market downturns, inflation, and world pandemics have increased the attractiveness of a steady guaranteed income. Many people want to ensure they have financial security for themselves and their spouse for the rest of their lives, no matter what happens to the market or the economy.

In many real-life situations, annuitizing a portion of your retirement holdings is consistent with a desire for security. It provides a stable income that, combined with Social Security, will offer a minimum base of income and a sense of financial security not available with other strategies.

Timing of Annuitizing

The income you receive from annuitizing a certain amount of money is mainly determined by two factors: your age (or the age of you and your spouse, assuming you pick a two-life annuity) and the current interest rate.

The higher the interest rate and the older you are, the higher the annuity payment will be. As we go to press, interest rates, which had been historically low, have risen quickly in response to inflation. So now might be a good time to annuitize, but I am not a market timer. No one knows if interest rates will remain high, or if they will go even higher, or if they will plummet suddenly.

Also, I don't like the idea of annuitizing early in your retirement because, frankly, it is much harder to predict your needs and expenses. Going in, you might think you want to spend conservatively for the rest of your life and live where you are now. Maybe later, your daughter has a child and moves to Texas or somewhere you never even considered purchasing a second home. Your idea of conservative spending is out the window as you find yourself supporting two houses and helping your children with their expenses or the expenses of your grandchildren.

I have one client with two daughters, both of whom had children. One child moved to a warm, sunny Southern state and the other to a colder state in the North. Though my clients were native Pittsburghers and thought they would spend the rest of their lives in their Pittsburgh house, they now support two houses, and neither home is in Pittsburgh. They bought houses in the same cities as both of their children and are enjoying the snowbird life. They spend roughly six months with each child and their families. This lifestyle also allows an "endless summer."

Please note that even though I continue to work full-time, my wife and I spend about half our time in Tucson and the other half in Pittsburgh. So, we are supporting two households, three if you include my daughter, and having financial flexibility is important.

My point here is that if you are in the early stages of retirement, down the road, you might end up in a situation that you could never have anticipated today. Since annuitizing can't be undone after you make that election, I would prefer you

In many real-life situations, annuitizing a portion of your retirement holdings is consistent with a desire for security. It can provide a stable income that, combined with Social Security, will offer a minimum base of income and a sense of financial security not available with other strategies.

have a better handle on what your retirement years will look like before making an irrevocable decision.

Annuitizing Worked Out Well for Many Older Investors

Annuitizing worked out well for many of my older clients, many of whom have since passed, who retired in the 1980s or before and were forced to annuitize most of holdings. (They may also have been able to take some taxable withdrawals.)

I am particularly familiar with professors who had to annuitize because one of them was my mom. When she retired from her job as a professor of journalism (back then in her department, retirement was mandatory at age 70), she had to annuitize her retirement plan accumulations. My dad predeceased her, so I recommended taking out a one-life annuity without a guaranteed number of years. Since I preferred she receive more income, I told her to forget the survivorship feature and just get the most possible for herself. Against my advice, she chose an annuity with a survivorship feature.

If she died within 10 years of her retirement, my brothers and I would have received some income until she would have turned 80. But she died at age 95. The reduced payment she received on the survivorship guarantee for her children was wasted, but she took great delight in knowing that the insurance company still lost a bundle of money on her. I don't know the formula that the retirement plan used to calculate the amount they paid for the monthly benefit of annuitizing. But they certainly didn't assume she would live till age 95. But whatever it was, they had to pay her for many more years than they likely expected. Between her Social Security, her annuity payment, and the payment that I made to her for the purchase of the family home where I live now, she had a great income for her retirement years, though she never had a lot of money.

In case you are wondering, I bought "the family homestead," where I was born and grew up when my wife and I were looking for our first house. It is a big old house in Squirrel Hill, a neighborhood within walking distance of Carnegie Mellon

> **I am particularly familiar with professors who had to annuitize because one of them was my mom.**

University (CMU) and the University of Pittsburgh (Pitt). Many professors live in Squirrel Hill and enjoy a walking or bicycle commute to CMU or Pitt. I could walk or bike to work also, but since I am usually running late and tend to work well into the night—as with writing this book—I drive.

Annuitizing: A Risky Strategy?

Another view of annuitizing is that it is not a conservative strategy but rather a gamble. Since most annuities are based on actuarial life expectancy, you are gambling that you will outlive your actuarial life expectancy, and the insurance company providing the annuity is gambling that you will not. (To quickly calculate your actuarial life expectancy, visit: **https://www.ssa.gov/OACT/population/longevity.html**.)

But the tables don't consider information you know about your own health and the longevity in your family. The insurance companies also don't take those factors into account—but *you* should.

- If you have reason to believe that you will not survive your actuarial life expectancy, then annuitizing is probably a mistake.

- If you think, however, that you and your spouse are going to substantially outlive your actuarial life expectancy and the life expectancy of people who have chosen to annuitize, then annuitizing on a two-life basis, that is the payment will continue for your and your spouse's life, which is longer, will provide both of you an assured income stream for a long life.

- If you have a terminal illness and your spouse has a long life expectancy, consider having your spouse purchase an immediate annuity on their life only. If you do that, please ensure the spouse with the reduced life expectancy will still be financially okay if you die. If not, consider term life insurance for the healthier spouse.

Although annuitizing will provide fixed monthly amounts for a lifetime, there are other risks involved that make even this conservative strategy a gamble. One risk is that the issuing insurance company will go bankrupt and be unable to meet its obligations to pay the annuity. State governments provide guarantee funds to protect consumers against insurer insolvency, but many such funds are stretched to the maximum.

You can minimize your risk by choosing insurance and annuity companies with Standard & Poor's quality ratings of at least AA or preferably AAA, even if it means that the interest rate offered to you is not as high as through a lesser-rated insurance company.

Another risk involves the effect of inflation on fixed annuity payments. If the payout is the same amount every month, the long-term effects of inflation can lead to the annuity income becoming inadequate to meet growing expenses in later years. As I mentioned above, many insurance companies offer inflation-protected options, but at a cost. The cost is starting payments that may be significantly lower than the fixed option.

In theory, at least in the early years, the annuity payment will be somewhat higher than RMDs since it reflects a return of principal. So, if you do not need the money, annuitizing retirement plan assets can needlessly accelerate income taxes on your retirement accumulations.

Also, suppose you incur unexpected expenses and need more than your monthly annuity payment amount but have no other savings. In that case, you are just plain out of luck unless you can borrow from a bank or other lending institution. That is the fundamental risk of annuities. If you are taking RMDs from a retirement plan, you can always eat into the principal for a larger distribution if you need it.

Finally, let me end this chapter by reiterating the excellent advice Larry Kotlikoff gave me regarding when to take Social Security because it also applies to annuitizing. "If you die young, you are dead and dead people don't have financial problems. The legitimate financial fear is not dying young but outliving your money." Annuitizing addresses this legitimate fear. For most retirees, Larry is a fan of annuitizing at least some of your accumulations, as are Jane Bryant Quinn, a popular financial writer, now retired, known as a champion for consumers, and Jonathan Clements, former personal finance writer for *The Wall Street Journal*.

I have worked with a number of clients who had already made all of the critical decisions regarding annuitizing their retirement assets prior to becoming clients or who, despite already being clients, made those decisions without seeking input and recommendations from our accounting firm. For some of those clients, their decisions regarding whether to annuitize, how much to annuitize, and which options they ultimately selected worked out well for them.

However, I have also seen my fair share of financially disadvantageous consequences befall investors who made bad decisions about the timing, amount, or retirement plan options. I have also seen investors whose bad choices weren't disastrous but gave up a great opportunity they couldn't undo.

And I have seen people in situations similar to the Davies who decided not to annuitize *any* portion of their retirement assets, which unnecessarily restricted their disposable income during retirement. Obviously, consulting our, or any, team of experts doesn't guarantee perfect results. But, when consulted, we do use our experience, subject-matter expertise, and nuanced understanding of the complexities of each client's financial situation and goals to ensure they are aware of all the options available to them and what the potential long-term financial pros and cons of each option are. To learn more about what we do for our clients and how to take the first step towards working with us, read the section at the back of the book titled *When your Child has a Disability...Save More, Have More, and Leave More to Your Child in a Tax-Advantaged Manner that Preserves Government Benefits! The Lange Edge: A Truly Integrated Long-Term Financial Masterplan for Parents Who Want to Ensure That Their Child Is Financially Secure for Life—Even After Mom and Dad Are Gone.*

KEY IDEAS

- Annuitizing a portion of your retirement accumulations is sometimes a good strategy to ensure that you never run out of money.

  Take time to understand *all* of your options *before* you commit to something you can't undo.

- Usually, since you will certainly want to leave money behind, you don't want to annuitize too much.

- There are arguments for purchasing an annuity for the life of your child, but I have never seen it done in practice.

9

What Happens to Your IRA When You Die? Contrasting the Old Regulations and When the Beneficiary has Special Needs and the New Rules within the SECURE Act

"Certain things they should stay the way they are.
You ought to be able to stick them in one of those big glass cases
and just leave them alone."

—J.D. Salinger,
The Catcher in the Rye

The following information is critical for parents of children with disabilities. Put simply, if you don't make proactive plans for your IRA and retirement plans, your estate will take a huge unnecessary tax hit. This is especially true if your retirement plans are the largest asset in your estate.

Not understanding how the change in the law will affect your beneficiaries and not taking proactive measures to protect yourself and your family could mean a difference of hundreds of thousands of dollars.

What Hasn't Changed: The Basic Transfer of Retirement Accounts After the Death of the First Spouse

Let's start with a simple case. You are married, and if your IRA and/or retirement beneficiary form is completed correctly (it often isn't) and there is appropriate estate administration after your death (there often isn't), your IRA or retirement account accumulations will likely pass to your spouse as the primary beneficiary. Your surviving spouse can transfer your retirement account assets into their own IRA using a technique called a spousal rollover, but it is better to make the transfer using a similar, but safer, process called a trustee-to-trustee transfer.

The trustee-to-trustee transfer electronically moves the funds from your IRA or retirement account directly to your surviving spouse's IRA, avoiding the potential mix-up and withholding tax problems caused by cutting a check. This trustee-to-trustee transfer, assuming it is done correctly, eliminates the possibility

> Your surviving spouse can transfer your retirement
> account assets into their own IRA using a technique
> called a spousal rollover, but it is better to make the
> transfer using a similar, but safer, process called a
> trustee-to-trustee transfer.

of horrendous tax consequences caused by human error. This was true before the SECURE Act, and it is still true.

If you were taking Required Minimum Distributions (RMDs) from your IRA or 401(k) account before your death and your spouse is your beneficiary and roughly your age, he/she must continue to take RMDs from the IRA (which is now his/hers after the trustee-to-trustee transfer). His/her RMDs will be similar to those you received because they will also be based on a joint life expectancy. This time, though, it's the joint life expectancy of your spouse and the life expectancy of someone deemed ten years or younger that determines his/her RMD. There are also special rules that apply to spouses who are more than ten years younger than their spouse. Please see Chapter 6 for more information on RMDs while you are still alive.

Required Minimum Distribution of the Inherited IRA Under the Old Law (Which is the Same for A Child with a Disability)

If you have a child with a disability, and your child meets the requirements to qualify as an eligible designated beneficiary, the old law will still apply to the IRAs and retirement accounts your child inherits. We'll cover this in more detail in Chapter 10. If your child—or other beneficiary—qualifies under one of the exceptions, this section will demonstrate the tremendous tax savings that can result from savvy planning.

Under the old law (for deaths prior to 2020) and depending on your situation, it was probably to your spouse's and your family's advantage to continue to defer the taxes and take only the RMDs from the IRA for as long as possible. Pay taxes later. The benefits of doing so are illustrated in Chapter 1, where we show the advantage of keeping the money in the IRA while spending after-tax money first. But what happens after both spouses are gone, or you leave at least a portion of your IRA to a non-spouse beneficiary, most likely your child or children? Or, what happens if one spouse "disclaims" to the children and/or the children disclaim to the grandchildren? (We will explore disclaimers more in Chapter 15.) This is

where the intense pain of the SECURE Act should strike terror in the hearts of most parents.

Under the old law, if your beneficiary were a child, grandchild, or anyone other than your spouse, they had the option to "stretch" distributions from the Inherited IRA over *their* lifetimes. (An IRA that is inherited by a non-spouse beneficiary becomes a special asset called an Inherited IRA.) The RMD for the Inherited IRA was calculated by dividing the balance in the Inherited IRA as of December 31st of the previous year by the beneficiary's life expectancy found in IRS Publication 590B. Even though they were required to begin taking taxable distributions from the Inherited Traditional IRA the year after their parents or grandparents died (the beneficiary of an Inherited IRA was not permitted to defer distributions until age 70½ as the original owner was), the RMDs of the Inherited IRA were much smaller than the RMD of the original IRA owner because of the child's/grandchild's much longer life expectancy. These rules allowed your Inherited Traditional IRA to continue to grow tax-deferred *for a very long time*. Don't pay taxes now. Pay taxes later. And even after you're dead, we still want your beneficiaries to pay taxes later too.

Required Minimum Distribution of the Inherited IRA Under the SECURE Act

Inherited Traditional IRA (Non-Spouse Beneficiary)

Under the SECURE Act, an Inherited Traditional IRA, subject to exceptions, must be fully distributed and taxed by December 31st of the year that includes the tenth anniversary of the IRA owner's date of death. For shorthand, we will typically refer to this date as ten years after the IRA owner's death. This new rapid distribution schedule causes a massive income tax acceleration and many lost years of income-tax-deferred growth compared to the pre-SECURE Act law.

As I'll cover in more detail later in the next chapter, one of the important exceptions to the 10-year rule applies to beneficiaries with a disability. If your child with a disability inherits your IRA and meets certain other IRS requirements, your child will be allowed to stretch those IRA distributions over their lifetime. And, as I'll describe more fully in Chapter 11, this exception for children with disabilities is a key component of how my wife and I are ensuring that our daughter will live a financially secure life after we are gone.

According to Proposed Regulations released by the IRS in February 2022, beneficiaries who do not qualify for one of the exceptions to the 10-year rule are split into two groups, depending on whether the original account owner was already taking distributions or not. If the account owner was 72 or older at the time of their death and had begun taking distributions, the regulations require beneficiaries to take *annual* distributions for nine years in addition to completely emptying the account within ten years after the death of the IRA owner. The proposed regulations state the annual distributions are to be made "at least as rapidly" as the account owner was taking them before he died.

What does "at least as rapidly" mean? It means that distributions for the first nine years will be made as if the original account owner were still receiving them. For example, suppose the decedent died at age 75 and had been using the IRS Table III for calculating distributions. That means that the following year, when the beneficiary needs to take the first distribution, she would divide the account balance by 23.7, which would be the factor for a 76-year-old account owner, to get the minimum amount of the first distribution. The beneficiary could also take a larger distribution, maybe one-tenth of the balance, but he would need to take a distribution of at least 1/23.7 of the account balance.

There is confusion surrounding the timing of annual RMDs in years 1 through 9. While the IRS proposed regulations require successor beneficiaries to continue taking RMDs if the original beneficiary was already taking them, the IRS guidance has provided transitional relief for these RMDs until 2024 when distributions will be required.

If the retirement account owner dies before she starts taking distributions, the beneficiary does not need to take annual distributions but must empty the account completely by the end of the tenth year.

Granted, there are some additional tax-planning opportunities for the beneficiary of the Inherited IRA, especially if the beneficiary is only subject to the 10-year rule and does not need to take annual distributions or has been provided with transitional relief through 2024. For example, if the beneficiary of the Inherited IRA is in a lower tax bracket but expects to be in a much higher tax bracket soon, it would likely make sense to make some taxable distributions of the Inherited IRA while the beneficiary is in a lower tax bracket even before he is required to do so. Depending on circumstances and tax bracket, the beneficiary of the IRA owner dying before age 73 may choose to take distributions roughly equally over the ten-year period to smooth out the income taxes paid on the distributions.

For beneficiaries subject to the annual distribution requirement and the 10-year rule, those annual distributions can serve as a floor for planning the most tax-efficient method for emptying the account within ten years. As above, it may make sense to make larger distributions in years when the beneficiary is in a lower tax bracket, and smaller ones when the beneficiary's tax bracket increases. Or it may make sense for the beneficiary to take roughly equal distributions over ten years, provided those annual distributions are greater than his RMDs.

Inherited Roth IRA (Non-Spouse Beneficiary)

In the case of an Inherited *Roth* IRA, the distributions to the beneficiary are not taxable because the original Roth IRA owner paid the taxes. Inherited Roth IRAs continue to grow income-tax-free. Under the old law, the Roth IRA beneficiary could "stretch" the tax-free distributions over his or her life expectancy, similar to an Inherited Traditional IRA.

Under the SECURE Act, an Inherited Roth IRA, subject to exceptions, must be fully distributed within ten years of the original owner's death. This doesn't cause a massive income tax acceleration, but it does mean the beneficiary is losing many years of income-tax-free growth that were available to him under the old law. This also means ten years after the death of the Roth IRA owner, future dividends, interest, or realized capital gains are subject to income tax, just like a regular taxable investment.

While you might not think that the old mechanism for stretching an IRA was all that important, those rules allowed owners of IRAs and other retirement plans to create tax-deferred and tax-free dynasties that ultimately provided lifetime incomes in the millions of dollars to their children and grandchildren. Even with more modest Inherited IRAs and Roth IRAs, it allowed children of IRA owners to have a lifetime of income that was a valuable supplement to their own income. Now it will be much harder to leave that kind of legacy to your heirs through your retirement accounts.

In 2019, time took its toll, and sadly, a number of our clients died. Some of the deceased IRA owners had more than $2,000,000 in IRAs, and some had substantial Roth IRAs. Children of clients who died in 2019 had enormous opportunities for income tax deferral. Children of clients who died in 2019 with Roth IRAs had enormous opportunities for tax-free distribution deferral.

We had a death in the last few days of 2019 of a tax-savvy client who we all liked, and while we were genuinely sad, we had the same thought—much better that the client died before year-end than after. Because he died before the effective date of the SECURE Act (January 1, 2020), his children were ultimately left in a much better position because they could "stretch" both the Inherited IRA and Roth IRA over their lifetime instead of being forced to withdraw the entire balance within ten years of his death. Going forward, children will have fewer opportunities to maximize the Inherited IRA you leave them.

One lesson from reading these rules is that the status quo is likely to cause massive income tax acceleration of Inherited IRAs, so consider methods to reduce the amount of money you leave to your non-spousal heirs through IRAs.

Demonstration of RMDs With Old Law or a Qualifying Beneficiary

Figure 9.1 below demonstrates the advantage of inheriting an IRA under the old law or if the beneficiary is an eligible designated beneficiary (EDB). (See Chapter 10). It assumes the beneficiary elects only to take RMDs from the Inherited IRA. As shown in the chart below, the first year is the RMD of the IRA owner, who died at age 80. His 45-year-old beneficiary must take an RMD from the Inherited IRA the year after the owner's death when she is 46. We skipped some middle years and picked up towards the end of the beneficiary's life to save space. Look at the bottom line…

Under the old law, the total distributions to the beneficiary of this $1M Inherited IRA could have been $2,433,471.

What Happens to Your IRA When You Die Now Under the SECURE Act?

With the new 10-year rule for distributing an Inherited IRA, one class of beneficiaries (e.g., beneficiaries of the original owner who had not started taking distributions) could take zero distributions for the first nine years after the death of the parent or grandparent. Still, they would have to take out the entire amount in the tenth year. Depending on the amount of the Inherited IRA, that would likely push the beneficiary to a higher income tax bracket. Or, if the IRA owner was already taking distributions before they died, the beneficiary will be required to take annual distributions "at least as rapidly" as the account owner was receiving

Figure 9.1

Old Law for IRA Distributions

YEAR	AGE	INHERITED IRA BALANCE	ANNUAL DISTRIBUTIONS	TOTAL DISTRIBUTED
2020	*80*	*$ 1,000,000*		
2021	46	$ 1,063,566	$ 26,132	$ 26,132
2022	47	$ 1,074,284	$ 27,060	$ 53,192
2023	48	$ 1,084,468	$ 28,022	$ 81,214
2024	49	$ 1,094,066	$ 29,020	$ 110,234
2025	50	$ 1,103,025	$ 30,055	$ 140,289
2026	51	$ 1,111,287	$ 31,128	$ 171,417
2027	52	$ 1,118,791	$ 32,242	$ 203,659
2057	82	$ 471,136	$ 100,242	$ 1,994,933
2058	83	$ 390,216	$ 105,464	$ 2,100,397
2059	84	$ 301,514	$ 111,672	$ 2,212,069
2060	85	$ 203,815	$ 119,891	$ 2,331,960
2061	86	$ 94,870	$ 101,511	$ 2,433,471
2062	87	—	—	**$ 2,433,471**

Detailed assumptions can be found in the Appendix.

distributions. As noted earlier, the IRS has provided transitional relief until 2024 to take the annual distributions. To make things simple for this example, I treated the distributions to come out more evenly. Look at the bottom line…

Though it isn't exactly an apple-to-apple comparison because I am not properly accounting for the time value of money, please note that in the example above, the beneficiary inheriting under the old law or as an EDB received $1,161,876 more in distributions from a million-dollar Inherited IRA than the beneficiary under the new law.

Please note that in the figure above, I have assumed the beneficiary chose to take the distributions evenly over ten years. In reality, the best time to take a taxable withdrawal from a Traditional Inherited IRA would be when your beneficiary is in their lowest tax bracket, as long as it is within ten years of the IRA owner's death.

Figure 9.2

IRA Distributed Under the SECURE Act*

YEAR	AGE	INHERITED IRA BALANCE	ANNUAL DISTRIBUTIONS	TOTAL DISTRIBUTED
2020	*80*	*$ 1,000,000*		
2021	46	$ 927,500	$ 142,500	$ 142,500
2022	47	$ 849,925	$ 142,500	$ 285,000
2023	48	$ 766,920	$ 142,500	$ 427,500
2024	49	$ 678,104	$ 142,500	$ 570,000
2025	50	$ 583,071	$ 142,500	$ 712,500
2026	51	$ 481,386	$ 142,500	$ 855,000
2027	52	$ 372,583	$ 142,500	$ 997,500
2028	53	$ 256,164	$ 142,500	$ 1,140,000
2029	54	$ 131,595	$ 131,595	$ 1,271,595
2030	55	—	—	**$ 1,271,595**

*Detailed assumptions can be found in the Appendix.

Planning for the Inherited Roth IRA

A beneficiary of an Inherited Roth IRA should have a completely different distribution strategy than the beneficiary of an Inherited Traditional IRA. Unless they meet one of the exceptions to the ten-year rule (which I discuss in Chapter 10), the entire balance of an Inherited Roth IRA will also need to be withdrawn within ten years of the original owner's death. If the beneficiary of a Roth IRA doesn't need the money currently, he should just let the Inherited Roth grow income-tax-free for ten years after the death of the original Roth IRA owner.

To oversimplify, if the beneficiary inherited $1,000,000 in a Roth IRA and the money was invested at 7%, he would have a $2,000,000 account after ten years. Again, the distributions from that account are not taxable, but dividends, interest, and realized capital gains would be taxable for earnings after the 10-year period. At that point, the money in the Inherited Roth IRA becomes a plain after-tax brokerage account.

The new law governing post-death RMDs for most non-spouse beneficiaries is not at all advantageous—in fact, it is the opposite.

> **... the beneficiary inheriting under the old law or as an EDB received $1,161,876 more in distributions from a million-dollar Inherited IRA than the beneficiary under the new law.**

Unless you take proactive measures, a massive income tax acceleration, which I have spent much of my career trying to help people avoid, is precisely what this law accomplishes. If you have a substantial IRA or 401(k) account, the effect on your heirs will be devastating—unless you make significant changes to your retirement and estate plan. Roth IRA conversions are one important defense against the SECURE Act.

But, if you are an EDB, taking the minimum distribution of the Inherited Roth IRA over your lifetime is usually the best strategy.

Planning for the Small Stretch that Survived is Still Critical

At this point, let me also add this cautionary note. Even with its diminished value, *taking full advantage of the 10-year limited stretch is still important.* Unfortunately, the "stretch IRA" is more often botched than done correctly. If the beneficiary meets one of the exceptions to the SECURE Act, taking advantage of the stretch IRA is even more critical.

Someone, whether the attorney, advisor, CPA, or client, usually makes a mistake that destroys the stretch IRA, causing a major tax acceleration for the beneficiary. For example, if Dad dies leaving his IRA to Junior and the advisor unwittingly titles Junior's Inherited IRA as "Junior, IRA," the ability to stretch the Inherited IRA would likely be reduced from a ten-year stretch to a five-year stretch. Consequently, Junior suffers a significant tax acceleration. The correct name for the account should be something like "Inherited IRA of Dad for the Benefit of Junior." If you don't have the magic language in the new account title or don't do exactly as you should in many other ways, your heirs will be taxed—literally and figuratively.

To realize the "stretch IRA," however limited, you need appropriate estate planning *and* administration after the IRA owner's death. This was true under the old law and remains true with the new.

Please note there are special "stretch" opportunities for minors, beneficiaries with disabilities or chronic illnesses, and beneficiaries who are ten or fewer years younger than the owner, which I will cover in Chapters 10 and 11.

What if the Beneficiary of the IRA or Roth IRA is a Trust?

If the end beneficiary is a trust, it must meet certain technical requirements to be deemed a designated beneficiary and receive "stretch IRA" status. We strongly encourage you to consult with a knowledgeable estate planning attorney in this area for the proper guidance. Otherwise, the trust may suffer enormous income-tax acceleration. In the case of an Inherited Roth IRA, it could cause a needless acceleration of tax-free distributions. In addition, if the beneficiary of the trust has special needs, then that trust must also be drafted in a manner that will protect government benefits.

Please note that many attorneys, banks, and even CPAs are touting the benefits of "IRA Trusts." They typically name the bank or financial institution as the trustee. I generally prefer to name a family member as trustee; that way, you can achieve the same tax result but still have the advantage of a family member as trustee. The benefits of having a family member as a trustee or executor are keeping control in the family and usually lower fees. On the other hand, sometimes there are no good choices for the trustee in the family or acquaintances, and you must look to some type of corporate trustee.

Remember that there are critical exceptions to the 10-year rule for beneficiaries with chronic illnesses or disabilities. For more information about those exceptions, please see Chapters 10 and 11. A special needs trust is often the best way to leave money to a beneficiary with a disability or chronic illness. An essential goal of a special needs trust is to provide money to the beneficiary in a way that does not interfere with any government benefit(s) the beneficiary might be receiving or may receive in the future. In Chapter 13, my colleague Julieanne Steinbacher delves into the many benefits of establishing a special needs trust for your child with a disability.

Drafting a special needs trust to name as the beneficiary of your IRA requires special language to protect the beneficiary's government benefit and minimize income-tax implications. When drafting a trust for a beneficiary with a disability or chronic illness, your attorney must understand the consequential language that allows beneficiaries to (1) continue to qualify for government benefits and (2) qualify as a designated beneficiary to the pre-2020 lifetime stretch for the trust. Please see Chapter 13 if you have a beneficiary with a disability or chronic illness.

Another common situation is naming minor children as beneficiaries of a trust. As I'll discuss in more detail in the next chapter under *Exceptions to the SECURE Act*, minor children of a deceased IRA owner are only *partially* exempt from the income tax acceleration rules. Under current law, a minor child (or a trust for a minor child) may defer distributions of the Inherited IRA or Roth IRA until they reach the age of majority at age 21. At that point, the 10-year clock starts ticking. Therefore, if a 10-year-old inherits an IRA from a deceased parent, they could have 21 years of income-tax deferral.

So, it is crucial that the trust be drafted appropriately.

Accumulation Trusts vs. Conduit Trusts and the Potential Need to Redraft Your Trusts

Accumulation trusts are typically permitted to accumulate income. This type of trust might be appropriate if the income from the trust exceeds the needs of the beneficiary, and the trustee doesn't want to give the beneficiary more money than he or she currently needs (or the owner of the IRA wanted to keep total control over the money from the grave)! So, while the trust does not have to pay out all the RMDs to the beneficiaries, the minimum distribution amounts that are not distributed to the beneficiary will be taxed within the trust at trust tax rates that are generally significantly higher than individual tax rates.

An accumulation trust still falls within the 10-year income-tax acceleration requirement of the SECURE Act. The advantage of an accumulation trust after the SECURE Act is that the trustee will have more discretion over when and how the income and principal are distributed during the 10-year term following the IRA owner's death and after. For instance, if a beneficiary is in college and has little or no income, the trustee may want to distribute income before the beneficiary graduates from school and gets a job that will put them in a higher tax bracket.

In contrast, a conduit trust requires the trustee to distribute all income from the trust. In the example of the college student who might do better to receive money before graduation, the trustee of a conduit trust has less control over the timing of the payout. If a conduit trust is named a beneficiary of the IRA, all the RMDs from the Inherited IRA must be paid to the trust and then to the beneficiaries who will pay tax at their income tax rate (avoiding the higher taxes on undistributed RMDs). Many conduit trusts with an IRA as the underlying asset have been drafted specifically to avoid the high income-tax rates on undistributed RMDs that would be triggered if the money was just left in the trust.

However, after the SECURE Act, with the loss of the lifetime stretch, beneficiary designations of IRAs and retirement plans that have conduit trusts as the beneficiary must be re-examined and probably changed to accumulation trusts. Even though conduit trusts avoid high trust tax rates, any control the IRA owner was trying to exert will be moot both during and after the ten years in which the balance must be distributed. If your current trust is a conduit-type trust, that alone might be a good reason to review your wills, trusts, and the beneficiary designations of your IRAs and retirement plans with a knowledgeable estate planning attorney.

The trustee may want to keep money in the trust for the same reasons that the trust was set up in the first place. That might include protecting the money from a spendthrift beneficiary, creditor protection, preserving a government benefit, protecting a beneficiary from a no-good spouse, or, for that matter, a future ex-spouse. (By that, I mean your current son or daughter-in-law who is likely to become an ex-son- or daughter-in-law.) In such cases, a trustee might not want to distribute the remaining balance of the trust within ten years of the IRA owner's death. If you want to give the trustee options for more control, and if your current trust is a conduit type trust, that alone might be a good reason to review your wills and trusts and beneficiary designations of your IRAs and retirement plans and possibly add a codicil or redo at least a portion of your estate plan. The recommended change would often be to change the conduit trust to an accumulation trust. If you don't even have a conduit trust now, you can go straight to the best choice and skip your intermediate estate plan and set of wills and trusts. That is like going from a young baseball player skipping the minor leagues and going straight to the major league. That might be true of many readers in many areas of their retirement and estate plan.

On the other hand, by the time you finish reading more of this book, you will likely want to completely redo your entire retirement and estate plan, so I suggest you not do anything until you have read the book or at least Chapter 15, *Lange's Cascading Beneficiary Plan*. For many families, it would be advantageous to have your current documents reviewed by a skilled and experienced professional to make sure things are done right. Based on the documents our firm has reviewed, so this is somewhat anecdotal, 50% or more of the more current plans and 90% or more of the older plans do not have everything right.

Examples of Estate Plans That May or May Not Need Attention

Here is an example of an estate plan that includes a trust that urgently needs attention. Assume a spendthrift trust is the primary beneficiary of a multi-million-dollar IRA. Please also assume that if the money were to be left outright to the beneficiary of the trust, he or she would buy a new guitar and spend money on drugs and alcohol before paying rent. Then, assume that the spendthrift trust is a conduit trust and the IRA owner is old and sick. That is an urgent situation that needs immediate attention. The terms of the trust should be reviewed, and it should likely be changed from a conduit trust to an accumulation trust.

On the other hand, an existing conduit trust for the benefit of young grandchildren, who are the second contingent beneficiaries after the spouse and the children, would not be as pressing. Particularly if there is not much money in the IRA and both the spouse and the children have significant needs, perhaps that estate plan doesn't merit spending any time and money to amend the estate plan with a type of trust that is more appropriate for this post-SECURE Act era. Of course, these two situations represent the extremes; most of our readers and clients are somewhere in between.

The point, however, is if you have a conduit trust as the beneficiary, or even the contingent beneficiary, of your IRA or retirement plan, you may need to update your wills, trusts, and beneficiary designations of your IRAs and retirement plans.

If you are getting the idea that the rules around trusts are complicated and that any estate plans that include trusts need special expertise, you are right. This is especially true when the underlying asset is an IRA. The unfortunate news is that many attorneys botch the basic rules for drafting trusts to qualify as a designated beneficiary of an IRA. This is particularly surprising because many of these trusts are drafted by attorneys that often have good reputations and work for large, expensive law firms.

The Consequences Of Getting It Wrong Can Be Dire For Disabled Beneficiaries

We have rarely given our seal of approval when we have seen estate plans prepared by other attorneys.[1] Part of it is we are particular and we like to see the strategy optimized. The beneficiary designations of 401(k)s, IRAs and other retirement accounts usually need the most attention. Many clients assume that the primary problem with their current estate plan is that it is outdated. However, more often than not, when we review these older existing plans prepared by other firms, we find they were already terribly flawed the day they were prepared.

Getting the strategy and the exact language in the documents right is critical for all individuals, but particularly for those with large retirement plans when the end beneficiary is a Special Needs Trust.

As I said earlier, in the majority of cases, even if expensive downtown firms prepared the documents, there are usually huge gaps. One of the biggest issues is not having the proper language to help the beneficiaries get the most out of their Inherited IRAs, and retirement plans.

---

1   There is no solicitation being made for legal services by James Lange nor by Lange Legal Group, LLC.

> Many clients assume that the primary problem with their current estate plan is that it is outdated. However, more often than not, when we review these older existing plans prepared by other firms, we find they were already terribly flawed the day they were prepared.

A common mistake since the passing of both the SECURE Act and SECURE Act 2.0 is whether your current estate planning documents still meet your wishes. Unintended tax consequences can result if the documents are not properly drafted. A major drafting error could result in the loss of a lifetime stretch for an eligible designated beneficiary, especially if it is a child with a disability or chronic illness.

We can provide estate planning ideas that you can give to your local estate attorney, who drafts, redrafts, or updates your estate plan. We have even identified excellent estate attorneys in a number of states across the country to whom we refer our clients who need to establish or amend their estate plans.

KEY IDEAS

- If the largest asset in your estate is your IRA or retirement plan, the beneficiary designations of your IRAs and retirement plans are the most important estate documents you have. Please be sure the beneficiary designations on all your retirement accounts are filled out appropriately.

- The SECURE ACT does not change the surviving spouse's ability to roll over or make a trustee-to-trustee transfer of an IRA inherited from a spouse.

- Subject to exception, the surviving spouse should continue to limit withdrawals to the RMDs for as long as possible.

- Taking advantage of the 10-year limited stretch is still critically important.

Key Ideas continue on the following page.

KEY IDEAS
(continued)

- If your child has a disability, they can have a lifetime stretch if everything is done right.

- If your IRA or retirement plan is the underlying asset for a trust, you should consider reviewing the trust with an estate attorney who understands the concepts and the requisite language discussed in this chapter.

- Conduit trusts drafted before the SECURE Act (which became law effective January 1, 2020), when such instruments were a reasonable choice, should probably be redrafted as accumulation trusts to protect the trust's beneficiary.

10

The Impact of the SECURE Act on Your Family Followed by a Special Section on the Proposed Regulations

"The more hidden the venom, the more dangerous it is."
—Margaret of Valois

Effective January 1, 2020, The SECURE Act Accelerates Taxes on Inherited IRAs and Retirement Plans—Trump's and Congress' Devastating Penalty on Hard Working Families

A Special Asset—The Inherited IRA or Inherited Retirement Plan

If you die and the beneficiary of your 401(k), IRA, or other retirement plan is not your spouse, he or she will own a special asset called an *Inherited IRA*. It could be an Inherited 401(k) plan that may still be invested with your employer's plan. Essentially, what that means for the beneficiary is that the same basic tax rules that apply to IRAs inherited by non-spousal beneficiaries also apply to other Inherited retirement plans. A non-spouse beneficiary may not roll an Inherited IRA or Inherited 401(k) into his or her own IRA or 401(k). Since the distributions from a Traditional Inherited IRA are taxable, our accounting office routinely, subject to rare exceptions, encourages IRA and other retirement plan beneficiaries to "stretch" or defer taxable distributions to the maximum allowed by law.

The old law allowed beneficiaries to "stretch" the Inherited IRA, at least to some extent, for their entire lives. The SECURE Act mandates that, subject to exception, the distributions of the Inherited IRA be fully distributed and taxed by December 31st of the year that includes the tenth anniversary of the IRA owner's date of death. From here on, we will simply refer to this date as "within ten years of the IRA owner's death." Of course, the critical exception to the ten-year rule is if your beneficiary is a special needs EDB or a qualifying trust.

The SECURE Act was an attack on taxpayers who have the majority of their portfolio in IRAs and retirement plans. The impact of this legislation will be devastating for the children and grandchildren of anyone who has accumulated a significant amount of money in their retirement plan.

By passing this act, the government is essentially picking the pockets of children of retirement investors who played by the rules for years and diligently saved as much as they could in their retirement plans. The deal all along was if you contribute money to your retirement plan, not only would you get tax benefits during your lifetime, but your heirs would enjoy the ability to defer taxes on your Inherited IRAs and retirement plans, to some extent, for the rest of their lives. Accordingly, you were prudent, made financial sacrifices, and put in as much money as you could afford or were allowed to contribute to your retirement. You had good reason to believe you were being smart and prudent in planning for not only yourself but also passing money on to your family in a tax-efficient manner after your death.

However, as we have mentioned elsewhere in this book, if your IRA or retirement plan beneficiary is your child with a disability, this change may give way to effective tax planning. Read on to learn about an important exception to this confiscatory law.

Then, late in the game for many older investors, President Trump and Congress changed the rules. The new rules will seriously jeopardize your legacy.

Quantifying the Difference Between the Past and the Current Law

Figure 10.1 shows the difference between inheriting $1 million from an IRA that could be "stretched" over a lifetime under the old law (solid line) vs. a child who inherits $1 million that is subject to the 10-year rule (dashed line).

Figure 10.1

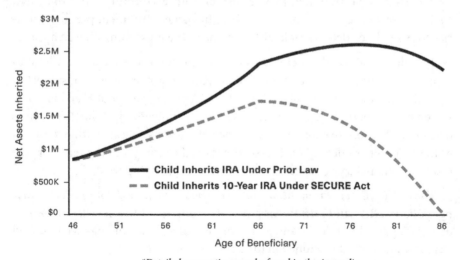

Impact of The SECURE Act—10 Year Distribution*

*Detailed assumptions can be found in the Appendix.

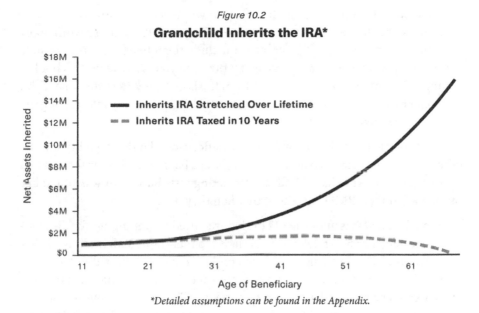

Figure 10.2

Grandchild Inherits the IRA*

*Detailed assumptions can be found in the Appendix.

The only difference between these two scenarios is when the child pays taxes.

Do you think that's devastating? Wait until you see the next graph, which shows what the ability to stretch the IRA could have meant to your grandchildren.

The solid line depicts what would have happened if the IRA was left to a grandchild and the grandchild stretched the distributions over 55 years. The dashed line shows what happens now that the grandchild must withdraw the IRA and pay all the taxes within ten years. In both cases, the grandchild immediately reinvests the withdrawals into a taxable brokerage account. The difference in wealth by the time they reach age 70 is an astonishing $16,245,105!

The old rules were a lot more fun for planners like me. I loved doing a series of Roth IRA conversions, and then, through the use of disclaimers (please see Chapter 15), we protected the surviving spouse but left open the possibility for a tax-free dynasty to the next two and sometimes three generations.

But the more common result of the SECURE Act is (without the aggressive intervention that this book is advocating) it just hurts the children of hard-working IRA and retirement plan owners who played by the rules and got burned.

Proposed Regulations from the IRS Released in February 2022

As I mentioned in the last chapter, Proposed Regulations from the IRS released in February 2022 would remove some of the flexibility that beneficiaries had for timing their distributions within that ten-year window to minimize taxes. As we go to press, the IRS has announced that these Proposed Regulations won't apply until they are finalized in 2024 or later. I include them here because I strongly suspect they will become law, possibly by the time you are reading this book. I am repeating some of the information from the last chapter to ensure that if you only read this chapter, you are aware of how the IRS is currently interpreting the changes generated by the SECURE Act.

The Proposed Regulations split IRA beneficiaries who don't qualify for one of the exceptions detailed below into two groups based on whether the original retirement plan owner had already begun taking distributions or was still under the age when their RMDs were to start when they died.

If the decedent was under age 72 or their required beginning age for distributions, the beneficiary can take distributions from an Inherited Traditional IRA whenever they want, as long as the account is completely emptied in ten years. They can take zero distributions until year ten and take everything out at the end, or they can take regular distributions every year. They can take bigger distributions in years when they will be in lower tax brackets and smaller distributions in high tax bracket years.

But suppose the decedent was already taking distributions. In that case, for the first nine years, the beneficiary of the Inherited IRA will be required to take annual distributions that are at least as large as the decedent's annual distributions. Whatever is left will have to be withdrawn in year ten. These Proposed Regulations will force owners of Inherited Traditional IRAs to take taxable distributions every year, even if that leads to a tax bomb. However, if the original owner died in 2020 or 2021, the beneficiary won't need to start taking distributions until 2024 at the earliest.

Those Proposed Regulations also reduce the games I planned to play in timing the Inherited IRA distributions.

The good news is that these Proposed Regulations don't apply to an Inherited Roth IRA because the original Roth IRA owner didn't have to take a distribution. So, the beneficiary of an Inherited Roth IRA, assuming they have other funds to spend, can just let the Inherited Roth IRA grow for ten years and then withdraw it tax-free. If the investments earn 7% per year, the Inherited Roth will double by the time it has to be withdrawn. On the other hand, like the Inherited IRA, the Inherited Roth IRA must be distributed within ten years of the Roth IRA owner's death.

Now that you've seen a demonstration of the SECURE Act's horrendous impact let's look at the few exceptions that Congress included that will still allow advantageous tax treatment for inherited retirement plan assets.

Exceptions to The SECURE Act

The following section could be extremely critical to protecting your non-spouse beneficiaries, especially your child with a disability.

Unless the beneficiary of your IRA meets the new definition of an Eligible Designated Beneficiary (EDB), the Inherited IRA will have to be fully distributed within ten years.

Eligible Designated Beneficiaries include:

- a surviving spouse
- an individual with a disability or chronic illness
- a child of the IRA owner who has not reached the age of majority (age 21), or
- an individual who is not more than ten years younger than the IRA owner.

Charities and charitable trusts are also exempt. Let's look into each of these categories in detail.

The Surviving Spouse

Thankfully, surviving spouses will still be able to do a spousal rollover or, preferably, a trustee-to-trustee transfer of your IRA or retirement plan. However, this doesn't necessarily mean that you should simply plan on having your surviving spouse inherit your retirement assets and then, at the second death, pass those assets on to your children.

Your surviving spouse will be required to take minimum distributions from the Traditional retirement plans they inherit from you as well as from their own IRAs and retirement plans. Remember, those minimum distributions will increase as the surviving spouse grows older, also increasing their taxable income.

Another option from the SECURE Act 2.0, which was passed in December 2022, allows spouses to elect to be treated as if they were the deceased spouse for the purposes of timing RMDs from an IRA or 401(k) inherited from that spouse. This provision is most useful when the decedent is younger than the surviving spouse because this allows the surviving spouse to postpone RMDs until the younger spouse would have started taking their RMDs.

And suppose you have accumulated a significant amount of wealth in Traditional retirement plans. In that case, the survivor (who now must file as single instead of jointly starting the year after you die) might move up to a significantly higher tax bracket. So, even though your spouse is exempt from the accelerated tax provision of the SECURE Act, it may make sense to plan on passing part of your Traditional retirement assets directly to your children at the time of your death either by leaving your IRA or other money directly to your children or, more likely, doing it by disclaimer.

The disclaimer solution allows you, the IRA or retirement plan owner, to avoid the difficult issue of predicting "who should get what." Disclaimers let the surviving spouse decide "who gets what" within nine months of the IRA or retirement plan owner's death. We cover the details of this type of planning—which we call disclaimer planning—in Chapter 15, *The Best Estate Plan for Most Married Couples Before and After the SECURE Act.*

Beneficiaries With Disabilities or Chronic Illness

This exception will be of chief importance for parents of children with disabilities. In addition to surviving spouses, beneficiaries with disabilities or chronic illnesses are also exempt from the devastating rules of the SECURE Act. If you have a child with a chronic illness or disability, you are in a specialty area that offers enormous opportunities and pitfalls. If you do have such a beneficiary, it is critical to read Chapter 11, *Critical Information for Beneficiaries with Disabilities.*

It is also critical that you consult with an estate attorney[1] and a trusted financial advisor and/or CPA familiar with planning for beneficiaries with disabilities or chronic illnesses.

In short, qualified beneficiaries with disabilities will meet the standards to use the old "stretch IRA rules," which, as demonstrated above, are life changing. As readers will learn in Chapter 11, the rules for qualifying a beneficiary as disabled or chronically ill are rather narrow and may require substantial effort on your part before your death. But favorable Proposed Regulations regarding beneficiaries with a disability could make that effort pay off by hundreds of thousands of dollars. In my personal situation, my wife and I have a daughter with a disability who will qualify as an EDB. In our estate planning, either our daughter or a trust for her benefit is the end beneficiary for our retirement accounts. Because of our planning for her in just two areas, she will be better off by $1.9 million measured in today's dollars than if we had not taken proactive measures.

Even if your beneficiary does qualify as disabled or chronically ill, you will have to put in place additional measures to ensure their financial security. First,

---

1   There is no solicitation for legal services being made by me, James Lange, nor by Lange Legal Group, LLC.

at least in the case of Supplemental Security Income, usually referred to as SSI, your beneficiary must meet income and asset limitations to qualify and ensure that your beneficiary remains eligible for government benefits.

To get around these income and asset limitations, funds left to SSI recipients will most likely need to be left to a carefully drafted trust known as a special needs trust (SNT trust). Ensuring that this trust meets all the qualifications to be treated as a SNT is a big deal, so I highly recommend you consult with at least one, if not two, attorneys with expertise in this field. If your child with a disability is not yet qualified for SSI, you will need to find a professional with the appropriate skillset to help shepherd your child's initial application through the approval process and/or to help win an appeal after a denied application. If your child is already qualified for SSI and thus considered disabled or chronically ill, you should seek out an attorney with expertise in drafting the appropriate wills, trusts, beneficiary designations, etc.

Our CPA team has expertise in tax and financial planning for parents with a disability, but not the skill set in winning the case to be considered disabled or chronically ill which is required to get the favorable tax treatment that is so critical for beneficiaries with a disability or chronic illness. But my colleague Deborah McFadden has that expertise, and in Chapter 12, she reveals her secrets for helping young adults with disabilities win the Golden Ticket of SSI or SSDI eligibility.

Because many beneficiaries with disabilities or chronic illnesses face challenges with long-term gainful employment, they tend to depend more on inherited funds to finance their basic living expenses than the average person who receives an Inherited IRA. Getting it right can make the difference between living in poverty—as many Americans with disabilities currently do—and having a secure future. It's heartbreaking to know how much misery for these individuals could have been prevented with appropriate estate planning by parents, grandparents, or other caring individuals had they had the right information and/or hired the right team to help them.

You can also understand why getting this right is crucial if you have a child with a disability who can use the old rules to "stretch" the Inherited IRA.

Fortunately, resources are available for families of children with disabilities or chronic illnesses. If your child can secure that Golden Ticket of SSI or SSDI eligibility, that will open many doors to financial, health, education, work support, and housing assistance. It is often more difficult than you might expect to navigate the Social Security programs' application and approval processes. Depending on your child's particular situation, their disability may not fit perfectly into the

SSA's criteria for what constitutes a disability or chronic illness; you may also experience significant issues generating the proof of that disability or chronic illness. We address those and many other matters related to the SSI/SSDI qualification process in Chapter 12.

This issue is close to my heart because I have a daughter with a disability. But I want all readers to be aware that planning for your child or beneficiary is critically important. The difference between the optimal plan and something that is just okay can have an enormous impact on your beneficiary's quality of life after you are gone.

One potentially critical piece to the puzzle in the mess of the SECURE Act is that under the Proposed Regulations if your beneficiary has already qualified as disabled for the purposes of the Social Security Administration, that beneficiary also meets the definition of disabled for the SECURE Act. This will allow your beneficiary to stretch out Inherited IRA distributions over their lifetime like the pre-2020 rules instead of being forced to empty the account within ten years.

That component of the Proposed Regulations was big news in our household. Though we had already won our daughter's Social Security benefits case, we had no assurance that, by virtue of the SSDI status, she would qualify for the SECURE Act exception, allowing her to stretch her Inherited IRA after we die. Since we have a 7-figure Roth IRA, it will be even more valuable for her. Assuming the Proposed Regulations become law, and our daughter can maintain her status with the Social Security Administration, we know she will qualify for the Inherited stretch IRA and Inherited stretch Roth IRA after we are gone. That will give her access to hundreds of thousands of additional dollars (thanks to her ability to allow most of the funds in that Inherited IRA to grow income-tax-free throughout her lifetime) that she would not otherwise have had.

That significantly lowers "the number" that we feel obligated to leave her at our death to feel secure that she will be fine financially for the rest of her life.

Minor Children as The Beneficiary of An IRA or Retirement Plan

Minor children of the IRA owner are also partially exempt from the SECURE Act's 10-year rule. The rules affecting children who have not yet reached the age of majority are complex. The SECURE Act potentially allows a minor child beneficiary to stretch an Inherited IRA like the old rules until they reach the age of majority. While the age of majority varies from state to state, Proposed Regulations, released by the IRS in February 2022, define this as age 21. Once reaching that age, however, the 10-year rule kicks in. So, you could theoretically

> **... if your beneficiary has already qualified as disabled for the purposes of the Social Security Administration, that beneficiary also meets the definition of disabled for the SECURE Act.**

leave an IRA to your newborn child, and the child would be able to "stretch" it like the old rules until they turn 21. They would then be required to withdraw the remaining balance within ten years of turning 21.

For most readers, however, the new law will have the most dramatic effect on your adult children and potentially your grandchildren. Let's look at why that is.

How The SECURE Act Affects Children Inheriting IRAs and Roth IRAs

As stated before, an IRA that passes to a *non-spouse* beneficiary becomes a special asset called an *Inherited IRA*. Subject to some exceptions listed in this chapter (for minors, persons with a disability, etc.), an Inherited IRA or retirement plan will have to be entirely disbursed within ten years following the death of the original IRA owner. Period.

If the Inherited IRA is a Traditional pre-tax account, all distributions are taxable. And if the Inherited IRA is large enough, the income from the accelerated distributions could force your non-spouse beneficiary into a significantly higher tax bracket even if the distributions are taken evenly over ten years. This tax acceleration can be devastating, as we saw above in Figure 10.1.

If the Inherited IRA is a Roth account, your child (or other non-spouse beneficiaries) won't have to pay taxes on the distributions because Roth account distributions are tax-free.

Assuming your beneficiary leaves the Inherited Roth IRA account where it is, any distributions from the account and income received from interest, dividends, and capital gains will all be tax-free for ten years after the death of the Roth IRA owner.

After ten years, the principal would not be taxed, but any accruing income would be taxable because the principal is no longer under the tax-free Roth umbrella. That's a big change. The idea that Roth accounts could compound over many years and distributions would be tax-free was a huge benefit for your heirs. So, in the case of an Inherited Roth account, there is an enormous incentive for your beneficiary to not take any withdrawals until they are absolutely required to—and there is no penalty for waiting until the very last minute, either.

The Ten Years Younger Exception

Another exception to the ten-year income acceleration on IRAs dictated by the SECURE Act is for a beneficiary who is no more than ten years younger than you. This exception would likely apply if you were leaving your IRA, or a portion of your IRA or retirement plan, to a sibling or an unmarried partner.

If you and your partner are unmarried please, please read Chapter 25 where I present a strong case for the financial benefits of getting married. Before the Court's 2015 decision in Obergefell, I wrote two financial planning books for same-sex couples. Among other things, the books quantified the value of the many forms of preferential tax treatment that federal and state law extend to married people.

Today, when same-sex couples can legally get married in all 50 states, the main thrust of those books is obviously moot. That said, it is still very true that unmarried couples are missing out on many opportunities to protect and build wealth. So, regardless of sexual orientation, most partners in committed, long-term relationships should seriously consider tying the knot. I have even toyed with the idea of writing a book titled *Get Married for the Money*. In the meantime, Chapter 25 will have to do.

Charities and Charitable Trusts

Charities and charitable trusts are a critical exception to the 10-year income acceleration rule for IRAs and retirement plans.

The charitable trust exception can create enormous opportunities for many readers, especially if you are charitably inclined.

In brief, a charitable remainder trust allows you to split the money in your IRA between your child and a charity. Your child will receive distributions from the trust over his or her lifetime, and at your child's death, the charity receives the balance in the trust. This is one way that an IRA beneficiary who is not an EDB can still stretch IRA distributions over their lifetime.

However, a charitable remainder trust will have few advantages for your child with a disability, especially if your child qualifies as disabled for the purposes of being an EDB, because that child will already be able to use the lifetime stretch. A special needs trust, which you can read about in Chapter 13, is likely a more suitable vehicle for providing for your child with a disability after you are gone.

The Disaster of the SECURE Act

Notwithstanding these fantastically helpful exceptions for some, the party for the rest of us is over.

The SECURE Act is a horrible piece of legislation that is miserable for retirees and their families. Losing the ability to stretch their Inherited IRA will be devastating for IRA and retirement plan owner's beneficiaries because the income tax on the Inherited IRAs will be significantly accelerated.

Now that you understand the gravity of the situation and why I find it such a deplorable change for most retirees, please read on to see what you can do about it.

KEY IDEAS

- An IRA that passes to a non-spouse beneficiary is a special asset called an Inherited IRA.

- The SECURE Act mandates that an Inherited IRA must, subject to exceptions, be totally disbursed and taxed within ten years of the IRA owner's death.

- One of the critical exceptions for our purposes is a qualifying beneficiary with a disability.

- The Inherited Roth IRA must also be distributed within ten years of death, but distributions are tax-free.

Key Ideas continue on the following page.

KEY IDEAS
(continued)

- The new Proposed Regulations make things even worse for beneficiaries inheriting IRAs from an IRA owner who was 72 or older.

- Eligible Designated Beneficiaries are not subject to the ten-year rule. EDBs include:

  - Surviving spouses

  - Minor beneficiaries of deceased parents

  - Qualifying disabled or chronically ill beneficiaries

  - Beneficiaries who are not more than ten years younger than the retirement account owner

  - Charities and charitable trusts

  - The new proposed regulations are very favorable for clarifying the terms of the exception to the ten-year rule for beneficiaries with disabilities or with chronic illnesses.

- Under the SECURE Act, your IRA and retirement plan legacy will be decimated if you don't take aggressive action.

11

Three Critical Steps to Protect Your Child's Financial Security After You Are Gone...and More

If you have a child with a disability, there is likely no better use of your time than to read this section of the book and implement at least some of the recommendations.

The next four chapters have vital information for parents of children with disabilities. This chapter outlines the steps that my wife and I have taken to ensure the financial security of our daughter Erica, who has a disability. Chapter 12, written by Deborah McFadden, an internationally known expert in the disability arena, explains her strategies for helping young adults win approval for SSI or SSDI, which she calls "The Golden Ticket." In Chapter 13, we will hear from fellow attorney Julieanne E. Steinbacher on the strategies and mechanics of Special Needs Trusts. Lastly, John Montoya and Julieanne E. Steinbacher will explain how ABLE accounts work in Chapter 14.

These four chapters can be read independently, but I strongly recommend carefully studying them all because the concepts build on each other. Implementing the ideas in one chapter will be better than doing nothing at all, but implementing the strategies in all four chapters—when they apply to your unique family situation—will help ensure your child has the maximum financial resources available to live the best life possible.

To illustrate the life-changing difference between pro-active and passive planning for your child with a disability, I am sharing my family's personal story. Our daughter, Erica, has a disability and will never be able to support herself unless there is an unforeseeable significant change in her condition. She is currently receiving SSDI. One of the most important things for me and my wife, as it is for practically all parents of a child with a disability, is to ensure we properly provide for our child while we are alive and, perhaps even more importantly, after we are gone.

Let's start at the end of the story.

Because of our actions on three critical fronts, our daughter will be $1,890,544 better off (measured in today's dollars) than she would have been had we not taken these proactive steps—and this is without factoring in any supplemental government benefits. A secondary consequence is that my wife and I will also be better off by $491,829.

The three things we did were:

1. We made a large Roth IRA conversion and a series of Roth IRA, backdoor Roth IRA, and Roth 401(k) contributions.

2. We won our Social Security Disability Insurance (SSDI) appeal with the Social Security Administration (SSA) formally establishing Erica's status as disabled.

3. Our attorney drafted an optimized estate plan with appropriate wills, trusts, and IRA and 401(k) and Roth IRA beneficiary forms that will allow Erica to "stretch" or defer distributions of her Inherited IRA or Inherited Roth IRA.

We are also setting in place measures to ensure our estate will be appropriately administered after we die. A key measure was to establish Erica's status as an eligible designated beneficiary. That will ensure she will be able to "stretch" her Inherited Roth IRA.

Why is this status as an EDB so important? As I described in Chapter 10, one of the consequences of the 2020 SECURE Act was the end of the stretch IRA. Before the SECURE Act, when someone inherited an IRA or other retirement plan, they could take distributions over their entire lifetimes. That meant that IRA or retirement plan assets could grow tax-free, in the case of Inherited Roth IRAs, or tax-deferred for decades. But under the SECURE Act, unless a beneficiary qualifies for one of a few exceptions, Inherited IRAs and other retirement plans must be entirely distributed within 10 years of the original owner's death, resulting in a massive income tax acceleration.

Fortunately for parents of children with disabilities, when the beneficiary qualifies as disabled or chronically ill with the SSA and the IRS, they become an Eligible Designated Beneficiary (EDB). Any EDB who inherits an IRA, Roth IRA,

> **Because of our actions on three critical fronts, our daughter will be $1,890,544 better off (measured in today's dollars) than she would have been had we not taken these proactive steps—and this is without factoring in any supplemental government benefits.**

or other retirement plan can still take full advantage of the stretch IRA, which can make a tremendous difference in the amount of money that person has access to over their lifetime, as I demonstrate below.

Figure 11.1 demonstrates the dramatic contrast between Erica's current projected financial future, the consequence of our effective planning (using Roth strategies, qualifying her as an EDB, and optimizing our estate plan), and the future she might have had with ineffective planning. It begins with our (mine and my wife's) projected deaths when she is age 46 and continues to her projected death at age 86.

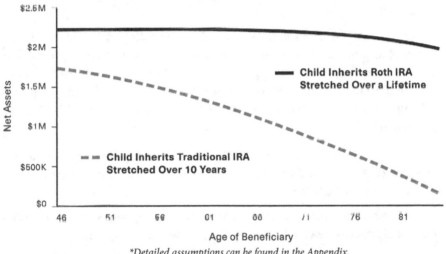

Figure 11.1

Benefit for an Eligible Designated Beneficiary Inheriting a Roth IRA with Lifetime Stretch vs. Inheriting a Traditional IRA with 10-Year Stretch* ($1.9 million difference in my daughter's case)

*Detailed assumptions can be found in the Appendix.

You can find the complete list of very reasonable assumptions we used to make these calculations in the Appendix. It is important to know that we factored the money we paid in taxes on the Roth conversion as well as the resulting loss of growth on that money into these calculations.

These projections represent a true "apples to apples" comparison. The bottom line is that had we not taken these proactive measures, at age 86, Erica would be broke but because we did, she will still have a comfortable $1,890,544 (measured in today's dollars). Or more to the point, she will be able to spend much more money over the course of her life and still not worry about running out of money. She will be able to afford many more services and a much better lifestyle, both for her health and comfort, in ways that would have otherwise been impossible. She will not have to worry about money, and now neither Cindy nor I worry about her financial security after we are gone.

An IRA Owner With $500,000 Can Provide $239,000 More for Their Beneficiary With Proactive Roth Conversion Planning

I realize not everyone reading this book will have as large an IRA as Cindy and I have accumulated over the years. We did a $249,000 Roth IRA conversion in 1998 (more on that story later), which really turbocharged the growth of our retirement assets. It's possible, even likely, that you haven't made *any* Roth IRA conversions to date, or haven't made any that were *as big as* the one Cindy and I made. But don't dismiss these strategies because you see a big difference between our circumstances and yours. Taking these steps could still provide tremendous value to your child.

Scenario A

Let's say you die at age 85 with a $500,000 Traditional IRA when your child, who has a disability, is age 54. Let's also assume your estate plan was not optimized to allow the "stretch IRA," and you did not make any Roth IRA conversions. Under these circumstances, your child would run out of money at age 88. (Assumptions for Figure 11.2 can be found in the Appendix.)

Scenario B

Let's say your child received the SSDI status, qualifying her as an EDB under the SECURE Act, and will be able to stretch distributions from Inherited IRAs or Roth IRAs over her lifetime.

Let's also assume you completed a series of Roth conversions of your $500,000 Traditional IRA before you died and got the estate planning right.

Under these circumstances, at age 88, your child will still have $239,068 in today's dollars. By sharp contrast, in Scenario A, she would have $0 at age 88. In Scenario B, if your child lives beyond 88, she will have even more additional financial resources to live comfortably for another 12 years or longer. Perhaps more realistically, thanks to your tax-savvy planning, your child has nearly a quarter of a million more dollars that she can spend for needed care between your death and her own.

Figure 11.2 plots the different outcomes from these two scenarios.

The Dread That Once Kept Us Up at Night is Now Gone!

Our daughter, Erica, is a very sweet and smart 27-year-old who has a disability. Our concerns for her long-term security and safety kept us up at night. We

Figure 11.2

EDB Child with An Inherited Stretch Roth IRA vs. Traditional IRA*

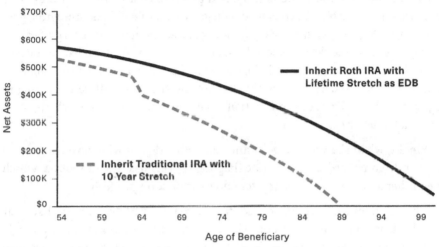

Detailed assumptions can be found in the Appendix.

could not rest easy until we were convinced we had planned appropriately and substantively for Erica. I know that as the parent of a child with a disability, you have these same fears.

At first, our general plan was to make more money, work longer, spend less, buy life insurance, and hope there would be enough. Then, we got strategic and came up with a plan. I want to share the strategies we used and the proof that, given reasonable assumptions, our strategies are not only sound, but could be extremely beneficial for you and your family.

It saddens me to think of children with disabilities who will end up in terrible financial shape simply because their parents failed to plan appropriately, often because they didn't know any better. Fortunately, as a CPA with Roth IRA conversion and SECURE Act expertise, I had the technical knowledge to plan for our daughter's long-term financial security.

Under these circumstances, at age 88, your child will still have $239,068 in today's dollars. By sharp contrast, in Scenario A, she would have $0 at age 88.

A Brief Summary of Erica's Health History for Context

One day Erica was acing her SAT, and two days later she got so sick that she had to quit school. To be fair, she had problems before this, but they were somewhat manageable. We consulted with gastroenterologists, neurologists, pain docs, cardiologists, psychiatrists, psychologists, acupuncturists, energy healers, chiropractors, Lyme disease specialists, and on and on. We traveled to specialists in New York, Cleveland, Toledo, Minneapolis, Salt Lake City, San Francisco, and more. Spoiler alert: none of the doctors and therapists offered anything to significantly help Erica beyond partially managing her symptoms, which, to be fair, is a lot better than nothing.

Finally, when she was 17, we connected with a doctor who gave us what we are firmly convinced is an accurate diagnosis. Erica has dysautonomia, which means her autonomic nervous system doesn't function properly.

The autonomic nervous system controls involuntary body functions like your heartbeat, breathing, and digestion. That explains why she has so many seemingly unrelated problems. Unfortunately, there hasn't been much that the doctors have been able to do to improve her situation. It has been a heartbreaking journey for our family. We attempt to control her symptoms—there are better days and worse days—but she has no real prospect of holding down a job.

Erica, now age 27, is comfortable sharing her/our story and has given my wife and I her blessing to do so. She hopes that sharing our story will help provide financial security for other children with disabilities.

Acquiring Disability Status

After a grueling legal marathon with the Social Security Administration (SSA), we won our Social Security Disability Insurance (SSDI) case. That was a significant step in protecting her financial security.

At the time, if we'd had Deborah McFadden's guidance, we might have avoided some of our struggles getting Erica qualified for SSDI. You'll find her critical recommendation and advice for the SSI or SSDI application process in Chapter 12. Winning SSI or SSDI approval for your child is the Golden Ticket that opens the door for many other financial and healthcare benefits.

We are confident that Erica's disabled status with the SSA will fast-track her status as an Eligible Designated Beneficiary (EDB) under the SECURE Act once she inherits our retirement accounts. This is largely because of proposed regulations released by the IRS in February 2022 that explain how that agency plans to interpret the SECURE Act. While those regulations aren't officially the law of the land, we feel confident they will be adopted. In effect, they say that beneficiaries who have already been qualified as disabled by the Social Security Administration will also qualify as an EDB for the purposes of the SECURE Act. So, if your child is already qualified to collect SSI or SSDI, you won't have to prove disability again beyond the required periodic updates.

This proposed regulation is a very big deal for us and, if your beneficiary has already qualified as disabled for Social Security, it should be a big deal for you too. Though we had already won our SSDI case, we were not assured that this would be sufficient for our daughter to qualify as an EDB (allowing her to stretch the Inherited IRA and Roth IRA that we will leave her) without having to jump through more hoops. Now, we are quite confident that our daughter will be on the fast-track for favorable EDB treatment once she inherits our retirement accounts.

Our Journey to Ensure Erica's Security—Roth IRA Conversions, Winning SSDI Case, and Appropriate Estate Planning and Administration

The first proactive thing we got right was optimizing our Roth IRA conversions and Roth contributions. Please note that our accounting firm has four number-crunching CPAs who routinely do this optimization work, as demonstrated in the detailed chapters on Roth IRA conversions in Chapters 16 and 17. Our Roth IRA analysis is usually focused on optimizing conversions for the benefit of the client. The benefit for the child that will inherit the Roth is a bonus. Many clients, however, are interested in Roth IRA conversions for their children and grandchildren. For clients who have a child with a disability, our emphasis significantly expands to optimizing Roth IRA conversions not only for the client but also for their beneficiary with a disability.

The second proactive step was winning Erica's SSDI case, which will likely fast-track her EDB status. The third proactive step was getting our estate planning right; specifically, we put measures in place to ensure optimal estate administration in response to the SECURE Act and the proposed IRS regulations.

Beneficiaries with disabilities or chronic illnesses who have EDB status are one of the critical exceptions from the SECURE Act's mandatory 10-year disbursement rule for Inherited retirement accounts. If the parent's estate documents are also prepared optimally and if the estate is administered correctly, beneficiaries with a disability—or trusts for the benefit of a child with a disability—can treat an Inherited IRA or Roth IRA as any beneficiary could in 2019 (before the effective date of the SECURE Act), i.e., take advantage of "stretching" Inherited retirement assets over a lifetime.

> The Roth conversions will be worth $1,297,500, and the 'stretch' feature on the Roth conversions will mean an extra $386,300.

Under the proposed regulations for the SECURE Act and assuming the appropriate planning and estate administration at our deaths, our daughter will likely qualify to enjoy a massive distribution deferral of her Inherited IRAs and Roth IRAs. Even without the Roth conversions, this deferral would mean an extra $206,700 for her at age 86, again measured in today's dollars.

The Roth conversions will be worth $1,297,500, and the 'stretch' feature on the Roth conversions will mean an extra $386,300. The synergy of the Roth conversions and the Inherited "stretch status" for our Inherited IRAs and Roth IRAs, and getting our estate planning right has led to the approximately $1.9 million total savings (in today's dollars) that we project for Erica using reasonable assumptions.

The third proactive step was getting our estate planning right and putting in place measures to ensure optimal estate administration in response to the SECURE Act and the proposed IRS regulations.

While our projections for Erica do not include every variable of our financial life, the result is clear. We made a $249,000 Roth IRA conversion, have contributed to backdoor Roth IRAs, and since 2006, the assumptions for the calculation assumed I contributed all my 401(k) contributions to a Roth 401(k). The math used to make the projection can and has been reproduced by the number crunching CPAs in our office.

The most critical information to convey is the potential benefits for your child that result from getting the three things right—optimal Roth planning, formal status as disabled leading to EDB status, and optimal estate planning and estate administration.

Your Child's Gain, Uncle Sam's Loss

In our analysis, each dollar your child gains, including interest and growth, is exactly equivalent to how much Uncle Sam loses. Basically, these strategies involve a massive wealth transfer from Uncle Sam to your beneficiary with a disability. To be fair, since I did include an investment rate of 6.5% and inflation of 3.5% on the IRAs and Roth IRAs, I assume the government would have earned the same rate on the money you used to pay for the Roth IRA conversion to arrive at the total tax savings. Please note if we had used a higher investment rate, or if tax rates increase in the future, the benefits to the child would be much bigger.

The Critical Role Roth IRAs and Roth Conversions Play in My Story

Our Roth story begins in 1997 when the mechanisms for Roth IRA conversions were just in the proposal stage. When the Roth was first introduced in 1998, I knew this would be huge for clients and readers with IRAs and retirement plans.

On February 16, 1998, right at the beginning of tax season, my office suffered a devastating fire.

At the time, my wife and I had combined Traditional IRAs and 401(k)s of $249,000. I wanted to convert all of it to a Roth IRA. My wife Cindy, who has a master's degree in electrical engineering from Carnegie Mellon University (CMU) and has excellent quantitative thinking skills, strongly resisted because she didn't want to pay the taxes on the Roth conversion.

Then, we "ran the numbers" (my firm's specialty) using the same methodology we used for the peer-reviewed article and still use today to some extent. After seeing convincing proof that our family would be much better off by hundreds of thousands of dollars in the long run, we went ahead with the conversion. Also, to be fair, this was before we knew Erica had a disability. On the other hand, back then, adult children *without* disabilities could "stretch" Inherited IRAs and Roth IRAs over their lifetime, and we always intended the Roth to be for Erica unless we got desperate.

I wrote a detailed article on the advantages of making Roth IRA conversions, including all the calculations. In May 1998, *The Tax Adviser*, the peer-reviewed journal of the tax division of the American Institute of CPAs, published my article—the first peer-reviewed article on Roth IRA conversions—and it won article of the year. So, while the analysis presented in this book is not peer-reviewed, the basis of the reasoning and calculations has been peer-reviewed.

> **The most critical information to convey is the potential benefits for your child that result from getting the three things right—optimal Roth planning, formal status as disabled leading to EDB status, and optimal estate planning and estate administration.**

Figures 11.1 and 11.2 demonstrate the impact of making a series of Roth conversions, contributing the maximum to your Roth 401(k) account, making "back-door" Roth conversions (while they are still permitted), and having your disabled child qualify as an EDB, and getting the rest of her estate planning right to be eligible for the Inherited "stretch IRA" or "stretch Roth IRA."

Your (Not Your Child's) Benefits from Getting the Roth Right

What do Figures 11.1 and 11.2 tell us, and what does this mean for you and your child with a disability? First, it means you will be able to spend more money in your lifetime and still provide for your child with a disability. The benefits of the Roth conversion and contributions to you, not including the benefit to your child, at least consistent with my assumptions in my case, will be roughly $491,829 in today's dollars, which was an intermediate step to the calculation to determine how much Erica would benefit.

To be fair, it is also easy to convert too much money to a Roth. Without the benefit of knowing some of the tax intricacies, it is easy to get far less than optimal conversions. Jen Hall, one of our number-crunching CPAs, points out that, depending on the facts of the situation for each client, it could be optimal to make a million-dollar conversion in year one or two, $500,000 conversions in years one and two, ten $100,000 conversions in years one through ten, or even no conversion at all.

Multiple Roth conversions over a series of years often produce the best results for the client and child. The other factor is some people don't want to write a huge check to the IRS. Even if the projections show that writing a big check is optimal, they prefer doing a series of smaller conversions over time, and that is fine with us.

For the strategy to work, it has to pass the math test and the stomach test. One of the ideas of this type of planning is to not worry at night. If writing a whopper check for the conversion is going to keep you up worrying, that is a significant factor. Fortunately, in many cases, we recommend doing a series of conversions over time, again depending on the individual circumstances. A series of Roth conversions tend to pass the stomach test much better than one massive conversion.

Besides writing a big check to the IRS, Roth conversions done later in life—when you're on Medicare or soon to be on Medicare—can have an impact on how your Medicare Part B premiums are calculated. Be sure to read Chapter 17 carefully if this applies to you.

The financial benefits from the conversion(s) will allow more money for caregivers for your child while you are alive, which might provide you with more

> **In our analysis, each dollar your child gains, including interest and growth, is exactly equivalent to how much Uncle Sam loses. Basically, these strategies involve a massive wealth transfer from Uncle Sam to your beneficiary with a disability.**

flexibility. For us, it has meant that we can afford certain services that allow Erica to live outside our home with her boyfriend. It also means we can afford to pay her other expenses so she can have a good life living outside of our house. To be fair, Cindy still spends much of her day taking care of Erica's needs from a distance and she frequently visits Erica. Most of that time is care-related, not just family vacation time.

In addition to a lot more money that we can afford for her current care, we are taking advantage of the tax savings to enhance our lives. We bought a place in Tucson to spend our winters, and now I am a working snowbird. You may be able to imagine things that would improve the quality of your life if you had to pay far less in taxes. Because we got the Roth IRA and Roth IRA conversion strategies right, we can enjoy additional spending without worrying about jeopardizing Erica's future. Perhaps you could enjoy some of these benefits too, all because of optimizing Roth conversions and, if you are still working, investing in Roth 401(k)s instead of the Traditional 401(k)s.

Let me also mention the issue of whether to convert and how much and when to do a Roth conversion isn't a matter of opinion. It is a matter of math. We believe in peer-reviewed science and math. One of the reasons we publish in peer-reviewed CPA and legal journals is to give readers the comfort that we did the math, and the peer-reviewers checked the math and confirmed its accuracy. You can disagree with our assumptions. In addition, I will concede we are making projections with a lot of unknown variables, like future tax laws and future tax rates. The stomach test (can you stand writing that big check to the IRS) is also important. That said, our approach is to make reasonable assumptions, do the math, and show the client the result of the different options. We can also do the math using the client's assumptions. But again, the main point of this paragraph is that Roth analysis is a matter of math, not opinion.

The benefit that is hardest to quantify is the greater peace of mind you will experience from acting on the steps we advocate. *Imagine letting go of the fear that your child will run out of money after you and your spouse are gone.* These steps are a game changer! To be fair, my wife and I still have worries about what will happen to Erica after we are gone—but running out of money is no longer one of them.

Benefits to Your Child

After you are gone, instead of running out of money, your child could enjoy enormous financial benefits just from the strategies mentioned above. Imagine your child being able to afford private social workers, nurses, a concierge medicine doctor, healthy organic meals specifically designed for her condition delivered to her door, out-of-network specialists, alternative treatments, medicines, and modalities that aren't covered by insurance, good housing, personal transportation services, mental health services that may not accept insurance, etc. Depending on the circumstances, your child or someone looking after your child will be able to prioritize what would serve them best. If your child already lives or will eventually live in some type of group home, your child will be able to easily afford the most desirable housing, where he or she will be happiest.

If you know other parents who have IRAs or other retirement plans and who have a child or grandchildren with a disability, please point those people to **https://DisabledChildPlanning.com** where they can download a copy of a Special Advisory Report we wrote that summarizes the most important information in this book. You would be doing them and their child an enormous service by recommending this report to them.

The Challenge of Coordinating All of the Moving Pieces for the Best Result

To make sure that all the pieces are correctly aligned, I think it is prudent to attempt to understand the most crucial principles, and I advise you to do the following:

- Work with pro-active CPAs or financial advisors who really understand and appreciate Roth IRA conversions and the benefits of the "stretch IRA." They should also be able to "run the numbers" to quantify the results of different Roth conversion amounts and determine the optimal timing for you and your child. Ideally, the same number-crunchers will integrate many other strategies, like the ABLE account (see Chapter 14). There are wonderful software programs available today, but you still need a highly skilled "number-cruncher" to do the kind of analysis I think should be done. I have had great success training razor-sharp CPAs to do this work. Trying to train a financial advisor or an attorney without deep tax knowledge to do these calculations seems improbable.

> **...the SNT must be drafted to ensure that the beneficiary will receive all the tax benefits and, if necessary, that the proceeds will not jeopardize your beneficiary's eligibility for any government assistance the beneficiary may receive in the future.**

- You might consider working with a specialist attorney or another expert (they don't have to be an attorney) to get your child formally qualified as disabled and ultimately as an EDB, but most frequently, an attorney only becomes necessary if an initial application is denied. Alternatively, you can work with an SSI/SSDI specialist like Deborah McFadden, who can help you secure the Golden Ticket of SSA approval. You can also do this on your own, and if you carefully follow the advice Deborah Mc Fadden gives in Chapter 12, your chances of a speedy approval the first time are greatly enhanced.

- You will also need an estate attorney[1] who knows how to draft and plan for a child with a disability to ensure the child doesn't lose their EDB status due to an improperly drafted estate plan. This attorney must have the specialized legal skills and knowledge required to get all the terms of the trust exactly right, assuming a trust is appropriate. You may need a special needs trust, and if so, the SNT must be drafted to ensure that the beneficiary will receive all the tax benefits and, if necessary, that the proceeds will not jeopardize your beneficiary's eligibility for any government assistance the beneficiary may receive in the future. The SNT must meet the technical requirements referred to above that most attorneys miss.

- In addition, you must make sure the executor or person handling the estate either understands these concepts or at least plans to employ advisors and attorneys who understand these concepts and who understand how critical it is to get the estate administration right after you and your spouse's deaths.

If all the pieces come together correctly, qualified beneficiaries with disabilities will meet the standards to use the old "stretch IRA rules," which, as shown above, are life changing.

---

1 There is no solicitation for legal services being made by me, James Lange, nor by Lange Legal Group, LLC.

The Burden of Proving Disability

The government administrative process puts a huge burden on the family to prove the need for SSI, SSDI, or Medicare. And if you haven't gone through the process of formally qualifying your beneficiary with a disability with the SSA, the law's definition of who qualifies as an Eligible Designated Beneficiary (EDB) under the SECURE Act is quite narrow. Caring for individuals with a disability is already a financial and emotional burden, and the medical system is already straining. But if you read Chapter 12, you'll learn Deborah McFadden's secrets for getting young adults relatively quickly and easily qualified for SSI or SSDI.

If you are the parent of a disabled child, please make sure you have appropriate experts working for your and your child's benefit.

Why Appropriate Estate Planning is So Critical

The contrast between the treatment of Inherited IRAs under the SECURE Act and the old law is bad enough for a beneficiary *without* a disability. Because their disabilities often preclude them from entering or remaining in the workforce, many beneficiaries with disabilities severe enough to qualify for the SECURE Act exemption are far more dependent upon inherited monies to finance their basic living expenses than the average recipient of an Inherited IRA might be. It is challenging enough to live with a disability, but to suffer that and be broke is tragic. And it is particularly devastating to know that there will be potentially millions of Americans with disabilities who will live in poverty whose long-term financial security could have been insured if their parents/grandparents/loved ones had only known about and used the appropriate retirement and estate planning tools. Below, we address some of the many technicalities involved in getting things right.

Our Challenges Gaining Social Security Disability Insurance (SSDI)

In our case, our daughter was first turned down for benefits and did not qualify for Medicare. With only weeks remaining for our appeal, our attorney fired us because she didn't think she could win the case. Upon a close examination of the record of the original case, my wife noticed glaring errors and omissions. Luckily, we got another attorney on short notice for the appeal.

My wife compiled a huge binder of accurate and detailed documentation and exhaustively reviewed the work of the first attorney. With the help of that second attorney, we eventually won the case on appeal. As my colleague Deborah McFadden has so meticulously described in Chapter 12, the language used to report an applicant's condition is so important.

Because of this immense effort and our other steps, Erica is assured of a much better life with no money worries. She will have the funds to pay for high-quality housing, concierge medical care, private nurses, social workers, specialists, treatment modalities not covered by insurance, and healthy food. In short, she will be financially cared for just as well after our deaths as she is while we are still alive.

Social Security Means-Testing

A quick note about Social Security assistance for your child with a disability: Supplemental Security Income (SSI) is means-tested, but Social Security Disability Insurance (SSDI) is not means-tested. For example, to receive SSI, there are limits on both the child's income and their assets. To qualify for SSDI, the child could have both high income (though not high earned income) and high assets.

Once one of the child's parents is receiving Social Security retirement (or disability) benefits, or, for a deceased parent, if receiving benefits at the time of death, the adult child with a disability can claim SSDI based upon that parent's work history. In order to qualify, the adult child's disability must have begun before age 22. It does not matter that your child does not have any work history. Our daughter qualified under SSDI. SSDI doesn't put a limit on the amount of assets or unearned income. There are constraints on earned income.

New Definitions Used to Qualify as an EDB

Frankly, I think the definitions that the IRS uses to determine who is disabled are far too limited, and attorneys who work in this area will tell you benefits are often denied for deserving beneficiaries. Parents of a child with a disability have enough challenges in their lives that they should not have to worry about meeting the IRS's and the administrative judge's overly strict view of who qualifies as having a disability. Let's look at some of the definitions.

Disabled Beneficiary

A disabled beneficiary is defined in Code Section 72(m)(7): "For purposes of this section, an individual shall be considered to be disabled if he is unable to engage in any substantial gainful activity by reason of any medically determinable physical or mental impairment which can be expected to result in death or to be of long continued and indefinite duration. An individual shall not be considered to be disabled unless he furnishes proof of the existence thereof in such form and manner as the Secretary may require."

This definition is quite limited. The intended beneficiary must have substantial health challenges which result in a limited capacity for earning a living. However, if the beneficiary can engage in "**any substantial gainful activity**," even if very limited, that person will not qualify as an EDB and will not be eligible for the exception to the 10-year rule. Partial disability doesn't count, nor does a disability that prevents the heir from working in a previous line of occupation but does not preclude some other type of gainful employment. We know of a parent whose son had low-functioning Down Syndrome who was denied benefits because, with substantial support, he could work bagging groceries.

The other issue IRA owners should worry about is that the beneficiary with a disability may not be inclined or able to prove their disability without your help. That is a frequent problem when it comes to proving disability for other benefits like SSDI. If you have a beneficiary with a disability and would like your child to enjoy the benefits of deferring your IRA over their lifetime, it would be prudent to establish proof of their disability while you are still alive, and the sooner, the better.

In our case, our daughter, while bright, could never have assembled the exhaustive documentation her mother assembled to prove her disability—not to mention the grueling work it entailed. I believe that effort made the difference between winning and losing our case. My wife took on that Herculean task. In the feedback we received from the judge, some of the most valuable information we presented were the personal stories from family and friends that described the real-life impact of her disability and the questionnaires completed by her medical providers. This information provided real-life evidence of her disability and ended up being most persuasive in helping win our case. It is important to mention that this sort of information gathering should continue, particularly from regular doctor visits, during the disabled child's life so that disability can be confirmed during the periodic reviews by Social Security.

Chronically Ill Beneficiary

A chronically ill heir who will receive the same tax benefits as a beneficiary with a disability is defined in Code Section 7702B(c)(2) with certain modifications. This Code Section provides: "(A) In General—The term "chronically ill individual" means any individual who has been certified by a licensed health care practitioner as—(i) being unable to perform (without substantial assistance from another individual) at least two activities of daily living for a period of at least 90 days due to a loss of functional capacity, (ii) having a level of disability similar (as determined under regulations prescribed by the Secretary in consultation with the Secretary of Health and Human Services) to the level of disability described in clause (i), or (iii) requiring substantial supervision to protect such individual from threats to health and safety due to severe cognitive impairment.

If you have a beneficiary with a disability and would like your child to enjoy the benefits of deferring your IRA over their lifetime, it would be prudent to establish proof of their disability while you are still alive, and the sooner, the better.

Such term shall not include any individual otherwise meeting the requirements of the preceding sentence unless within the preceding 12-month period a licensed health care practitioner has certified that such individual meets such requirements. (B) Activities of daily living for purposes of subparagraph (A), each of the following is an activity of daily living: (i) Eating (ii) Toileting (iii) Transferring (iv) Bathing (v) Dressing (vi) Continence."

I would offer the same caution I mentioned in the previous section on beneficiaries with disabilities. I think it is prudent for you to establish proof of your beneficiary's chronic illness while you are still alive.

As Martin Shenkman wrote in *Forbes*: (**https://www.Forbes.com/Sites/Martinshenkman/2020/12/29/Secure-Act**):

> *"The above definition suffers from the same overly restrictive terms as the definition of 'disabled' above. Many intended heirs are living with challenges that may limit or even prevent gainful employment, but they are not so severely incapacitated as to meet the requirements of chronically ill according to the above definition. Yet, these same people who need the protections of a trust, and who may desperately need the economic benefits from the plan assets to be bequeathed, will be forced to have the plan balance distributed in 10-years and lose the continued tax deferred growth, etc."*

Any IRA owner planning on an heir meeting the requirements of being "disabled" or "chronically ill" to qualify as an EDB under the SECURE Act should carefully evaluate the stringent requirements involved.

The Three Critical Steps to Qualify as an EDB

What must happen under the new law for a beneficiary with a disability or chronic illness to qualify for the exception to the ten-year acceleration of income taxes?

- First, you must have a favorable finding of the beneficiary being considered disabled or chronically ill.

- Second, you must have appropriate estate planning, and, more specifically, you must have the correct language for assigning the beneficiary of your IRA and retirement plan. In addition, it may be prudent to have a special needs trust, but even then, that trust must also meet the four conditions required to qualify for Inherited "stretch IRA" status.

- Third, you must have appropriate estate administration after your and your spouse's death.

A Critical Extra Step for Ensuring Qualification as EDB

In order to qualify as an EDB under the IRS Proposed Regulations, a disabled or chronically ill beneficiary of an Inherited IRA or retirement plan must be disabled or chronically ill as of the date of death of the original IRA or retirement plan owner.

The Proposed Regulations also require documentation supporting the disabled or chronically ill diagnosis of the beneficiary be submitted to the IRA custodian by a certain date.

Under the current proposal, the documentation supporting the diagnosis of a disability or chronic illness *must* **be provided to the custodian of the account** no later than October 31 of the calendar year following the calendar year of the IRA owner's or employee's death. That means if your disabled child or a trust for the benefit of your child is the beneficiary of your IRA and you die on July 1, 2024, the IRA custodian must be provided with documentation supporting the disability of your disabled beneficiary no later than October 31, 2025.

Although this will not apply to most readers and their children, the Proposed Regulations also discuss how the terms of the SECURE Act will be applied to disabled or chronically ill individuals who inherit an IRA or retirement plan from a parent when they are under the age of 21. As stated above, in order to qualify as EDBs, proper documentation verifying that a minor was disabled or chronically ill as of the date of death of their parent who was the original plan owner must be submitted to the IRA custodian or plan administrator no later than October 31 of the calendar year following the calendar year of the death.

Therefore, if the parent of a 3-year-old boy were to die with that child as a named beneficiary of his or her IRA or retirement plan, or with a minor's trust for his benefit as a named beneficiary, and then at age 10 he was to be deemed disabled or chronically ill, despite having acquired a 'disabled' designation, at age 21, he will no longer be considered an EDB for the purposes of that asset and will be forced to begin taking distributions from it in accordance with the SECURE Act's accelerated timeline.

You may be wondering why that is the case; after all, the boy obtained the proper documentation to be deemed an EDB at age 10. So, what's the problem?

The problem is two-fold:

1. the boy was not deemed disabled *as of the date of the original plan owner's death*

2. the documentation of his disability was not submitted to the plan administrator on or before October 31 of the calendar year following the year of his parent's death

So, while this boy *will* be eligible to stretch any IRAs or retirement plans he might inherit *after* his diagnosis (which was made at age 10), he will never be able to acquire that EDB status with respect to the plan he inherited at age 3.

Regardless of whether your disabled or chronically ill beneficiary is under or over 21, if this legislation passes and becomes law, we recommend you provide the documentation for your disabled or chronically ill beneficiary to the custodian or plan administrator while you are still alive. If you cannot provide the documentation itself, even asking the custodian to make a notation in your account file regarding the disabled or chronically ill beneficiary's status is better than nothing. Minimally, if you at least have a plan in place for a designated person to obtain and produce this information to the custodian after you pass away, it can help ensure that this vital deadline is not missed.

The documentation and the timing of providing the documentation is critical, and if not done properly, the lifetime stretch could be eliminated, and your disabled beneficiary would be limited to the 10-year rule. All of the painstaking efforts you took to provide for your child with a disability or chronic illness could go up in smoke if the documentation is presented too late.

Under-Publicized Inherited 401(k) Strategy for IRA Owners in a High Tax Bracket with a Disabled Child Who Will Be in a Low Tax Bracket

There is an entire discussion of the benefits of a one-person 401(k) plan over an IRA discussed in Chapter 7, and that information would be a good background for this idea that some readers will absolutely love.

This fascinating strategy entails planning for your beneficiary to make a Roth conversion of an Inherited 401(k) or 403(b) after you die. By the way, we also use this strategy for clients who don't have a child with a disability. The specific asset type matters here; this does not work with an Inherited IRA. It only works with non-IRA 401(k) and 403(b) retirement plans, provided it is allowed under that plan. This strategy works particularly well if you are in a high-income-tax bracket, but your beneficiary will be in a low-income-tax bracket and your beneficiary will not need to qualify for any government assistance program with an income and/ or asset eligibility limit. That is, if it makes sense for the disabled beneficiary to receive means-based government benefits, then the income generated from the Roth IRA conversion after your death (see below) will likely need to be recognized at the higher trust income tax rate rather than the individual level, reducing some of the strategic tax benefits of this strategy.

If your child is receiving or will receive government benefits, you will want to read Chapter 13, which discusses special needs trusts, and Chapter 14, which explains how ABLE accounts work.

Please note that we like to create our own one-person 401(k) plans and specifically choose plans that allow this post-mortem conversion feature.

Converting Your Inherited 401(k) or 403(b) Retirement Plan to an Inherited Roth IRA After You Die

We had a client with a high required minimum distribution and tax bracket. He ran a small consulting practice as part of his post "retirement" activities. We recommended he roll his entire IRA into a new one-person 401(k), which has practically the same rules as an IRA. But, when he dies, his disabled beneficiary (who is not receiving public benefits) will be able to make an Inherited Roth 401(k) conversion or even a series of Inherited Roth 401(k) conversions at their low tax rates. This plan could result in the savings of hundreds of thousands of dollars or even more for the beneficiary.

The big distinction between keeping the money in the IRA vs. a Solo 401(k) is that your beneficiary cannot do Roth conversions on an Inherited IRA account, but assuming the plan allows it, your beneficiary could do Roth conversions on an Inherited 401(k) account. If you are creating your own 401(k) plan, you can incorporate that provision. In the old days, it was expensive and time consuming to have your own 401(k) plan. Not anymore. It can be done with a minimum of time and money and could end up being extremely favorable for your child.

This will likely work better for a beneficiary receiving SSDI who doesn't have an income cap to remain eligible for benefits. If this is not your situation, you will need to carefully evaluate the decision to do a Roth conversion and plan for the big jump in income for the beneficiary in the year of conversion so that the conversion does not jeopardize needs-based assistance.

Why we like the idea of moving the assets into a Solo 401(k) vs. an IRA is to have the *flexibility* to do a low-cost Roth conversion or a series of low-cost Roth

> **This fascinating strategy entails planning for your beneficiary to make a Roth conversion of an Inherited 401(k) or 403(b) after you die.**

conversions over a period of time, but only if it makes sense. The advantage of having this option is you can have the Roth account continue to grow tax-free, and your child will be able to take the *stretched* required minimum distributions, providing you with the peace of mind that they will be cared for long after you and your spouse are gone. Another advantage of utilizing the one person 401(k) plan is it is part of a strategy to convert after-tax dollars inside an IRA to a Roth without having to pay the taxes, which we discuss in Chapter 7.

The beauty of the Roth conversion either while you are alive or even after you are gone (which is only possible with an Inherited 401(k) or 403(b) account and not an IRA) is your beneficiary can get all the benefits of 'tax-free' and 'stretched' required minimum distributions of the Inherited Roth IRA for their entire life just like under the pre-2020 rules before the effective date of the SECURE Act.

Potential Downsides of the 401(k) vs. the IRA

The biggest downside of a 401(k) plan designed to be used as an Inherited 401(k) is it is subject to the required minimum distribution rules while you are alive. This is assuming you own more than 5% of the company that had the earned income that is needed to establish the 401(k) plan. You can get around that by transferring that money to a Roth IRA, but then the child won't be able to make an Inherited IRA conversion after your death. You might consider maintaining as much money in the 401(k) as you think your child should convert.

Another caveat to mention, a potential downside to having the Roth conversions done post-death is the inherent income tax liability on the conversion cannot be deducted on your federal estate tax return or possibly your state inheritance tax return (for example, Pennsylvania).

Another possible downside to this plan is it is foreseeable they will change the rules on converting Inherited 401(k)s. Consequently, we still see doing the conversions yourself as the primary Roth strategy, not just relying on your beneficiary or trustee to perform the conversion after death.

This is one of the reasons why it is so important to do proper planning and run the numbers ahead of time to see what makes sense for your particular situation.

While the above strategy could be extremely useful for a limited number of readers, it is usually secondary to making Roth IRA conversions while you are alive.

Another downside to this strategy that we learned from a column by Jeffrey Levine is that you can't do a Qualified Charitable Distribution (QCD) with a one person 401(k) plan.

In Conclusion

We have tried to provide as much information as possible for either the do-it-yourselfer or for the parent who wants solid information to help choose and work with appropriate financial professionals and special needs attorneys. We hope that either on your own or working with an appropriate team, you implement at least some if not most of these ideas and enjoy the benefits of knowing you took critical steps towards providing for yourself and your child with a disability.

KEY IDEAS

- My daughter, Erica, has a disability that will prevent her from providing for herself. My wife and I worried endlessly, as do most parents of a child with a disability, about ensuring her safety and prosperity after we are gone. Using just three strategies, we took care of that worry. Consequently, Erica will have close to an additional $1.9 million dollars measured in today's dollars to support her over her lifetime. Using the same strategies, someone with a $500,000 IRA can provide their child with an additional $239,000.

The three strategies are:

1. Make a Roth IRA conversion (or several) and contribute to Roth IRAs, backdoor Roth IRAs, and Roth 401(k)s. $1.3 million of the $1.9 million dollar savings for Erica came from us doing a large Roth IRA conversion and contributing to Roth IRAs and Roth 401(k)s.

2. Formally establish your child's status as disabled with the SSA. Remember, however, that the definitions are extremely narrow and may not cover your beneficiary who you consider disabled or chronically ill. We are confident

---

Key Ideas continue on the following page.

KEY IDEAS
(continued)

that the SSA designation will fast track a child's status as an Eligible Designated Beneficiary (EDB) under the SECURE Act. The EDB status will allow the child to stretch distributions from retirement accounts over a lifetime. These qualifying beneficiaries are in effect deferring distributions on their tax-deferred Inherited IRA or their tax-free Inherited Roth IRA to some extent for their entire lives. The additional deferral of the Inherited Roth IRA was worth an extra $600,000 for our daughter.

3. Draft an optimized estate plan with appropriate wills, trusts, and IRA and 401(k) and Roth IRA beneficiary forms that, to a large extent, will allow your child and/or a trust for your child's benefit to "stretch" or defer distributions of any Inherited IRAs and/or Roth IRA for life. Please be sure the trust has the four technical provisions to qualify as an EDB and the right language to protect government benefits for your child. Please also have plans in place for competent estate administration after you are gone.

- Be aware of the documentation requirements and timing required by the custodian of your IRA or employer plan to support your disabled or chronically ill beneficiary. If possible, provide the required documentation to the custodian as soon as you have it, so nothing is compromised later after your death.

- Consider planning for a posthumous Inherited 401(k) Roth conversion that would be taxed at the beneficiaries' rate, not yours.

12

How to Win the Golden Ticket of SSI or SSDI Approval

By Deborah McFadden

As other chapters in this book explain, taking advantage of favorable stretch payment options for Inherited IRAs is a huge benefit from winning approval through the Social Security Administration (SSA) for SSI or SSDI. But there are many other financial benefits that your child will also be eligible for once they get that Golden Ticket. Besides monthly SSI or SSDI payments for life, your child will also be eligible for Vocational Rehabilitation (VR) assistance, which can pay for college or other job training programs, as well as things that allow your child to work. The total of vocational benefits by themselves could be as much as $150,000. In addition, benefits could include the cost of making a vehicle accessible. Your child will be eligible for Medicaid or Medicare and other medical benefits. Your kids can stay on your insurance after age 26 if they have a disability. Personal care attendants, SNAP benefits, and even respite care for parents are also available, among many other benefits that will help your child live their best life.

Beyond Finances

I would be totally remiss if I did not also spend some time in this chapter addressing some of the psychological and emotional experiences that accompany parenting and providing for a child with a disability. Raising a child with a disability is expensive. Much of the information in this book can help with that. But in my experience, many parents and children too have quieter and less spoken-of concerns that I have also experienced personally. Giving my daughters (two of whom have disabilities) the best chances in life has meant navigating a system that none of us have been trained in. We have examples of what it means to be a parent; there is scads of advice for parents, but having a child with a disability brings a whole lot of different challenges.

In this chapter, I'm sharing what I've learned from navigating the labyrinthine rules and regulations of the Social Security Administration and helping both my own children and hundreds of other children obtain approval for SSI and SSDI.

Parents of children with disabilities are so often worn out from fighting for their children and being constantly shut down. You fight and struggle for healthcare, for inclusion, for fairness, and for your children's best interests. Getting these benefits will not only make a huge difference for your child, but also for you. The quality of my life would have been much worse had I not received these benefits for our daughters.

So, while I do get to the specifics of applying for disability benefits, I also share aspects of my personal journey to present a fuller picture of why getting the help you and your child deserve and are entitled to is so important.

I can't personally work with all the families who need this help, so I'm sharing this information so that many other families can get the help they need.

The Golden Ticket

When your child is approved for SSI or SSDI, they qualify for many programs. It's a Golden Ticket. Your child may not need to use all the benefits, but isn't it reassuring that these benefits are available if he or she does need them?

Many (like Jim's daughter Erica) get denied the first time. The Social Security Administration states that in 2022, 65% of first-time applicants were denied. But this shouldn't happen if you know how to present your application. I've been helping families get approved for SSI or SSDI for years and have a 95% success rate.

I'm the mother of three daughters, two with disabilities. Tatyana was born with spina bifida, but she has also won more than 20 medals—eight of them gold—as a paralympic wheelchair racer. If she wins two more medals at the 2024 Paris Paralympic Games, she'll be the most decorated track athlete ever. Hannah was born with a hip and leg deformity so severe that we had her leg amputated when she was six. Hannah competed alongside her sister as a wheelchair racer at the 2012 London Paralympics and is currently ranked third in the world as a para rock climber.

I was able to get both of my daughters approved for SSI. Vocational Rehabilitation (VR) funds paid for college for both. For some families, this can be worth almost a quarter of a million dollars. I quit keeping track of the financial statistics after I helped families secure $25 million in total benefits.

Jim's comment: Deborah's success rate helping qualified candidates get approved for SSI and SSDI on their initial application really speaks for itself and I don't know that there is anyone in the world who could come close to her experience and knowledge in this area. I only wish that we had known Deborah before Erica submitted her first application for SSDI.

If this sounds like a recommendation to strongly consider her services if your child is applying for SSI or SSDI, it is. I predict she will soon have way more demand for her services than her capacity to do the work, so I wouldn't think too long about using her services. Please see page 467 to learn more about working with her.

(back to Deborah)

My Path to Becoming an Expert Helping Children and Adults with Disabilities

When I was in college, I contracted Guillain-Barré syndrome and was paralyzed from the chest down. I was in a wheelchair. It affected both of my hands, and I drooled. It was a different time then, and I experienced the discrimination and obstacles that prevented many people with disabilities from living successful, independent lives.

Before my disability, I was a straight-A student on the honor roll. After the onset of my disability, I needed someone to help me take notes in class and write out answers for exams, which the administration said was unfair. I agreed with them that it was unfair. It was horribly unfair that I had to speak clearly and compose my answers to essay questions verbally and without being able to make notes to organize my thoughts. We were still a long way away from academic institutions making accommodations for students with disabilities.

The college administration didn't want me to graduate with a degree. They said I was unemployable. They said I could get some job training to be a phone operator, using a device attached to a baseball hat that I could use to dial a phone. At that time, they couldn't imagine that I would ever be a manager and supervise people. They certainly couldn't imagine that I would serve in the federal government as a U.S. Commissioner for Disabilities or that I would go on to serve on advisory boards across the country and around the world to help improve the lives of people with disabilities.

With a lot of effort, I slowly recovered, and today, you likely wouldn't be able to tell that I was once in a wheelchair.

I met Tatyana at an orphanage while working in Russia to distribute aid for the U.S. State Department. She was five years old and had been born with spina bifida. This was during the time when Russian President Gorbachev was promoting more open communications with the West, and President George H. W. Bush was very supportive of all his efforts. My objective was to distribute aid to those who were most in need and with the fewest advocates. Those included people with disabilities, orphans, and the elderly. I had no intention of adopting a child, let alone one with a disability, until I met Tatyana. She had these bright eyes, and although I spoke English and she spoke Russian, I felt she was following along with every word I said. At my hotel that night, I could not get her out of my mind. The orphanage director told me she'd put a Polaroid picture of me up on a shelf, and Tatyana was telling everyone, "That's my mom!" Little did we know she was prescient!

It was the same experience with my other two daughters. With each child, my first thought was, "This is my daughter." It was love at first sight, much as it is with all moms and dads. I did not go through any calculation with Tatyana or Hannah of what it meant to adopt a child with a disability (Ruthi does not have a disability). These were my children. I adopted the children who were meant to be my children, two of whom just happen to have a disability.

When I met Hannah at an orphanage in Albania, she couldn't walk because of the severe deformity in her left leg. However, this did not stop her from crawling all over the orphanage. I saw her taking care of the younger kids and protecting them. She made sure that they got the food and especially the candy that I brought with me. She took the treats I brought and made sure that those children who were not able to get out of their cribs also got these treats. At a young age, she was a "caregiver" to children younger than her and even older children who just needed a bit more help; it was amazing.

Like all parents of children with disabilities, my next thoughts for Tatyana and Hannah centered on how to treat the disability and give them the best opportunities for success in life. For Tatyana, that meant lots of surgeries because her health had been neglected for the first five years of her life. For Hannah, that included making the decision to amputate her leg. I was totally focused on adapting to their needs and getting them the necessary medical help. I had decided that I needed to make them strong and healthy to help them deal with their disabilities as best as they could.

For me, that meant getting them both involved in sports because I knew that sports make people stronger, not just physically, but in the many ways that would help them deal with things in their lives. So, I got them both involved in wheelchair track, swimming, sled hockey, wheelchair basketball, and any other sport we could adapt to their abilities. I found that sports were an excellent way to improve their strength and integrate them into the schools and the community.

From that bleak orphanage in Russia, Tatyana brought with her an attitude of *Ya Sama!* This Russian phrase can be translated as "I can do it!" She'd already taught herself to walk on her hands and use her arms to scoot around the orphanage.

Even at that age, she was developing upper body strength and was not letting anything stop her.

At home with me and my wife Bridget O'Shaughnessey in the U.S., she faced many hurdles as a young child. In elementary school, I had to fight for her right to play on the playground equipment and to participate in physical education classes with the other kids. The kids marveled at her upper body strength and always wanted her on their team for any games where that was an advantage.

Among all the sports she tried, wheelchair racing was where Tatyana truly excelled. By the time she was 13, she was competing at the national level. At age 15—before she even started high school—she qualified as the youngest U.S. track and field team member for the 2004 Paralympics in Athens, where she won silver and bronze medals. Four years later, at the 2008 Paralympic Games in Beijing, she won four more medals; in London in 2012, she won another four. So far, she's won 20 Paralympic medals: eight gold, eight silver and four bronze. She even competed in the 2014 Winter Games in Sochi as a cross-country skier, winning a silver medal with her birth mother in attendance.

In 2009, she raced in her first marathon in Chicago and won. Since then, she's won 24 major marathons and is the only person to have won the Grand Slam (Chicago, Boston, London, and New York) four consecutive times.

Today, besides training for the 2024 Paris Paralympics, her passion is advocating for others with disabilities. One of her favorite sayings is, "Life isn't about what you don't have. It's about what you do with the gifts you're given."

Hannah also has been a lifelong athlete. Like her older sister, she excelled at wheelchair running and, at age 16, qualified for the U.S. track and field team at the 2012 Paralympic Games in London as the team's youngest member. Not only was this her first international meet, but she competed with her older sister Tatyana, marking the first time siblings have competed together in the Paralympic Games. She also raced in the Rio Paralympic Games in 2016.

Shortly before the tryouts for the Tokyo games in 2020, she 'fell out of love' with wheelchair racing and stepped away. A friend suggested that she try rock climbing, and to everyone's astonishment, she was a born natural at the sport. At her very first event in 2021, just after she started climbing, she won! Although it frightens me to death when I see pictures of her far up on a cliff face, just a tiny dot in a vertical expanse of rock, I am grateful she has found something she excels at. Today, she's ranked number three in the world in para-climbing.

While her achievements in para-climbing show off her upper body strength, it's her inner strength that is truly amazing. She does not let anything hold her back. Today, she works at Achilles International, and is an example of "get over it, and just do it."

Fighting for the Right to Participate

Life as an elite athlete hasn't always been easy for either Hannah or Tatyana. When Tatyana started high school on her return from the Athens Paralympic Games, she wanted to join the track team. Track teams in high school usually let just about anyone with an interest in track participate. It's not like there are only a few spots available for long jumpers, pole vaulters, or discus throwers. But the athletic director told her, "Sorry, but you can't race with the team. There are clubs for kids like you."

So, we sued the school district, not for money, but for her right to be on the track team. That court battle wasn't easy. Not everyone at her school supported her lawsuit. As a fifteen-year-old girl in a wheelchair, she had to face the school district's lawyers in suits and hear them say openly in court that it was okay for the school to treat her differently because of her disability. She wasn't fighting just for herself but for her younger sister Hannah and all the other kids with disabilities who would come after her.

After Tatyana won her lawsuit, we pushed for the passage of the Fitness and Athletics Equity for Students with Disabilities Act (a.k.a Tatyana's Law) in Maryland, which later became a federal mandate.

Throughout her life, and to this day, Tatyana's attitude of *Ya Sama!* has been a key to her success. Likewise, Hannah has always had a gutsy attitude and never liked people giving her pity. She says, "it is what it is," and does not dwell on the fact that she has lost a leg. Though Tatyana and Hannah are thriving, they both deal with the challenges of living in a world that isn't always accessible. Whenever they leave their homes to go to a store or restaurant or fly in an airplane and stay in a hotel to participate in an athletic event, they face many of the same challenges that your child with a disability might also face. That internal attitude of "I Can Do It!" has allowed both Hannah and Tatyana to excel.

It is my hope with this chapter that some of Hannah's "Can Do" and Tatyana's *Ya Sama!* attitude will rub off on you and your child. Everything I learned over the years in my own life with a disability and helping my girls thrive and excel provided the foundation for my evolution as a strong advocate for young people with disabilities.

How One Event Triggered an Awakening

When Tatyana was applying to colleges, several schools offered her a full-ride scholarship because of her success as a wheelchair racer. The financial aid package for most of these schools was around $50,000 per year. That scholarship money was clearly a godsend, but because Tatyana was approved for SSI, I knew she could get close to $20,000 in VR funding for college. So, I told the schools that they should be offering Tatyana half the amount because we could get the other half paid for with VR funds. That government support meant the university could offer another $25,000 scholarship to a deserving prospective student.

As we toured the school, I stopped to speak with other students who had disabilities, and I inquired if they were on SSI and working with VR. Alarmingly, most had never heard of the program. This is still the case. Even though SSI and SSDI have been around since the 1930s, these programs are not well known.

Now I had a new mission: to help students and parents of children with disabilities get qualified for SSI and SSDI. It started with helping students at Tatyana's school qualify for SSI. These students were all extraordinarily capable individuals. But that didn't change the fact that because they couldn't do some things the way a person without a disability could, or because they needed help or accommodations for some activities, they fit the criteria for approval for SSI or SSDI.

I started telling other parents at wheelchair athletic events about how VR funds could help them pay for their children to go to college. When you have a child with a disability, there are always a lot of extraordinary expenses. A prosthetic leg can cost tens of thousands. High-quality wheelchairs start around $3,000 and can run as high as $30,000 or even more. Modifying a van to accommodate a wheelchair can cost a minimum of $10,000. Adding tuition and room and board on top of that puts college out of reach for many parents without the added assistance from the government programs.

Soon, colleges and universities began referring students to me, and over time, my name spread across many disability communities. I've worked with hundreds of young adults with disabilities and have a track record of getting 90% of clients approved, sometimes as quickly as in just a few weeks.

An Overview of SSI and SSDI

- SSI is for people who don't have a sufficient work history to claim benefits on their own. Monthly benefits under SSI are up to $914 as of January 2023. Your child may also be eligible for additional state benefits, depending on where you live. This is a poverty program. SSI is not intended to make your child wealthy. Your child cannot have more than $2,000 in assets, and their income is strictly limited. But if your child applies after they turn age 18, SSA no longer counts the parents' income or assets when they evaluate your child's application.

- SSDI is for people who have worked at least 10 quarters (for the SSA, a quarter equals 13 weeks) or who have a parent who is receiving retirement or disability benefits or a parent who is deceased and who worked at least 10 quarters (thus qualifying for benefits). SSDI has no asset limits, but your child will still be subject to strict income limits if they work. In addition, if your child is claiming benefits on your work record, your child's disability must have begun before age 22.

- SSDI benefits are often higher than SSI. That's why I recommend getting your child on SSI before you begin receiving benefits and then switching to SSDI when you start receiving benefits. The approval process for both programs is the same. The difference is which benefits your child qualifies for based on your specific family situation.

- If your child is collecting SSDI benefits under their own work record, their monthly benefit will be calculated using a method similar to what is used to calculate Social Security benefits at full retirement age. Average benefits in January 2023 were around $1,483, according to the SSA.

- If your child is collecting benefits based on a parent's work record, they will receive 50% of the parent's retirement or disability benefit or 75% of a deceased parent's benefit. SSDI benefits are subject to a family limit. The total benefits paid to a family are generally between 150% and 180% of the parent's benefit. This means that if you have more than one child with a disability, each will likely receive less than the full 50% of the parent's benefit.

Overview of the Vocational Rehabilitation Program

Vocational Rehabilitation (VR) is a program designed to help people be gainfully employed. When your child is approved for SSI or SSDI, they will also be eligible for VR benefits. This program is administered by the states. Many of the families I work with use VR benefits to pay for college for their child. This program provides money towards tuition and living expenses and can be worth up to $150,000 or more per person over their time in school. This means you can send your child to college and continue saving for your own retirement. Furthermore, if you've been putting money into a 529 Plan for your child's college, you can roll funds from that into an ABLE account or a Roth IRA, as Jim explains in Chapters 14 and 23.

VR services are wide-ranging, depending on the individual's abilities and goals. Both of my daughters, Tatyana and Hannah, used VR funds to pay for bachelor's degrees and then went on to get their master's degrees. VR also pays for other kinds of employment training, such as technical schools or certifications. They can also help pay for the modifications to a car to make it accessible for your child so they can get to work.

You don't need to be on SSI or SSDI to get VR assistance, but like SSI, VR considers your financial means. So, you might as well get your child qualified for the Golden Ticket of SSI or SSDI because he or she will also automatically qualify to be a client of VR funds.

SSI and SSDI are Not Welfare Programs

I don't like to talk too much about SSI being a poverty program because many parents mentally equate that as meaning it is a welfare program, and they don't want their child on welfare. But this is a harmful misconception. SSI and SSDI are not welfare programs. They are entitlement programs that you, as a parent, have paid into with your payroll taxes. If you developed a disability, you would receive SSDI. SSI is for people who haven't paid into the system, but our children are entitled to this because we have paid into the system. Now that Tatyana and Hannah are successful professionals, they're not on SSI anymore, and they have paid far more into the system through taxes than they received as benefits.

There aren't many advantages to having a disability, but these programs can help level the playing field for our children and provide them access to the things they need. These resources can help children to become the best version of themselves.

This is not just a problem for the parents. Some children will resist qualifying for SSI or SSDI because they see it as a way of admitting to a "weakness" they don't want to acknowledge. This is devastating because they are not only hurting themselves, but they are hurting their parents. One of my professional roles is talking to these adult children directly and explaining the process of qualifying for SSI or SSDI. I try to help them understand that receiving these benefits is not stigmatizing; it is empowering and could make a big difference in their lives and their parents' lives.

Getting Support Is an Act of Empowerment, Not an Act of Resignation

Parents I have worked with have expressed unwarranted fears that they are resigning their child to a dependent future by getting SSI or SSDI benefits for their child. If I apply for this, does that mean there is no hope for them? Going on SSI or SSDI has nothing to do with hope. There is always hope. Your child can go on this program and go off this program if they are ultimately able to work. I got my daughters on this program because I knew this would work out well financially for both of them. But as soon as they got jobs, they both went off it.

I think of the experience Jim and his wife had with their daughter Erica and how she had good days when she was doing okay, but more often she had bad days when she was not. The unpredictable nature of the good and bad days is what keeps Erica from having a steady job or even completing college. I'm sure that all three of them still have hope that she will get better. But she may not. The outcome, however, will be determined by factors unrelated to her SSDI status.

While SSI, SSDI, and VR programs are meant for people with permanent disabilities—disabilities that will never go away—these programs can help your children to become as independent as possible. These programs will provide a safety net for your child and can help them live to their fullest potential, whatever that may be.

Who Qualifies for SSI or SSDI?

The legal definition of disability that SSA will use is "the inability to engage in any substantial gainful activity (SGA) by reason of any medically determinable physical or mental impairment(s) which can be expected to result in death, or which has lasted or can be expected to last for a continuous period of not less than 12 months."

Both SSI and SSDI are programs for people with permanent disabilities who likely need assistance with many of the activities of daily living, such as taking a shower, preparing food, dressing, carrying things, and using the bathroom. They're not for someone who was in a car accident, and after six weeks or six months in a body cast and rehab they will recover. Hannah's leg is not growing back. Tatyana may be the fastest wheelchair runner in the world, but her spina bifida is never getting better. How Tatyana and Hannah accommodate for their disabilities may get better, but there are some things they will never be able to do without help or some kind of accommodation. They will always be dependent on others or on some kind of accommodation or device.

You Must Speak the Language of SSI and SSDI

The language of SSI and SSDI approval is **"I CAN'T."** If you don't speak the right language, you don't get the benefits. You have to take off the hat of *Ya Sama!* and put on the hat of **"I CAN'T."**

When applying for SSI, the emphasis is on all the things your child can't do. Let me make it clear that we never lie or misrepresent when talking to Social Security. We answer things based on "the norm" (which I'll define below). If

Both SSI and SSDI are programs for people with permanent disabilities who likely need assistance with many of the activities of daily living, such as taking a shower, preparing food, dressing, carrying things, and using the bathroom.

I asked Hannah, "Can you climb a flight of stairs?" she'd say, "Yes, of course, I can." She can either hop up on one leg or use her prosthetic leg. Tatyana would lean back in her chair and go down. But that doesn't count. This is not the norm.

When applying for SSI or SSDI, you have to focus on what your child can't do compared to the norm. You have to wear the hat of "I CAN'T."

It's true my daughters are both able to do what they want as long as they have the proper accommodations. But compared to the norm they "CAN'T." They travel around the world and compete in elite athletic events. But compared to the norm they "CAN'T."

I talked to a family who has a child with cerebral palsy, but no one at her school knows she has it because she is so minimally affected. Because that child's disability does not put her outside the norm of what children can do, that family will most likely not be eligible for benefits.

SSI and SSDI Norms Established in the 1930s

SSI bases everything on the norm. I call SSI and SSDI "the crippled, lame, and infirm law." This law was written back in the 1930s. Back then, if you were born with spina bifida, as Tatyana was, you most likely would be in an institution for the rest of your life. Someone would need to take care of you. You would not be employable in the traditional sense.

Of course, that's not the way it is now. The statute for SSI didn't contemplate the many advances in accommodations we have today, many of which came about as part of the 1990 Americans with Disabilities Act, an act I happen to know a bit about. I was fortunate to be one of the main authors of the ADA during my tenure when I was the United States Commissioner of Disabilities.

If I use my daughter Tatyana as an example, she needs a shower with grab bars, a shower chair, and an accessible shower handle. If she has those things, she can manage quite well. Now Tatyana travels all over the world for athletic events, and sometimes she doesn't get those things. But she still manages because she has learned how to accommodate for her difficulty balancing and not having the use of her legs. She also has incredible upper body strength from a lifetime of using her arms to get around, and she has learned how to be careful in situations where she might lose her balance. The caution she has developed is akin to the way a person without a disability learns to walk on black ice.

But for SSI purposes, compared to the norm, she can't shower on her own.

Tatyana lives on her own and cooks for herself, but she needs adaptations in her kitchen to do that. If I asked Tatyana to help me with Thanksgiving dinner and asked her to carry the 35-pound turkey on my grandmother's antique china serving platter with hot gravy all around it, she couldn't do it.

Because she has spina bifida, compared to the norm for SSI purposes, she can't cook for herself.

As another example, what if I asked Hannah to help me with laundry? If I lived in a four-story townhouse and asked her to bring the laundry from the third floor to the basement, she wouldn't be able to do that in the "normal way."

For SSI, they're *not asking about how your child manages to do things*. They're asking if your child can do it based on the norm. Remember, SSI is the "crippled, lame, and infirm law," which means that he or she can't accomplish tasks when compared to the norm. The definitions for eligibility were written a long time ago. It's the standard of the 1930s, which meant your child would be in an institution and would need people to take care of them.

What is the Process for Applying for SSI/SSDI?

Now that you understand the language that the SSA uses and the mindset shift required when preparing to apply for benefits, let's talk about how the process works.

First, the timing: When working with a family, I generally start the process the month after a young adult turns 18. By the SSA's definition, they're independent adults the month after they turn 18. It doesn't matter if your child's eighteenth birthday is October 1 or October 31. According to SSA, on November 1, your child is now an adult. Your household's income and assets will no longer automatically disqualify your child from eligibility for SSI. You can't start the process—even by simply requesting an appointment—until the first day of the month after your child turns 18, or they will treat the entire application as that of a dependent child. And this rule applies to all applicants who start the process too early, even if the applicant in question is of age based on the SSA's definition when the application itself is submitted.

The exception to waiting until the child turns age 18 is if your income is low enough that they can be on SSI or if they are eligible for SSDI. If your child falls into one of the categories listed above, then you can apply for SSDI before they are age 18 because SSDI is not means-tested. SSA does not consider your income or assets for SSDI applications. With SSDI, your child is not limited to $2,000 or less in net worth but will be subject to limits on employment income.

The reason you want to start the application for either SSI or SSDI as soon as possible is that the benefits begin accruing as soon as you start the application process. If it takes a year to approve the application, your child will receive a year's worth of benefits when it is approved.

This is a Recipe for Successful SSI/SSDI Applications

The families who follow these directions exactly, without thinking too much about the reasons for doing it this way, tend to be the ones who are most successful when they do this on their own. It's like learning how to bake, and you have a recipe for a chocolate cake from a master baker. If you substitute lemons for the chocolate on your first try, you won't get the chocolate cake. After you've mastered baking, you can tweak the recipe, but at least the first time through, you need to follow the recipe exactly.

It's the same with the process I've developed over years of working with families to get benefits for their children. If you don't follow the recipe exactly, you might not get the desired result—approval for SSI or SSDI for your child.

Jim's comment: The following section is absolute gold. My advice is don't try to improve Deborah's process. Just follow it.

How to Get Started

The process for applying for either SSI or SSDI starts out the same. The SSA employees you work with will help you determine which benefit your child is qualified for. **You can start an application in three ways:**

1. Make an appointment and go to a physical office

2. Apply online

3. Call and make an appointment

The clock for benefits starts ticking as soon as you do any of these three things. If you look on the Social Security Administration's website, they'll ask you to fill out a form online because they say it will be faster. In reality, it's not faster. It's just easier for them. Instead, I get on the phone with the child (who is now 18 and one month and considered an adult by Social Security) and call for an appointment. I ask for a phone appointment because I often don't live near the families I work with. I'm also on the phone with the young adult when the initial phone appointment happens.

During that initial call, they will ask the applicant to describe the nature of their disability and date of onset to make sure this person is applying for the right program. Sometimes, people don't know the official medical name for their disability, so the SSA person will ask questions to make sure this young person has a permanent disability. I usually add generic descriptors, like "This person uses a wheelchair to get around" or "They're blind," to help the SSA person develop a picture of the disability.

The SSA person will also ask for the following information to verify the applicant's identity:

- Full name
- Social Security number
- Address
- Date of birth
- City and state of birth
- Mother's maiden name and date of birth
- Name of disability and onset

After they have all that information, they will help you set up an appointment for a second call.

What Happens During the Second Call?

During that second call, which is about a 45-minute interview, the SSA person will first collect basic information, including your child's name, date of birth, and Social Security number (again). The interview starts as an application for both SSI and SSDI, so they will begin by asking work-related questions.

I use the word "child" here, but remember it will be necessary for them to be on the phone as they are now an "adult." If you have guardianship of your child, then you can be on the phone talking for them.

Do you Qualify for SSDI?

- The SSA person will be trying to see if your child qualifies for SSDI, so they will ask if your child has the 10 quarters of work history required to be eligible for benefits on their own record.

- Many of the young adults I work with have tried out summer jobs, just like their friends, or are trying a job to see if they can work. The jobs turn out to be too demanding because of their disability, so they usually end up quitting after a few weeks or months. Your child can't be working when you apply for benefits because if he or she is working, then clearly, SSDI is not needed. If your child *has* worked, the SSA person will ask when they worked, how long they worked, what their job title was, how much they were paid, and why they left—which is usually because of their disability.

- If your child doesn't qualify based on their own work history, the SSA person will ask if there is a parent on whose work record a benefit can be collected. If the answer is no, then your child isn't qualified for SSDI, and the process switches to the SSI application.

- A child who is eligible to receive benefits based on their parent's work record will generally lose their benefits if they get married.

Do you Qualify for SSI?

What Income and Assets Does Your Child Have?

First of all, SSA wants to determine whether your child qualifies from the point of view of income and assets. SSI is means tested, so your child will only qualify if their total assets are worth less than $2,000. They will ask your child questions along these lines:

- Do you have a bank account? How much is in it? Is it savings or checking?
  - Remember that SSI is a poverty program, and because your son or daughter cannot have more than $2,000, he or she likely won't need a savings account.
  - An ABLE account (which is discussed in Chapter 14) won't disqualify your child from SSI as long as the balance is under $100,000.

- Are you currently working? Are you receiving benefits from the Veterans Administration or the Railroad Retirement Administration?
  - Income from any of these sources may limit or even disqualify your child from SSI.

- Have you been in jail?

- Are you married? Or do you live with someone where you present yourself to the world as a married couple (*this question would apply to applicants residing in states that recognize common law marriage*)? Do you have a child?

- – SSA wants to make sure the applicant isn't getting assets from a spouse.
- Next, they will ask about owned property. Do you own a vehicle? Do you own a house?
    - – Technically, owning a car or a home won't disqualify your child. In most cases, the kids don't have cars that they bought and paid for, but the parents purchased a vehicle and paid for any needed modifications. If this is the case, then the answer is no, your child does not own a car.
- Do you have collectibles like baseball trading cards or coins? Do you own something you could sell for money?
- Do you have a trust?
    - – A Special Needs Trust won't disqualify your child as long as it is set up and administered correctly. A testamentary trust you set up in your will or revocable trust won't disqualify your child, at least while you live. You can change that will or revocable trust at any time, and your child will not have access to the funds until your death. However, unless that trust is set up as a Special Needs Trust, it may jeopardize your child's eligibility for government programs after you are gone.
- Do you have life insurance?
    - – A life insurance policy will be counted as a resource if your child owns the policy and the policy has a cash surrender value. However, life insurance policies can be excluded if the total face value of all policies owned by your child insuring any one person's life does not exceed $1,500.

Once the SSA person establishes that your child's net worth is under $2,000 and that they don't have other sources of income, they will finally start asking about your child's disability.

What Is the Nature of Your Child's Disability?

- They will ask about the onset of the disability and at what age the disability began. They will also ask for a list of all the doctors who are treating the child and the dates of the first and most recent visit.
    - – Be prepared to have all the doctors' names, addresses, and phone numbers. If the doctor has been seeing your child for many years, SSA just needs the year of the first visit, not necessarily the month and day. SSA will send form letters to your child's doctors and medical facilities asking about the disability. In addition to those form letters, I always ask parents to get

additional letters from their child's doctors. I'll explain below why those letters are key to approval.

- The SSA person may ask whether your child has an IEP or a 504 plan at school, and they may want to contact the teachers or counselors at the school.

  - This is not always helpful for the application. If they do ask, it may be useful to get in touch with the teachers and counselors and coach them on what language they should use if they are contacted. Remember, the language for SSI and SSDI approval is **"I CAN'T."** Teachers and schools always have hope for their students with disabilities, so the tendency will be to cast everything in a positive light—how this child can do anything and what a delight they are to have in class! Just as we want to make sure doctors use the SSA's language of disability, we want teachers and counselors to be equally careful to use the correct language.

What Are Your Child's Living Expenses?

- SSA will also ask about household expenses like rent, food, and utilities and about other household members.

  - The benefits from SSA are in two pieces: they pay about $600 for living expenses and about $300 per month for rent and utilities. Your son or daughter may have to go back to SSA and ask for the rent piece. I don't know anywhere that anyone can find a place to live for just $300, but that's what SSA allows. SSA will only allow the full monthly benefit if your child is paying their full share of the household living expenses. They will reduce the monthly benefit if your child is living above their means because this implies they are getting support from other household members. This means that if your child is living with you and you're paying all their living expenses, SSA will reduce your child's benefit by the rent piece, or about $300.

- SSA will ask about the monthly rent or mortgage for the home your child is living in and how many people live in the house.

  - Let's say your child lives with you, and the monthly mortgage and utilities cost $2,000. If four people live in the house, SSA will divide $2,000 by four to come up with $500 per month as your child's share of living expenses. Since this is more than $300, your child's benefit will most likely be reduced.

Final Permissions and Waiting for Approval

At some point, the SSA person will ask permission to contact your child's bank, employers (if there have been any), and doctors.

At the end, the SSA person usually asks if there is anybody besides a doctor who knows about the child and their situation. I will usually give them the name and contact information of the applicant's mother or father.

Once SSA has all the materials, they will send it to a Determination Officer (DO), who will review your child's applications. In some cases, the DO will ask the child to see one of the doctors who works for SSA. This may be because your child's doctor didn't fully explain the disability. Or it may be a random check like we sometimes get in TSA lines. Approval may take between 8 and 13 months. Many of the people I work with are approved in three months. My fastest approval was just three days, and my longest was ten months. However, with the backlog from COVID, approval may take longer. Benefits will be calculated starting with the date of the initial application.

Presumptive Disabilities Get Quicker Decisions

You can get a much quicker decision if your child has a progressive illness that will limit their life expectancy or has a condition that is considered a presumptive disability. Severe diseases like Duchenne muscular dystrophy and total deafness or blindness are examples. In those cases, SSA can expedite payments while you wait for the DO to make a decision. I worked with the family of a young woman with muscular dystrophy who was age 18 at the time we applied, and she was receiving benefits within a week.

Doctor Letters Are the Key

While SSA may inform you that additional letters are unnecessary as they will contact the doctors directly, *I have found that these additional letters are absolutely key to a successful application.* I ask parents to start gathering these even before speaking with the SSA, so they have letters ready to send to the SSA right after the 45-minute interview. Make sure to get letters from all of the doctors who have seen your child in the last six months.

As I have said, the language of disability is "I CAN'T." The mistake many doctors make is that their letters don't speak the right language—which is why the parent needs to provide specific guidance. Doctors generally don't emphasize the "CAN'T" enough. These letters need to highlight what your child can't do, not what they have been able to achieve through accommodations. And they need to emphasize that there is no hope for improvement from this disability. Tatyana's spina bifida will never get better. Hannah's amputated leg will never grow back. However, how they accommodate will improve. But the disability doesn't get better.

Doctor's letters should always point out the activities of daily living that your child cannot do— cooking, personal care, shopping, laundry, eating, paying bills—all the activities that most people do without even thinking.

Providing a comprehensive view of your child's situation is vital. Additionally, guiding the doctors on communicating effectively about your child's limitations prepares them for interactions with the SSA. I suggest families provide the following information to doctors regarding what to include in their letters.

Outline for Doctors:
- Name of the disability
- Age of onset
- Confirmation of the disability as permanent with no chance for improvement
- Specifics on the impact of the disability on Activities of Daily Living (ADL)
- Dates of first and most recent visits

These doctor letters should not brag about how your child is playing sports, how they're getting top grades in school, or how they manage to help around the house. If your child's doctor focuses on how well your child is doing despite their disability, you risk your application being denied.

I have heard of children who are double amputees or quadriplegics who have been denied SSI because the doctor's letters talked about how these kids were playing sled hockey or wheelchair football and what amazing athletes these children are. Both of these conditions, by the way, are on a list of medical conditions that should automatically trigger SSI approval.

If your child is seeing a psychologist or another mental health professional, you have to be careful about asking them to write letters. SSA contact with those providers may not be helpful. As with the teachers and counselors from your child's school, these professionals always have hope that their patients or clients will get better. The overriding message from any letters should be that this child has a permanent disability that will not get better—it's all about the "CAN'T," not "CAN."

Remember, the SSA will tell you that these letters are unnecessary because they will be contacting the doctors themselves. But you want to paint a complete picture of why your child deserves these benefits. And you're also training the doctors about how they need to communicate about your child's abilities when SSA contacts them.

The Emotional Mindset Shift You Have to Make

My goal with these letters is to make mom cry—you need to feel like they are describing a helpless child who is unrelated to the child you know and love. Remember that the objective is to "win that Golden Ticket," which will open doors for your child for the rest of his or her life.

You've probably told your child, "**You CAN do it.**" You've probably also told your son or daughter that you believe in them, and they will get a job and have a great life. But for SSI and SSDI approval, you and your child both will have to take off that hat and put on the hat of **"I CAN'T."**

As a person who worked tirelessly on the passage of the ADA, as a woman with a disability, and as a mom with kids with disabilities, I know people with disabilities can do everything. I know there are tons of accommodations, and we can figure out how to accommodate just about everybody.

But for SSI and SSDI approval, we're talking about a law that was written a long time ago, when there weren't all these accommodations, and when the traditional sense of being employable was highly dependent on physical abilities. The approval process is still based on the language of **"I CAN'T."**

This is a complete mindset shift for most parents because you have encouraged your child to do as many things as they possibly can. Most parents are incredibly proud of what their children can do. This is not about being proud of your child. This is about getting them the financial assistance they will (potentially) need for the rest of their lives.

The Mindset That's Required for SSI and SSDI Benefits is Not Recommended for Life

One of the reasons my daughters are successful is because I told them over and over, "You can do it, you can do it." I started with Tatyana in elementary school when I fought for her right to play on the playground. You've told your child to get up if they fall or to try again if they fail. You've been encouraging your child to be as independent as they possibly can be. And if you're not pushing them to do things, you've got to start.

I speak to many parents with kids in wheelchairs and advise them to encourage increased self-reliance. A common response is, "But they get tired; I have to push them." If you always push them, it will be difficult, or even impossible, for them to achieve whatever peak independence would look like for them.

One way to think about it is to imagine you're walking in the mall with a three-year-old. You're holding hands and walking with them, and they fuss, so

My goal with these letters is to make mom cry—you need to feel like they are describing a helpless child who is unrelated to the child you know and love.

you pick them up, carry them for a little bit, and put them down. Maybe you put them in the stroller for a bit. But you understand that if you're going to a mall with a three-year-old, you'll have to walk slowly, pick them up occasionally, and give them time to develop their strength and ability.

It's the same for a child in a wheelchair. Let her push herself. When she gets tired, when she needs your help, assist. But let her experience these challenges because they build resilience and independence.

For me, nothing has been more illustrative of the value of this kind of thinking than my experience helping my daughter Hannah learn to walk.

Hannah was born with Proximal Femoral Focal Deficiency (PFFD), which means she has no femur, hip socket, or knee. They told us she'd never walk because she doesn't have the hip to rotate. When she was six, we had her leg amputated. She got her first prosthetic leg soon after that, but it was still really hard for her to learn to walk.

As soon as Hannah's leg was healed enough to be fitted, she got her first prosthetic and started learning to walk. Because she doesn't have a hip, it was and continues to be hard and painful for her to walk. One day, while she was learning, she came to me and, with all the desperate urgency that only a child can summon, informed me that she *needed* to visit the Build-A-Bear store at our local mall. So, I told her, when you can walk, we will go "Build-A-Bear." Now that was motivation!

In the subsequent weeks, she made real progress, and soon, we were headed to the mall. At this point in the learning process, she was walking, but not with complete mastery, and it was painful for her. But you probably wouldn't have known she was in pain if you'd seen her navigating the mall that day with her purple crutches in the shiny red patent leather shoes she loved so much, her prosthetic leg covered in puppy stickers, and a huge smile lighting up her face. She was just so happy to be walking.

Then she fell, really hard. I bit back my tears, turned to her, and said, "Good fall, Hannah!" because she fell the way she had been taught to protect herself from

You've probably told your child, "You CAN do it." You've probably also told your son or daughter that you believe in them, and they will get a job and have a great life. But for SSI and SSDI approval, you and your child both will have to take off that hat and put on the hat of "I CAN'T."

injury. She was down on that hard floor, working on getting up and trying so hard not to cry—I was so very proud of her courage and perseverance. When this woman came up to me, all in a fury, and angrily asked, "Why aren't you helping her?" to which I replied, "I am." I was helping her by supporting and encouraging her efforts to learn how to get up when she falls down. Trust me. We are not always going to be available to step in and assist our children; fostering independence is vital. That is a strong motivating impetus for this book!

Besides helping your child learn to get up when they fall, you and your child have most likely found accommodations that help them do as much as they can and stay comfortable. As a teenager, Hannah loved to go to the mall with her friends, but all that walking was hard for her. Instead of looking for pity, she'd tell her friends that she was hungry and would meet them at the food court later on. That was her accommodation for not being able to walk as much as her friends.

SSI And SSDI Applications Engender Cognitive Dissonance— For the Parents and the Child

To get your child approved for SSI or SSDI, you have to put on the hat of **"I CAN'T."** It engenders cognitive dissonance—you know how very capable your child is, and it can be emotionally difficult for parents to view their children through the lens of **"I CAN'T."** When I started helping college athletes qualify for SSI and asked them to get letters from their doctors that listed all the things they couldn't do, they experienced cognitive dissonance. These students would say, "Oh, no, I can do everything!" While that might have been true, it couldn't happen without accommodations or modifications—climbing on top of the counter to cook or to get things out of a cabinet isn't the norm that SSA uses to judge whether or not someone can do something.

Like all parents, you want your child to be successful and independent. Using the rubric of twenty-first-century America, being independent usually means

> **It's the same for a child in a wheelchair. Let her push herself. When she gets tired, when she needs your help, assist. But let her experience these challenges because they build resilience and independence.**

having a job, and in today's world, there are many, many examples of people with disabilities who live independent lives and have successful careers. Receiving SSI can facilitate that eventuality. But SSI is a poverty program, and to get approved, you need to shift to the mindset that your child can't do the things that will help them become independent and successful. It is a bit twisted, but true.

You have to make that shift if you want a successful application that gets you that Golden Ticket for your child. You have to put on your emotional armor and do what it takes. Remember that when we talk about SSI and SSDI, your child will qualify because of all the things your child cannot do based on the norm. Don't forget that for the purposes of the definitions SSA is using, being able to *do* an activity with significant modifications is not the same thing as being able to do that activity. For SSI and SSDI, the question is, can your child do an activity in the same, accommodation-free way that is described in the norm?

I know that Jim and his wife see their daughter Erica as an amazing young woman. On her rare good days, she can do anything. But she has her bad days as well when she can't do much of anything, and those days are frequent and unpredictable. I am sure that it was the emphasis on those more common bad days in the letters from family, friends, and doctors that Jim and Cindy gathered for their appeal that made the difference.

I also want to mention again that since my daughters are both working, they're no longer on SSI. But that Golden Ticket helped them get where they are now.

SSI Is Means-Tested, SSDI Is Not

Remember that SSI is not designed to make you or your child wealthy. There are income limits and limits on the assets your child has access to. Your child can't have more than $2,000 in assets. SSDI, on the other hand, has no limits on assets.

Depending on your family situation, it might make sense to apply for SSI when your child is an infant. But most families make too much money or have too much money in the bank to qualify. That's why I wait until the month after my young clients turn 18 to apply.

> **To get your child approved for SSI or SSDI, you have to put on the hat of "I CAN'T."**

Alternatively, your child might be eligible for SSDI, which doesn't have limits on assets. If your adult child worked enough before they developed a disability, they could collect SSDI based on their work history. A child can also collect SSDI based on a parent's work history if that parent is receiving SSA benefits (either retirement or disability benefits) or if the child has a deceased parent who qualified for benefits. These rules for claiming SSDI benefits based on a parent's work history apply to children under 18 and over 18. But if your child is claiming SSDI benefits on your work history, the onset of the child's disability must have occurred prior to age 22. SSI and SSDI both lead to the Golden Ticket. It just depends on how your child qualifies.

The Lifecycle of an Application

It may be helpful for families to think about the application process in three stages.

1. In the first stage, the family consists of a young child who has a disability and at least one living, working parent. In this stage, the parent's income and assets will "count" and disqualify the child from receiving SSI. The parents, who are still working and have not reached the SSA's full retirement age, are not receiving retirement or disability benefits, so the child will not be eligible for SSDI. It is not yet time for an application.

2. In the second stage, the family consists of an adult child (over age 18) who has a disability and a living, working parent. In this stage, the parent's income and assets won't "count," so SSI is an option for the child. The parent is still working and not receiving retirement or disability benefits yet, so the child will not be eligible to apply for SSDI on the parent's work record. It is time to apply for SSI.

3. In the third stage, the family consists of an adult child (over age 18) who has a disability and a living parent who is eligible for SSA benefits, either retirement or disability.

    a. If the parent also has a disability, it is time to apply for SSDI for both the parent and the child.

b. If the parent does not have a disability, it is time to analyze when the parent *should* apply for retirement benefits, which can be as early as age 62 or as late as age 70.[1] Applying early comes with the price tag of an actuarially reduced benefit but the reward of making the child eligible for SSDI sooner. Applying late comes with the reward of a benefit that includes credit for delaying the application but the price tag of making the child eligible for SSDI later. The right time for the applications will depend on each family's situation.

A Change in Qualifying Circumstance Will End SSI Eligibility

Once your child is approved for SSI, your child gets everything, and he will stay on SSI for the rest of his life until he has a change in qualifying circumstances. Those qualifying circumstances include:

- Getting married
- Winning the lottery
- Inheriting money (unless it's in a Special Needs Trust)
- Getting a job and earning money

To be eligible and remain eligible for SSI, your child can't have ready access to more than $2,000 in assets. In practical terms, that means your child must spend almost all of their monthly benefit payment on living expenses.

You always want to tell the truth to the SSA, but that truth should always be framed according to the norms, laws, and regulations that the SSA follows.

How Do You Keep Your Child's Assets Under $2,000?

- **Charge Them for Living Expenses**

  Once your child is approved for SSI, he or she will start receiving monthly benefits. Maximum monthly benefits starting in January 2023 will be $914. Your child can use those benefits to pay for their living expenses. If your child lives with you, you can charge them up to $350 per month for rent and utilities. You can also charge your child for many other living expenses, such as their cell phone or transportation. I give my clients guidelines for calculating those monthly bills, so they don't run afoul of the SSA's picky rules.

  When your child writes a check to you, and you cash it, it's now your money. You can do what you want with it. Your child can't ask you to buy her a car

---

1   Full retirement age for Social Security varies between age 66 and 67 depending on the calendar year in which you were born.

> You always want to tell the truth to the SSA, but that truth should always be framed according to the norms, laws, and regulations that the SSA follows.

with "her money." It's your money. Remember, SSI is not intended to create wealth for your child.

You can also open an ABLE account for your child. As this book explains in Chapter 14, ABLE accounts don't count against the $2,000 limit, provided the balance remains below $100,000.

- **No Joint Bank Accounts**

Your child cannot have a joint bank account with a parent. If your child still has the bank account you opened with them as a minor, SSA will consider your salary and assets. You can't just ask the bank to take your name off the account when your child turns 18. Social Security will look at the prior six months' history of any bank account your child has when they apply. If they find a bank account with your name on it, it's an automatic disqualification. You have to close the bank account that was established when your child was a minor and open a new one when they turn age 18.

The only exception to this rule is if your child cannot manage a bank account on their own. In that situation, a parent can be a representative payee of that bank account.

- **What About Trusts?**

The key to trusts is that your child cannot have ready access to the funds. A properly drafted and administrated SNT will allow you to amass funds for your child without counting against the $2,000 means-testing limit used by SSI. Jim and Julieanne go into more detail in Chapter 13, but the key is that a Special Needs Trust must be set up and administered carefully so that it does not jeopardize eligibility for SSI.

- **What About Modified Vehicles or Special Wheelchairs or Other Devices?**

These don't count. Technically, your child can have a car in his or her name, but in most cases, this vehicle was purchased by the parents. So, from the perspective of SSA, your child has the use of a vehicle that you purchased for them.

- **What Happens if Your Child Gets a Job?**

If your child starts work and starts earning over the SSI income limit—as Hannah and Tatyana do now that they are working—you are obligated to notify Social Security right away about the change in circumstances. Currently, your child can earn up to $1,350 per month before they lose all of their SSI benefits. The calculations SSA uses to determine how much monthly benefits will be reduced by outside income are complex and kick in at really low levels, so be sure to notify SSA right away. It will take about four months for benefit payments to stop. Once they stop, you have to pay back the benefits you received, so make sure you don't spend it.

Your child's Medicaid or Medicare benefits will continue as long as your child has a disability that prevents him or her from working. If your child starts working, SSI has certain incentives to help him enter or re-enter the workforce. Monthly income plus Medicaid or Medicare benefits will continue for a finite period of time. If your child goes back to work but finds that it's really not feasible and that there is no good way to make the needed modifications so that they can earn a living, their full benefits can be reinstated if it's been less than five years. Your child will start receiving benefits right away while the SSA reviews the case.

What Happens If Your Application Is Denied?

If your application is even just a bit outside of SSA's parameters for acceptance, it will be denied. If it is denied, there is an appeal process. The appeals process can be costly and exhausting. Best to do things right in the first place.

The strict parameters the SSA sets for an application to be successful means that if you make even a tiny mistake, you risk your child being denied. Because I've been doing this for years, I know how to get people approved. I can alleviate the stress of having to fight yet one more bureaucracy to get the benefits your child deserves.

As I indicated, you can appeal the decision. You can do this on your own, but your best bet is to hire an attorney, as Jim and his wife did.

Final Words

To make it through this process and get your child approved for SSI or SSDI, you have to keep your eye on the big picture: qualifying for the Golden Ticket. Getting approved for SSI or SSDI not only provides your child an income stream they can rely on or just a safety net while they need it, but it also opens the door

> **The appeals process can be costly and exhausting.**
> **Best to do things right in the first place.**

to VR assistance, which can truly launch your child to their best future.

While SSI is not a huge amount of monetary support, for many families, this provides a financial lifeline. A lifeline that can help parents handle the many extraordinary expenses of caring for a child with disabilities and give them the financial room to save more for retirement. Plus, as Jim explains in Chapter 11, when your son or daughter is approved for SSI or SSDI, this also qualifies them as an Eligible Designated Beneficiary which can mean that after you are gone, they will have better distribution options for Inherited IRAs. Those favorable distribution options can potentially provide your child with hundreds of thousands of additional funds from your IRA over his or her lifetime.

Just remember, I can't stress this enough: after a lifetime of telling your son or daughter **you can do it,** you need to embrace the cognitive dissonance of **"I CAN'T."** It is a temporary "thought" accommodation, not a change of philosophy. It can be hard, but it is essential.

KEY IDEAS

• Winning SSA approval for SSI or SSDI benefits for your child is a Golden Ticket that opens the door to many other financial benefits.

• SSI is for individuals who cannot qualify for benefits on their work record or the work record of a parent. SSI is means tested: your child cannot have more than $2,000 in assets and cannot have significant monthly income.

• SSDI is for individuals who have worked at least 10 quarters (for the SSA, a quarter equals 13 weeks) or who have a parent whose work record a benefit can be collected. SSDI is not means tested, but your child is still subject to strict limits for earned income.

Key Ideas continue on the following page.

KEY IDEAS
(continued)

- SSI and SSDI are not welfare programs. They are entitlement programs that parents and workers pay into with payroll taxes.

- A good strategy is to get your child on SSI before you begin receiving benefits, then switch to SSDI when your benefits begin. Benefits under SSDI are generally higher.

- To win approval for SSI or SSDI, you have to speak the language of "I CAN'T." Even if your child has found accommodations, compared to the norm of a person without disabilities, your child can't do the normal activities of daily living.

- The best time to start an application is the first day of the month after your child turns 18, when SSA considers them to be independent adults. After a person turns 18, SSA will not consider the assets or the income of the parents when evaluating the application.

- The application process starts with a request for a telephone appointment for an interview. This can be done in person, online, or by phone.

- The telephone interview will last about 45 minutes and your child will be asked questions about their work history, disability, bank accounts and other assets, and household expenses.

- A key part of successful applications is letters from doctors that describe the disability in detail and the ways that your child can't do the normal activities of daily living because of the disability.

- Evaluation of the application may take anywhere from three months to eight months.

- Once approved, your child can stay on SSI or SSDI until they have a change in a qualifying circumstance. These circumstances include:
  - Getting married
  - Winning the lottery

13

Special Needs Trusts and Legal Considerations for Children with Disabilities

By James Lange, *CPA, Attorney with*
Julieanne E. Steinbacher, *Esq., CELA, LLM in Estate and Elder Law*

As parents, we want to provide our children with a safe space to grow and express themselves. And when your child has a disability, creating that safe space means setting up a protective legal framework to ensure your child has the financial resources and the support network he or she needs now, and vitally, after you are gone.

Beyond the strategic IRA planning considerations for children with disabilities, it is important for parents to have an overall understanding for how best to guide their disabled child through the labyrinth of lifetime planning considerations. My colleague, Julieanne E. Steinbacher, provides both practical considerations for parents who are assisting their adult child with a disability and recommendations for employing an attorney to help them successfully navigate these waters.

Throughout this book, we discuss the many ways parents can use trusts as an invaluable tool for estate planning and for passing wealth on to the next generation. They can also enable you to "rule from the grave" by putting conditions or limits on the beneficiary's access to money. In this chapter, we focus on special needs trusts or SNTs. For children with disabilities, SNTs can allow your child to inherit money or retirement accounts without jeopardizing their eligibility for government benefit programs.

My colleague Julieanne Steinbacher will start us off by explaining the terminology of trusts.

Learning the Legal Language

Where do I start? What should I do? These are the questions for which you should seek advice and direction from professionals who are experienced in these types of situations. Your first steps in planning for your child who has a disability may be with a knowledgeable, trusted financial advisor and with an attorney who practices in the area of special needs planning. Special needs planning for an adult child with a disability is more than just putting a trust in place. It's not simply about the documents. There is a lot of judgment involved in these situations. In addition, the estate attorney must be prepared for considerable handholding throughout this process. This legal engagement is much more consequential and critical than planning for children without a disability. This is why I don't think you can go to a general estate planning attorney, have a special needs trust slapped together, and get the same result as someone who used a fully engaged specialist who has done hundreds of these cases.

Also, the terms are confusing.

You may have heard about special needs trusts or supplemental needs trusts. Is there any difference between them? No, the terms are interchangeable for the most part. Supplemental often refers to the special language found in the trust which refers to the trust assets being used to supplement the benefits provided by government programs such as Social Security, Social Security Income, and Medicaid. The idea is to supplement but not replace the benefits that may be available to the beneficiary with a disability. Special needs often refer to the purpose of the trust, which is to provide for a person who has "special needs."

There are several types of trusts. A trust may be self-settled or third-party. A trust may be testamentary or living/inter vivos. These different trusts are detailed below.

Self-Settled Trust

A *self-settled trust* holds the funds belonging to the individual who has the disability. These trusts may only be created by a parent, grandparent, legal guardian, or the court. In many states, the individual for whom the trust is established must be under the age of 65 when the trust is created. A self-settled trust may hold assets that the individual accumulated through gifts from family and friends, or the individual could have earned the money through employment.

Frequently, a self-settled trust can be funded from an inheritance when families have failed to plan ahead. This is unfortunate because of the pay-back provision needed. Self-settled trusts could also be funded from the proceeds of a lawsuit. Trust laws require that any assets remaining in the self-settled trust at the death of the individual with a disability be paid back to the state to reimburse Medicaid for paying benefits to the individual. Any funds remaining after Medicaid is paid back can be inherited by family or friends.

Third-Party Trust

A *third-party trust* is established with the funds of someone other than the individual who has a disability, such as a parent, grandparent, or friend. The parents might create this type of trust to be funded upon their death with an inheritance in cash, IRAs, and retirement plans, including Roth IRAs, life insurance, or other assets. This trust can also accept gifts made by others for the benefit of the individual with a disability. This trust does not have an age restriction.

Whereas a self-settled trust requires a pay-back provision to Medicaid, a third-party trust does not require a pay-back provision to Medicaid once the individual with a disability passes away. At the individual's death, the assets remaining in the trust can go wherever the person who created the trust directs. For this reason, a third-party trust is usually a better option as compared to a self-settled trust.

Inter Vivos Trust

An *inter vivos trust* is one that is established during the life of the person creating the trust. An inter vivos trust cannot be established without holding assets. Some assets will have to be transferred immediately to this type of trust, but a small amount of cash will usually suffice. A good reason to have an inter vivos trust for a disabled beneficiary is if you want to make a gift while you are alive but you still want all the protections of a trust. An inter vivos trust could be named in your will or in another person's will if he or she wanted to leave assets for the individual who has a disability. Usually, clients like to hold money themselves while they are alive, figuring they could pay for all the child's needs but still have control of the money.

However, if a parent wanted to make a gift but still allow the child to receive government benefits, they might consider an inter vivos trust. Some parents like to buy their child a house, which is an example of the kind of lifetime gift that could be placed in an inter vivos trust.

Testamentary Trust

A *testamentary trust* is not technically created until someone dies; therefore, the terms are found in someone's will or beneficiary designation of an asset like an IRA or Roth IRA that typically is passed on through beneficiary designation rather than a will or a revocable trust. In that case, the trust in the will or named as the IRA beneficiary does not contain any assets until the person creating the trust passes away. That type of will or beneficiary designation as well as the trust within the will or beneficiary designation is considered revocable.

Irrevocable Trust

Whereas a revocable trust can be changed or amended in many more circumstances, an *irrevocable trust* is a trust that tends to be difficult to amend or revoke without court intervention. Self-settled trusts are typically irrevocable, while third-party trusts can be revocable or irrevocable.

Pooled Trust

A *pooled trust* is administered by a nonprofit organization that holds or "pools" the money from many enrolled individuals who have disabilities. The organization generally understands the eligibility rules for the various government programs and manages and disburses the funds in a way that will not disqualify the individual from public benefits. Often, a pooled trust is used when an appropriate individual cannot be found to serve as the trustee or if funds are too small for a bank to manage. This trust can be set up by the individual, parent, grandparent, guardian, or by the court.

Why a Special Needs Trust? *(back to Jim)*

There is a very good chance that it would be most prudent to leave money intended for a disabled beneficiary in a Special Needs Trust (SNT) rather than leaving the money to the beneficiary outright. There are conflicting definitions in the literature about what a SNT is, so for the purposes of this chapter, I am talking about a very specific type of trust. A SNT can be drafted either as a testamentary trust or as an inter vivos trust (defined above).

There is a reasonable chance that either now or at some point in the future, your beneficiary who has a disability or a chronic illness will qualify for some type of government aid that places limits on the beneficiary's income and/or assets. It might be Supplemental Security Income (SSI), Medicaid, or another essential federal or state public benefits program. The goal of the SNT is to make sure that the trust is not considered an *available asset* as defined by public benefit agencies. The attorney preparing the trust must be mindful of income and principal because, without the appropriate provisions, too much of either could result in your child losing benefits (or potentially even being required to return some portion of benefits that have already been distributed).

Over the years, competent attorneys who work in this area have found language that works for these purposes. Unfortunately, that isn't enough. If the underlying asset of the trust is an IRA or a Roth IRA, then the trust must also meet four specific conditions that are required in order for it to qualify for the "stretch" treatment.

A detailed explanation of those conditions is beyond the scope of this book, but here they are in brief. Please work with a competent attorney to ensure your SNT qualifies.

1. The trust must be valid under state law.

2. The trust must be irrevocable, or by its terms become irrevocable upon the death of the original IRA owner.

3. The trust's underlying beneficiaries must be identifiable as being eligible to be designated beneficiaries themselves.

4. A copy of the trust documentation and the proof of disability must be provided to the IRA custodian/plan administrator by October 31 of the year following the year of the IRA or retirement plan owner's death.

Lange Legal Group has reviewed hundreds of these types of trusts that other attorneys have prepared, and we estimate that 50% or more of the trusts where the IRA or retirement plan is the underlying asset have significant flaws that, if discovered, could disqualify the beneficiary from being able to stretch the Inherited IRA or Roth IRA.[1]

The biggest and most expensive flaw we see is not having all the conditions in the trust to qualify for the stretch IRA, which allows able-bodied beneficiaries to stretch distributions out over 10 years and beneficiaries with a disability to extend those distributions over their entire life.

Ideally, the person drafting the trust to be named as the beneficiary of an IRA or retirement plan will know the rules and use the language required to protect the beneficiary's government benefit and preserve the "stretch" of the Inherited IRA.

Extreme Caution in Estate Planning is Warranted

Remember, in this and practically all cases when we are talking about an IRA or retirement plan asset, the key document is *not the will or revocable trust* but the **beneficiary designation of the IRA or retirement plan**. One drafting technique is for the beneficiary designation of the IRA to refer to a testamentary trust inside your will or revocable trust that is specifically designed to receive IRAs and retirement plans. But, if that isn't done right (even if your will and the trust instrument have all the correct language), if the beneficiary designations for your IRA or other retirement plan assets are not correct, all that careful planning could go down the toilet, and your child with a disability may end up broke.

---

1   There is no solicitation for legal services being made by me, James Lange, nor by Lange Legal Group, LLC.

Designation as Disabled or Chronically Ill Plus Special Needs Trust as IRA Beneficiary

The first strategy is to do everything you can to ensure your child receives the necessary designation as disabled or chronically ill. Then, if appropriate, work with a special needs attorney to draft a SNT with your child as beneficiary of the trust. Next, make sure that SNT is the designated beneficiary of the portions of your IRA, Roth IRA, and other retirement assets you have earmarked for your child with a disability. Most of the time, but not always, a SNT will be the best way to ensure your child has access to the funds they need, that the funds are administered appropriately, and that their access to government benefits is not jeopardized.

Since a SNT will often be funded by someone other than the disabled beneficiary, it will typically be referred to as a third-party special needs trust or a supplemental needs trust (there is also a first-party special needs trust funded with assets already owned by the disabled beneficiary or received from an outright inheritance). As I stated above, and Julieanne concurs, drafting this trust requires the expertise of an attorney who is experienced in these matters.

If the beneficiary is a grandchild or the disability issue isn't the primary focus of the estate plan, our firm likes a combination of our classic favorite estate plan for Traditional families, Lange's Cascading Beneficiary Plan (LCBP), but to include a Special Needs Trust in lieu of leaving money to a grandchild outright. See Chapter 15 to read about how LCBP offers your heirs the flexibility to distribute the assets in your estate based on the actual financial and life situations of your heirs at your death.

The Enormous Risks and Penalties of Not Doing Your Special Needs Trust Correctly

If not drafted correctly, the SNT will not stand up under the scrutiny of the IRS and the public benefits agencies. Two bad things can happen if the trust isn't drafted appropriately.

First, the trust will be considered an asset available to the child, which could result in government benefits being terminated and may even require that the government be reimbursed for past benefits the child received. Second, your beneficiary will lose the ability to stretch distributions of the Inherited IRA or retirement plan, triggering massive taxes at the very high trust income tax rates.

When planning for this trust, it may also be prudent to consider making a Roth IRA conversion on a portion of the pre-tax retirement monies. By doing so, you can leave the tax-free Roth IRA to your child with a disability and the remaining pre-tax retirement monies to your other children. The advantage of leaving the Roth IRA to the child with a disability—if they are an EDB—is that the money can grow tax free over their lifetime. On the other hand, if your other children inherit the IRA, they will have to pay taxes on the money within ten years, and most likely at a higher tax rate than your child who is an EDB. It is best to run the numbers to determine which child should get which IRA.

In some situations, parents may choose not to leave their IRA or Roth IRA to a trust but will leave it to the child directly.

Special Needs Trust Funded with Life Insurance

Another strategy is buying life insurance[2] and making a SNT the beneficiary of the life insurance policy. An advantage of this approach is that it may work well if your beneficiary needs special assistance but does not qualify as an EDB for the purpose of stretching the Inherited IRA.

Also, the life insurance strategy is almost always just one part of the plan. Most of our clients use a combination of the various strategies presented in this book. My wife and I have life insurance as an important part of our estate plan. The benefits of the life insurance are not included in our projection of saving $1,890,544 in taxes for our daughter Erica, as described in Chapter 11. One of the benefits of also having the life insurance policy is it gives us "permission" to spend more money while we are still alive, as we have comfort in knowing our daughter is provided for. Before we had the insurance, the Roth conversions, and proper estate planning in place, my wife was more frugal because she wanted to leave more than enough money for our daughter. She is still far more frugal than I am but less frugal than she was. Running the numbers also helped her feel more comfortable with spending more money. That said, I think she would only eat rice and beans before spending one dollar of our Roth IRA.

Avoid Entrusting Siblings with Resources Intended for a Child with a Disability

In my practice, I have seen IRA owners try to get around all these complications by naming a sibling as the beneficiary of the IRA or other funds. The tacit assumption is that the named sibling will use the money to benefit their sibling with a disability and not themselves. This might work, but it could also be disastrous.

---

2   Life insurance can be offered by a member of Lange Life Care, LLC for those interested. These are not legal services. The protection of an attorney-client relationship does not exist with respect to insurance services. There is no solicitation being made for legal services by James Lange nor by Lange Legal Group, LLC.

What if the named beneficiary falls victim to a lawsuit, bankruptcy, or divorce and loses the money that was intended for their sibling with a disability? What if there is a dispute with the siblings? What if a greedy relative, like Fanny Dashwood in Jane Austen's novel *Sense and Sensibility,* interferes? The other problem with this approach is that only the beneficiary with the disability or chronic illness will qualify as an Eligible Designated Beneficiary who can "stretch" the Inherited IRA or Roth IRA over his or her lifetime. So, this "oral trust" approach is a particularly bad idea under the SECURE Act when the underlying asset is an IRA or Roth IRA.

Critical Mechanical Issue if You Are Using a Special Needs Trust

You and/or your attorney will work together to decide whether a SNT is appropriate. Once a SNT is established or planned for a disabled beneficiary, if the goal is to protect government benefits, it is particularly imperative to coordinate all anticipated future assets that the beneficiary might receive so that the terms of the SNT will control them all. Because of sloppy estate planning, this often doesn't happen. For example, if the beneficiary form of just *one* of the IRAs or 401(k)s names the child rather than the trust for the benefit of the child, the child could lose critical government benefits.

Flexibility In Planning with the Toggle Trust

As we have discussed here, it is essential to plan for the future needs of a family member with a disability or chronic illness, particularly when that person is already receiving or qualifies for means-based government benefits. That being said, you might be in a situation where your young child is diagnosed with a disability that may or may not qualify that child for SSI. It might be unclear whether the disability will prevent the child from working in the future or if the child will simply need some modest accommodations or assistance in order to work. In the case of a young person with mental or emotional health concerns that may or may not get worse later on in life, it might be unclear today whether they will need someone else to oversee a future inheritance.

Such circumstances create an uncertain future. Special needs trusts are typically even more restrictive than a general creditor protection trust. So, depending on things you can't predict now, you might prefer a special needs trust for your child or a more typical general creditor protection trust.

It is possible to include a trigger or toggle within your will or trust that allows the disabled person's inheritance to be directed to a SNT based on the circumstances known at the time of distribution (generally the date of your passing). Alternatively, the money could be directed to a different type of trust or even to the child directly, depending on circumstances that would be determined after death.

This sort of planning is available for other scenarios where trust protections may also be necessary and is not only for disability planning. These are important considerations to discuss with your estate attorney and other trusted advisors.

Accumulation Trusts vs. Conduit Trusts and the SECURE Act

One way to think of trusts is as a way station for the income generated by the assets they hold. An accumulation trust can hold on to a portion of the income and pass the rest to the beneficiary according to the terms of the trust. Income retained or accumulated by the trust will be taxed at the trust tax rate, which is usually higher than the beneficiary's tax rate. Income passed to the beneficiary will be taxed at the beneficiary's tax rate. This can be ideal for a SNT because this kind of trust is designed to provide supplementary support for the beneficiary so the trustee can exercise discretion over the amount and timing of distributions.

A conduit trust, in contrast, is required to distribute all of the trust income to the beneficiary every year. The trustee has essentially no discretion over the timing of the payout, which makes this kind of trust less than ideal for a SNT.

Fortunately, the SECURE Act does allow accumulation trusts for chronically ill or disabled beneficiaries who also qualify as EDBs. The upside is that the trustee can stretch distributions over the beneficiary's lifetime and has discretion over the timing and amount of those distributions to ensure that the beneficiary remains eligible for government benefits. The downside is the higher taxes that the trust will pay on the retained income. Under 2023 tax rates, the maximum rate of 37% kicks in with just $14,451 of income.

As attorneys and CPAs, we typically get around the high trust rates by making a distribution to the beneficiary and claiming a deduction for the distribution on the trust tax return. Then, the trust files a Form 1041 tax return and sends a K-1 to the beneficiary, who must then report the distribution as income on their own return. The upside is that the distribution will now be taxed at much lower individual tax rates instead of trust income tax rates.

Who Should be Trustee? *(back to Julieanne)*

One of the most difficult discussions is trying to figure out who the trustee should be for the trust. There is a strong preference among professionals to appoint a corporate trustee because SNTs can be complex to work with. Corporate trustees also have insurance which can cover any mistakes that are made which could affect government benefit eligibility or the ability to "stretch" the Inherited IRA. A trust can be in place for 25 to 30 years, or even longer, so flexibility is important. A corporate trustee may be more permanent and provide consistency of administration for an individual who is expected to outlive their parents and likely many other loved ones.

Families will often want to name a family member, especially a sibling of the individual with a disability. Family members are also good choices for the trustee because they have a more intimate understanding of the person with a disability, and they can make sure the person is receiving everything he or she needs. However, if a family member makes a mistake because he or she didn't know the rules, the family member will likely not have the money to cover the mistake. Families are almost always concerned with the cost of a corporate trustee. However, the costs associated with mismanagement by a family trustee can be much more costly if mistakes occur.

Another option could be to appoint a corporate trustee and family member trustee to manage the trust together. The details of this relationship would have to be approved by the corporate trustee beforehand. The corporate trustee and family member trustee could be appointed as co-trustees, or the corporate trustee could be responsible for managing most of the trust while the family member trustee must be kept involved and has the power to change the corporate trustee to a different corporation. If the corporate trustee agrees to the terms, there can be a considerable amount of flexibility in making this work with the corporate trustee and the family member trustee together. On the other hand, the corporate trustee will likely want to get their normal trustee fee and not split it with a family member co-trustee.

Additional Things to Consider When Planning for an Adult Child Who Has a Disability

In most states, a child is considered an adult once they reach the age of 18. At this time, they are their own legal person. It doesn't matter if they have a severe disability or what type of disability it is. The law presumes they are competent/capacitated until proven in court that they are not. If you, as parents, have not planned ahead, you will no longer have the right to make decisions for your child with a disability. This includes both medical and financial decisions. You cannot continue to sign documents or make banking decisions without the legal authority to do so; thus, planning becomes very important. You also may not have access to health care information or be able to make decisions.

A few things to keep in mind when planning for your child with disabilities include:

- Consider whether your child will have sufficient resources to financially support themselves in the future.

- Evaluate the ability of any support services and the cost of those services or needed residential care.

- Consider whether life insurance could be a valuable resource to pay for your child's financial needs when you are no longer around. See Chapter 26 for a discussion on life insurance.

- Re-examine any trusts that you previously put in place to verify that the provisions are still appropriate for yourself and for your child.

- Visit a special needs planning attorney to help you determine what your child's financial and legal needs will be when you are no longer with them.

- Determine whether a guardianship will be necessary or whether alternatives to a guardianship are available.

Planning for the Care of Your Child After Your Death

One of the most important considerations as you age is preparing your child who has a disability for the fact that one day, you will die. The following are a few important steps that should be considered at this time to protect your child in the future:

1. In the appropriate documents, name who should be the successor trustee or guardian to avoid a time when there is no one to make decisions for your child if you should suffer a sudden illness or die unexpectedly. Plan now for the possibility that you will have an unexpected change in your health. This will avoid anxiety for your child and will make sure that someone else has the authority to step in if necessary.

2. Have a plan for succession in case those who have agreed to take over for you can no longer serve as the advocate for your loved one. Name these successor(s) in your legal documents.

3. Review and update your legal documents every three to five years or anytime there is a significant life or health change.

4. Determine a plan for your child's future, such as where he or she will live and whether he or she will be able to continue with his or her routine if you are not around.

5. Prepare a "summary of our wishes" document to guide the trustee, guardian, family, and caregivers. A template of the worksheet used by Steinbacher, Goodall & Yurchak can be found at **https://DisabledChildPlanning.com.** It covers such things as the family history, medical history, housing, education, religion, values, recreation, daily routine, likes, dislikes, and triggers for your child's various emotions or behaviors.

6. Come up with a plan to address how your assets will be distributed once you pass away. Determine whether your child with a disability will receive an inheritance and how it will affect their public benefits. Think about what share of your estate will be inherited by your child who has a disability and whether this could cause problems among your other children.

What You Need to Know Before Meeting with an Attorney

Here is the preparation I recommend for your meeting with a special needs attorney. Sit down, organize yourself, and make a list of the following.

1. What type of government benefits is the child receiving now and/or will the child receive in the future? Also include the estimated value of those benefits.

2. What other income is available to the child?

3. What is the family's current financial situation?

4. Is the child mentally competent/capacitated?

5. Is the child already under a guardianship/conservatorship, and what are the details of this arrangement?

6. What is the child's condition? Is it stable or worsening? Are they more likely to need long-term care than the average person?

7. What type of accommodations need to be in place for the child?

8. What is the child's daily routine?

9. Is the child planning to receive SSI, SSDI, or long-term disability?

10. What are the current sources of support?

11. How is your health? Is long-term care imminent?

12. What are the family dynamics? Who is available for support in the long term?

13. What medicines is the child receiving? Who are their doctors?

14. Have you, the parent, completed your own specialized estate planning centered around your child with a disability?

A discussion about special needs planning is often about planning for multiple generations—you, the parent, the child with a disability, and other children or grandchildren. Any plan must also address the potential for being taken advantage of, especially since those with disabilities are a highly vulnerable population. Honest conversations about the availability and willingness of family members to provide support and/or oversight is essential.

Guardianship and Conservatorship

Seeking a guardianship should not be taken lightly. In some states, a guardianship will apply to both health and financial decisions. In other states, the process is bifurcated, and a guardianship only applies to decisions about the person, which includes medical decision making. A conservatorship would be required if a person needed to make decisions about the estate, which includes financial decisions.

By granting guardianship to another person, the individual with a disability is deemed unable to make these decisions on their own. The person appointed as guardian will now step into the shoes of the individual with a disability and will make health and/or financial decisions on his or her behalf.

Guardianships are a legal process that require the involvement of a court to make a determination that a person is incompetent. Each state has its own laws and requirements for implementing guardianships. Many individuals who have developmental or intellectual disabilities can manage their own affairs with some assistance. They may only need a limited guardianship if a guardianship is needed at all. A guardianship needs to be implemented on an individual basis depending on the person's needs. Often, a guardianship may only be necessary when there are behavioral issues that will result in a person revoking more informal alternatives. Another reason for obtaining a conservatorship is to protect the person from those who would prey on the financial status of the person who has a disability. Other reasons for obtaining a guardianship or conservatorship could be:

- When there is no clear understanding of the individual's ability to consent to treatment or services. Unfortunately, it is often a medical provider's concern over liability as to whether the person has the capacity to provide informed consent that is the issue.

- If health providers are concerned over releasing records and information without a clear grant of authority under HIPAA, and if there is a concern of capacity to grant that consent.

Alternatives to Guardianship for an Adult Child with a Disability

There are several less restrictive options available as alternatives to seeking a guardianship or conservatorship. A representative payee may be appointed to deal with Social Security payments or government or military payments. By having a representative payee appointed, you can also limit the risk of financial exploitation when the individual with a disability is unable to manage his or her own money. The Social Security Administration will require regular accounting and the person appointed is liable if the money is mismanaged.

Joint ownership of property is another way to make sure that taxes, insurance, and other real estate ownership issues are taken care of. However, there is always a risk in joint ownership. For example, creditors of any of the joint owners could claim an interest in the property, including if the property is subject to divorce proceedings. Joint bank accounts can also be set up and can offer a simple way to pay bills automatically and prevent excessive spending of money. However, the risk is still present if any of the owners have creditors. A trust account could also be a good alternative to a guardianship.

Executing certain legal documents is another alternative to guardianship or conservatorship. A Health Care Proxy, also referred to as a Durable Power of Attorney for Health Care, Living Will, or Advanced Health Care Directive, addresses the medical treatment that an individual wants or does not want to receive if he or she is unable to speak with the medical professionals or is deemed incapacitated. Some of these documents also address the life-sustaining measures that an individual wants or does not want if they are diagnosed with an end-stage

medical condition or end up in an irreversible coma or vegetative state. The execution of one of these documents when a person is competent can avoid the necessity of obtaining a guardianship.

The Durable Power of Attorney or Financial Power of Attorney is a document that names someone else to handle a person's financial affairs. If validly executed, this document will avoid the necessity of obtaining a conservatorship or guardianship of the estate. Because it is durable, it will survive a person's subsequent incapacity.

KEY IDEAS

- Trust terminology can be confusing. Here are brief explanations of the main terms you may come across:

  - A *self-settled trust* holds the funds belonging to the individual who has the disability.

  - A *third-party trust* is established with the funds of someone other than the individual who has a disability, such as a parent, grandparent, or friend.

  - An *inter vivos trust* is one that is established during the life of the person creating the trust.

  - A *testamentary trust* is not technically created until someone dies; therefore, the terms are found in someone's will, and the trust does not contain any assets until the person creating the trust passes away.

  - An *irrevocable trust* is a trust that tends to be difficult to amend or revoke without court intervention.

  - A *pooled trust* is administered by a nonprofit organization that holds or "pools" the money from many enrolled individuals who have disabilities.

- Special Needs Trusts allow your child to inherit IRA funds without jeopardizing their eligibility for government aid. However, they must contain the four conditions required to ensure they function as intended and to preserve the "stretch" of an Inherited IRA. A majority of the trusts we have reviewed

---

Key Ideas continue on the following page.

KEY IDEAS
(continued)

fail to meet the four conditions meaning the stretch IRA is in jeopardy because of poor drafting.

- Naming a sibling of your disabled child as the beneficiary of your IRA with the understanding that the sibling will help to support their disabled brother or sister can backfire. This should only be done as a last resort.

- Keep in mind that most states consider a child an adult when they reach the age of 18. That means that after age 18, your ability to make decisions and get information about their health may be limited.

- Start planning now to protect your child with a disability after your death. Besides ensuring your child will have adequate financial resources, you may also need to name a successor guardian or advocate when you can no longer fulfill that role. Plan for where your child should live and provide a summary of your wishes to guide your successor.

- We recommend a team to help you with your planning. You will likely want to work with a number-crunching CPA and/or financial advisor to optimize Roth conversion strategies. You will also want to work with an estate attorney who specializes in working with parents with a child with a disability. Before meeting with an attorney, gather information about your child's condition, current and future financial resources, daily routine, and other family sources of support, among other crucial details.

- Familiarize yourself with the differences between different types of trusts and how they are created and funded.

- In some situations, granting guardianship to another person for your disabled child may be appropriate. Granting a limited guardianship can help support your child in managing their own affairs. This is not a decision to be made lightly.

- Alternatives to guardianship include appointing a representative payee to deal with government payments, establishing joint ownership of assets, and executing legal documents such as a Durable Power of Attorney for Health Care.

14

Tax-Free Savings
Under the ABLE Act

By John Montoya, *Esq., with*
Julieanne E. Steinbacher, *Esq., CELA, LLM*

Achieving a Better Life Experience accounts, better known as ABLE accounts, are wonderful planning tools that are often underutilized. Understanding the concepts of this chapter and implementing appropriate planning for the ABLE account will help with the finances of practically all children with a disability. This chapter, while perhaps not life-changing, will still help you and your child get the most out of what you've got.

Getting your child with a disability qualified for SSI is the Golden Ticket that will open doors for many financial benefits. If your child is on SSDI, the ABLE accounts are still a good idea, but they work best for people receiving SSI. As Milton Friedman said, "there's no such thing as a free lunch." SSI comes at the expense of means testing, which means your child, subject to exception, cannot accumulate cash or valuables that exceed $2,000 in value. Fortunately, ABLE accounts offer an additional way for parents or persons with disabilities to save funds but not interfere with asset limitations to qualify for SSI. These are easier to manage than a Special Needs Trust and still protect eligibility for government benefits. There are also more liberal provisions on how your child could spend money in an ABLE account without interfering with other benefits. This is not the case for distributions from a Special Needs Trust.

What is an ABLE Account?

The easiest way to think about an ABLE account is that it is like a 529 plan for a child with a disability. The ABLE Act is a federal law passed in 2014 (26 U.S.C. §529) that allows states to enact legislation to allow individuals with disabilities to fund an account that is not countable for SSI or Medicaid eligibility. Today, 46 states and Washington, D.C., offer their own ABLE account plans. These accounts are literally modeled on state 529 plans. While these are administered by state agencies, many allow residents from other states to participate.

An ABLE account can be opened by a person with a disability or anyone trying to provide for a child with a disability, presumably a parent or someone looking out for the benefit of the child with a disability. It is important to note that there can only be one ABLE account per person with a disability. While more than one person can contribute to an ABLE account, there can only be one ABLE account. This differs from the rules for 529 plans, where a beneficiary can have several 529 plans. You can learn more under *Opening an ABLE Account* and *Contributions and Funding* later in the chapter.

After an ABLE account is opened, this special savings account can accumulate up to $100,000 without jeopardizing government benefits. This program was designed with a goal ofpromoting independence by giving the account owners more control over the account and the usage of the funds.

One of the beauties of the ABLE account is you can make a contribution, which can grow tax-free and then be used later to pay for a qualifying expense without any taxes on the principal or the growth, and then replenished.

Contributions grow income-tax-free as long as withdrawals are used for "Qualified Disability Expenses," which I'll describe below. Any withdrawals that aren't used for qualified expenses will be subject to income tax and a 10% penalty.

Who is Eligible for an ABLE Account?

The account owner must have a disability with an onset prior to turning age 26, although the account can be opened at any time. Starting in 2026, as part of the SECURE Act 2.0, the disability onset age will increase to 46. If your child is already receiving SSI or SSDI benefits for a disability and meets the cutoff age for onset, he or she is automatically eligible to open an ABLE account. If not, then to qualify as disabled, you or your child will need to submit a Disability Certification to the Social Security Administration (SSA) that includes documentation from a physician that describes the nature of the disability and the date of onset. This Certification will state that your child meets the SSA's definition of disabled, and for most, this will prove to be an easier process than obtaining approval for SSI benefits.

SSA considers an individual to be disabled if not able to participate in any substantial gainful activity (SGA) because of a medically determinable physical or mental impairment or impairments that are expected to result in death or that have lasted or are expected to last at least 12 months. Substantial gainful activity is an economic and income test. If your child has too much earned income, he or she will fail to qualify as disabled. For 2023, the income limit is $1,470 per month for non-blind persons with disabilities.

ABLE accounts have a lower bar for eligibility than getting SSI or SSDI benefits.

All that is needed is documentation of a disability with an onset earlier than age 26—or age 46 starting in 2026. In contrast, as Deborah McFadden explains in Chapter 12, SSI approval is only granted if the person with a disability meets the income and assets tests. So, it is possible for someone to qualify for an ABLE account by having a medical provider confirm the disability but not qualify for SSI due to the income and asset tests. Until your child with a disability is 18, SSA will look at your income and assets to determine eligibility. If your child is approaching age 18 and is likely to qualify for SSI on their own, this may be a good time to open an ABLE account to transfer any assets your child has accumulated that would exceed the SSI limit of $2,000. These assets might include wages from part-time jobs or gifts of cash from family members.

SSDI benefits are for people who have worked enough to qualify for benefits on their own work records, or who have a parent on whose record they can qualify either because the parent is receiving retirement or disability benefits or because the now-deceased parent worked enough to qualify for benefits.

Opening an ABLE Account

If your child is competent to handle financial matters, he or she can open and fund an ABLE account. If not, a parent, legal guardian, or an agent under a Power of Attorney can create the account for the disabled beneficiary.

As stated earlier, a beneficiary can have only one ABLE account. The ABLE account programs in many states allow residents of other states to open accounts under their programs, but there may be benefits to opening an account in the home state. The limitation of one ABLE account per beneficiary applies across states as well: your child cannot have multiple accounts in different states.

Investment choices are selected by the beneficiary from the range of options offered by that particular state's program. The ABLE National Resource Center has a tool that allows you to compare ABLE programs from different states, which you can find here: **https://www.Ablenrc.org/Compare-States/**

Contributions and Funding

The contribution limit is set to the current federal gift tax exclusion. For 2023, this limit is $17,000 per year. Contributions can be made by any person or persons using after-tax dollars. The contribution limit is *per beneficiary, not per donor.* This is different from contributions to a 529 plan where multiple family members can make annual contributions per year for the same beneficiary.

There can only be one ABLE account per disabled beneficiary. This means if there are multiple family members wanting to contribute to a disabled family member's ABLE account, the combined contributions cannot exceed the annual contribution limit. Contributions to an individual's ABLE account may be made by an individual, trust, estate, partnership, association, company, or corporation. The contributions are not tax deductible on the federal level, but some states may provide a state income tax deduction.

Contributions to an individual's ABLE account are considered to be completed gifts of a present interest (one that the beneficiary has an immediate and unrestricted right to use). Contributions made on behalf of a beneficiary are not considered income, and one of the great features of the ABLE accounts is they do not count against limits for SSI or Medicaid.

The maximum value of an ABLE account is limited to the state's 529 program limit, which can range from $235,000 to $550,000. However, if the balance exceeds $100,000, this will result in suspension of SSI benefits. Medicaid benefits are not impacted by account balances over $100,000. Benefits for SSDI recipients are not impacted by high balances in ABLE accounts, as long as those accounts remain under the state's limit. For Pennsylvania, the maximum ABLE account balance in 2023 is $511,758.

However, as we explain below, state ABLE account programs may come with payback provisions, which means that any balance left in the account at the account owner's death may be used to reimburse the state for Medicaid-related expenses. The goal should be to spend ABLE account funds for the benefit of the account owner while they are still alive.

If your child with a disability is working and does not participate in the employer's retirement plan, he or she can contribute additional funds above the annual contribution limit. Your child can contribute the smaller of his or her earned income for the year or up to the Federal Poverty Level for a single person. For 2023, the Federal Poverty Level for single-person households in the continental US is $14,850. In Alaska, that level is $18,210, and for Hawaii, it's $16,770.

Let's say that Jonathan earned $5,000 in 2023 from his job and is not participating in his employer's 401(k). If his parents contribute the maximum of $17,000 to Jonathan's ABLE account in 2023, Jonathan can also contribute up to $5,000 for a total of $22,000. The funds that Jonathan contributes to his ABLE account from his income are counted as income but not as an available resource under the means testing for SSI and Medicaid.

If you think about it, an ABLE account or even a college savings 529 plan is a lot like a Roth IRA. You contribute after-tax dollars. The fund grows tax-free, assuming the eventual distribution is for a qualifying purpose. Even better, the accounts will likely not be included and taxed in your estate. Most states have their own college savings 529 plan and ABLE plans. You don't need to pay an advisor for the investments because you can use whatever the state has set up. Pennsylvania, for example, has a variety of asset allocation options, including Vanguard funds, and all the options have low fees.

How is an ABLE Account Different from a Special Needs Trust?

One difference between eligibility for an ABLE account and a Special Needs Trust (SNT) is the age of the onset of a disability. To be eligible for an ABLE account, the disability must have had an onset prior to age 26, or age 46 beginning in 2026. SNTs are less restrictive—the disability must have had an onset prior to funding the trust. However, a self-funded SNT can only be established if the beneficiary is under age 65.

ABLE accounts can be funded by the beneficiary or, as discussed above, by almost anyone who wants to help out, as long as the total contributions for the year are below the annual federal gift tax exclusion. In contrast, there is no limit, annual or otherwise, on the contributions to a SNT.

Self-funded SNTs are funded by the beneficiary or someone acting on their behalf using the beneficiary's funds. Funds are subject to "payback," i.e., any funds that remain in the trust at the time of the disabled individual's death must be paid to the state to reimburse for the cost of Medicaid benefits paid on behalf of the beneficiary. Depending on the state, ABLE accounts may have a payback provision for Medicaid. In either case, any funds remaining after the state has been reimbursed for Medicaid will most likely pass to the beneficiary's estate.

A third-party SNT is funded with someone else's funds that are not related to the beneficiary's assets. Third-party SNTs are not subject to payback, which makes these a better vehicle to transfer large sums of money than an ABLE account.

The biggest difference is the issue of control. The trustee for a SNT is in control of all trust decisions, including distributions to the beneficiary. ABLE account owners, or their legal guardians or legal representatives, have complete control over investment choices and distributions.

What can ABLE Account Funds be Used for?

ABLE account funds (whether cash or investments) grow income tax-free and are not subject to income tax when distributed so long as the funds are used for qualified disability expenses. Most normal expenses would qualify, so you probably don't have to worry that the distributions will be taxable. Qualified disability-related expenses include education, housing, transportation, employment training and support, assistive technology, personal support services, health, prevention and wellness, financial management and administrative services, legal fees, funeral and burial expenses, and basic living expenses. If you're interpreting this to mean that it covers basically everything, you are right!

The ABLE account does not impact the beneficiary's means-tested SSI benefits if the account balance is less than $100,000. Depending on the state, the limit for Medicaid benefits may be higher. If you are not concerned about means-tested benefits, the balance can be higher, subject to state-specific limits.

Accordingly, Jim's plan for his daughter is to use this tax-free vehicle, the ABLE account, to accumulate more money for Erica, but also to spend it at an appropriate time, then replenish it and then spend it again and not just let it sit there for the rest of her life.

Coordinate an ABLE Account with a Special Needs Trust for Extra Benefits

If a disabled beneficiary qualifies for government benefits, coordinating a SNT with an ABLE account provides advantages to the disabled person. Generally, funds from a SNT should not be used to pay for basic costs of living that would typically fall under government assistance (food and groceries, rent or mortgage, utilities, and basic medical care). If SNT funds are used for these purposes, the monthly SSI benefit may be reduced.

However, distributions from an ABLE account for housing expenses are not considered to be in-kind support and maintenance, so this does not reduce the SSI payment. A best practice is to make sure that distributions from an ABLE account are used in the same month of withdrawal to avoid being counted as an available resource. There are exceptions to this requirement to spend ABLE account funds in the same month of withdrawal, as long as the funds are used for non-housing qualified disability expenses, and you can track the distribution to its eventual permissible use.

But by coordinating an ABLE account with a SNT, your child with a disability can get the best of both worlds. Under current law, a trustee of a SNT can contribute funds from the SNT to the ABLE account up to the annual contribution limit. For 2023, this limit is $17,000. As explained above, funds from an ABLE account can be used for an expansive list of qualified disability expenses—which includes almost everything—without jeopardizing your child's SSI or Medicaid. This workaround allows your child with a disability to use SNT funds to help pay for their basic costs of living without any negative impact on his or her government benefits, provided they pass through the ABLE account first. If you do choose to follow this route, be sure to first consult with an estate attorney, financial advisor, or other trusted professional who is familiar with planning for a disabled beneficiary to make sure you have all the pieces set up correctly.

Please note that while the law allows this transfer from the trust, the trust itself might not allow the transfer. That is likely one good reason to make sure the SNT is up to date and has all the important provisions that you want. None of the trusts drafted before 2014 allow that transfer because the ABLE account didn't exist back when the older trusts were drafted. Many of the trusts drafted after 2014 still don't have that provision because sometimes it takes a while for the impact of a new law to be realized by advisors or attorneys.

Fund an ABLE Account with a Rollover from a 529 Plan

The Tax Cuts and Jobs Act allows tax-free rollovers up to the current gift tax exclusion amount (currently $17,000) from a 529 plan account to the ABLE account through the end of 2025. The $17,000 rollover limit replaces the $17,000 contribution limit. This means you cannot contribute $17,000 to an ABLE account in a given year and initiate a $17,000 rollover from a 529 plan in the same year. Funds distributed from the 529 plan must be contributed to the ABLE account within 60 days to count as a tax-free rollover. If the contribution limits are exceeded, there is a 10% penalty tax plus, even worse, it could adversely impact the ABLE beneficiary's eligibility for certain public benefits.

To put the paragraph above into perspective, if you or a family member have several children with multiple 529 plans and one of your children becomes disabled before age 26 and does not attend college, you could transfer any leftover monies from any of the other children's 529 plan into the disabled child's ABLE account, subject to the limitations described above. This means that if the leftover 529 plan has more than $17,000 (or the annual gift tax exclusion), you may have to perform several rollovers to get the 529 money into the ABLE account. The IRS will allow you to do this kind of rollover once every 12 months for the same ABLE

> If you or a family member have several children with multiple 529 plans and one of your children becomes disabled before age 26 and does not attend college, you could transfer any leftover monies from any of the other children's 529 plan into the disabled child's ABLE account.

account beneficiary.　That being said, you should discuss the matter with your advisor to make sure you receive the best advice for your particular situation.

What's more, there are some additional benefits that a 529 plan has over an ABLE account, and it may make more sense to retain funds in the 529 plan—higher contribution limits, higher total funding limit, additional ownership options, no state agency recapture, and a waiver of the IRS 10% penalty if used for care and support of a disabled beneficiary (though still liable for income tax on earnings). When transferring a 529 plan to a disabled family member's ABLE account, the IRS rules consider a family member as a son, daughter, stepson or stepdaughter, brother, sister, stepbrother or stepsister, father or mother, son-in-law, daughter-in-law, father-in-law, mother-in-law, brother-in-law, sister-in-law, spouse, first cousin, or adopted child.

Subject to certain conditions and restrictions, beginning in 2024, leftover 529 plan monies can also be transferred over into a Roth IRA account. One of the main conditions is the beneficiary has to have 'earned income' in order to qualify for the transfer. Some disabled beneficiaries do have jobs with earned income, so they may be eligible for the transfer. Before making any decision to do so, we would highly recommend you consult with an estate planning attorney, financial advisor, or trusted advisor who is knowledgeable and up-to-date on the rules so means-tested monies received from federal or state programs are not reduced or eliminated as a result of the transfer.

What are the Pros and Cons of ABLE Accounts?

Until legislation for ABLE accounts passed, SSI recipients had almost no way to accumulate funds for the future. These are a great savings vehicle for SSI recipients with modest employment as a way to boost savings. There are also great for small lawsuit settlements or inheritances as long as the proceeds are under the annual contribution limit. For larger lawsuits, the first $17,000 can fund an ABLE account, and the rest can go to a Special Needs Trust. Then, the SNT can make additional ABLE contributions of $17,000/year.

But ABLE accounts are not ideal for all situations. ABLE accounts are not allowed for individuals who become disabled after age 26 or, starting in 2026, after age 46. With the limits on annual contributions, they're not suitable for the proceeds of larger lawsuits or inheritances. They are also not the best primary savings vehicle for parents to accumulate funds for their children with a disability. ABLE accounts are also not the best way for individuals with disabilities to accumulate wealth to eventually pass to their children.

If the balance of an ABLE account exceeds $100,000, that could limit your child receiving means-tested government benefits. So, they aren't a perfect solution, but they can be a key piece of the overall financial plan for your child.

Additional Considerations with ABLE Accounts

Our colleague Julieanne Steinbacher has a few additional pieces of advice concerning ABLE Accounts.

If the disabled beneficiary opts for continued education, ABLE accounts are not considered as a resource under the Free Application for Federal Student Aid (FAFSA) program.

Also, if the individual is able to work or may be able to work in the near future, we recommend leaving room in the ABLE account to allow the disabled individual to contribute his or her own earnings to their ABLE account.

An important consideration when looking into enrollment into an ABLE account is how your state handles the death of the individual with disabilities. In some states, when an individual dies, funds remaining in the ABLE account, after the payment of outstanding Qualified Disability Expenses (expenses such as funeral and burial costs), may be used to reimburse the state for Medicaid-related services. Medicaid payback amounts can be calculated based on amounts paid by Medicaid after the creation of the ABLE account and exclude amounts paid by the beneficiary as premiums to a Medicaid buy-in program. This Medicaid payback provision has been prohibited by law in some states. Remaining ABLE funds are payable to the designated heir under the estate.

Because of these payback provisions in some states, our office doesn't automatically recommend ABLE accounts. For a minor child, an alternative we consider is contributing money to a third-party Special Needs Trust that includes a provision allowing the trustee to distribute funds to an ABLE account. That said, while a third-party Special Needs Trust could be a great solution for larger sums of money, the cost of drafting and maintaining that special needs trust should also be a consideration.

It is important to look at your specific state's rules about ABLE accounts. In some states, like Pennsylvania, for example, the entire ABLE account (both savings and growth) is exempt from Pennsylvania inheritance tax. Also, in most cases, the ABLE account is protected from creditors. Since this is a complex area, we strongly recommend you consult with an advisor who has experience with disabled beneficiaries and Special Needs Trusts before making any decisions.

KEY IDEAS

- ABLE accounts are universally underutilized. You should likely start an ABLE account if you haven't already.

- ABLE accounts allow persons with disabilities to accumulate up to $100,000 without jeopardizing means-tested government benefits such as SSI and Medicaid.

- Only one ABLE account is allowed per beneficiary.

- To qualify, the disability must have had an onset prior to the age of 26 or, starting in 2026, prior to the age of 46.

- The total annual contribution to an ABLE account from all sources cannot exceed the annual gift exclusion limit. For 2023, this limit is $17,000.

- If the ABLE account owner is working, he or she can contribute additional funds above the annual limit, up to the smaller of:

    – The account owner's earned income, or

    – The Federal Poverty Level for a single-person household.

- Funds in an ABLE account grow tax-deferred and can be withdrawn tax-free as long as they are used for qualified disability expenses.

- ABLE account funds may be used for a wide variety of qualified disability expenses, including education, housing, transportation, employment training and support, assistive technology, personal support services, health, prevention and wellness, financial management and administrative services, legal fees, funeral and burial expenses, and basic living expenses.

- Pairing a Special Needs Trust with an ABLE account allows for additional financial benefits, but be sure to consult with a knowledgeable CPA, attorney, or other financial advisor before implementing this.

Key Ideas continue on the following page.

KEY IDEAS
(continued)

- Through the end of 2025, you can also fund an ABLE account with a rollover from a 529 plan. The rollover and any other contributions to the ABLE account cannot exceed the annual limit for contributions. For 2023, this limit is $17,000.

- At the death of the account owner, any balance in an ABLE account may first be used to reimburse the state for Medicaid benefits received by the account owner, depending on the state of residency.

- ABLE accounts are best for SSI recipients with modest employment.

- The annual contribution limits make ABLE accounts less suitable for lawsuit settlements or inheritances unless the total proceeds are under the annual contribution limit.

15

The Best Estate Plan for Most Married Couples After The SECURE Act

*"Planning is bringing the future into the present so that
you can do something about it now."*

—Alan Lakein

*For the life of me, I can't understand why the plan I am recommending in this
chapter is not the "standard" estate plan for many, if not most, married couples
who have IRAs and retirement plans.[1] The other thing I don't understand is
why the thousands of attorneys, including many estate attorneys, whose work
our firm has reviewed haven't incorporated the concepts of this chapter into the
estate plans they draft.*

*I would read and, if necessary, re-read this chapter, as it could make an enormous
difference for you and your family. It is also likely to make you want to change your
wills, trusts, and the beneficiary designations of your IRAs and retirement plans.*

*Please note we have a separate chapter for Special Needs trusts. Please see Chapter
13 for that information. This chapter is more foundational and not specific to
parents with a child who has special needs. For parents of a child with a disability,
combining some of the concepts of this chapter with a special needs trust like those
described in Chapter 13 could be a powerful estate planning solution.*

Choosing the Right Beneficiaries for Your Retirement Plan

What follows is an important concept that a surprising number of people and
even estate attorneys get wrong. *Your will (or your trust documents, if you have
them)* **does not** *control the distribution of your retirement plans or IRAs after your
death.* Any account with a specific beneficiary designation will be distributed to
the individuals listed on the beneficiary designation form, *regardless* of what your
will or trust says. In other words, the beneficiary designation of any retirement
plan trumps your will (no pun intended, sorry about that).

In my practice, clients often came in with sophisticated wills or trusts,
sometimes 20–30 pages or more, drafted with every possible contingency in

---

1   There is no solicitation for legal services being made by me, James Lange, nor by Lange Legal Group, LLC.

mind. When I asked them where most of their money was, they usually replied, "in my retirement plan." Then, when I asked them about the beneficiaries of their IRAs and retirement plans, I found that, despite all of the time and money they had spent on these wills and trusts, the beneficiary designation form that controls the majority of their wealth (which I often found out the client had filled out themselves) had just two simple lines:

1. **Primary Beneficiary** – My surviving spouse
2. **Contingent Beneficiary** – My children equally

A little better is:

1. **Primary Beneficiary** – My surviving spouse
2. **Contingent Beneficiary** – My children equally, *per stirpes*

(The *per stirpes* protects the children of a deceased child so that the grandchild or grandchildren would receive what their predeceased parent would have received.)

This simple beneficiary designation, while better than nothing, is nowhere near optimal. Unfortunately, documents with those instructions are not likely to accomplish the family's goals because the beneficiary designations listed on their retirement accounts were not part of a coordinated and integrated estate plan. In situations such as this, the best option for the family is often to completely redraft or, at a minimum, make significant changes to their wills.

Here's another scenario. The client comes in with a basic "I love you" will and beneficiary designations. The "I love you" will says I leave everything to you (my spouse), and at the second death, everything goes to the children equally, *per stirpes*. Owners of "I love you" wills often have their beneficiary forms filled out like the above—and again, though much better than nothing, this is nowhere near optimal.

Unfortunately, the difference between effective and ineffective planning can mean the loss of hundreds of thousands, sometimes even millions, of dollars for your heirs. By the way, the problem with this simple beneficiary designation existed before the SECURE Act, but the passage of the SECURE Act compounds the problem.

The Elephant in the Room of Estate Planning

The problem with estate planning is uncertainty. One uncertainty is that you don't know when you are going to die. You don't know what the tax law on Inherited retirement plans will be at the time of your death. Or, with respect

Your will (or your trust documents, if you have them) does not control the distribution of your retirement plans or IRAs after your death.

to the SECURE Act and the SECURE Act 2.0, you may know where the law stands now, but what you don't know is whether the Proposed Regulations will be ultimately approved or what the next round of legislation will bring. Other huge uncertainties are the future needs and resources of your heirs, most likely your children, and for parents of children with disabilities, what income-tested governmental programs they may be benefiting from at the time of your death.

One final considerable uncertainty is the issue of both general tax rates and the specific tax rates of some of your different beneficiaries. Investment performance, future spending, and inflation rates are also unpredictable. Perhaps a terrible and expensive illness strikes one spouse, and most of the resources of the marriage pay that spouse's expenses, leaving the surviving spouse much worse off than previously projected.

In an alternative and more positive scenario, there is a lot of money left after the death of the first spouse. If so, it might make sense to have at least some of the money go to children or grandchildren after the first death instead of waiting for both spouses to die before anything goes to children or grandchildren.

We also don't know what the future tax laws are going to be. The SECURE Act was bad enough, but who is to say it won't be changed at least one more time before you die, or perhaps multiple times with multiple changes between now and the time of your and your spouse's death?

Whether it is an IRA, a Roth IRA, a 401(k), a brokerage account, life insurance, an annuity, a house, or another asset, there might be compelling reasons for who should get what at the first and then at the second death. If you draft traditional estate planning documents that "fix in stone" the distribution of your assets to your heirs, they are not likely to get the full benefit of your legacy.

Better decisions regarding who should get which assets can be made after your spouse dies when circumstances are current and clear. Furthermore, if your estate planning documents are drafted in the way I am going to propose, your surviving spouse will have nine months after your death to consider a myriad of options and discuss the best strategies with an advisor and other family members.

Similarly, for a "traditional family" after you both die, providing your heirs (usually your mutual children) with as much flexibility as possible is also optimal. So, what can you do to give yourself and your heirs maximum flexibility?

For most married parents with traditional families, I assume that your primary goal in your estate plan is to first provide for your surviving spouse and to ensure your child with a disability is left with adequate financial resources. Leaving money to your other children and grandchildren, while potentially beneficial in terms of tax savings and giving them money earlier in their lives when they are likely to need it more, is usually secondary. But perhaps you can potentially save hundreds of thousands or even millions of dollars for your family and get money to all of your children when they need it more, and still protect your surviving spouse. Doesn't that seem like a better solution than the traditional fixed-in-stone class approach?

Lange's Cascading Beneficiary Plan (LCBP)™

Lange's Cascading Beneficiary Plan (LCBP) is for parents and IRA owners who have traditional marriages with children from that union, and potentially grandchildren—what I like to call the "Leave it to Beaver" marriages. The plan outlined here is not for couples in second marriages who have children from the first marriage. While some of the concepts of this chapter will apply to non-traditional families, those situations require additional strategic thinking that I don't address in this book.

Starting in the mid-nineties, I began recommending additional flexibility to traditional wills and trusts and the beneficiary designations of IRAs and retirement plans. In 1998, I described my plan in *The Tax Adviser*, the peer-reviewed journal of the American Institute of CPAs. An adaptation of that article is available by going to **https://PayTaxesLater.com/Reading/Roth-Iras-Accumulating-Tax-Free-Wealth**. The Roth IRA conversion and the flexible estate plan I recommended were both extremely well received by the peer-reviewers and readers, and that article won Article of the Year.

Then, in 2001, immediately after a change in the law passed, I received explosive coverage for that same strategy that I called Lange's Cascading Beneficiary Plan (LCBP). The recommendations I made in the 1998 article worked out even better after a new law was passed in 2001. I am still recommending that plan today.

At the time, the concept was groundbreaking. Since then, it has been covered many times in national publications with attribution to me in such journals as *The Wall Street Journal*, (twice) *Newsweek*, *Kiplinger's*, *Financial Planning*,

Trusts & Estates, and many others. If you type Cascading Beneficiary Plan in Google, there are hundreds of entries that mostly point back to me.

The concept takes complete advantage of delaying making critical decisions until after someone dies and allowing the surviving spouse to make better decisions when more information is known. The idea is simple but is intended to preserve maximum flexibility and provide the opportunity to get much more value from the assets you leave behind. My plan gives your spouse nine months after your death to make important decisions and the power to act on them.

If it's set up properly, LCBP can give your heirs an enormous amount of flexibility. Under my plan, your surviving spouse can make decisions based on his or her own needs, the needs of the family, the status of your special needs child, and the tax laws in effect at the time of your death. And my plan is as simple as this: start by naming primary and contingent beneficiaries* to your IRAs and all retirement plans and, for that matter, potentially all your wills, trusts, etc., according to the following hierarchy:

1. Primary beneficiary: your spouse,

2. your child (or children equally) as the contingent beneficiary or beneficiaries, per stirpes. (*If you have a child with a disability, a special needs trust for their benefit could be a contingent beneficiary.*)

3. the grandchildren, though, depending on their ages, likely a trust for their benefit. There would be a separate trust for the children (your grandchildren) of each of your children. (*If you have a grandchild with a disability or chronic illness, you could name a special needs trust for the benefit of that grandchild.*)

Perhaps the best description of my plan from a noted source comes from *Kiplinger's* (with slight modifications for clarity).

> "*Lange paints this scene: You are married with children and grandchildren. You name your wife as the primary beneficiary. The first contingent beneficiaries are your children equally. The second contingent beneficiaries are trusts for your grandchildren. Each set of grandchildren has their own trust. At your death, your wife could roll over all or part of the IRA into her IRA. Your wife could also disclaim a portion, which would be distributed to your children. Your wife could also disclaim non-IRA assets. Finally, if neither your wife nor your children need all the money, your children could disclaim all or a portion to a trust for the grandchildren.*"

The key concept here is *disclaiming.* You can't force anyone to accept a bequest—and if you don't lay out a contingency plan, a bequest that is refused might not end up where you would prefer it to go. My plan allows the beneficiary of the IRA (or of the 401(k) or other assets listed above) to accept the IRA for themself or to say, "I don't want that IRA—give it to the next person on the list."

Successful professionals frequently accumulate a significant amount of money in their retirement plans and money outside their retirement plans. And in many cases, it just doesn't make sense to have the surviving spouse inherit more money than they could possibly spend during the remainder of their lifetime.

If the surviving spouse says, "I only need this much money," we look to see who is next in line or, if we want to use the legal term, the contingent beneficiary. The primary beneficiary can accept all the money but can also make a "partial disclaimer." This means that they can accept part of the asset and let the contingent beneficiary or beneficiaries have the rest.

Laying the Groundwork Now for A Post-Mortem Tax Planning Strategy

We also recommend disclaimers because sometimes, when the surviving spouse is left a big IRA, the new tax brackets of single instead of married filing jointly will likely push the surviving spouse into a higher tax bracket. Your child with a disability will hopefully qualify to stretch IRA distributions over his or her lifetime, but any other children would have to withdraw the Inherited IRA in ten years. So it often makes sense to disclaim a portion of the Inherited IRA to a special needs trust or child with a disability at the first death for income tax savings for the family.

Think about how it would work. If your surviving spouse needs all the money, that's fine. She can keep it—end of story. But if your spouse doesn't need the money, or more likely doesn't need all of the money, then she can disclaim either all or a portion of it in favor of the next beneficiary on your list—usually your children.

If you have two children with unique needs, one might accept the disclaimed inheritance while the other disclaims their inheritance or a portion of it to your second choice—which could be a trust for the benefit of their own children (the IRA owners' grandchildren). I know I said it earlier, but it deserves repeating: each beneficiary down the line can have a partial disclaimer if they want to retain some, but not all, of the Inherited IRA or other assets.

When drafting wills, trusts, and beneficiary designations of retirement plans, it is critical to make it crystal clear and specify that each beneficiary has the right to disclaim all or part of the Inherited IRA and other assets, and also what happens to the Inherited IRA or other assets if the beneficiary chooses to do so.

In addition to having specific disclaimer language in the will, revocable trust, and all the beneficiary designations, this plan anticipates the possibility of a child or grandchildren or a special needs trust inheriting IRAs or other assets even if their parents are still alive.

With traditional planning and traditional estate administration, the children don't get anything until both parents are gone. The grandchildren don't get anything unless their parents are gone. The additional flexibility in the LCBP that allows children or a special needs trust to receive money at the *first* death often not only has tax advantages but can also help them out when they are younger and need the money more than if they have to wait for the second death to get any money.

With traditional documents, the only way a grandchild typically receives an inheritance is if both the grandchild's grandparents died and their parent died before the grandparents. With LCBP, we anticipate the possibility that a grandchild could inherit money even though there is a surviving grandparent or parent.

That gives us the ability to name your children as trustees for the grandchildren. As long as you trust your spouse to disclaim any part of the inheritance that he or she doesn't need, and if all of the parties involved understand the reasons for it, disclaiming can not only reduce taxes after your death but also increase the amount of wealth passed on to future generations. It can also get money in the hands of adult children who need the money sooner rather than having to wait for both of their parents to die to spend any of the inheritance.

In practice, people love this plan both conceptually and after someone dies.

As a result of the advance planning, drafting an LCBP, and strategic planning after the first and second deaths, people with these plans saved hundreds of thousands, sometimes millions, of dollars for their families. You can accomplish all of this while fully protecting, or even overprotecting, the surviving spouse.

As a consequence of the SECURE Act, using the power of disclaimers will require more strategic thinking. Since your grown children and grandchildren will have to withdraw everything from the Inherited IRA within ten years unless they qualify for the lifetime stretch, it might no longer make sense for the surviving spouse to disclaim a large IRA to a child.

So, let's assume you want the maximum flexibility possible for your heirs. You have established an LCBP for your estate planning documents. Now, let's look at how the LCBP can work to your advantage in conjunction with the SECURE Act.

Looking at LCBP in Conjunction with the SECURE Act

For this example, we will assume the husband dies first. He leaves a large IRA and a more modest after-tax portfolio. The legal documents give you, his

> **As a result of the advance planning, drafting an LCBP, and strategic planning after the first and second deaths, people with these plans saved hundreds of thousands, sometimes millions, of dollars for their families. You can accomplish all of this while fully protecting, or even overprotecting, the surviving spouse.**

surviving spouse, complete discretion. You have the option to keep the entire IRA and after-tax funds, disclaim part of it to your children, or even have a portion of the IRA pass to a grandchild or grandchildren who your husband named as a second contingent beneficiary. Ideally, with the help of an attorney[2], the appropriate advisor, or even a family member, you (the surviving spouse) will begin by assessing your current financial position.

Let's assume you have more money than you will be able to spend over your lifetime and that after splitting off an adequate portion to fund a special needs trust for your child with a disability, your other children don't have any need for their father's money either. Under the old law, more than likely, it would have made sense for you to disclaim a portion of your IRA to the beneficiaries with the longest life expectancies—specifically, your grandchildren. Because of the SECURE Act, though, the better plan now might be for you to disclaim a portion of the after-tax portfolio. That is because we must now evaluate which generation will pay less tax under the new law and when they will pay the taxes on the Inherited IRA. Will it be the surviving spouse, the child with a disability, any other children, or the grandchild (or, more than likely, a trust for the grandchild's benefit)?

The surviving spouse will have a slower or longer payout period than other potential beneficiaries of the IRAs or retirement plans. This is because his or her minimum required distributions will be spread out over their lifetime. The payout period for a child or grandchild who doesn't qualify as an EDB is only ten years.

Here is another important consideration. Maybe minimizing taxes may not be your family's most pressing need. Perhaps your kids need some money after your death. Their financial situation is desperate due to a job loss. They need money now, and your surviving spouse wants to provide that support. In that case, he or she could disclaim a portion of your IRA or, possibly, after-tax assets.

---

2   There is no solicitation for legal services being made by me, James Lange, nor by Lange Legal Group, LLC.

Another scenario is that the person who receives the disclaimed asset could fall into one of the exceptions to the 10-year rule, such as a child or grandchild with a disability. Furthermore, there may be changes to the SECURE Act or even the tax code that we can't anticipate. All these factors point to the value of decision-making flexibility. I don't know a better or more flexible plan than the LCBP. If I did, I would be writing about that plan. Of course, LCBP or even a variation of it isn't appropriate for everyone, but it is a great starting point for traditional families.

The Concept of Disclaimer, but Outside the Traditional Marriage

Suppose you are single and don't have any children. Let's assume you want to provide for your biological family. A reasonable plan would be to have your wills, trusts, and beneficiary designations leave money to your siblings equally. Let's also assume if one of your siblings predeceases you, the share of the predeceased sibling would go to the children, if any, of the predeceased sibling. Further, if that niece or nephew also predeceased you, their share would go to your grandnieces or grandnephews of that predeceased nephew or niece, presumably in a trust if the grandnieces and nephews are still young.

You could still maintain the basic intent of the above-mentioned plan but add disclaimer provisions. In the event one of your siblings didn't want or need the inheritance or even part of the inheritance, you could have a clause that allows that sibling to "disclaim," presumably to his or her children, your nieces and nephews from that sibling.

Then, you could have each niece and nephew have the right to "disclaim" into a trust for the benefit of their children, your grandnieces and/or grandnephews from that niece or nephew.

Do You Need Disclaimer Provisions in Your Documents to Disclaim?

Legally, there is no requirement that wills, trusts, or beneficiary designation forms must have disclaimer language in order for the survivor to disclaim. However, I like attorneys to include the disclaimer language for several reasons:

1. Putting the language in there at least makes the issue of whether to disclaim or not part of the conversation after a death. Although all heirs have the right to disclaim even if the decedent's estate planning documents do not include disclaimer language, in practice, that right is rarely exercised when the language is not included in the documents.

2. I like to make it crystal clear to the parties what can happen to the money and/or other assets if there is a disclaimer.

3. It is often the true intent of the parties to give the survivor choices and including these choices in the documents makes a lot of sense.

But let's say someone drafted a document that made you the beneficiary and for some reason you wanted to have the money go "next in line." You could disclaim and get the same result as if disclaimer language was included and you disclaimed. That said, it is rare to see an heir exercise that right to disclaim assets unless there is disclaimer language in the documents.

Forcing Ten-Year Payout for Successor Beneficiaries of Existing and Future Inherited IRAs

This is a technical point that could probably be skipped, but definitely read this section if you inherited an IRA and/or have an interest in the New York Yankees. In addition, it is part of the SECURE Act. The SECURE Act allows for the continued stretch of an Inherited IRA if the original owner died on or before December 31, 2019. However, it makes no accommodations for grandfathering those rules with respect to successor beneficiaries. We had quite a few clients die in 2019 and earlier, leaving balances of more than a million dollars in their retirement plans. In many cases, we recommended that the surviving spouse make significant disclaimers—saving heirs hundreds of thousands, perhaps millions of dollars over their lifetimes. We might look back on these days as the good old days in terms of when to die (not that there is ever a good time to die).

Some people do die at the right time in terms of tax law. George Steinbrenner, the former owner of the (for me) hated New York Yankees, died in 2010, the only year there was no estate tax. The timing of his death saved his family hundreds of millions of dollars in estate taxes.

For you long-time Yankee fans, all I have to say is 1960. That is the year the dark horse Pittsburgh Pirates won the seventh game in the ninth inning when Bill Mazeroski, known as a great fielder but not a great hitter, hit the winning home run that clinched the World Series for the Pirates. Go Bucs!

At the time, the capacity of Forbes Field, the site of the winning home run in Pittsburgh, was 41,000. There are at least 60,000 surviving Pittsburghers, including my brother, who claim to have been present for that game. You do the math.

The beneficiaries of IRAs in which the IRA owner died on or before December 31, 2019, are grandfathered. For example, if you inherited an IRA prior to or on December 31, 2019, you are still permitted to "stretch" that Inherited IRA over your own lifetime because the original IRA owner died before the effective date of the SECURE Act.

But let's say you inherited an IRA from your parent prior to or on December 31, 2019, and are appropriately taking an RMD from the Inherited IRA every year. Once you die and pass your Inherited IRA on to your own beneficiaries, they will be subject to the 10-year rule.

Under the old rules, your beneficiary could have "stretched" that Inherited IRA over what remained of your actuarial life expectancy, even though you were dead. If you pass when you are age 60, that means your beneficiaries will lose decades of tax-deferred (or, in the case of a Roth account, tax-free) growth compared to the old law.

This entire "Death of the Stretch IRA" was a huge money grab by Congress, and this provision just rubs salt in the wound.

Unfortunately, even some of your heirs who initially qualified for exemptions from the accelerated IRA taxation rules will eventually fall victim to them. For example, once a minor beneficiary reaches 21, the 10-year rule kicks in. Furthermore, if your minor beneficiary dies before reaching the age of majority, then any subsequent beneficiaries are subject to the 10-year rule immediately— even if they are not of the age of majority themselves! The same is true for the heirs of an individual with a disability who inherits an IRA. Any subsequent beneficiary must withdraw and pay taxes on the IRA within ten years. So, while some accommodation is available for individuals with disabilities and for individuals who have already inherited IRAs under the old law, they will not extend the privilege to their beneficiaries.

Beyond what we have covered so far, is there anything else you can do to reduce the impact of the SECURE Act, as well as the looming specter of rising tax rates? The answer is yes. The chapters that follow explore some options that can help minimize the bite of this tax bill, including naming trusts that you establish for the benefit of your heirs as the beneficiaries of your IRAs and retirement plans, Roth IRA conversions, and lots more. Read on!

KEY IDEAS

- A flexible estate plan offers multiple advantages to your surviving spouse and non-spousal heirs, including children and grandchildren with disabilities or chronic illnesses.

Key Ideas continue on the following page.

KEY IDEAS
(continued)

- The LCBP allows heirs to strategically disclaim to subsequent beneficiaries to take care of needs and minimize taxes.

- This plan provides or overprovides for the surviving spouse but also allows important options.

- The SECURE Act makes it even more urgent to plan for the long term.

- Though the LCBP is more popular with traditional families, the concept of disclaimers can be used in many situations.

16

Roth IRA Conversions
Before and After the SECURE Act

"If there is one thing that marks families with money in the long term, it is this: delayed gratification."

—Bill Bonner

For many IRA owners, proactively developing a long-term Roth IRA conversion strategy is one of the best financial decisions you can make. This was true before recent tax-law changes, and it is still true. For parents of a child with a disability, it is even more important to develop a long-term Roth IRA or other Roth conversion plan while you are alive and perhaps even after you are gone!

You Can Trust this Information on Roth IRA Conversions

I wrote the first peer-reviewed article on Roth IRA conversions which was published in 1998 and won *The Tax Adviser's* article of the year award. We also wrote an entire book on the subject, *The Roth Revolution, Pay Taxes Once and Never Again* which you can download without cost by going to **https://PayTaxesLater.com/Books/**. Some of the highly skilled number crunching CPAs on our team participated in writing the Roth chapters in this book and created some of the graphs and charts.

After the Tax Cuts and Jobs Act (TCJA) of 2017, the value of Roth IRA conversions surged. The TCJA reduced income tax rates effective from 2018 through 2025. The TCJA includes a "sunset" date. Unless Congress takes action, many of its provisions, including the lowered tax rates, will expire at the end of 2025. At that point, without intervention, tax rates will go back up to the much higher 2017 levels plus inflation.

The lower tax rates of today often allow taxpayers to execute larger Roth IRA conversions at a lower tax cost. *Forbes* magazine featured my strategies on a front cover story in 2019 that emphasized the tax rates and the long-term value of a Roth IRA conversion. I also published several articles on the subject for Forbes.com, where I am a paid contributor. I don't mean to brag (ok, maybe a little), but I don't want you to disregard the information because you question my expertise or the expertise of the team contributing to these chapters. Roth IRA conversions are likely a good strategy for most IRA owners at some point in their lives even with steady income tax rates. With income tax rates likely to increase in the future, a series of Roth IRA conversions before 2026 could add significant wealth for you, your family, and your child with a disability. In addition, Roth IRA conversions are an important defense to the dreaded SECURE Act that has occupied a major portion of this book because it is so devastating to IRA and retirement plan owners with children who don't have a disability.

Roth IRA conversions usually make sense with steady income tax rates. But, with tax rates likely to rise in the future, they make even more sense now. Please see the following chart showing the difference in tax rates for 2017 and 2023. If the sunset provisions take effect in 2026, which will happen unless Congress intervenes, the income tax rates will revert to the higher rates of 2017 plus inflation.

Comparative Tax Rates for 2023 and 2017 (2026) for "Married Filing Jointly"

2023				2017 (2026)			
$ 0 – 22,000	x	10%		$ 0 – 18,650	x	10%
22,001 – 89,450	x	12%		18,651 – 75,900	x	15%
89,451 – 190,750	x	22%		75,901 – 153,100	x	25%
190,751 – 364,200	x	24%		153,101 – 233,350	x	28%
364,201 – 462,500	x	32%		233,351 – 416,700	x	33%
462,501 – 693,750	x	35%		416,701 – 470,700	x	35%
693,751 *and above*	x	37%		470,701 *and above*	x	39.6%

As I just mentioned, the TCJA temporarily reduced personal income tax brackets. For example, in 2023, your taxable income could be as high as $364,200 and you would still be in the 24% marginal tax bracket. That same income in 2017 would put you in the 33% bracket. Even if your income was closer to $100,000, that means in 2023 you could potentially make a $264,200 Roth conversion and pay tax at the marginal rates of 22% and 24%. Please note this is a simplified example that doesn't take into account some of the other taxes and costs that occur with increased income such as an increase in your Medicare Part B premium and net investment income tax. That said, please keep in mind, these are still substantially reduced tax rates that might go up even before the end of 2025 as Congress struggles to find a way to fund the interest on the federal deficit, let alone the deficit, the national debt, and the unrecognized debt that we have already incurred.

After the SECURE Act passed, we began recommending that many 72-year-old+ clients consider executing Roth conversions, even though they were taking RMDs and receiving Social Security benefits. Basically, it makes sense for many retirees to execute Roth conversions in the 24% tax bracket because we know that their future RMDs will be more heavily taxed when/if the current tax rates revert to their 2017 levels. Of course, every situation is unique, and the decision needs to be evaluated on an individual basis, but there are significant commonalities also.

Many people are surprised to discover that their taxable income in retirement is often higher than when they were working. Take a simple example of a married retired professional who has $2,000,000 in his or her retirement plan or IRA. The RMD on that amount starts at roughly $80,000 and gets higher as he/she ages. If you add this RMD to the income from two Social Security checks and some interest and dividends, the couple's taxable income is often higher than when they were working.

Many people have their retirement plans outside of an IRA, perhaps in a 401(k). Depending on the employer plan document, it might be possible to make a Roth 401(k) conversion, which would be almost identical, conceptually, to a Roth IRA conversion.

Hopefully, you already have part of your retirement assets in Roth accounts. I have been attempting to get many of my clients to be proactive about Roth strategies. These clients now have a lot of money in these tax-free accounts, and many of their families will be hundreds of thousands of dollars, perhaps even millions of dollars, better off because they did.

Our family will be hundreds of thousands of dollars better off even measured in today's dollars because of the large Roth conversion we made in 1998 along with additional Roth IRA and Roth 401(k) contributions and Roth conversions since that time. If you are reading this book, you likely have a significant amount of money in Traditional retirement accounts because your employer's matching contributions were deposited there and up until at least 1998 and likely much longer, that is where your contributions went also. If so, you should consider integrating a long-term Roth IRA conversion strategy into your retirement and estate plan.

The creation of additional Roth contribution opportunities was written into SECURE Act 2.0 in an effort to raise more tax revenues. The new legislation can benefit those who are higher earners who want to contribute more to their Roth accounts, especially when there is a consideration for providing for a child with a disability. As I explain in Chapter 11, leaving Roth accounts to your child with a disability can potentially provide hundreds of thousands more over your child's lifetime after you are gone. Under the SECURE Act, if that child is deemed an eligible designated beneficiary due to their disability or chronic illness, they will be able to stretch the Inherited retirement plan over their lifetime.

This makes it important to accumulate more money in a Roth account when you are planning for the future of your child with a disability. Combining Roth accounts with a special needs trust and an ABLE account as we explain in Chapter 14 can prevent the Roth funds from being counted as an available financial resource for your child so that the Inherited Roth account does not compromise any federal or state assistance programs.

Effective in 2023, employee plan participants can now elect to have their employer matching contributions be made into a Roth account; under the prior rule the money had to go into the Traditional retirement account. Of course, the employer must modify their plan document in order to allow this feature, and the employee must pay taxes on the matching contributions made into the Roth account in the year the employer matching contribution is made. This change will not happen quickly, especially in smaller companies. If you are an employer or have some clout in your company, try to have this option become part of your plan.

Beginning in 2026, if an employee earns more than $145,000 and is over age 50, employee catch-up contributions are required to be directed into a Roth account instead of the Traditional retirement account. Initially, SECURE Act 2.0 required this change for 2024 but has since provided a two-year transition period until 2026 due to the administrative complexities of this requirement.

We cannot stress the importance of directing more money into your Roth account when planning for the long-term future of your child with a disability. One of the things we like to do for our clients is to have our CPAs "run the numbers" as part of a Financial Masterplan. This is our affectionate term for detailed quantitative analysis comparing many different scenarios into the long-term future. Though we have several specialty software programs to help

> **Effective in 2023, employee plan participants can now elect to have their employer matching contributions be made into a Roth account; under the prior rule the money had to go into the Traditional retirement account.**

> **Frequently, our clients arrive with an unintegrated "financial plan" that is the product of many independent financial decisions. Each individual decision probably made sense at the time, but they do not necessarily work together effectively.**

us test different conversion amounts and timing, it is more of a manual process than one might imagine.

One reason we do this is to determine an ideal long-term Roth IRA conversion plan. Of course, Roth IRA conversions are only one aspect of running the numbers; a well-integrated Financial Masterplan will include strategies for Social Security, spending, gifting, etc.

A well-integrated financial plan is usually the "after" picture for most of our accounting clients. The "before" picture tends to be far less integrated. Frequently, our clients arrive with an unintegrated "financial plan" that is the product of many independent financial decisions. Each individual decision probably made sense at the time, but they do not necessarily work together effectively.

Does the Following Scenario Seem Familiar?

Either on your own or with an advisor, when you first started working, you picked an asset allocation for your retirement plan that seemed quite appropriate at the time. Then, either on your own or with another advisor, you picked investments for your money outside your retirement plan. Perhaps you contributed to a Roth IRA or even made several Roth IRA conversions.

At some point, you may have switched your allocations in your retirement plan. At a different point in time, you may have seen an insurance agent and purchased some insurance. At another point, you saw an attorney and had wills, trusts and hopefully the beneficiary designations for your retirement assets drafted.

Maybe you took Social Security before age 70 or maybe you read an article that made sense and held off taking Social Security until you turned 70.

In other words, what you likely have now is *not* part of an integrated Financial Masterplan that takes everything into account, including money, desires, family situation, taxes, etc. It is the end result of what seemed to be a lot of reasonable independent decisions made at different times, often without thought as to how those decisions had an impact on your total plan.

We think you will get a much better result if you develop a Financial Masterplan that takes your entire financial and family situation into account. Though it sounds self-serving, few firms provide this type of planning. One of the advantages that we enjoy is the close association of number-crunching CPAs, with expertise in IRAs and in mathematically oriented financial planning, combined with investment experts and wonderful money managers.[1]

Your Financial Masterplan should be updated at least every several years, even if the original plan was a multi-year plan. We see many quantitative professionals, especially engineers, who attempt some primitive version of "running the numbers" using Excel spreadsheets.

Sometimes they find a better solution than doing nothing. On the other hand, they aren't tax experts, and they often neglect to factor in critical considerations. But, of course, we have a significant advantage. We possess excellent software and highly skilled CPAs who know tax law inside out and have many years of experience "running the numbers" to develop Financial Masterplans.

We want all our clients to have a synergistic plan that accounts for all assets, income, goals, dreams, family situations, etc. This is especially important for someone who wants to provide a long-term plan for their child with a disability. But I digress.

Back to the subject: the basic premise of this chapter is to show you that at some point in your life, a partial Roth IRA conversion will likely be a good strategy for both you and your heirs. Under the current law (lower income tax rates combined with accelerated income taxes on your Traditional IRAs when you die), making a series of Roth IRA conversions is likely to improve your and your spouse's financial position while you are alive. It is also more likely that it will significantly improve your children's financial situation after you and your spouse die, especially when planning for your child with a disability. You want to make sure you got the planning just right in this case. Evaluating the impact of making Roth IRA conversions for the long-term benefit of your child with a disability is a key consideration to your overall planning.

---

1 Please see restrictions and disclaimers at the end of the book in the section titled *"When your Child has a Disability…Save More, Have More, and Leave More to Your Child in a Tax-Advantaged Manner that Preserves Government Benefits! The Lange Edge: A Truly Integrated Long-Term Financial Masterplan for Parents Who Want to Ensure That Their Child Is Financially Secure for Life --- Even After Mom and Dad Are Gone.""*.

Please note that if you engage Lange Accounting Group, LLC for our Financial Masterplan service or receive Financial Masterplan services as part of our assets-under-management arrangement with Lange Financial Group, LLC, these services are provided by employees in their capacity as CPAs and are not legal services. The protection of the attorney-client relationship does not exist with respect to these accounting and asset management services. There is no solicitation for legal services being made by me, James Lange, nor by Lange Legal Group, LLC.

Do the Math

One of the reasons we "run the numbers" is because I don't believe that decisions about Roth IRA conversions should be based on opinions: i.e., "I like the idea of a Roth conversion, let's do it." Whether you should make a Roth conversion and for how much and when is not just a matter of personal preference. Maybe you like Celine Dion, and I like Whitney Houston. There isn't a way to objectively prove who is the better singer. Whether to make a Roth IRA conversion, on the other hand, is a matter of math, not opinions; it is possible and imperative to make objective projections.

We believe in peer-reviewed math, science, and following proven academic data-driven planning to enhance your finances. Yes, the results will depend on the assumptions used to make the projections. We address that by starting with assumptions that we think are reasonable. But as the client is frequently present when we run our numbers, all assumptions can be modified or changed with the client's input. In addition, the goal of running the numbers is to arrive at the best solution given your personal values and your individual financial situation. But, given certain values and other parameters, the best results can be obtained by "running the numbers" rather than guessing.

Many factors should be considered when planning the ideal Roth IRA conversion strategy for your family. I will be the first to admit that Roth IRA conversions are not perfect or appropriate for everyone. But I believe that, with the help of projections of different amounts and timings of Roth conversions, coming up with the ideal Roth IRA conversion plan for you and your family can provide most parents and their families enormous financial rewards.

Critics of Roth IRA conversions will point out that the SECURE Act reduces the potential long-term benefits of Roth IRA conversions because the beneficiary will no longer benefit from the lifetime stretch of an Inherited Roth IRA. However, for parents of a child with a disability, if your child can qualify for the lifetime stretch, Roth conversions can mean hundreds of thousands of dollars more for your child over his or her lifetime.

Even if your child doesn't qualify as an Eligible Designated Beneficiary (EDB) and the lifetime stretch, in most cases, inheriting a Roth IRA is much better than inheriting a Traditional IRA. Of course, for those who do not qualify as EDBs, both types of Inherited accounts must be distributed within ten years of the death of the IRA owner. That said, Traditional retirement accounts are taxable, leading to potentially massive acceleration of the income taxes for the beneficiary.

While the greatest benefit of Roth conversions is often assumed to be conferred on

> We believe in peer-reviewed math, science, and following proven academic data-driven planning to enhance your finances.

your beneficiaries, we have found surprising benefits for IRA owners who are willing to learn when and how much of a Roth IRA conversion to make. I have wealthy clients who either don't have children or aren't particularly interested in providing for the next generation who are still making substantial Roth IRA conversions.

The irony is even though these conversions will allow the clients to spend a lot more money over their lifetime, they probably won't. We address that frequent unwillingness to spend anywhere near what you can afford in Chapter 24.

The math usually works even if tax rates are steady. If you believe like we do that the reduced tax rates established by the Tax Cuts and Jobs Act will not be in place permanently and tax rates will go up in the future, the Roth conversion is even more advantageous. Running the numbers will demonstrate that it is often beneficial for you to pay taxes *now* on money that, at some point in your lifetime, you know you will be required to pay taxes on anyway—potentially at a much higher rate. There have been times in history when Congress was not shy about taxing your hard-earned money. In 1944, the top tax rate peaked at 94 percent! We already have insurmountable financial problems as a country, and I think betting on future tax increases is a much better bet than future tax decreases, at least in the long run.

Roth IRA conversions give you some control over your tax planning by reducing the balance in your Traditional IRA accounts, which then reduces your RMD—an advantage during times when future tax rates are likely to increase. Furthermore, Roth conversions reduce the amount of money held in Traditional IRAs that will be subject to the SECURE Act's accelerated income tax at your death. Inherited Roth IRA distributions are tax-free—which will seriously reduce the pain of accelerated taxes on Traditional IRAs. Developing a long-term Roth IRA conversion strategy is most likely an extremely valuable use of your time and/or money if you choose to work with a Roth IRA conversion expert. Even if you go through the appropriate steps and determine a Roth conversion isn't for you, at least you will know and won't have a nagging feeling you should be doing something that you aren't doing. So, how do you move forward?

Know the General Principles First, Run the Numbers Next

Making changes to a retirement plan can be scary and overwhelming. You don't want to make a mistake, and it can seem safest just to stay put. I get it. I have a reputation for being a strong advocate for Roth IRA conversions for people of all ages. That reputation doesn't really reflect my beliefs. I believe this is a more accurate statement—*I am the owner of an accounting firm that "runs the numbers" for our clients to make objective recommendations that often include making a series of Roth IRA conversions over several years.*

The advice that follows comes from me having overseen our "number running" literally thousands of times. I have trained thousands of financial advisors, CPAs, attorneys, and consumers on the benefits of Roth IRA conversions. Our team of number crunching CPAs have also made major contributions to the Roth conversion chapters of this book.

I mention some of these things because Roth IRA conversions can be so valuable that I would hate readers to conclude "Oh that's his opinion. My CPA or advisor said they weren't a good idea or at least not a good idea for me." This isn't a matter of opinion. It is a matter of math. I cannot overemphasize the potential benefits of an objective math-oriented approach for producing an ideal long-term Roth IRA conversion plan. If math indicates that not doing a conversion is best, then that is likely what you should do. That said, the math has to be done right.

The Secret: Quantifying the Benefit of Roth IRA Conversions Using the Concept of Purchasing Power

The following section could be a game changer for you. I would read this section carefully and you might have to read it more than once to fully absorb this critical concept. It is worth the time to keep reading until the concept is clear.

Of course, if you have been following my work, you have heard me drone on and on about this point for over 25 years. I have been teaching this concept to IRA and retirement plan owners, financial advisors, CPAs, and attorneys. The CPAs and engineers usually get it fairly quickly. You have to explain it multiple

> **I am the owner of an accounting firm that "runs the numbers" for our clients to make objective recommendations that often include making a series of Roth IRA conversions over several years.**

times to attorneys who have a harder time with it than even the IRA owners who attend our workshops. Despite having taught it to thousands, it is still a general secret that millions would benefit from understanding.

"The Secret" involves determining the most accurate measurement tool for wealth. I am not interested in increasing your total dollars nearly as much as I am interested in increasing your purchasing power.

I am not talking about inflation here either.

Critical to evaluating the costs and benefits of Roth conversions as well as understanding your true wealth is thinking in terms of "purchasing power" vs. "total dollars."

For example, if I have $1 million in my IRA, and you have $900,000 in an after-tax account, then using a total dollar approach, I have more money than you. But what if we both want to make a large purchase? I must cash in my IRA and pay the taxes. Let's assume a flat income tax rate of 24%. I know that isn't realistic, but this is to demonstrate a concept. After paying the taxes, I'd end up with $760,000 in cash. (This ignores the tax on the money needed to pay the tax, but I want to keep this simple.) Unless there are capital gains that need to be paid, there will be no tax consequences when you cash out your $900,000. Even if you have to pay some capital gains taxes, they will be much lower than my tax bill. That means you can purchase more goods and services with your $900,000 after-tax dollars than I can with my $1 million IRA. You have more purchasing power than I do, even though I have more total dollars.

This is a critical concept, and I recommend rereading the prior paragraph until you understand it before moving on.

Now, let's look at Roth conversions in terms of purchasing power:

Assume that both of us have $100,000 in our Traditional IRAs and $24,000 outside our IRAs. I will assume a flat income tax rate of 24%, as I did previously. If I don't make a Roth IRA conversion, I have $124,000 when measured in "total dollars." But, if I think of that amount in terms of "purchasing power," I have $100,000.

> "The Secret" involves determining the most accurate measurement tool for wealth. I am not interested in increasing your total dollars nearly as much as I am interested in increasing your *purchasing power*.

Here's a breakdown of that purchasing power math:

$100,000 Traditional IRA dollars + $24,000 non-IRA dollars = **$124,000 *"Total Dollars"***

$124,000 "Total Dollars" - $24,000 non-IRA dollars that I will use to pay the tax due when I cash in the $100,000 IRA = ***$100,000 in "Purchasing Power"***

---

*The non-IRA dollars will be used to pay the tax due when the $100,000 IRA is cashed.

Now let's assume that you start with the same $100,000 in your Traditional IRA and $24,000 outside your IRA, and you execute a Roth conversion of your entire IRA. Because you converted your Traditional IRA (which you haven't yet paid taxes on) to the Roth IRA, you will have to fork over $24,000 of after-tax dollars to Uncle Sam ($100,000 times 24% tax rate). But, after the conversion, you also have $100,000 measured in both total dollars and purchasing power because there will be no tax due when you cash in your Roth IRA.

Below shows that, when measured in terms of purchasing power and using simple assumptions, the breakeven point on Roth IRA conversions is Day 1, regardless of your age.

Roth IRA After Conversion		$ 100,000
Traditional IRA	$ 100,000	
Other Non-IRA Funds*	$ 24,000	0
Total Dollar Value of Accounts	**$ 124,000**	**$ 100,000**
Less Taxes Paid on IRA *(if distributed)*	$ 24,000	0
Purchasing Power	**$ 100,000**	**$ 100,000**

*Non--IRA Funds of $24,000 used to pay taxes on either cashing in the Traditional IRA or a Roth IRA conversion.

Again, I can't overemphasize the importance of this concept. The failure to understand this concept is one of the reasons why many so-called experts and advisors give clients advice regarding Roth IRA conversions that is completely wrong for them. And many of the free calculators available on the internet calculate the value of Roth conversions in terms of total dollars which, again, leads to underestimating the financial benefit that could be derived from a series of Roth IRA conversions.

If your measurement tool is total dollars, instead of the better measure of wealth which is purchasing power, then your inevitable conclusion will be that Roth IRA conversions are only good for younger taxpayers who have many years for the tax-free growth to accumulate in their Roth IRA, which will outweigh the money they paid to convert their Traditional IRA to a Roth IRA. Using the same measurement tool of total dollars will also lead you to conclude that Roth IRA conversions are bad for older taxpayers.

Measuring value in total dollars instead of purchasing power is a very common but very costly mistake.

Let's look at this issue in a different way, but one that will lead to the same conclusion. If you were a farmer, would you rather deduct the cost of the seed but be required to pay tax on the harvest or pay tax on the seed and reap the harvest tax-free? A Roth IRA conversion is like paying tax on the seed—that is to say, paying tax on the amount of your Traditional IRA that you want to convert. Then, after you pay the tax, you plant the seed (open your new Roth IRA account with the money you have converted), and over many years, you watch it grow. Then when you or your heirs distribute or harvest the crop (the amount you converted plus all of the growth), the *entire harvest or distribution is income-tax free.*

If you're already retired, is the tax-free advantage of the Roth conversion great enough to write a big check, or perhaps a number of smaller annual checks over a period of several years, to Uncle Sam before necessary, let alone deal with all the paperwork? Paperwork can be quite time-consuming. And most of my clients are as interested in saving time as well as money, which is one of the reasons why I appreciate your reading this book.

To address this question of whether the value of Roth conversions might outweigh the hassle and time required to execute the strategy, let's look at the comparison outlined in Figure 16.1. In this example, we "ran the numbers" for two married couples whose circumstances (including financial history, annual income, annual spending, etc.) are identical in every way except that one couple did a series of Roth IRA conversions, and the other couple did not. Have a look at the figure below, which shows the outcome for the first couple who made a series of Roth IRA conversions of $175,000 over five years starting at age 65, compared to no Roth IRA conversions. Again, we measure in purchasing power, not total dollars.

> **Measuring value in total dollars instead of purchasing power is a very common but very costly mistake.**

Keep in mind that the current tax rates are set to "sunset" and return to 2017 rates at the end of 2025. For the couple in this example, it made sense to maximize annual conversions over five years before the tax rates are scheduled to increase even though their income will remain relatively low for an additonal two years.

Since 2025 is rapidly approaching, and so is the potential of increased tax rates, time is of the essence. The sooner you are able to begin Roth conversions, the more years you have to maximize these current lower tax brackets. For those of you still employed and who don't have IRAs that you could convert to Roth IRAs, check with your retirement plan administrator and see if you are allowed to make Roth 401(k) conversions inside your retirement plan. If you know you are going to be in a higher tax bracket in future years, it might be profitable to start Roth conversions in your retirement plan at work, potentially either before or after you retire.

It is hard to see, but this shows that the IRA owner (that is you, not your kids) is better off measured in purchasing power by $266,890 if you make five $175,000 Roth conversions starting as late as age 65 and assuming you and/or your spouse survive until age 90. This assumes a 7.5% rate of return and 2.5% inflation, and we are measuring in today's dollars. If we measured without taking inflation into account, the advantage would be much higher.

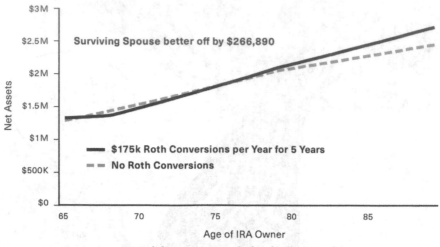

Figure 16.1
Original IRA Owner After Roth Conversions*

Detailed assumptions can be found in the Appendix.

This figure measures the accounts in terms of their purchasing power, which we believe is the only appropriate way to compare the value of a taxable IRA to that of an after-tax account. Of course, much depends on your personal circumstances. Still, you will likely benefit during your lifetime by making a Roth conversion or, more likely, a series of smaller Roth IRA conversions over a period of years. And the longer you and your spouse live, the more that benefit grows, and the greater the potential benefit for your child with a disability. There is a great benefit to going through the exercise of evaluating the different types of assets your child with a disability could inherit and the overall impact on their long-term financial security. By doing so, you can further evaluate the benefits of incorporating a Roth conversion plan and/or making Roth contributions over your lifetime.

If you would like to learn more about why Roth IRA conversions are good for you and your heirs, please see our book, *The Roth Revolution, Pay Taxes Once and Never Again,* which you can download for free by going to **https://PayTaxesLater.com/Books/** or purchase on Amazon. Please note that while that book was written before the SECURE Act and is therefore dated, virtually all the concepts remain the same, and it can still be a valuable resource. We also have a video focusing on Roth IRA conversions before and after the SECURE Act. Please see **https://PayTaxesLater.com/Roth-Workshop/**.

Please note, a number-crunching CPA in our office did this analysis and when I reviewed it, I thought it was wrong. I would have guessed that doing Roth conversions up until age 73, not age 70 would have been optimal. I thought she made a mistake forgetting that RMDs didn't start until age 73 under the SECURE Act 2.0. When I questioned her on it, I saw she was a step ahead of me. She used the right year for the RMD calculation but in this case, the additional income from collecting Social Security made the optimal plan to stop converting at age 70, not age 73. I bring this up to point out that "running the numbers" is very fact specific and even experts can guess wrong without "running the numbers."

Roth IRA Conversions are Definitely Good for Your Heirs

Let's continue with the example above. Assume you begin making Roth IRA conversions of $175,000/year at age 65 and continue until you begin taking RMDs from what remains of your Traditional IRA, at age 73. You die at age 80 and your spouse dies at age 90, leaving the remaining estate to your son who is 56 when the second spouse dies. Let's also assume that both you and your spouse are dead and that your Roth IRA is now worth $800,000. Let's also assume you did not do any of the special planning regarding disclaimers covered in Chapter 15. Your only child is named as the beneficiary of the Roth IRA. Your child now owns a special asset called an Inherited Roth IRA. Under the SECURE Act, the entire Inherited Roth IRA account must be disbursed within ten years of your death, assuming the child is not an EDB.

Let's assume that although your child has a disability, they do not qualify for eligibility under the stringent rules for the lifetime stretch and will be required to drain the account within 10 years of your spouse's death. Losing the long-term tax-free growth on the Roth IRA over their lifetime as was possible under the pre-SECURE Act rules will be costly to your child, but inheriting a Roth account is still way more advantageous than inheriting a Traditional IRA.

The following figure projects the difference between your completing the five $175,000 Roth IRA conversions versus doing nothing as measured in the life of your child. Though we have more details for this figure in the Appendix, the most important detail is that this figure considers the taxes you had to pay to make the Roth IRA conversions before you died and the taxes that would be paid by the beneficiary if no Roth IRA conversion had been done.

The above figure continues the scenario from Figure 16.1 and shows what would happen after your death. The bump at age 66 is when all assets from the Inherited IRA have been disbursed. The solid line shows what would happen if you completed the series of Roth IRA conversions by age 70, as depicted in Figure 16.1, and the dashed line shows where your child would be if no Roth IRA conversions had been done. As Figure 16.1 shows, with a Roth IRA conversion,

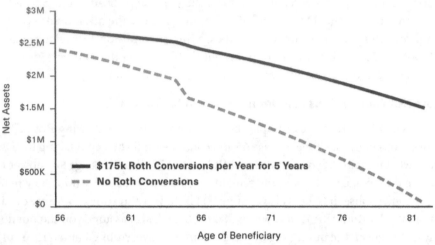

Figure 16.2
Child Inherits Roth IRA vs. Traditional IRA after The SECURE Act*

*Detailed assumptions can be found in the Appendix.

your child will inherit a Roth IRA with a higher balance than if no conversion had taken place. During the first ten years after the death of the last surviving parent, this difference gets even bigger because the beneficiary of a Traditional IRA has to pay tax on the distributions while the inheritor of a Roth IRA can leave the assets in place to continue to appreciate tax-free until the tenth year.

Even though both of these IRAs are stretched for only ten years, inheriting the Roth (the solid line) gives your child well over an additional $1,000,000 over their lifetime. Again, please note that if you complete a Roth IRA conversion and if tax rates increase after the conversion, the value of the Roth IRA conversion to you and your children will be even higher because we do not assume increasing tax rates for this analysis. If you are leaving the Roth IRA to a beneficiary with a disability or chronic illness who qualifies to stretch the Inherited Roth over their lifetime, the difference would really be enormous, as I demonstrated in Chapter 11, where, over her lifetime, my daughter Erica will have an additional $1.9 million of purchasing power measured in today's dollars.

Our Process for Running the Numbers

You can skip to the next subhead if you have no interest in how our accounting firm "runs the numbers" and why we recommend running the numbers.

Are you considering Roth conversions? We recommend that unless you are an extremely skilled amateur number cruncher that you consider working with a firm that has great expertise in running the numbers on Roth IRA conversions to make objective recommendations.

We have a lot of clients who would rather have a root canal than pay an advisor. Often, they try doing some financial analysis and Roth IRA conversion analysis and don't come up with the right conclusion. They often make significant mistakes that lead them to far-from-optimal results. That being said, they may come up with a better conclusion than doing nothing. Investors who measure in total dollars often come to the conclusion that a Roth IRA conversion is not appropriate for them. We might conclude that if they had used the more accurate measure of wealth, that is purchasing power, they might have come to a completely different conclusion.

Please be wary of internet financial calculators. As I mentioned before, many, if not most, of the ones I see don't consider the concept of purchasing power and lead to the wrong conclusion. If you measure in total dollars instead of purchasing power, you will often conclude that Roth IRA conversions are not good for older individuals. A young person will likely have a long enough time to make up for the fact that they had to write a check to the IRS to make the conversion. Seniors, on the other hand, will have less time, and they might not make up for the taxes they had to pay on the conversion. However, both examples are based on total dollars instead of the more appropriate measurement of purchasing power. When you take purchasing power into account, Roth IRA conversions are often advantageous for seniors, as demonstrated in the analysis above.

Completing a Financial Masterplan, at least the way we do it, taking multiple variables into account, is a fairly complicated calculation that has to consider timing, taxes, and Social Security benefits. (I know this sounds self-serving, but there are very few firms that can thoroughly run the numbers and come up with the right answer, and we pride ourselves on our skillset.)

We also make it our practice to run the numbers with the client present, at least part of the time, either in the room or, in recent years, when our practice has transformed from a basically local practice to a national practice, on Zoom. Of course, even with our long-time local clients many of our financial reviews may be on Zoom, at the client's request, as a result of the pandemic. This allows the client to see how we arrive at our recommendations. And it allows them to evaluate the assumptions and choose the ones that best reflect their circumstances. In practice, when we run the numbers, Roth IRA conversions are only one of many factors that we consider. For example, we often compare different Social Security strategies, gifting strategies, spending strategies, and lifestyle issues like buying or renting a second home in a warmer climate. We also work backwards to determine how much money a client can safely spend. Evaluating the merits of Roth IRA conversions, though critical, is only one variable when we run the numbers. Our goal is to develop a long-term Financial Masterplan for our clients.

You might assume that in today's world, there would be killer software where all you need to do is enter a few numbers and *poof!*, the ideal Roth IRA conversion recommendation pops out. Unfortunately, that isn't even close to the truth. Though we use the finest software available, running the numbers is much more hands-on than you would imagine, and the skill of the person running the numbers is more important than the quality of the software they are using. Believe it or not, in addition to a variety of the excellent specialized software now on the market, for certain applications, we still use an Excel template that we developed years ago because we haven't found anything better. Other times the person running the numbers is using an Excel spreadsheet because no software can adequately handle certain situations, and we must make "manual" calculations.

It is also prudent to test your hypothetical results. Preparing mock tax returns will show the impact of alternative courses of action. For example, after arriving at a conclusion for the amount and timing of a Roth IRA conversion, we test that amount using all the facts and figures of a client's actual tax return in a mock tax return with different levels of Roth IRA conversion amounts included.

Even for veteran number crunchers, there are often surprises in this last step that cause us to change our recommendations, such as discovering we can reduce or eliminate the alternative minimum tax with a Roth IRA conversion. If you are curious about whether a Roth IRA conversion is something you should think about, here are some points to consider.

You may be able to minimize the sticker shock and stay in a lower tax bracket if you make a series of small conversions over several years rather than converting one large lump sum. One overly simplistic—though useful—idea would be to convert, each year, only enough to bring you to the top of your existing bracket, only moving into the next bracket if it made good long-term sense.

But that rule of thumb is overly simplistic. For example, right now, after running the numbers we often recommend that a taxpayer in the 22% bracket makes a large enough Roth IRA conversion to take them to the 24% bracket. This recommendation may be made because when evaluating the taxpayer's long-term tax bracket, we may project them to be in the 25% - 28% tax bracket in the future so it makes sense to make the conversion to the top of the 24% tax bracket now.

The Classic "Window of Opportunity" for Roth Conversions

The classic window of opportunity for Roth conversions has conventionally been after you retire but before your minimum distributions. You won't have the taxable income from your wages, nor the income from your RMDs. This will be even more critical for those of you who took advantage of the early retirement buyouts that happened across many industries at the onset of the Covid-19 pandemic. Delaying your Social Security benefits until age 70 also widens this window of opportunity.

If you have accumulated after-tax savings that you can live on, or you can survive on your spouse's income, without applying for Social Security, you may have some years when you can convert more money to a Roth IRA while still staying in a lower tax bracket.

Related to this topic, one of my clients had a dilemma. He desperately wanted a low-income year to make more Roth IRA conversions. But he didn't want to retire, even though he was in his 80s. He asked the University of Pittsburgh if he could work but not get paid anything for the calendar year. They said no! He had to get paid whether he liked it or not. In his case, we partially made up for the fact that he had to accept his salary by making a sizable charitable contribution, which he wanted to do anyway.

Charitable contributions--depending on if you itemize your deductions or do qualified charitable deductions (QCDs) (please see Chapter 20)—and Roth IRA conversions sometimes go together like peas and carrots. The reduced income from the charitable deduction or the QCD that reduces the minimum distribution often allows a bigger Roth IRA conversion at a lower tax rate.

If you plan, you can sometimes manipulate your income before or during retirement to ensure that the taxes you pay on a Roth conversion are as low as possible. Please note that we make similar calculations with regard to optimizing your Social Security strategy. Optimizing Social Security and Roth IRA conversions is often a synergistic calculation. For more about the various Social Security strategies, please download our best-selling Social Security book,

> One overly simplistic—though useful—idea would be to convert, each year, only enough to bring you to the top of your existing bracket, only moving into the next bracket if it made good long-term sense.

The $214,000 Mistake: How to Double Your Social Security & Maximize Your IRAs, for free by going to **https://PayTaxesLater.com/Books/**.

Finally, consider that tax rates are likely to increase in the future. The value of paying taxes now at lower rates and making tax-free withdrawals at a later date will be even more favorable than indicated by the analysis presented here. Current tax regulations are set to "sunset" at the end of 2025. At that time, the federal tax brackets are scheduled to return to 2017 levels plus inflation. For a married couple, the top of the 24% tax bracket for 2023 ends at $364,200. After 2026, that same couple will be in the 33% tax bracket at that income level. It might make sense to maximize every penny of the 24% tax bracket now with Roth conversions in an effort to reduce future RMDs and paying 33% tax. As we approach 2025, the window to take advantage of the current favorable tax brackets is getting shorter and shorter. The sooner you start Roth conversions, the more years you have to take advantage of these reduced rates.

There are so many variables to consider when making Roth IRA conversions for retirement and estate planning. It has been our longstanding practice, when running the numbers, to determine the best long-term strategy for when and how much to convert to a Roth IRA. And while the advantages to your heirs can be impressive, our primary focus can be on the advantages of the conversion for our clients and not their heirs.

On the other hand, the truth is most clients are interested in the best conversion advice for both them and their heirs. We usually ask what income tax bracket your children are in, as well as which state they are living in, both of which are relevant questions for our calculations. We usually run our calculations through a reasonable projection for the life of your child or children.

For a child with a disability, whether they are an EDB or not, running projections over their lifetime can help you decide the best strategy for when and how much to convert to a Roth. Acting on this information can make a major difference on the financial resources your child will have after you are gone. You may think you have sufficient resources for your child, but you really don't know until you "run the numbers."

I started out the chapter by stating not all assets are created equal. This is especially true when evaluating the long-term projections of your child with a disability and how long those assets are projected to last. Of course, your child with a disability should be better off inheriting a Roth IRA account instead of a pre-tax retirement account because the taxes would have already been paid. In addition, you would not have to be as concerned about the impact of the taxable retirement distributions on your child's future federal or state benefits, provided that the distributions from the Inherited Roth IRA pass through a special needs trust. While Inherited Roth distributions will not count as income for your child, they do count as an available financial resource, which can reduce or entirely eliminate your child's eligibility for government benefits.

It is also possible that after running the numbers, it may become clear that you are not a good candidate for a Roth IRA conversion. For example, it might not be beneficial for taxpayers who have no money to pay the income tax on the conversion except by invading their IRA. Paying for the conversion with IRA dollars isn't great, but there may be some long-term benefits in terms of reduced future RMDs and potential savings for your heirs, though if that is your situation, please keep reading.

What you might need is a nontaxable source of funds to pay the taxes on the Roth conversion. But what if you don't have sufficient funds to live comfortably and pay taxes on your Roth IRA conversion because all your money is already in a retirement plan or even a Roth IRA? Should you just give up?

Let Your House Pay for Your Roth IRA Conversion

You could borrow the money to pay the taxes on a Roth IRA. The borrowed money would not be considered income. The most likely source of the borrowed money would be to borrow money from the bank, usually in the form of a home equity loan like a line of credit, a HELOC, a mortgage, or even a reverse mortgage. You can use the nontaxable money from that loan to finance your short-term living expenses and to pay the taxes on a series of Roth IRA conversions. Most people balk at this suggestion. I get it. It is a lot easier for our accounting firm to "crunch the numbers" than for you to go out and borrow against your house.

I also recognize this advice goes against most everything you have read or heard and likely goes against your instincts.

Even Shakespeare said, "Neither a borrower nor a lender be." Dave Ramsey quotes Proverbs 22:7 "the borrower is slave to the lender" and wants you to pay off your mortgage early and not to go back into debt after retirement.

If there is any reasonable chance you won't be able to make the payments, obviously this would be a terrible strategy. On the other hand, the bank probably wouldn't lend you the money if they thought you couldn't make the payments. They don't want to foreclose.

I also always say for a tax strategy to work, it must pass the "math test" and the "stomach test." This strategy for more than half of the clients I have brought this up to fails the "stomach test."

> I also always say for a tax strategy to work, it must pass the "math test" and the "stomach test." This strategy for more than half of the clients I have brought this up to fails the "stomach test."

But if you *are* interested in this strategy, I suggest you download an article I published three years ago with Forbes.com titled *Let Your House Pay for Your 2020 Roth IRA Conversion*. Unfortunately, Forbes.com has become a paid site but you could get that article by going to **https://PayTaxesLater.com/langes-advice-column/let-your-house-pay-for-your-2020-roth-ira-conversion**. We have saved a lot of families tens if not hundreds of thousands of dollars with this strategy.

By the way, disclaimer, disclaimer, disclaimer. Do this strategy only after talking with a qualified financial expert who will likely try to talk you out of it.

Who Else Would Not Benefit from A Roth IRA Conversion?

Another example of someone who might not benefit from a Roth IRA conversion is someone who plans on leaving all their money to a charity. Again, this is because charities are tax-exempt, and the conversion would result in unnecessary taxes when the Traditional IRA and the money that would have been used to pay the tax on the Roth IRA conversion could have gone to the charity tax-free.

There are certainly other IRA owners who would not benefit from a Roth conversion. That said, we find that most of the IRA owners that we see will benefit from developing and implementing a Roth IRA conversion strategy. Determining your best plan is a great use of your time, and if you find the right advisor to help you, a great use of your money.

Please keep an open mind when going into the process of determining how much and when to convert to a Roth IRA. It is okay to have preconceived notions, but please be data driven in this area.

One client was unhappy when the results of the projections of our best recommendations still left him with a significant IRA at the end of his lifetime. He was hoping for a plan that would have converted everything to a Roth. In his case, doing so would have pushed him into too high of an income tax bracket. Then, when he hit age 72, since there would be so little Traditional IRA left, his income would be down. Both he and his family would have been worse off if we blindly followed his wishes of gradually converting everything to a Roth before he died. Remember, in God we trust; all others bring data.

Of course, this short chapter can't tell you everything you need to know about Roth IRA conversions, which is why we have several more in-depth chapters. Also, I encourage you to download my book, *The Roth Revolution: Pay Taxes Once and Never Again* at **https://PayTaxesLater.com/Books/**.

KEY IDEAS

- Most IRA owners should be proactive about at least considering and more likely developing a long-term Roth IRA conversion strategy.

- To better appreciate Roth IRA conversions, we recommend you measure wealth in purchasing power rather than total dollars.

- The current low tax brackets and inevitable tax increases add incentive to explore Roth IRA conversions, especially when you are considering the impact on the life of your child with a disability.

- Act now, the window is getting shorter and shorter before tax rates are scheduled to increase.

- Your heirs will benefit more from inheriting Roth IRAs than Traditional IRAs.

- Running the numbers can result in much better decisions than winging it.

- An integrated retirement and estate plan that takes your assets, income, goals and dreams, family situation, etc., into account is decidedly advantageous. Roth IRA conversions are not for everyone, but the only way to really assess the situation is to "run the numbers." We recommend not only evaluating the impact of a Roth conversion plan on your and your spouse's lives, but also on the lives of your heirs, including your child with a disability.

17

Roth Conversions and the Effects of Medicare Income-Related Monthly Adjustment Amounts (IRMAA)

by Steven T. Kohman

Certified Public Accountant*

We all would like to have more in Roth IRAs than Traditional IRAs since they grow tax-free and there are *no* Required Minimum Distributions (RMDs) for the owner. Additionally, if your children or grandchildren inherit your Roth IRA, the Inherited Roth IRA can continue to grow income-tax free for ten years after the death of the IRA owner. In contrast, with an Inherited Traditional IRA, RMDs over the ten years may cause higher income and higher tax rates for the beneficiary during those years. To get more in Roth IRAs and less in Traditional IRAs, a taxable Roth conversion is the only option for most retirees.

The costs of making a Roth conversion must be considered when deciding how much to convert in any given year. For people who are under age 63, higher income taxes are the primary cost of doing a conversion. Why age 63 and not age 65? This is not a typo. Please read on for more information. For people who are older and who will be on Medicare in 2025, increasing income in 2023 with a Roth conversion may make their 2025 Medicare premiums higher. These Medicare Income-Related Monthly Adjustment Amounts (IRMAA costs) should also be considered as an extra cost of doing the conversion. In this chapter, we will look at how significant these additional IRMAA costs are in relation to the Roth conversions. All the costs discussed in this chapter are based on the Married-Filing-Joint (MFJ) costs for married couples.

Roth Conversions Can Increase Your Taxes in Multiple Ways

Without IRMAA costs, the current federal income tax bracket rates of 10%, 12%, 22%, 24%, 32%, 35%, and 37% are useful as a guide to quantify your conversion costs. There are, however, additional costs beyond the income tax in these brackets. For example, the additional income from the Roth IRA conversion

---

* Steve is our veteran number-crunching Roth IRA expert.

increases other taxes like net investment income tax when your AGI exceeds $250,000. For higher income taxpayers, the additional conversion income could trigger the higher 20% capital gains tax rate rather than the normal 15% capital gains tax rate on qualified dividends and long-term capital gains when your taxable income exceeds $553,850.

For lower income taxpayers receiving Social Security income, Social Security income may not be fully taxable up to 85% without a conversion, but with a Roth conversion, up to 85% of Social Security income may then be subject to federal income tax. The additional income from the Roth IRA conversion could also add to the tax cost of the conversion by changing tax-free qualified dividends and/or long-term capital gains to amounts taxable at 15% when *ordinary taxable income* is below $89,251 before the conversion. *Ordinary taxable income* is taxable income less the qualified dividends and long-term capital gains.

How Roth Conversions Impact Future Medicare Premium Costs

In November of each year, the Social Security Administration determines how much Medicare premiums including IRMAA costs you will have to pay for the coming year based on the most recently filed tax return. For 2023, Medicare premiums are based on your 2021 income because that was the most recently filed tax return as of November 2022. Similarly, the 2025 Medicare premiums will be based on your 2023 income which may include Roth conversion income. Because of this two-year lag between the time you file your income tax return and the effect it has on your Medicare premiums, tax planning during the year you turn age 63 impacts the amount of Medicare premiums you pay when you are age 65.

This means that taxpayers who are age 63 and older must consider what the possible impact of additional income from a Roth conversion in the current year might be on their Medicare premiums two years in the future. Because the IRMAA cost increases and the income levels where the increases take effect are not known until well after the year of the conversion, calculating the impact of Roth conversions on future costs of Medicare premiums must be estimated.

IRMAA costs increase the Medicare premiums when your Modified Adjusted Gross Income (MAGI) exceeds certain amounts. MAGI is the AGI plus tax-exempt dividends and interest on your tax return plus some other less common income exclusions. For 2023 Medicare premiums, the IRMAA cost increases start when MAGI on a 2021 MFJ tax return exceeds $194,000. As MAGI increases, so do the additional costs for Medicare premiums.

These extra 2023 IRMAA Medicare premiums cost increases for a MFJ couple on Parts B and D of Medicare for a full year are as follows:

- $1,874 for 2021 MAGI over $194,000 but under $246,000

- $4,711 for 2021 MAGI over $246,000 but under $306,000

- $7,546 for 2021 MAGI over $306,000 but under $366,000

- $10,382 for 2021 MAGI over $366,000 but under $750,000

- $11,328 for 2021 MAGI over $750,000

It is important to know that if you are over the MAGI limits by any amount you will be charged the extra Medicare premiums. For example, if you convert $1 too much and make your MAGI $194,001, you will have the extra $1,874 of Medicare premium costs. This is different than how your income tax rates increase where the first dollars are taxed at a certain rate, say 10%, and then the next dollars are taxed at 12%, and so on. By earning only $1 more in income, a big difference in the effective cost of your Roth conversion could result. It makes sense to keep the conversion low enough to safely stay under the applicable income level in most cases.

It is also important to know that for the last few years, these MAGI levels have increased for inflation. By the time they calculate the IRMAA increase levels for 2025 Medicare premiums based on 2023 income, these levels will likely be higher since they are now indexed to inflation. For example, due to inflation in 2022, the first increase level changed from $182,000 to $194,000. For 2024, the IRMAA levels will be increased for one more year's inflation beyond the 2023 levels, and for 2025 there will be two years of future inflation increases.

They also change the extra premium increase amounts from year to year so the extra IRMAA premiums could be higher by 2025 or 2026. These extra charges are not based on normal inflation. From 2021 to 2022 the extra IRMAA costs increased by over 12% and in some of the lower income thresholds by 14.5%! However, between 2022 and 2023, these IRMAA costs actually decreased by about 3% due to lower than projected Medicare spending in 2022.

Avoiding IRMAA Costs Initially

What happens if your income drops between year 2021 (the year that Medicare uses to determine your premium costs for 2023) and in year 2023, when you pay those premiums? Fortunately, the Social Security Administration offers a way out—but it is fairly restricted. These IRMAA increases can potentially be avoided in the first year after you have a "life-changing event" that causes your income to decrease by filing Form SSA-44. A life-changing event includes retirement, death of a spouse, marriage or divorce, loss of pension, and a few other rare circumstances. Roth conversions are not counted as life-changing events. The most common reason to file Form SSA-44 is when you retire from a highly compensated position, and now that you have retired, your income will be less.

Using the 2021 tax return with high income before retirement may not be representative of the lower income you will have in 2023 after retirement. The SSA-44 is a way for you to get excused from the IRMAA Medicare premium increases in that situation, possibly saving you thousands of dollars.

Quantifying the Impact of Roth Conversions on Medicare

These extra IRMAA costs affect the overall cost of Roth conversions. As a basic example, let's assume that without the Roth conversion, the 2023 MAGI for a married couple filing jointly is $139,500 and taxable income is $108,800. For this example, we're ignoring the complications of investment income, state income tax, and other factors, so ordinary taxable income is also $108,800. This is in the 22% tax bracket for 2023. We will also make the reasonable assumption that the 2025 IRMAA cost increases will increase by about 6% (3% per year) for inflation for the two years between when they measure the IRMAA costs for 2025 from the 2023 actual amounts.

- A Roth conversion of $54,000 can be done to keep the MAGI under the first Medicare premium increase level at a tax cost of 22% since the taxable income is still in the 22% tax bracket. *The IRMAA cost—which will affect Medicare premiums to be paid in 2025—is zero.*

- A Roth conversion of $106,000 can be done to keep the MAGI under the next Medicare premium increase level at an incremental tax cost of 22.93% above the $54,000 conversion, since this is partly in the 22% and partly in the 24% tax bracket. But the estimated extra Medicare premiums of $1,992 makes the incremental cost 26.76%. *The IRMAA cost is 3.83% of the extra conversion.*

- A Roth conversion of $166,000 can be done to keep the MAGI under the next Medicare premium increase level at an incremental tax cost of 24% above the $106,000 conversion, since this is in the 24% tax bracket. But the estimated extra Medicare premiums of $3,000 makes the incremental cost 29.0%. *The extra IRMAA cost is 5.0% of the extra conversion.*

At this point, the couple may want to convert only $106,000 instead of $166,000 because this extra IRMAA cost is higher than the first level of IRMAA cost.

In addition, if this couple has investment income, they may also be subject to the 3.8% net investment income tax because their AGI exceeds $250,000.

Net investment income tax applies to the extent that AGI exceeds $250,000 MFJ ($200,000 if Single) and to the extent that you have investment income. In this example, AGI is $245,500 with the $106,000 conversion but becomes $305,500 with the $166,000 Roth conversion. If the income included $30,000 of investment income, there is an extra $1,140 of tax cost to consider. This is 1.9% of the incremental conversion amount on the $166,000 conversion, making the total incremental cost 30.9% of the additional $60,000 conversion amount.

- A Roth conversion of $226,000 can be done to keep the MAGI under the next Medicare premium increase level at an incremental tax cost of 24% above the $166,000 conversion, since this is still in the 24% tax bracket. But the estimated extra Medicare premiums of $3,024 makes the incremental cost 29.0%. *The extra IRMAA cost is again 5.0% of the extra conversion.*

- If a larger conversion is done to the top of the 24% tax bracket, it would only be a $255,400 conversion or $29,400 more than the $226,000 conversion. The extra Medicare premiums result in an incremental cost of 34.12% which is the 24% tax cost plus an extra 10.12% for the IRMAA cost. This is very high, so if the couple wanted to convert at least this much, it may make sense to convert $353,700 to the top of the 32% tax bracket at an incremental cost of only 32% because there would be *no additional IRMAA cost* over the $255,400 conversion. Similarly, if it makes sense to convert to the top of the 35% tax bracket with a $584,950 conversion, there is again *no additional IRMAA cost* over the $353,700 conversion.

As you can see, the IRMAA increases typically add about 3.83% for exceeding the first IRMAA level or 5.0% for exceeding the higher IRMAA levels to the cost of Roth conversions unless you do a very large conversion or if you have high IRMAA costs even without a Roth conversion (MAGI over $366,000).

Recovering IRMAA Costs Paid on Larger or Multi-Year Conversions

On the other hand, doing larger Roth conversions all at once or over a period of years will lower your future taxable RMDs. For a 76-year-old person, reducing the balances in Traditional IRAs by $500,000 through Roth conversions will reduce the annual RMDs by about $21,000 initially, and likely by more in future years. By reducing your annual RMDs, your MAGI will be less, and thereby your IRMAA income level and Medicare premiums you pay will be less. Whereas without the conversions, you would be over certain IRMAA income levels due to the higher RMDs and pay more in Medicare premiums over a longer period of time. In addition, if the $21,000 of extra income without the conversions is in a higher tax bracket (say 32%) than the tax bracket level with the conversions (say 24%), there could be additional income tax savings from the conversions to help offset extra IRMAA costs of the conversions done.

If your child is qualified as an Eligible Designated Beneficiary (EDB) due to their disability or chronic illness, IRRMA costs may be less of a concern. If your plan is to do Roth IRA conversions and die with them and let this child stretch the Inherited IRA over their lifetime, additional IRRMA costs might pale in comparison to the long-term benefits of a more aggressive Roth conversion strategy.

Determining the actual amount of Roth conversions optimal for your situation is beyond the scope of this chapter—too many factors are involved in the decision. If Roth conversions generally make sense in your situation, and if you are or will be covered by Medicare in two years, keeping conversions small enough to stay under the applicable IRMAA income level may help you determine the optimal amount to convert in any given year. But in other situations, converting larger amounts to Roth may make sense despite these additional IRMAA costs. For example, if you are taking into consideration the benefit for your heirs of making Roth IRA conversions, the extra IRMAA costs might not weigh so heavily. If you're wondering whether a Roth conversion makes sense and would like some expert help in running the numbers, please read the letter in the back of this book titled *When your Child has a Disability…Save More, Have More, and Leave More to Your Child in a Tax-Advantaged Manner that Preserves Government Benefits! The Lange Edge: A Truly Integrated Long-Term Financial Masterplan for Parents Who Want to Ensure That Their Child Is Financially Secure for Life—Even After Mom and Dad Are Gone* to learn more about the services we offer and how you can take advantage of a free consultation with me.

Whichever method you use to calculate Roth IRA conversions, however, you should be taking the additional IRMAA costs created by the conversion into the calculation.

KEY IDEAS

- Determining how much and when you should make Roth conversions becomes trickier if you consider IRMAA costs.

- Many taxpayers will get the optimal result not by doing just one conversion in one year, but a series of smaller Roth IRA conversions over multiple years.

- One method you may consider is to develop a long-term Roth IRA conversion plan that may involve a partial Roth IRA conversion over a series of years. Then, update the calculations every year based on changes in investments, taxable income, tax rates, IRMAA rules, liquidity to pay the taxes, and any other factors which impact your family's financial situation.

- Finally, the math will change if the goal is to leave an Inherited Roth IRA to your child who is qualified as an EDB due to their disability or chronic illness and will stretch the Inherited IRA over their lifetime.

18

Roth Conversions and Inflation

by Steven T. Kohman
Certified Public Accountant

Inflation erodes the value of the spending power of all assets including after-tax savings and investments, Traditional IRAs, as well as Roth IRAs. A common measure of inflation is the All Urban Consumer Price Index or CPI-U. Inflation increased 8.58% from May 31, 2021 to May 31, 2022 and it was up 4.99% from May 31, 2020 to May 31, 2021. While inflation has eased from its peak in 2022, the current rate is still higher than the two decades prior to 2021, when inflation was mostly less than 2-3%. Between February 28, 2022 and February 2023, inflation was up 6.0%.

Inflation Reduces the Purchasing Power of All of Your Investments

Using our prior examples from Chapter 16 of the purchasing power of money with and without a Roth conversion, on day one after the conversion they are equal as shown below:

Before Inflation	Without Roth Conversion	With a Roth Conversion
After-tax Investments	$ 24,000	0
Roth IRA	0	$ 100,000
Traditional IRA	100,000	0
24% Tax Allowance on IRA	(24,000)	0
Value Day One After Conversion	**$ 100,000**	**$ 100,000**

As you can see, immediately after the Roth conversion, purchasing power is identical. In both cases, $24,000 of cash outside the IRA, is used to pay tax, either on the conversion itself or when funds from the IRA are withdrawn as a distribution. But what happens when inflation is taken into account after the conversion? Ignoring the effects of future investment returns and income taxes, and assuming a 20% inflation rate where the value of a dollar becomes 80 cents, the relative value of a Roth conversion is not changed just due to inflation as shown below.

329

The inflation adjusted purchasing power of the money is lower, but still equal with and without the conversion as shown below:

After Inflation	Without Roth Conversion	With a Roth Conversion
After-tax Investments	$ 19,200	0
Roth IRA	0	$ 80,000
Traditional IRA	80,000	0
24% Tax Allowance on IRA	(19,200)	0
Purchasing Power After Inflation Only	**$ 80,000**	**$ 80,000**

So, inflation in isolation should not impact the decision of whether you do a Roth IRA conversion or not.

But the economic reality is that inflation does not occur in isolation. There are other factors related to inflation that will affect the future success of Roth conversions such as:

- Future tax rates on RMDs and distributions (from the IRA not converted) could be lower since the tax brackets are adjusted for inflation. If you drop to the 12% tax bracket after inflation from your prior 22% tax bracket, you paid higher taxes on the conversion than you will owe in the future on the incremental RMDs, so it may appear that the Roth conversion was not as effective as planned. In fact, you could potentially be worse off.

- An interesting quirk, however, is that for retirees with lower income in the 12% tax bracket, there are potential advantages from Roth conversions. After a Roth conversion, your RMDs from your Traditional IRA will be lower, which will increase the tax-free portion of capital gains and qualified dividends from your after-tax investments. This typically lowers the tax by 27% which is the 12% tax bracket on ordinary income plus the 15% tax on capital gains. Reducing taxable income may also mean that less than the full 85% of your Social Security income will be taxable. This factor alone typically makes the tax savings 22.2% for someone in the 12% tax bracket. These factors frequently result in an effective marginal tax rate of much less than 12% even though technically in the 12% tax bracket. If both of these factors apply together, the actual incremental tax savings rate could be even more than 27% for someone in the "12%" tax bracket.

- IRMAA cost levels are increased for inflation. As discussed in Chapter 17, Roth conversions may increase your IRMAA costs in the second year after the conversion year if the converted amount boosts your income to the next level of Medicare premium costs. Inflation could be an advantage for a Roth conversion if the IRMAA cost levels increase with inflation to the extent that even with the conversion, your future IRMAA costs do not increase. Conversely, additional IRMAA cost is a disadvantage for the conversion if your income in the conversion year pushes you into a higher Medicare premium cost bracket for the second year after the conversion. But in future years with less RMD income (from the IRA converted) the conversion has an advantage if you end up below the future threshold for an extra IRMAA cost. Higher inflation for future IRMAA increase levels help to make this happen.

- If there is a long-term advantage calculated for Roth conversions, in inflation adjusted dollars, that advantage becomes less due to higher inflation, although it would still be an advantage.

The real advantage or disadvantage of doing Roth conversions is not due to inflation directly, but due to the rate of returns on investments, the tax and IRMAA costs of the conversion, future income taxes including taxes on investment income, and to some extent future estate or inheritance taxes.[1]

Advantages of Roth Conversions

In general, as converted Roth IRAs grow, you will have the advantage of paying less tax on investment income. This is because the tax paid to the IRS for the Roth conversion is normally taken out of other after-tax accounts, which reduces your taxable investment income, composed of interest, dividends and capital gains This tax creates a second layer of tax when a conversion is not done. In contrast, the assets converted to a Roth IRA have no such tax.

Also, starting at age 72, 73, or 75, depending on your birth year, Traditional IRA owners must take RMDs, and the transfer of money from tax-deferred Traditional IRAs to after-tax investment accounts increases this second layer of tax. Roth IRAs have no such RMDs during the lifetimes of the owner and spouse, so more wealth can be protected from taxation.

---

1   All investing involves risk, including the potential for loss of principal. There is never any guarantee extended that any investment plan or strategy will be successful. Please see additional disclaimers in the letter in the back of this book titled *When your Child has a Disability...Save More, Have More, and Leave More to Your Child in a Tax-Advantaged Manner that Preserves Government Benefits! The Lange Edge: A Truly Integrated Long-Term Financial Masterplan for Parents Who Want to Ensure That Their Child Is Financially Secure for Life—Even After Mom and Dad Are Gone.*

If future tax rates increase, performing Roth conversions under today's relatively low tax rates offers the advantage of paying less tax overall. Of course, if the Roth IRA money is placed in investments with a higher rate of return than the pre-conversion IRA and after-tax accounts provided, that's another advantage of doing Roth conversions. This would also be true if the value of the Roth IRA declines less than the IRA and other investments in a declining stock market. However, this is not usually the case unless market timing adjustments are made to the Roth IRA portfolio for protection.

Roth Conversions in Times of Market Declines

While the stock market as of April 2023 has recovered somewhat from the 20 percent drop in mid-2022, it is still well below its high. After a steep decline in 2022, the bond market is showing signs of recovery, although rising interest rates may keep prices down.   This follows several years of great returns as measured by the S&P 500 index: **https://www.upmyinterest.com/sp500/**. Roth conversions done over the last decade have resulted in tremendous tax-free growth and have provided our clients and other IRA owners who made conversions greatly increased wealth compared to not doing the conversions. This holds true even if the rates of return on the Roth IRA and other investments are the same. Many have benefited even more by having the Roth IRAs invested more aggressively than the other investments.

However, market declines are not good for Roth IRAs after conversions. For example, if we look at the first quarter of 2023, the S&P 500 was down over nine percent, which means it recovered somewhat since its dramatic drop of more than 20 percent in late 2022. If there is a negative rate of return on the Roth IRA at a future measurement date after the conversion, it initially may result in a disadvantage for the Roth conversion. Suppose your tax bracket is 24% and you paid $24,000 in tax on a $100,000 Roth conversion, but the market later declines. If your Roth IRA is now worth only $80,000, then your tax cost of the conversion on the resulting Roth IRA would actually be 30% ($24,000 / $80,000). If you had done the conversion after the market decline, you would have paid much less tax. With hindsight, a conversion done in July 2022 generally would have been much better than a conversion done in January 2023 as the market begins to show signs of an upswing.

Many investors consider Roth IRAs to be long-term investments, perhaps for the benefit of children and grandchildren who inherit those assets much later. The stock market has historically recovered from significant market declines, so over the long term, the stock market generates positive returns if invested in a well diversified portfolio. So, if conversions are done annually over many years, it is a form of dollar cost averaging, which makes the long-term result more favorable when there are swings in the stock market.

The disadvantages of Roth conversions caused by market declines can be offset, recovered, or turned into an advantage in the long run by the following:

- Obviously, if your Roth IRA increases in value over time, you will compensate for any temporary market declines.

- Your personal tax rate increases, due to your circumstances or a general tax rate increase, which we think is likely, will favor a Roth conversion.

- The lower RMDs in the future after the conversions reduce your additional Medicare premiums caused by IRMAA increases.

- In many cases, investors who are subject to the 3.8% net investment income tax could save this much in future tax from the reduced income that comes with lower RMDs.

- If your Roth IRA beneficiaries are your children who are in a high tax bracket, they will still enjoy a benefit from the conversion since they could easily be in the 32% or higher tax bracket in the future when they have not only their own income, but also income from Inherited Traditional IRAs. This tax savings could well surpass the higher tax rate caused by a post conversion decline (30% rather than 24% in the previous example).

We do not claim to be market timers, but there is a strong argument that the best time to do Roth conversions is after a market decline.

Again, as stated in Chapter 16, we love making Roth conversions, dying with them, and leaving them to a child with a disability or a trust for that child. The combination of the "stretch" and the tax-free distributions of the Inherited Roth IRA could last for decades.

KEY IDEAS

- Inflation in isolation neither increases the value of the Roth conversion, nor does it decrease it. But, in reality, inflation does alter other variables that will determine if a Roth strategy is for you, and if so, how much and when.

Key Ideas continue on the following page.

KEY IDEAS
(continued)

- Inflation reduces the purchasing power of all your investments, including Roth IRAs, Traditional IRAs, and other after-tax investments.

- Assets transferred to the Roth environment are protected from a second layer of tax on investment gains.

- Because Roth IRAs do not have RMDs, you will not be forced to transfer wealth from a tax-deferred or tax-free environment to a taxable environment.

- If tax rates increase in the future, making Roth conversions now will save you taxes over the long run.

- If the market declines after you make a Roth conversion, you will have paid more taxes than you would have if you had been able to time the conversion just right.

- Roth conversions can have the following advantages:

  1. The tax burden over your lifetime and your heirs may be lower, both over the lifetime of a married couple and for the surviving spouse as well as the end beneficiary, especially if the beneficiary is an eligible designated beneficiary or a trust for that child in which case they can "stretch" the tax-free Inherited Roth IRA over their lifetime.

  2. Medicare premiums may be lower.

  3. You may pay less of the additional 3.8% net investment income tax.

  4. Your children who are in a higher tax bracket will pay less tax for inherited Roth IRAs than for Inherited Traditional IRAs.

19

Who Gets What?
Maximizing Bequests to Charity and Children with Different Financial Needs

"Some people forget money and IQ points
often do not correlate."

— C.A.A. Savastano

The following content of this chapter is adapted (with some edits) with permission from ***Forbes.com***. The content of this chapter was originally published in an article I wrote that appeared in Forbes.com in January 2021.

"Who gets what?" is frequently an eagerly awaited question at someone's passing, especially when there is considerable wealth involved. How many movies have you seen with a dramatic "reading of the will" scene that introduced an unexpected plot twist? In reality, there is no "reading of the will" scene, but obviously beneficiaries want to not only know what they got, but what other beneficiaries got.

Most people seek an outcome that all beneficiaries will accept as fair and in character with the decedent's character. No one wants to set up a situation where the will is almost sure to be contested. Some attorneys might be attracted to the lure of additional billable hours. I can't stand conflict and would prefer spending my time helping people, not getting involved with siblings fighting over money.

Let's assume that you are preparing your estate planning documents and after you and your spouse are gone, you want to provide for your child with a disability, your other children, and your favorite charity. Let's also assume a large portion of your estate is in an IRA or Roth IRA. In effect, you will be cutting up a pie among your children, your favorite charity, and the IRS. This chapter is about reducing the size of the slice the IRS is getting and increasing everyone else's slice. If you are only focused on leaving money to your children, skip ahead to the section in this chapter titled *What if My Children Have Different Needs?*

In this chapter, I offer the suggestion that thinking ahead to the potential tax burden of the various assets in your estate that will go to different beneficiaries can help you decide *Who Gets What*. This will allow you to fulfill your charitable inclinations while also making sure your child with a disability and your other children will pay the least in taxes.

An Obvious but Frequently Missed Drafting Error

After reading this chapter, you are likely to think—that is so obvious. How could I and my estate attorney both have missed this? Don't feel bad. We have seen thousands of wills and trusts, and in our experience, hardly anyone gets this right. The mistake often costs families tens of thousands of dollars or more.[1]

I'm referring to the decisions that you make when you are crafting your estate plan and are trying to figure out *Who Gets What*. In this chapter, I want to focus on the smartest solution for donations or inheritances that you leave to a charity and to children with different needs after you and your spouse pass.

There are several critical ideas to cover, but the most fundamental is: what are the tax implications to each recipient if they inherit your money? By being very selective about who receives which type of money—whether Traditional or Roth IRAs, after-tax brokerage accounts, life insurance, etc.—you can dramatically cut the share that goes to the IRS and increase the amount going to your family.

In most cases, Traditional IRAs, subject to exception, are going to be fully taxable to your heirs. After the dreaded SECURE Act that effectively killed the stretch IRA, income taxes will be due on your IRA within ten years after your death. That is, unless the Traditional IRAs are left to a qualifying EDB, which may be either outright to your child with a disability or chronic illness or to a special needs trust (see Chapters 10 and 13). Inherited Roth IRAs have the advantage of being able to continue to grow for ten more years after your death and then can be withdrawn tax-free. If the beneficiary qualifies as an EDB, that tax-free Inherited Roth IRA can be stretched over their lifetime. After-tax dollars and life insurance proceeds are generally not subject to income taxes. All of these different types of inheritances have different tax implications for your beneficiary…unless your beneficiary is a tax-exempt charity.

First and foremost, a charity that is recognized by the IRS as being tax-exempt does not care in what form they receive an inheritance. They never have to pay taxes on the money they receive. To them, a dollar is a dollar. So, a charity will look at bequests of Traditional IRAs, Roth IRAs, after-tax dollars, or life insurance in the same light. In sharp contrast, your heirs will face substantially different

tax implications depending on the type of asset they receive and what type of

---

1   There is no solicitation for legal services being made by me, James Lange, nor by Lange Legal Group, LLC.

beneficiary they are after your death. Please note that in this chapter we are only addressing income taxes, not estate or transfer taxes.

Imagine this scenario. You want to leave $100,000 to charity after you and your spouse die. You have both Traditional IRAs and after-tax dollars. For the sake of simplicity, I am going to say that your child is in the 24% tax bracket. So, *Who Gets What?* In most of the estate documents that we have seen, we saw instructions directing that the charitable bequest comes from after-tax funds—usually found in the will or a revocable trust.

The problem is that your will (or revocable trust) does not control the disposition of your IRAs or retirement plans. By naming that charity as a beneficiary in your will or trust, you will likely be donating after-tax money to charity. The charity gets $100,000 so the "cost" of the bequest to your heirs is $100,000. Restated, the amount that your children inherit is reduced by $100,000 because you made that bequest to charity.

But what if you decide to leave $100,000 to XYZ charity through your Traditional IRA and/or retirement plan beneficiary designation? It makes no difference for the charity because they get $100,000 tax-free. If your heirs receive $100,000 from your IRA, they will have to pay taxes on the money. Forgetting about the 10-year rule for Inherited IRAs or the stretch IRA for qualifying beneficiaries and assuming that they are in a 24% tax bracket, that would be $24,000—leaving them with $76,000 after the government takes their share. And the tax bite is even worse if your heirs are in a higher tax-bracket or live in a state that taxes Inherited IRAs. So, if you were planning to leave $100,000 of your *after-tax dollars* to a charity but change the plan and instead leave $100,000 of your *Traditional IRA money* to that charity, you are in effect leaving your beneficiaries an extra $24,000 all at Uncle Sam's expense!

This is a simple tweak to your estate plan that can be very beneficial to your heirs. On a smaller bequest, smaller savings. On a bigger bequest, even larger savings.

Consider the purchasing power, after taxes, available to your beneficiary if you have $100,000 in a Traditional IRA, and $100,000 of after-tax dollars, and we switch who gets what.

Scenario 1

Leave $100,000 to charity through your will or revocable trust and $100,000 to your heirs as the beneficiary of your Traditional IRA.

- Impact on the charity: They get $100,000 and pay no tax.
- Impact on your heirs: $100,000 IRA money - 24% taxes = $76,000.

Scenario 2

Leave $100,000 to charity through your IRA beneficiary designations and $100,000 to your heirs in your will or revocable trust.

- Impact on the charity: They get $100,000 and pay no tax.
- Impact on your heirs: $100,000 and pay no income tax.

This simple switch of *who gets what* saved this family $24,000. The savings would be even greater with a larger bequest or if your beneficiary's tax bracket is higher.

Let's imagine another scenario. Suppose that your child is well off and, as a parent, you are totally comfortable with reducing the purchasing power of their IRA inheritance by $100,000. Does that mean you can leave even more IRA money to charity? Yes!

You could leave $131,579 to charity through your IRA or retirement plan beneficiary designation. The same tax implications apply. A $131,579 IRA bequest will only "cost" your child $100,000 ($131,579 times 24% = $31,579). If you left that $131,579 IRA to your children instead of charity, your children would have to pay $31,579 in taxes, leaving them $100,000.

By switching *who gets what*, you accomplish one of two things:

1. You save $31,579 in federal taxes for your child, or

2. If you increase your IRA bequest to the charity to $131,579, you still only remove $100,000 from the purchasing power of your heir's total inheritance, and the charity gets the additional $31,579 that would have otherwise been paid in federal income taxes.

Who loses out with this strategy? You guessed it. The IRS. You are dramatically cutting the share that the IRS receives—giving the IRS a smaller piece of the pie. And I think that all of us can safely agree that we want more money to go to our kids and favorite charities, and less money to go to the IRS.

If you are only leaving a minimal amount to charity, it probably isn't worth the time and aggravation to change your documents. If you are leaving a substantial amount to charity, it probably is worth it. I recommend starting a list of the changes you would like to make to your estate plan and having all of them incorporated into new wills, trusts, and beneficiary designations at once.

What if My Children Have Different Needs?

Hardly anyone uses this strategy, but I like it in a lot of situations. The application of the concept of *who gets what* can also sometimes save families hundreds of thousands of dollars in taxes even without any charitable bequest involved.

Many IRA owners have children for whom it can reasonably be predicted that they will be in significantly different tax brackets. The different income tax brackets of your beneficiaries may create an opportunity for tax savings by simply changing *who gets what*. For example, imagine you have two adult children, and one child is in the 12% tax bracket and the other in the 32% bracket. Let's also assume that though you might not know the details, you can reasonably predict one child will most likely always be in a higher tax bracket than the other child. It is also possible, even likely, that one of your children will qualify as an EDB and one will not. In this case your children will have much different IRA distribution requirements.

That said, let's also assume you want to divide the estate relatively equally between your two children. You may prefer to leave more money to your child with a disability, but bear with me to make this point. Situations like this sound like an opportunity to reduce the total taxes your family may have to pay, but rarely do we see any attorney or advisor recommend the following strategy.

Consider increasing the *purchasing power* of both of your children after you die and reducing the share going to Uncle Sam by switching who gets what.

Let's keep it simple and assume you have a $1,000,000 Roth IRA and a $1,400,000 regular IRA and that neither child qualifies as an EDB. The status quo is each of your children will receive 50% of both assets. If you forget growth, each child will get a $500,000 Roth and a $700,000 regular IRA. The IRS will get $308,000 which represents the taxes both kids will have to pay on the Inherited Traditional IRA. ($700,000 times 12%= $84,000 and $700,000 times 32% = $224,000.)

Let's assume instead you leave the $1,000,000 Roth to the child in the 32% bracket and the $1,400,000 in your regular IRA to the child in the 12% bracket. The IRS would get only $168,000 in taxes. This means your children would get an extra $140,000 worth of purchasing power, which is the difference between the amount paid to the IRS in the two scenarios. In addition, since hopefully, the children aren't planning on blowing their inheritance the year that you die, the extra $140,000 will continue to grow after you die.

Did I oversimplify this example and not take into consideration many things that would cause this estimated tax savings to change? Yes. But I wanted to make the point clearly. By shifting who gets what there might be a significant tax savings that could then be divided between your children.

You could attempt to get a basically "even division" of purchasing power and have the family enjoy the tax savings. You might consider careful planning and/or an equalization clause to ensure that your estate is split roughly equally between them *measured in purchasing power*. Frankly, the math is tougher when you do have a beneficiary with a disability, but the concept still applies. Careful planning will need to be done to determine the most tax-advantaged way to split up the pie, especially when considering children who will qualify for the full stretch and other children who will only receive the ten-year stretch.

By being creative about who gets what and dividing up the pie in an approximate method you think is appropriate, you can cut down the IRS's slice dramatically.

I suspect most estate attorneys do not suggest this strategy because they never think about it. Other times, they don't use it even if it makes sense because it complicates the estate and many clients want to keep things simple, even if it means more taxes. I like talking about this strategy more than estate attorneys like drafting the documents to realize the strategy.

It can also potentially increase the chances of fighting between children because it is nearly impossible to make the bequests exactly even after taking taxes into consideration. One child might end up with 51% and the other 49% but both would be ahead by well over 10%. Personally, I would prefer 49% of a much bigger number than 51% of a much smaller number, but some kids (or spouses) don't see it that way. But, as mentioned previously, for the right clients, considering all these factors is a way to potentially save the family a lot of money in taxes and approximate equality between children in different tax brackets.

Other Situations When You Might Consider Treating Your Children Differently

A similar situation where you might want to treat your children differently occurs if one of your children would benefit from a trust as opposed to leaving them money outright. They might need a trust because they are a spendthrift, have creditors, have a no-good spouse where they may lose money in a divorce, etc. Your child may also need a special needs trust so that the income from their inheritance doesn't jeopardize their means-tested government benefits. If another child doesn't need a trust, my preference is to draft a trust for the child that needs it and to leave the child that doesn't need a trust their share outright.

Life gets tricky when the math or the legal situation shows treating your children differently is a great strategy. That may be less of an issue when you have children both with and without disabilities. In the best-case scenario, your children without disabilities will want what you want: for your child with a disability to have all the financial resources needed for a full life. Naturally, I like the tax savings or added creditor protection if a trust is indicated for one child, but not the other. Then,

> By being creative about who gets what and dividing up
> the pie in an approximate method you think is appropriate,
> you can cut down the IRS's slice dramatically.

the poor drafting attorney has to face the client's natural preference to treat their children not only equally, but identically.

As a result, in the real world, attorneys often do not utilize *Who Gets What* even when the math indicates it is a great strategy. Attorneys also sometimes end up with a trust for a child who doesn't need a trust because the other child does, and Mom and Dad want to treat the children identically (though I hate the thought of attorneys drafting unnecessary testamentary trusts which take effect after you die because of the continued cost and aggravation of maintaining trusts over the lives of the children).

Planning out *Who Gets What* to achieve maximum tax savings might not be appropriate. This doesn't mean you should never treat sibling beneficiaries exactly equally when it comes to purchasing power, but it only makes a lot of sense when there is a large tax savings, a strong need for a trust for one child, understanding clients and, hopefully, understanding children.

I still like the tax savings and fewer trusts if they aren't needed. Unfortunately, it is often the financially weaker or less sophisticated child or the child who needs the trust that is most likely to object. That is true even though the plan I might prefer would put that child in a much better position.

Another circumstance to utilize *Who Gets What* could be if one beneficiary qualifies as an EBD (who can stretch the Inherited IRA or Roth IRA over his lifetime) and the other doesn't qualify. In many cases it might make sense to leave the IRA (Roth or Traditional) to the beneficiary who qualifies for the stretch and other assets (after-tax brokerage accounts, life insurance, real estate, etc.) to the beneficiary who doesn't qualify for the stretch.

Who Should Get Your Life Insurance and Who Should Get Your IRA?

Let's assume you have one child with a disability and another child without a disability. In that situation many parents would purchase life insurance for their child with a disability, thinking that is money that the child will receive no matter what. If there is IRA money left after the child with a disability is provided for, that money can go to their other child. Makes sense, but....

With that plan, assuming there is IRA money left over, we are leaving the IRA money to the child who will be forced to withdraw that money in ten years. If we switch who gets what, then the child without a disability can get the insurance and the child with a disability, if he/she qualifies as an EDB, can stretch the Inherited IRA over his/her lifetime. Of course, each situation must be looked at separately, but this is another example of a great potential in saving a lot of money by switching who gets what.

Another application of who gets what in the insurance vs. IRA decision is also based on tax bracket. Let's say one child is in a 20% higher tax bracket than the other child. Leave the IRA to the child in the lower bracket and the life insurance to the child in the higher bracket.

Sometimes grandparents leave life insurance to their grandchildren in irrevocable life insurance trusts. That may be a mistake. If we aren't worried about federal or state transfer taxes, it is probably better to leave IRA money to the lower income child/grandchild and the insurance to the higher income child/grandchild.

If we want to preserve flexibility because we don't know the brackets each beneficiary will be in and we aren't worried about transfer taxes, it might be best to preserve flexibility through a disclaimer in both the IRA beneficiary designation and in the life insurance beneficiary form.

Attention Grandparents: How to Leave a Longer Legacy

Grandparents have special planning opportunities to help provide for their grandchild with a disability that are rarely brought to their attention.

First, I will touch on the quality-of-life improvement both for you, your child, and grandchild if you get this planning right. Remember, your child's biggest financial problem is, likely, providing for their child with a disability. If you help your child with that enormous problem, you will relieve anxiety for you, and your child and when he or she comes of age, your grandchild. One common symptom is anxiety and part of the anxiety is financial if child with a disability is unable to work. If things are efficiently set up in a protective trust, grandparents, parents, and beneficiary can breathe a sigh of relief.

The Wrong Way for Grandparents to Provide for their Grandchild

There are different opportunities grandparents can employ to help provide for their grandchild with a disability. Here is the wrong way. Sometimes without thinking, the grandparent might assume, "Well, I'll leave my money to my child, and it will be up to my child to appropriately pass on the money to their child/ my grandchild."

A Better Way for Grandparents to Provide for their Grandchild with the Greatest Tax Savings

That is certainly understandable, but that strategy misses a great opportunity to potentially defer distributions on Inherited IRAs or Inherited Roth IRAs. So, for example, if Grandpa Joe left a Traditional IRA to his child, Son Joe, Jr. (assuming Joe, Jr. did not have a disability), Son Joe, Jr. must withdraw the Inherited IRA within 10 years of Grandpa Joe's death, causing massive income tax acceleration. That same amount left to his Grandson Joe III, who has a disability, in an appropriately drafted special needs trust can be distributed over the life of Grandson Joe III. This would mean a lot more money for the family and a lot less money for the IRS. We are assuming the grandchild with a disability qualifies as an EDB.

Preserve Flexibility for Your Child with the Same Great Tax Savings

One totally reasonable approach would be for Grandpa Joe to delay the decision about whether to leave the money to his son or his grandson. To do this, he would leave the IRA or Roth IRA for the benefit of Son Joe, Jr. Then, he would give Son Joe, Jr. the right to disclaim into a special needs trust for Grandson Joe III. After Grandpa Joe dies, Son Joe, Jr. has the choice to keep the money or to disclaim it for the benefit of Grandson Joe III. Please see Chapter 15 under the subheading *Lange's Cascading Beneficiary Plan* for the benefits of disclaimers in general.

That way, if Son Joe, Jr. absolutely needed the money for himself, it would be available. Likewise, maybe Grandson Joe III will have other sources, and it may make more sense for Son Joe, Jr. to keep the money for himself. But if Son Joe, Jr. could afford not to receive that IRA bequest or inheritance, or even part of it, it might be wise to disclaim all or part of it to the trust. The trust for Grandson Joe III could stretch that Inherited IRA or Inherited Roth IRA over Grandson Joe III's own lifetime.

> One totally reasonable approach would be for Grandpa Joe to delay the decision about whether to leave the money to his son or his grandson. To do this, he would leave the IRA or Roth IRA for the benefit of Son Joe, Jr. Then, he would give Son Joe, Jr. the right to disclaim into a special needs trust for Grandson Joe III.

> **It is critical that if the end beneficiary is a grandchild with a disability—and that grandchild is receiving SSI or some other government or health care benefit—that money left for the benefit of that grandchild is left in a special needs trust.**

Another thing that a grandparent should keep in mind is even if they decide to leave the money to their child, we always want to have a contingent beneficiary in the event that their child dies or chooses to disclaim to the next beneficiary in line.

If the grandparent is looking for a life insurance solution, we often find that they choose to leave the insurance to their grandchildren. It might be better to leave the insurance to their children and their IRA or other retirement plan to their grandchild who has a disability, because of the lifetime stretch available to EDBs. There's more on this above in the section titled *Which Child Should Get Your Life Insurance and Which Child Should Get Your IRA?*

Save Your Grandchild's SSI with a Special Needs Trust

It is critical that if the end beneficiary is a grandchild with a disability—and that grandchild is receiving SSI or some other government or health care benefit—that money left for the benefit of that grandchild is left in a special needs trust. This is to protect any government benefits that the child might be receiving. Chapter 13 discusses requirements necessary to prevent the Special Needs Trust from being considered an available asset when looking at SSI eligibility. Deborah McFadden tells the story of a grandparent who left $350,000 to a child receiving SSI and the child lost all their government benefits. That is tragic.

So, grandparents, please be smart about the money.

KEY IDEAS

- Thinking strategically about who gets what—specifically with regard to charitable bequests—can save the family 24% of the bequest if it comes from an IRA or retirement plan *and not* from the will or revocable trust controlling the non-qualified money.

- Considering your children's different financial situations offers an opportunity to divide your estate to leave all your children with more purchasing power and cut taxes.

- There are opportunities for tax savings by switching who gets what, when one child has a disability and the other one doesn't.

- Family dynamics and special needs may indicate that a trust would be a prudent method of leaving wealth to one or more children, while leaving money outright to others would work best.

- Setting up trusts for all children, even if they are not necessary, may feel fair, but will result in additional expenses for maintaining those unneeded trusts including annual tax filings.

- That said, sometimes seeking the perfect balance might not be appropriate even if there are tax savings and additional costs of having a trust for a child who doesn't need one.

- Look at all of the variables when choosing beneficiaries for your IRA and your life insurance.

- Grandparents:

  - Use a special needs trust when leaving money to a grandchild on SSI.

  - Consider leaving your IRA or Roth IRA to a special needs trust for your grandchild if they are an EDB and have the ability to stretch it over their lifetime.

  - Get the most flexibility by leaving your retirement plan to your child and specify your grandchild's special needs trust as a contingent beneficiary. Let your child decide if it's appropriate to disclaim to your grandchild's trust when the time comes.

20

Qualified Charitable Distribution (QCD) Rules Save Extra Money on Charitable Donations

by Steven T. Kohman
*Certified Public Accountant**

*"As you grow older, you will discover that you have two hands:
one for helping yourself, the other for helping others."*

—Sam Levenson

Charitable giving and bequests are a broad topic, and mostly beyond the scope of this chapter. Before you make any substantial gifts, whether to charities or to friends and family, you will need to first think about how much you want to give away while you are alive and how much you want to give to specific charities and individuals at your death. The focus of this chapter is on using Qualified Charitable Distributions ('QCDs') as a tool to satisfy your charitable giving intentions while you are alive. Later in this chapter, I will provide a broad overview of the points to consider for gifts you make during your life and bequests you make at death.

Many parents who are over age 70½ (not the RMD age 73 as you might think is logical) will have money in a Traditional IRA, and many will make annual donations to charity. If this describes you, you should be glad to know that the Qualified Charitable Distribution rules are now permanent tax laws, and we can safely put them to use.

QCD Rules and Limitations

A QCD allows you to donate to charity directly from your IRA or your Inherited IRA if you are at least age 70½. You must wait until you are officially age 70½ before donating to charity directly from your IRA using QCDs. Inactive SEPs or SIMPLE plans without any contributions being made can also be used so we will refer to these as part of your IRAs. QCDs can come only from distributions from IRAs, not other retirement plans like 401(k)s, 403(b)s, or active SEPs or SIMPLE Plans. So, for example, if you are age 70½ and still working, you cannot make a

---

* Steve is our senior veteran number-crunching CPA. Special thanks to Jen Hall, CPA, for her significant additions to this chapter.

QCD from your employer's retirement plan, as QCDs can only be made from IRAs. If your plan permits in-service withdrawals, however, you could transfer funds from your employer's retirement plan through a trustee-to-trustee transfer into an IRA account. You can then use QCDs through this 'back-door' method to use your work-related retirement plan money to take advantage of the favorable tax treatment by giving to charity through a QCD. Of course, you have to be charitably inclined to want to go through this extra step.

For retirees with RMDs who still have significant amounts in their former employer's retirement plans, we recommend transferring at least enough out of your retirement plan to an IRA so future RMDs from the IRAs will at least equal the amounts of the planned donations. Then the QCDs can fund the donations and provide significant savings.

When the QCD laws were established, you had to begin taking RMDs by age 70½. Even though the SECURE Act raised the RMD age to 72 and later to age 73 starting in 2023, it didn't change the QCD laws. Before the SECURE Act, if you were age 70½ and were making QCDs before you turned 72, your charitable contribution coming directly from your IRA counted as at least part of your RMD. Now, however, if you are age 70½, you may still make a QCD even though you aren't required to take an RMD until age 73. Using QCDs before you have RMDs inherently saves you income taxes because you are using pre-tax IRA money instead of after-tax money to make the donations. You also increase the cash flow in your bank account for other spending since the donations come from your IRA instead of your bank account.

Rules limit the types of charities that can receive QCD donations. Donations to donor-advised funds, private foundations, or a supporting organization under IRS Section 509(a)(3) are not permitted for QCD treatment. Unfortunately, this means that donations to a Fidelity or Vanguard Charitable Giving account or any other donor-advised fund cannot be used for QCDs. However, most other 501(c)(3) charities qualify. As we will discuss later in the chapter, SECURE Act 2.0 provided us with the opportunity to make a $50,000 once-in-a-lifetime transfer from your IRA to a charitable gift annuity or a charitable remainder trust beginning in 2023.

QCD rules limit direct IRA donations to charity to $100,000 per year per person. If you are married, you and your spouse can donate up to $100,000 each or $200,000 total. This amount has not changed since QCDs were first allowed in 2006, but starting in 2024, the maximum contribution limit will be indexed for inflation under the SECURE Act 2.0. If you are reading this book in 2024 or later, the QCD limit will be higher than the $100,000 figure we use here. For some clients, the best math solution for their goals was to aggressively use QCDs for the rest of their lives or at least to the point they wanted to continue making charitable donations.

For people who have after-tax contributions (basis) in their IRAs, any charitable contributions made through a QCD will not use up any of the after-tax basis. The pro-rata rules do not apply to these types of distributions, which is good news.

Savings When the Standard Deduction is Used

The "home run" created by QCDs is for people who take the standard deduction rather than itemizing. The Tax Cuts and Jobs Act of 2017, which cut tax rates but also restricted itemized deductions and increased the standard deduction, was a game-changer. Many taxpayers who used to itemize will no longer be able to do so. For the people who used to itemize but no longer can, QCDs provide a terrific way to save on taxes.

The standard deduction for people age 70½ or older for 2023 is $30,700 (for married, filing jointly) and an extra $1,500 each if blind. Combining the higher standard deduction and the increased limitations on other itemized deductions like the $10,000 maximum for state and local taxes paid, many more taxpayers now use the standard deduction than ever before.

If you have required minimum distributions from your IRA because you are age 73, or if you have RMDs from an Inherited IRA, using QCDs counts as fulfilling that part of your RMDs so you are taxed on less of the RMDs you otherwise would have to withdraw for yourself. Taking all or a part of your RMD as a QCD will reduce the AGI on your tax return because the QCD is not included in your AGI. While the standard deduction is not affected, your taxable income is reduced compared to making donations without using QCDs. This lowers your income taxes. For example, if you use the standard deduction and are in the 24% tax bracket, you will save $2,400 in income tax if you donate $10,000 to charity using a QCD rather than taking your entire RMD and writing a check from your bank account.

Watch Out for Limits on QCDs if You're Still Contributing to a Traditional IRA

There is a constraint I want to mention. With the passing of the SECURE Act, the age limit cap on making Traditional IRA contributions was removed. This means tax-deductible IRA contributions can be made for older investors up to their earned income or to the maximum of $7,500 for each spouse if their income is below the income thresholds. The SECURE Act also includes, however, an annoying anti-abuse provision that disallows you from making a tax-deductible IRA contribution and later taking a QCD for that amount. Basically, the IRS is saying you cannot 'double-dip' by taking a tax deduction for your IRA contribution and make a charitable contribution through a QCD. If you have earned income and contribute to an IRA after age 70½ and take a tax deduction, any future QCD will be reduced by the cumulative amount of deductible IRA contributions you made after age 70½.

For example, if you make a deductible IRA contribution of $7,500 to an IRA in the year you turn 70½, then make a QCD of $10,000 the next year, you will only be allowed to report a QCD of $2,500. The remaining $7,500 will be a taxable distribution from your IRA, which you can also deduct as a charitable contribution, but only if you are itemizing your deductions. If you are not itemizing, your taxable income will increase by the disallowed amount of your QCD with no offsetting deduction.

The purpose of the anti-abuse provision is to prevent individuals from deducting IRA contributions (an above-the-line deduction, thereby reducing AGI) and then making a donation of the contributions on a pre-tax basis as a QCD (also reducing AGI) - thereby, 'double-dipping.'

A planning technique if you are married and making tax-deductible IRA contributions and using QCDs as your annual gifting strategy, would be for one spouse to make a tax-deductible IRA contribution to their own account and the other spouse to make the QCD from their account.

Remember, notwithstanding the above, if you have post-tax contributions in your IRA, the QCD operates on a first-in-first-out basis, with the pre-tax contributions being distributed first. However, treating your $7,500 IRA contribution as non-deductible is not an effective way around this anti-abuse provision. By doing that, you are losing the $7,500 IRA deduction, and the $7,500 of basis created in your IRA will be watered down over the entire value of your IRAs.

Savings When Itemizing Deductions

If you itemize deductions, you cannot claim a charitable contribution that was given via a QCD as part of your itemized deductions (that would be double dipping too). Itemizers often think making a charitable donation through a QCD will not make any difference in their taxes, and, in some cases, it might not. However, even if you itemize, the advantage of using QCDs is that you lower your taxable IRA income and thus lower the Adjusted Gross Income (AGI) shown on your tax return. This is an above-the-line deduction. If you take only the required minimum distribution from your IRAs and you use a QCD, you will only be taxed on the remainder of your RMD above the QCD contributions. This provides many money-saving advantages over using the donation as a below-the-line itemized deduction in various tax situations, as discussed below.

Medical deductions are itemized deductions that are reduced by 7.5% of your AGI. If you have significant medical expenses and you itemize your deductions on your Schedule A, using QCDs to reduce your AGI and thereby increasing your medical deduction will be advantageous. By using QCDs, you reduce your AGI and taxable income.

Savings for Taxpayers Subject to Net Investment Income Tax or Alternative Minimum Tax

Higher income taxpayers with AGIs over $250,000 (married couple) or single taxpayers with AGIs over $200,000 incur additional taxes from the Net Investment Income ('NII') tax. The NII tax is a 3.8% tax on investment income above the AGI limits cited. By using a QCD, your AGI is reduced, which may reduce the amount of investment income subject to the NII tax. This NII tax savings can occur whether you itemize deductions or not. While it is rare to be subject to the alternative minimum tax after the passing of the Tax Cut and Jobs Act, it is possible that QCDs can save on Alternative Minimum Tax (AMT) for those subject to it.

Savings on the Taxation of Social Security

The 'Grand Slam Home Run' created by QCDs is for people using the standard deduction and whose Social Security income is not fully 85% taxable when QCDs are used. The taxable amount of Social Security is based on how much other taxable income you have to report on your tax return. Up to 85% of your Social Security may be taxable, but depending upon your other income sources, you may have less than 85% of your Social Security taxed. If you employ a QCD to reduce your AGI, you will further reduce the amount of Social Security that is taxed in addition to reducing the taxable IRA withdrawals.

Suppose a married couple, both over age 70½, had a combined income in 2023 of $70,000 from their Social Security and $71,000 of RMDs from their Traditional pre-tax IRAs. In this case, their Social Security income was not fully taxable up to the 85% maximum. If they had donated $5,000 to charity but did not have enough deductions to itemize (over the $30,700 standard deduction), their federal income tax would be $12,395 without using a QCD. By using a QCD for their $5,000 charitable giving, their taxable RMD would have been reduced by $5,000 which also reduces the taxable Social Security income, and now the taxes owed will be only $10,360. This is a $2,035 tax savings which is 40% of the donated amount!

Various Other Tax Saving Benefits of QCDs

Without getting too much more involved in the tax code, there are many other ways QCDs can benefit you by reducing your AGI whether you itemize deductions or not. Higher levels of AGI limit certain deductions and credits. *A tax credit example* is the lifetime learning credit for retirees taking college courses later in life. Using QCDs may help you qualify for that credit. *A deduction example* is the rental loss deduction that can become limited if your income is over certain amounts. Using QCDs can lower your income, potentially allowing for a larger rental loss deduction.

Last but not least, if you plan to donate to charity anyway, it may make sense to do so using a QCD to reduce the balances in your Traditional IRAs. This can have the effect of reducing future RMDs and lowering your income taxes in an environment of rising tax rates.

Savings on Medicare Premiums

Nearly all people age 70½ are on Medicare, and the premiums for Part B and sometimes Part D are usually deducted from their Social Security payments. If your Modified AGI (MAGI, which is AGI plus tax-exempt interest) is over certain amounts, these Medicare premiums will be raised for the second year after the tax-year. These additional premiums are called Income-Related Monthly Adjustment Amounts (IRMAA costs).

For married couples, the first income threshold for 2023 Medicare IRMAA costs is $194,000 of the MAGI shown on the 2021 tax return. If the couple's MAGI was $194,001 - only $1 over the threshold in 2021, the 2023 Medicare premiums would be increased for each spouse by $65.90 per month for Part B and $12.20 per month for Part D. This is a $1,874.40 extra cost for both spouses in 2023. If your MAGI was approaching that threshold of $194,000, using QCDs to lower your MAGI below that amount by lowering the taxable RMDs would provide significant savings—at no real cost if you planned to donate to charity anyway.

There are additional 2023 thresholds of increased Medicare premiums at MAGI levels of $246,000; $306,000; $366,000, and $750,000. The increases in Medicare premiums for parts B and D are larger at each of these thresholds. At $246,001, for example, the Part B premium increases to nearly two times the standard rate, from $164.90 to $329.70 per month. Using QCDs to get under these thresholds can save a significant amount of money.

Since 2020 is history, and no RMDs were required in 2020, we should now be looking at using QCDs in 2023 to lower the taxable RMD incomes in 2023.

This could have the effect of lowering the 2025 Medicare premiums if the QCDs result in income falling below the MAGI thresholds for 2025 Medicare premiums.

It is noted that the 2024 MAGI thresholds for IRMAA costs will not be determined until November 2023 and 2025 IRMAA cost thresholds will not be determined until November 2024. This makes it difficult to determine the IRMAA cost thresholds in 2023 for the 2025 Medicare premiums based on 2023 income.

In recent years, these MAGI thresholds have increased with inflation. Up to 2019, the first level was $170,000 of MAGI. Then for 2020 Medicare premiums, it was increased to $174,000. For 2021 it was increased less, to $176,000, based on lower inflation than the prior year. However, inflation in 2021 and 2022 pushed the first IRMAA threshold all the way to $182,000 and $194,000, respectively, a jump of $6,000 for 2022 and $12,000 for 2023.

Guessing the 2025 threshold early in 2023 would require a guess for the following two years of inflation increases. Guessing late in 2023 would only require a guess of one more year of inflation increase since the first year will be known in November 2023. If you are tax planning to stay under a MAGI threshold, using QCDs can also help to keep under the thresholds.

Of additional interest, while the first MAGI threshold has increased 3.41% for 2022, for example from $176,000 up to $182,000, the standard Part B Medicare monthly premium increased by 14.5% from $148.50 in 2021 up to $170.10 in 2022! Then, in an unusual situation, it actually decreased to $164.90 in 2023. Of course, all these rules and IRMAA costs could change for future years (likely increasing costs), based on increased funding needs for the Medicare program. Again, since IRMAA costs are so high, it makes sense to use QCDs to lower the MAGI.

Improved Roth IRA Strategy

QCDs can help in planning Roth conversions. Some people want to make Roth conversions but only up to the point that their Medicare premiums will not increase based on MAGI. Since MAGI is reduced by using QCDs, more can be converted to Roth IRAs. Others want to make Roth IRA conversions up to an amount that maintains a certain tax bracket, often 24%. Again, QCDs can lower your income, increasing the amount you can convert to a Roth IRA while staying within your desired tax bracket.

What if you are receiving earned income or self-employment income and are subject to the RMD rules and you would like to contribute more money to your Roth IRA, but you are slightly over the 2023 AGI income thresholds of $138,000 (single) and $218,000 (MFJ)? A good planning strategy would be to use a QCD for a portion of your RMD to reduce your AGI so you qualify to contribute the maximum to your Roth IRA.

A New Twist on QCDs from the SECURE Act 2.0: Fund a CRT with a QCD

As mentioned briefly in Chapter 10, the SECURE Act 2.0 allows investors to fund a Charitable Remainder Trust (CRT) with a QCD. However, this provision comes with so many restrictions that I don't see it as a particularly valuable option.

- Funding is limited to just $50,000 per person, and this is currently a once-in-a-lifetime opportunity.

- This contribution will only count as a QCD if the only contributions to this CRT come from QCDs.

- Income beneficiaries are limited to the IRA owner and his or her spouse. Even if both spouses contribute the maximum of $50,000, this would only result in a CRT funded with a maximum of $100,000. As I mentioned in Chapter 18, a good rule of thumb for the minimum contribution to a CRT is $1,000,000. The costs to administer a CRT don't make it worthwhile with smaller amounts.

No Downside or Costs of QCDs?

The downsides of using QCDs, which are minimal, are simply the procedures. There is no cost to using them. Usually, you only need to send your IRA investment manager or broker the name and address of the charity and tell them how much to donate. You will probably want to lower your other RMDs above the amount donated, so keep track of this. You will still need to get the documentation letters from the charities as you would with any other charitable donation. You will need to keep track of the QCDs and tell your tax preparer you made them. If you prepare your own tax return, you must follow the rules on presenting the QCDs on Form 1040. There is not any tax reporting for the QCDs on the annual 1099-R you receive.

Processing a QCD may add a slight burden on your IRA custodian. Because of the additional paperwork, you may want to use QCDs only for larger contribution amounts. You may even want to "bunch up" your charitable donations for the year, or even for two years at a time, to take advantage of the standard deduction and other advantages mentioned above.

I know of at least one brokerage firm that will give you a checkbook for your IRA, from which you can write a check directly to a charitable organization. I know some providers do not like this technique, and I am not certain all brokerages allow this, but it surely seems to simplify life for the IRA owner. One thing to remember is that the QCD checks need to clear before the year end, so you should not wait until the last minute to send them out.

Are There Situations When Giving Highly Appreciated Stock is a Better Strategy than Using QCDs?

Because QCDs are limited to just $100,000 plus inflation beginning in 2024, donating appreciated stocks to a charity will allow you to make more substantial donations during your lifetime. This can be a great way to reallocate your portfolio and to get rid of highly appreciated stock—before it goes down—without incurring capital gains taxes on the appreciation. If you are already itemizing your deductions, you get a deduction for the fair market value of the stock; however, your deduction will be limited to 30% of your AGI as of this book's writing. Any excess can be carried forward until used. The downside of this is that if your itemized deductions are less than the 2023 standard deduction of $30,700 for joint filers, $15,350 for single filers, you will not receive any tax benefit from the portion that brings your total itemized deductions up to those amounts.

However, in other limited situations, it may be more advantageous to donate highly appreciated stocks to a charity rather than using a QCD. If the portion of your wealth in the appreciated stock is designated to pass as a bequest to charity anyway, donating it during your lifetime will give you an income tax savings using the itemized deduction, whereas there is no tax savings when passing it to the charity when you are gone. Also, lowering your taxable income with a large donation of appreciated stock can increase the amount of lower cost Roth conversions you can do in the lower tax brackets.

Another situation that may warrant donations of highly appreciated stock over QCDs would be if your long-term estate plan is to have all the current amounts in Traditional IRAs become Roth IRAs for specific beneficiaries by doing future Roth conversions. If you give the IRAs to charity, there will be less to convert into Roth IRAs for this goal.

On the other hand, if your planned annual charitable donation is less than $100,000, a QCD could be the best strategy. If you do not have enough other deductions to itemize, a QCD is generally the best strategy. QCDs, as mentioned above, can be a great way to minimize income tax when you are simultaneously performing a Roth conversion. QCDs also make sense if you want to reduce your RMDs and stay in a lower tax bracket or to keep your future Medicare premiums down.

Once all your Traditional IRA assets are converted to Roth IRAs, there are no more opportunities to make QCDs and, of course, you will have no more IRA RMD income. We generally recommend a lifelong plan of Roth conversions to allow the IRAs to remain in sufficient amounts to fund future QCDs to maximize tax savings over your lifetime.

If you are planning a large charitable bequest, it is best to designate the charity as beneficiary of your Traditional IRA, as the charity will not pay any taxes on it. But if the planned bequest is larger than your IRAs, donating a large amount of appreciated stock while you are alive may be a better strategy because the additional itemized deduction will save you on income tax. If you donate that stock by bequest after your death, you will not save on income tax, though you may save on estate taxes.

Use QCDs!

Assuming you do not want to give more than $100,000 or meet the less common exceptions where donating highly appreciated stock may be a better strategy than using QCDs, we like QCDs. Because there are no significant disadvantages and no costs for using QCDs, you should use them to make most if not all of your charitable donations if you are over age 70½. If it is early in the tax year, you may not even be aware of how they will save you money for the current year.

I know this is a lot of technical information, and it is a shame the IRS makes you "jump through hoops" for QCDs instead of just allowing you to deduct all your charitable donations from IRA income. Using QCDs certainly makes sense if you were going to make the charitable donations anyway.

KEY IDEAS

- People often think making a charitable donation through a QCD will not make any difference in their taxes, and, in some cases, it might not make a significant difference if you itemize deductions. However, it may, and in many more cases, it will create significant savings.

- Because there are no significant disadvantages and no costs for using QCDs, you should, subject to limited exceptions where gifting highly appreciated stock to a charity might be a better strategy, use them to make your charitable donations if you are over age 70½.

- Depending on your financial circumstances and your overall gifting strategy, QCDs can be the best way to make planned donations to charitable organizations.

- The tax benefit of your QCD is diluted by the cumulative amount of any tax-deductible IRA contributions made to your IRA account after age 70½.

- Donating appreciated securities in addition to QCDs can be an effective way to reallocate your portfolio and save income tax, especially if you are already itemizing your deductions and doing Roth conversions.

21

How Should You Respond to High Inflation?

As this book goes to design, inflation has returned to 'normal' levels. In June 2022, US inflation peaked at 9.1% before dropping to 6.5% for the 12 months ending December 2022. That June peak was the highest rate since 1981. Most economists predicted that inflation will remain elevated for at least the next three years. With these types of predictions, many people worried about what that will do for their retirement plans. This fear is fully justified—even with modest 3% inflation, purchasing power drops by about 45% over 20 years. At the same time, inflationary pressures as well as other world-wide events can bring additional volatility to the stock market, so many investors saw their portfolios drop in value. Thus, we suffered both from inflation and, at certain times, a down market.

Don't Panic, But Don't Ignore Inflation

Just about any time the economy starts behaving in unpredictable ways, the natural instinct of many is to panic, so we batten down the hatches to prepare for the storm ahead. Today is no different, with some so-called experts ranging from Elon Musk to Jamie Dimon professing a "bad feeling" or predicting an economic hurricane. If too many people follow the counsel of these influencers, then a recession may be the predictable outcome. Joe's Widgets will lay off employees, who happen to be customers of Lana's Diner, which will cause Lana's Diner to lay off employees, and so on in an endless chain of recession-driving panic.

Others, however, including Larry Kotlikoff, an economist whose opinion I respect, point out some of the positive things about today's economy. We've got low unemployment. The labor-force participation rate, a measure of the number of working-age people with jobs, maintained a steady 62.6% rate from March 2023 to June 2023, just a bit shy of the pre-pandemic level of 63.3%. As of this writing, job growth is slowing down because there aren't many people left to hire. The Bureau of Labor Statistics says there are currently about twice as many job openings as unemployed people. So even though prices on many things are rising, Mr. Kotlikoff urges us not to panic, reminding us that "[t]he three big concerns with inflation are whether wages will keep pace with prices, the impact of inflation on retirees on fixed nominal pensions and on other creditors, and hidden inflation-based tax hikes."

We shouldn't be complacent about inflation, but as Mr. Kotlikoff says, "[w]hat can kill the economy is enough people, who should know better, talking it down." Inflation by itself will not wreck the economy, but enough people panicking just might.

Inflation roughly follows from the law of supply and demand. As the population increases, demand for goods and services increases across the board. If the supply of those goods and services cannot keep up with demand, and we are still experiencing enormous problems with our supply chain thus not being able to fulfill demand, then prices increase. As can be seen in the chart below, average inflation in the U.S. from 1913 to 2020 has been 3.1%. Except for the Great Depression of the 1930s, we've had price increases in every decade, with the highest rates in the 1970s and 1980s.

https://inflationdata.com/Inflation/Inflation_Rate/Long_Term_Inflation.asp

Figure 21.1

Average Annual Inflation by Decade

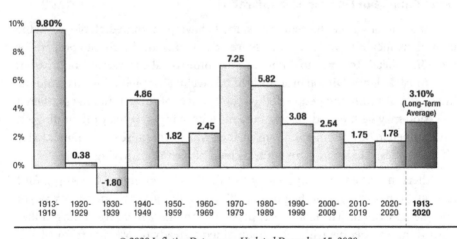

© 2020 InflationData.com - *Updated December 15, 2020*

That said, the U.S. carries a lot of debt and one of the best ways to pay off debt is to reduce the value of the dollar and pay your debt off in dollars that are worth less. But such a devaluation of the dollar would be inflationary. When I interviewed Burton Malkiel about a year ago, he feared inflation would really hurt retirees on a fixed income.

Inflation is The Enemy of Fixed Income

Inflation eats into purchasing power so the same dollars cannot buy as much. If the bulk of your income in retirement is from fixed income sources, such as fixed annuities, or a fixed pension from your employer, you may feel the pinch more than if you also have Roth accounts, Traditional IRAs and retirement plans, and after-tax investments to draw on to make up for any shortfall. Conversely, if you have a sound Financial Masterplan in place, you should have more than adequate financial resources to rely on to get you through most economic disturbances.

Inflation is generally uneven. It doesn't impact the prices of everything uniformly. The inflation percentage you see in headlines is measured by the U.S. Bureau of Labor Statistics on a broad "basket of goods," which includes items you may or may not be purchasing. While gasoline and electricity are up by 48.7% and 12.0%, respectively, medical care and housing show more reasonable increases of 4.0% and 5.5%. Yes, gas prices are high now. But they've been high before. In 1980, gas was $1.19 per gallon, which seems like a bargain. But measured in today's dollars, that's $4.33 per gallon, which isn't that much different from what we're paying now.

While inflation is the enemy of fixed income, the benefit of annuitizing a portion of your retirement funds is that you have a guaranteed stream of income for the period you elect, whether it's for a term of years, your life, your spouse's life, or for a certain period after your and your spouse's death. Just having that floor of guaranteed income to supplement your Social Security or other pensions can go a long way in ensuring that you and your spouse will never run out of money, no matter what the stock market does. If you want to learn more about the pros and cons of annuitizing your retirement funds, be sure to read Chapter 8 in detail.

What's Indexed for Inflation?

The good news with inflation is that the federal government indexes many things for inflation. The bad news is that there are also things that are not indexed for inflation. Let's look at those things that change with inflation, which can be the silver lining for inflationary periods.

Social Security Benefits

For 2023, the Social Security Administration increased payments by 8.7%, the biggest cost of living adjustment (COLA) in four decades. If your monthly benefit for 2022 was $2,000, you got a raise of $174 per month, or $2,088 per year, without considering any changes to Medicare premiums. At least so far, benefits have not ever gone down after they go up, so this counts as a big win for those

> That said, the U.S. carries a lot of debt and one of the best ways to pay off debt is to reduce the value of the dollar and pay your debt off in dollars that are worth less. But such a devaluation of the dollar would be inflationary. When I interviewed Burton Malkiel about a year ago, he feared inflation would really hurt retirees on a fixed income.

collecting—or soon to be collecting—Social Security. The projected 2023 COLA at the time this book goes to press is approximately 3.0%. A provision in the law prevents those benefits from going down, even if the inflation adjustment or the Medicare Part B premium would cause them to decrease. In the case of the cost of living going down, benefit amounts stay the same as the previous year.

I should also point out that in times of high inflation, income that is adjusted for inflation becomes much more valuable than income that is not. Social Security income is adjusted for inflation, but many pensions and annuities that are not adjusted for inflation are often fixed in amount and become less valuable in inflation adjusted dollars over time.

Social Security Wage Base

If your W-2 wages or self-employment income are greater than the current Social Security wage base, that income will not be subject to Social Security taxes. For 2022, that wage base was $147,000, and in 2023, the threshold increased to $160,200. However, be aware that among other fixes to Social Security that are under perennial consideration by Congress, that wage base limitation may be increased substantially or entirely removed.

Standard Deduction

In 2017, thanks to the Tax Cuts and Jobs Act (TCJA), the standard deduction for a married couple filing jointly was nearly doubled to $24,000. For 2023, that's now risen to $27,700. However, unless Congress acts to make the temporary provisions of the TCJA permanent, in 2026 the standard deduction will plummet to its 2017 level of $12,700 plus inflation since 2017. On the positive side, personal exemptions will come back if we would revert to the pre-TCJA law, so that will somewhat mitigate the drop in the standard deduction.

Tax Rate Brackets

Every year, the IRS moves the income ranges that a particular tax rate applies to. For example, in 2022, income for married joint filers between $178,151 and $340,100 was taxed at 24%. In 2023, that income range for the 24% rate moved up to $190,751 to $364,200. Without these inflation-related increases, many people would see any gains in annual income devoured by bracket creep, which is a kind of stealth tax increase.

Capital Gains Rate Thresholds

For 2022, joint filers with taxable income up to $83,350 paid no tax on net long-term capital gains. The 2023 threshold for joint filers moved up to $89,250. Above that bottom rate, joint filers with taxable income of up to $517,200 for 2022 and up to $553,850 for 2023 pay 15% tax on net long-term capital gains, and 20% when taxable income is over those thresholds.

AMT Exemption and Phaseout Thresholds

Since 2012, the Alternative Minimum Tax exemptions and other parameters have been indexed for inflation, and temporary changes in the 2017 TCJA made this parallel tax assessment regime applicable to many fewer people. Prior to those changes, between four and five million taxpayers were impacted by AMT. Now only about 200,000 taxpayers per year pay AMT, but unless Congress extends those changes, as many as seven million taxpayers may be trapped in AMT-land in 2026. In 2022, the exemption amount for joint filers under the AMT system was $118,100 and for 2023, the exemption amount is $126,500.

Contribution Limits for IRAs, 401(k)s, 403(b)s, and Other Retirement Plans

By statute, these go up only when the calculated increases from inflation are big enough to increase by $500 or more. The IRA contribution limit remained at $6,000 for years 2019-2022. As a result of higher inflation in 2022, the 2023 IRA contribution limits have increased to $6,500, with catch-up contributions for those over 50 limited to only $1,000 (unchanged). In 2023, this threshold was met for most other retirement plans, including 401(k)s, which increased from $20,500 in 2022 to $22,500 with the catch-up contribution increasing to $7,500. With the recent passing of the SECURE Act 2.0, beginning in year 2024, catch-up contribution limits will be indexed to inflation. Previously, catch-up contributions were static. Also, with the passing of the SECURE Act 2.0, catch-up contributions for workers ages 60 through 63 will increase up to the greater of $10,000 or 150% of the standard catch-up contribution limit beginning in year 2025, and that amount will be indexed to inflation. In addition, the income thresholds for making deductible Traditional IRA and Roth IRA contributions goes up every year as you can see in Figure 3.2.

Medicare Income-Related Monthly Adjustment Amounts (IRMAA)

Due to ever-increasing costs for healthcare, Medicare Part B premiums go up every year. Those premium amounts are based on income so that those with higher incomes pay more than those with lower incomes. Each November, the Social Security Administration determines the monthly premium amounts for Medicare beneficiaries based on their most recently filed tax return. This means that the premium amounts being charged in 2023 are based on 2021 income amounts. See Chapter 17 for more information about this and what steps you may be able to take if your income has decreased in the intervening years.

Qualified Charitable Contributions (QCDs)

With the passing of the SECURE Act 2.0, maximum Qualified Charitable Contributions limits will now be indexed annually for inflation beginning in 2024. QCDs were introduced with the Pension Protection Act of 2006, and the limit established at the time was $100,000 per year per individual. The limit has remained constant at $100,000 per individual until now with the passing of the SECURE Act 2.0. See Chapter 20 for more information about how making QCDs can help you fulfill charitable intent and save you taxes.

Estate and Gift Tax Exclusion Amounts

In 2017, the TCJA doubled the estate tax exemption, and this exemption amount will be indexed for inflation until 2025. Unless the 2017 increase is extended by Congress, this will drop back to the 2017 level plus inflation in 2026. The 2022 exemption amount—which is the size of an estate that can pass tax-free to beneficiaries—was $12.06 million per individual. For 2023, the exemption increased to $12.92 million. The annual gift tax exemption also increases in increments of $1,000 according to inflation. From 2018 through 2020, this exemption was stuck at $15,000, but finally in 2022, it increased to $16,000 per person per recipient, and in 2023, it increased to $17,000.

What's Not Indexed for Inflation?

Many other provisions of tax law are set by statute so those provisions can only increase when Congress changes the law. These include the following:

Exclusion of Capital Gain on the Sale of Your Primary Residence

Even though home prices soared during 2022, the amount of capital gain from the sale of a primary residence that you can exclude from taxable income has remained fixed at $250,000 for single filers and $500,000 for joint filers since the law was passed in 1998. Back then, the average price of a home was $152,500. Today, the average home has more than tripled in value to $507,800 (Source:

https://fred.stlouisfed.org/series/ASPUS.) If you sell your primary house at some point, you may be facing a substantial capital gain—and tax on that gain.

Deductible Net Capital Loss

Since 1978, investors with net capital losses can only deduct $3,000 per year and this has never been increased. Any losses remaining must be carried forward until completely used up, or until your death, at which point they simply evaporate.

Net Investment Income Tax

This additional tax went into effect in 2013 for taxpayers with modified adjusted gross income exceeding certain thresholds, which have not changed since the law was passed. For a couple filing jointly, this threshold is just $250,000 ($200,000 for single taxpayers) and results in an additional 3.8% tax. This tax is imposed on the smaller of a taxpayer's net investment income or the amount that their MAGI exceeds the threshold for their filing status.

Amounts Used to Determine the Taxable Amount of Social Security Benefits

Legislation passed in 1983 set the income limits for when Social Security benefits may be taxable, and those levels have not changed since then. Determining the taxable amount of Social Security starts by determining "combined income" which is essentially AGI adjusted by using only half of the gross Social Security income, plus tax-exempt income. If this "combined income" is $32,000 or less, none of the Social Security income is taxable. As the combined income rises, more and more of the Social Security income becomes taxable up to a maximum of 85% of the Social Security being taxable. The amount of "combined income" needed to make the maximum 85% of Social Security taxable depends on the amounts of Social Security and other income.

Trust Tax Return Exemptions

Similar to individual tax returns, trust tax returns are allowed to deduct a certain amount from gross income to arrive at trust taxable income. But unlike the standard deduction and personal exemptions on individual returns, the exemption amounts for trust tax returns have not changed in decades. Depending on the kind of trust, this exemption may be $100, $300, or $4,300 (the biggest exemption is for qualified disability trusts). These stingy exemption amounts combined with the extremely narrow tax rate brackets for trusts mean that the highest rate of 37% kicks in with taxable income at just $14,451 for 2023.

Strategies to Mitigate the Impact of Inflation

Inflation will likely be around for the rest of our lives. When our CPAs "run the numbers" for a client, we always take inflation into account. Because inflation has been relatively low for the last 20 years, with the exception of year 2022, the recent sharp increases in prices have taken many by surprise and as noted above, have been putting many investors and retirees on edge. But as Mr. Kotlikoff and other advisors counsel, this is not the time to panic, but it is still prudent to consider the possible impact of inflation on your retirement plans. Here are some ideas on what you can do to mitigate the wealth-devouring impact of inflation.

Presumably, if you have a well-developed plan in place, that plan should have taken into account future inflation that is occurring now, and arguably you may not need to do anything. That said, there is a certain anxiety that comes with inflation and a down market. In addition, you may not have a plan that has taken inflation into account.

If that is the case, or if you just want to be a belt and suspenders investor, here are a few potential action points.

Keep Working

While the Covid pandemic and the combination of remote work plus health challenges has driven many professionals to take early retirement, the threat of ongoing inflation is keeping many people in the workforce longer than they had originally planned. However, pay increases in some industries don't always keep up with inflation. Staying on the job also allows older employees to delay taking distributions from employer-sponsored 403(b) and 401(k) plans.

Also, the biggest threat of a down market is not for young workers contributing to a retirement plan. Presumably, with a long-term recovery, they are, in effect, contributing money to their retirement while the market is down and will reap the rewards when the market recovers as it has historically done.

The threat of a down market is for recent retirees who are forced to liquidate investments at low prices to pay their living expenses at high prices. That is another good reason to keep working and when I say keep working, I am talking about keeping your full-time job and not dropping down to part-time work.

Dropping hours to part-time usually means a huge cut in pay compared to your existing salary. You may also lose many of your workplace benefits. That is why, especially in an environment of high inflation and a down market, it may be wise to continue working full-time.

If you've already retired and feel the need for a bit of extra income, consider becoming a consultant in your field of expertise. You could also teach courses at your local university or community college as an adjunct professor, even if you don't have a background in academia. While many universities are increasing the number of adjunct professors they hire, you should be aware that these professors are not generally paid very well. However, a bit of extra cash in the bank can be welcome, particularly if you're not yet taking Social Security.

Delay Applying for Social Security Benefits

Each year that you wait from your full retirement age until age 70 will give you a permanent raise of approximately 8% in your monthly benefit. This increase is a slam-dunk, as I detail in my book, *The $214,000 Mistake: How to Double Your Social Security and Maximize Your IRAs,* which you can download for free at **https://PayTaxesLater.com/Books/**. As the title of my book implies, back in 2018, this difference could amount to an extra $214,000 in benefits by age 95. With the annual COLA increases to Social Security benefits since 2018, the financial windfall from delaying taking your benefits is even bigger today. So, before you apply for benefits, I encourage you to educate yourself on the topic to determine the best age for you to start receiving benefits based on your individual situation. There are various online calculators if you want to do this yourself, but you'll get a more accurate readout if your calculations look at your entire financial picture, as we do when we create a Financial Masterplan.[1]

At the same time, you should be aware that if nothing is done to the Social Security system, the most recent report of the Social Security Trust Fund (**https://www.ssa.gov/oact/trsum/**) says that future benefits may be cut. The report projects that the Trust Fund will be able to pay 100% of total benefits only until 2033. After 2033, the fund's reserves will become depleted and the continuing program income will be sufficient to pay only 77% of scheduled payments.

This could be an argument to start Social Security earlier, perhaps at age 67, applying the "get it while you can" strategy to add three more years of 100% benefits. Of course, there are many ways that the funding problem could be fixed, so this drastic cut in benefits may not happen.

Seek Out Low-Interest Debt

If you do need to borrow, make sure your interest rate is lower than inflation. The difference between inflation and your interest rate is essentially a discount on the payments you need to make. You're paying off debt with money that's worth less than it was when you borrowed it. The key to leveraging this is to pay off only the minimum and invest any extra cash you would have used to pay this off with.

---

1   Please note that if you engage Lange Accounting Group, LLC for our Financial Masterplan service or receive Financial Masterplan services as part of our assets-under-management arrangement with Lange Financial Group, LLC, these services are provided by employees in their capacity as CPAs and are not legal services. The protection of the attorney-client relationship does not exist with respect to these accounting and asset management services.

Keep Contributing to Retirement Accounts to Take Advantage of Dollar Cost Averaging

During inflationary periods, the stock market frequently drops in value as well. Companies struggle to turn a profit when their costs go up, so this is reflected in their market valuation. This means that if you continue to contribute to your retirement account, those same dollars will buy more shares when the price is low and fewer when the price is high. Over time, investors who continue to contribute to their retirement plan generally come out ahead. This reduces the risk that you'll miss the low-cost windows or that you'll pay too much for those equities.

Convert to a Roth

As we go to design, the S&P has increased so far in 2023. As of June 30, 2023 it is still down roughly 5.5% from the December 31, 2021 level. This current level is an increase of about 28.9% from the low point on September 26, 2022, when it was down about 22.4% year-to-date in 2022. Looked at in isolation, if you made a Roth conversion when the market was at the low point, and the market went back up, you ended up with more Roth dollars than if you had made that conversion when the market was holding steady or increasing. But if the market continues to drop after you make your Roth conversion, this will hurt you, not help you, at least in the short-term.

As Steve Kohman explained in Chapter 18, inflation in isolation neither increases the value of a Roth conversion, nor does it decrease that value. But it alters other variables that determine whether a Roth conversion is a good idea for you at a particular time.

Let's say you had a $100,000 Traditional IRA at the beginning of the year. If the market drops 20%, then it's worth only $80,000. If you then convert the entire IRA to a Roth, you'll pay tax on only $80,000 rather than $100,000. If the market recovers, you may end up with a $100,000 Roth for the price of an $80,000 conversion. But if the market continues to drop after your conversion, you will have paid too much in tax relative to the diminished value of your Roth.

However, the only thing that really matters with a Roth conversion is that the IRA grows in actual dollars. Inflation will reduce the purchasing power of your converted Roth, but it also reduces the purchasing power of your Traditional IRA and your after-tax investments as well. If you convert and pay taxes on $100,000, and the account value later drops to $80,000, you could have waited and paid less in tax.

Since I'm not a market timer nor an inflation timer, and I acknowledge I can't predict what will happen with the market, I usually do not take these factors into account. But if you consider the overall market, this may impact your thinking about whether this is a good time or a bad time to do a Roth conversion.

With a long enough investment horizon, performing a Roth conversion while the market is down can be a great strategy. Historically, down markets have been a good time to make Roth conversions. But over the short term, you'll come out ahead only if the Roth IRA investments outperform the IRA and after-tax investments. Otherwise, your purchasing power will be down until the market recovers sufficiently or the other advantages of Roth conversions occur. For a deeper look at the impact of inflation on Roth conversions, please see Chapter 18.

That said, I still like Roth conversions. But the decision to perform one during a period when the market is also down may require additional courage. Although we cannot predict whether a current Roth conversion will be done when the market is at a low point and will subsequently grow, we generally prefer a long-term Roth conversion plan. In some years, the conversions may be done when the market is low, and in some years, when the market is not. Over time, those conversions should average out for a good long-term result. You can even use this dollar-cost-averaging method by converting the recommended amount in increments during the year.

Rebalance Your Investments

The traditional thinking has been that allocating your portfolio 60:40 between equities and bonds is one method to preserve wealth from the hazards of market declines. But according to researchers who looked at the historical performance of different types of investments during inflationary periods, this may not perform as well as you might think.

According to research published in 2022, as summarized by Larry Swedroe in an article on the *Advisor Perspectives* website, "the best hedge against inflation—admittedly imperfect—has been a diversified portfolio of real assets including TIPS, real estate, commodities used sparingly, and certain equities selected for their ability to pass through cost increases to consumers. International equities and debt may also be a hedge against domestic inflation due to the currency effect."

More details can be found at: **https://www.advisorperspectives.com/ articles/2022/04/25/which-asset-classes-protect-against-inflation**.

Inflation Will Always be a Fact of Life

As I said at the beginning of this chapter, the best response to inflation is not to panic. But there's a substantial difference between inflation at the low levels of 2% or below that we experienced from 2000 - 2020 and the more than 8% we experienced in 2022. Depending on your financial situation, you may find it prudent to make some changes to ensure you make it through this inflationary period with little long-term harm to your finances. You may need to make some changes especially if your cash inflow isn't keeping up with the inflation-induced increases to your cash outflow.

Doing just one of the strategies I outlined above will help you guard against inflation. Doing some or all of them will help more. But the best strategy of all to make sure that inflation is a non-issue during retirement is to start planning early for your retirement so that you will have way more money than you can spend for the rest of your life. That means, during the accumulation stage, sock away as much as you can, and at least enough to max out your employer's match. Take advantage of any Roth options available to you. Then, during the distribution stage, make sure you're spending the right money first, as I outlined in Chapters 1 and 5. Before you make any changes, be sure to "run the numbers," either on your own or with a financial professional or possibly even our accounting firm. Please see the back of the book for more details about the possibility of working with us.

KEY IDEAS

- Don't panic about inflation. Too many people panicking can result in the self-fulfilling prophecy of a recession.
- Be aware of the tax attributes that are and are not indexed for inflation. Some increases to inflation may help you in the long run, while others can hurt you.
- Retirement income from Social Security and other sources that receive annual increases for inflation can help hedge against inflation.
- The best strategies to mitigate inflation will depend on where you are in your work-retirement journey:
  - If you're still working, consider delaying retirement.
  - Delay taking your Social Security until age 70 or at least as long as you can. Every year you wait will give you a permanent increase to your benefits.

Key Ideas continue on the following page.

KEY IDEAS

(continued)

- Keep contributing to your retirement accounts if you're still working.
- Consider the pros and cons of a Roth conversion.
- Rebalance your portfolio to make it more resistant to market declines.

22

Save a Bundle in Income Taxes by Offsetting Medical Expenses

This chapter is divided into two sections. The first is relevant if you are planning to use a private housing facility or private nursing at home. The second is for deducting more common medical and related expenses.

PART ONE

Take advantage of a Residential Home Facility Buy-In or Other High Medical Expenses

The general idea of this section is to make a Roth IRA conversion the same year that you incur a significant deductible medical expense, whether through a buy-in of a residential home or through incurring other substantial medical expenses.

Depending on your particular situation and the severity of your child's disability, your child's day-to-day care may be beyond your capacity, and you may have to consider other avenues for care. Home care support is one option, and a residential care facility is another.

Recognizing the need for additional support is the first step. But making the decision can be very difficult emotionally, however it may be necessary for the quality of life and quality of care for both you and your child. Then there are the costs. Both options are expensive, but there are tax-planning steps you can take to mitigate the financial burden and to better provide for your and your child's long-term financial future.

Residential care facilities generally offer various payment structures. Some may either suggest or require a payment structure that includes a large upfront payment. A portion of this upfront payment (potentially a large portion) might be attributable to medical care services. Ideally, the facility will provide a statement that provides details on what percentage or dollar amount of the total upfront fee is allocated to medical expenses. The potentially large medical expense for the buy-in to a facility or private nursing care offers windows to implement effective tax planning strategies.

Deductibility of Medical Care

In general, out of pocket medical expenses are allowed as an itemized deduction on your tax return for you, your spouse (if filing jointly), and any of your dependents. A child can qualify as a dependent if they meet the dependency requirements as prescribed by the IRS. In general, you can claim your child as a dependent if they are of any age and meet the definition of being "permanently and totally disabled", if:

- they didn't provide over half of their own support,
- they aren't filing a joint return or are filing a joint return but only to claim a refund, and
- they lived with you for more than half of the year.

But you may meet one of the exceptions. In a circumstance where your child who has a disability did not live with you for over half of the year (i.e., lived in a residential home) they may still qualify as a dependent on your tax return if:

- They had gross income of less than $4,700 (in 2023). This limit will be adjusted year to year. If your child was "permanently and totally disabled," certain income for services performed as a sheltered workshop may be excluded for this test.
- You provided over half of the person's support.
- The person was a U.S Citizen, U.S. National, or U.S. resident alien.
- They were not married or if they were married, they either do not file a joint return or they file a joint return only to claim a refund of withheld income tax or estimated tax paid.
- You and your spouse, if filing jointly, cannot be claimed as a dependent on someone else's return, unless the person who could claim you on their tax return is not required to file and isn't filing a tax return or is filing a return only to claim a refund of withheld income tax or estimated tax paid.

To take this one step further, the instructions for Schedule A allow a taxpayer to deduct medical expenses that were paid for someone who they can either claim as a dependent (see above) or who they could have claimed as a dependent except the person received $4,700 or more in gross income (2023 limit) or filed a joint return. Additionally, you can deduct medical expenses paid for anyone who you could have claimed as a dependent except that you, or your spouse if filing jointly, can be claimed as a dependent on someone else's return.

"The key takeaway here is that the parent of a child with a disability is entitled to include out-of-pocket medical expenses on their tax return as an itemized

deduction as long as they qualify to claim that child as a dependent. The expenses you claim as itemized deductions are net of any government subsidy payments or insurance reimbursements."

In many cases when you have a large deductible medical expense, you can make a large Roth IRA conversion in the same year at a reduced tax cost. The benefits of making this conversion versus doing nothing can sometimes amount to tens or in some cases hundreds of thousands of additional dollars that can be used for your child who will defer the tax-free distributions of the Inherited Roth IRA over their lifetime. (See below for a case study showing the difference between being proactive and doing nothing).

We have been recommending these types of conversions for years, though more commonly on a buy-in for a nursing home or a continuing care facility for older residents. The concept is quite similar, and we have saved clients tens, or if you include their heirs, hundreds of thousands of dollars.

Mechanically, a large (perhaps several hundred thousand dollars) medical expense deduction can offset the income on a Roth IRA conversion. As with many other things in life, the devil is in the details. To determine the optimal amount and timing of the Roth conversion, many factors have to be taken into consideration when you "run the numbers." But knowing the big idea and, even on your own or perhaps with professional help determining the ideal timing and amount, this technique could possibly be the difference between your child having money during their lifetime for their care versus running out of money during their lifetime after you are gone.

Though usually not as dramatic because the annual cost is less, the cost of a qualifying home medical care is also deductible as a medical expense and the same reasoning can be used in that situation.

How the Medical Expense Deduction Works

To get the tax benefit from medical expenses, your itemized deductions have to exceed your standard deduction. Assuming you are in a position to itemize deductions, the medical expense deduction is not a straightforward dollar for dollar deduction. Qualifying medical expenses are tax deductible to the extent they exceed 7.5% of your Adjusted Gross Income (AGI) for the year. To illustrate using round numbers, let's assume your AGI is $100,000. 7.5% would be $7,500. If you had qualifying medical expenses of $90,000 for the year, then $82,500 would be tax deductible, i.e., the portion of the medical expenses that exceed the 7.5% floor. To take this example a step further, let's assume all of the same facts but we add in a $150,000 Roth conversion during the year. This would increase your AGI to $250,000 and would also increase the 7.5% floor to $18,750. The deductible portion of medical expenses in this example would decrease to $71,250. In short, as AGI increases, the deductibility of medical expenses decreases. Nonetheless, a large deduction for medical expenses still exists in the latter scenario.

As mentioned above, the upfront cost for moving into a residential home or similar facility could be large. On a purely practical basis, you have to figure out where to get the money to fund the move. Ideally, you would have the cash reserves. Realistically though, most people do not have that much in cash reserves. Another option is to combine cash reserves and after-tax assets, i.e., assets in a taxable brokerage account. Selling assets in a taxable brokerage account could give rise to capital gains taxes if the assets sold have appreciated. To the extent possible, assets with the highest cost basis could be sold to help minimize capital gains. If there were significant capital gains on the sale of the highly appreciated stock, the deductible amount of medical expenses become diluted due to the 7.5% of adjusted gross income floor.

Additionally, if capital gains in the current year would give rise to additional taxes such as net investment income taxes or an increase in the capital gains tax rate for the year then you could consider a short-term margin loan against the assets in your brokerage account. This would provide liquidity in the short term. The loan could be satisfied in the following tax year with the sale of assets in your brokerage account. Capital gains may still need to be recognized in the subsequent tax year, but possibly at a lower tax cost if net investment income taxes do not apply or the capital gains tax rate is lower than in the previous year. As stated above, the devil is in the details. Interest rates would have to be considered and compared to the potential tax savings to assess whether this is a viable option in your situation. Unless you are very comfortable weighing all the variables, it would be most helpful to consult with a number crunching CPA or advisor.

Once you have enough after-tax assets to satisfy the entrance fee you will then want to determine how much of the total expenditure is allocated to medical care. The facility should be able to provide guidance on this.

We do not cover that issue in this book. Once this figure is determined you and/or your CPA can begin tax planning for the year. At this point, weighing options for a Roth conversion comes into play. Depending on your particular circumstances, a "number crunching" CPA should evaluate whether it would be possible to use the tax deduction—that you will be entitled to in the year you make the payment to the facility—to offset some of the income that will be generated by doing a Roth conversion in the same tax year.

Capitalizing on this circumstantial opportunity might offer multiple advantages:

- The medical expense deduction in conjunction with a Roth conversion helps move assets from the tax-deferred environment to the tax-free environment at a lower tax cost than if you didn't utilize the medical deduction.

- Your child will benefit from the tax-free growth of the Roth IRA between the time of conversion and the time of withdrawal. Ideally, the withdrawals will "stretch" over the lifetime of the child with a disability who, either directly or more likely as beneficiary of a special needs trust, inherits the Roth IRA.

- The Roth strategy offers an opportunity for a longer investment horizon as compared to tax deferred assets. Because Roth accounts are not subject to required minimum distributions (RMDs), the money in these accounts can compound tax-free for the life of the account owner (plus spouse if married and spouse is named as primary beneficiary). Under current tax law, tax deferred accounts (Traditional IRA, Traditional 401(k), Traditional 403(b)) are subject to RMDs once the account owner reaches their required beginning date (RBD). At that point in time, a minimum amount as calculated by IRS life expectancy tables must be withdrawn from tax-deferred accounts each year. Roth accounts are not subject to these RMD rules. Roth IRAs have never been subject to RMD rules. Roth 401(k) and Roth 403(b) accounts used to be subject to RMD rules, however SECURE Act 2.0 removed the RMD requirements for Roth 401(k) and Roth 403(b) accounts, placing them on similar footing to their Roth IRA counterparts.

- Please see Chapter 16 for more general information about Roth IRA conversions.

- The general rule for Inherited retirement accounts (excepting a spouse) is that the beneficiary must have the account emptied by the end of the 10th year containing the anniversary of the account owner's death. However, there is a special class of beneficiaries called "eligible designated beneficiaries" who are allowed to stretch distributions from Inherited retirement accounts over a longer period of time. "Chronically ill or permanently disabled" beneficiaries are included in the definition of "eligible designated beneficiaries" and are allowed to stretch distributions from Inherited retirement accounts over their lifetime. This could be a significant advantage and benefit to beneficiaries who have disabilities or are chronically ill, if executed properly. The Inherited Roth account could provide a tax-free income stream for the rest of the beneficiary's life.

- Please see Chapter 9 and 10 for information on stretching inherited IRAs and Roth IRAs if your child qualifies as an eligible designated beneficiary (EDB).

I'd be remiss if I did not take this scenario a step further to illustrate the thought process and the holistic type of planning that a proactive IRA owner or CPA helping the IRA owner can make. For the reasons mentioned above and throughout other sections of this book, we are big proponents of Roth accounts for parents of a child with a disability. We regularly and proactively look for opportunities for our clients to perform Roth conversions where possible. If you are a do-it-yourselfer, or use some service, we want you to utilize this information also.

However, there is such a thing as over converting to a Roth. In the case of parents of a child with a disability, it's likely that the parent or parents will be in a higher tax bracket than the child. For this reason, it could make sense to ensure that some level of tax-deferred dollars (i.e., Traditional IRA) are left to the child in order to take advantage of the lower tax brackets that the child will theoretically be subject to—it is a balancing act to decide how much to leave in each type of retirement account and there is no exact science to it. We cannot predict with 100% accuracy the growth rates of the assets, or life expectancies of all parties involved, or even their future tax rate. However, we can make our best guess and determine if action is recommended.

Let's now look at an example of someone who is "retirement plan heavy" and see how they may be able to use a large medical expense deduction to their advantage. "Retirement plan heavy" in this context means that a large portion of their assets are in IRAs or other taxable retirement accounts, and they do not have much in the way of after-tax assets. This is not an uncommon situation, at least for us. If you are in this situation, then you likely do not have enough available resources outside of your retirement accounts to pay for an entrance fee to a residential home facility for your child. A slightly modified version of the technique outlined above would involve taking a distribution from a tax-deferred retirement account (which would be taxable to you in the year of distribution) to pay for the entrance fee and using the portion of the entrance fee that is allocated to medical care as a deduction to help lower the tax burden on the taxable distribution. The retirement plan distribution and the payment of the entrance fee would of course have to occur in the same calendar year for this technique to work out as planned.

Case Study of the Potential Advantage of a Whopper Roth Offset by a Big Medical Expense

To illustrate this concept let's consider the following example: John and Jane Doe are a married couple. John is 65 and Jane is 64. They have one child, Jeff, who has a disability and is a dependent for tax purposes. John and Jane have decided that the time is right for them to move Jeff into a residential home facility that is nearby. Let's assume the cost on one of the higher end facilities is $600,000 and $300,000 of the cost represents the medical expense portion. John and Jane have both retired recently. Upon the advice of an expert, Jane has elected to begin collecting the Social Security benefit that she is entitled to (based on her own earnings record). This strategy was recommended to Jane for the purpose of getting their son Jeff qualified for Social Security Disability Insurance (SSDI). Amongst other things, getting Jeff on SSDI is important for helping to get him qualified as an "eligible designated beneficiary," so that he can eventually stretch any IRA that he inherits. Jane's gross Social Security benefit for the year is $17,000. Up to a maximum of 85% of gross Social Security benefits can be taxable. In addition, they will have $4,000 in interest income and $25,000 in dividends ($18,000 of which represents qualified dividends). With the $300,000 medical expense John and Jane will have enough to itemize deductions for 2023. In addition to the medical expense, they will have $10,000 in state and local taxes to deduct on schedule A.

John and Jane had a feeling that the payment of the entrance fee would have some impact on their tax situation, so before making the payment they made the wise decision to engage a reputable accounting firm that provides tax planning services. This firm was able to perform analysis and ultimately recommended that John and Jane combine the medical expense deduction with a Roth conversion. Though John and Jane wanted to stay in the 24% tax bracket, they could still do a $600,000 Roth conversion in 2023. Adjusted gross income (AGI) for the year is $643,450 which includes $14,450 of taxable Social Security benefits (85% of the $17,000 in gross benefits), $4,000 in interest income, $25,000 of dividend income, and $600,000 in Roth conversions. The deductible portion of the medical expense equals $251,741 (7.5% of $643,450 = $48,259). $300,000 gross medical expense less 7.5% floor of $48,259 equals $251,741 in deductible medical expenses. The calculation to get taxable income close to the top of the 24% tax bracket is as follows.

$ 14,450		Taxable Social Security income
$ 4,000	+	Interest income
$ 7,000	+	Ordinary dividends (the qualified portion is taxed as capital gain income)
$600,000	+	Roth Conversion
$625,450	=	Gross ordinary income
$ 10,000	-	Itemized deduction for state and local taxes
$ 251,741	-	Itemized deduction for medical expense
$363,708	=	Taxable ordinary income

By making a Roth conversion in 2023, John and Jane were able to utilize a large portion of the total medical expense they incurred during the year to help offset this additional income and begin to build up their Roth accounts. These Roth accounts will likely end up being a legacy asset for their son Jeff. The large medical deduction allowed them to do a sizable Roth conversion while still staying within the 24% marginal tax bracket.

In continuing with the above example, let's take a look at the potential benefit that this Roth conversion could have on the overall estate, assuming reasonable annual spending and a long-term rate of return. Let's assume that in 2023 John and Jane have a net worth of $5 million. This includes $2.5 million of after-tax assets (cash and brokerage accounts), a $500,000 house, and $2 million in Traditional IRA accounts. Let's further assume that John and Jane spend $175,000 annually, they realize a 6.5% annual rate of return on their assets, John lives until age 83 and Jane lives until age 87. Finally, let's assume a $600,000 entrance fee was paid out in 2023 for Jeff to enter a residential home facility. If we were to run a side-by-side projection using this set of assumptions with one scenario showing no Roth conversions and the second scenario showing a Roth conversion of $600,000 in 2023, the Roth conversion comes out ahead. In 2046 at Jane's death, the net estate value would be larger by just over $620,000 in actual dollars and just over $280,000 in inflation adjusted dollars. It is worth noting that the software used to prepare these projections automatically backs out estimates for federal income taxes. For state tax purposes we assumed the taxpayers in this example were Pennsylvania residents. Pennsylvania taxes earned and investment income but does not tax retirement income or Roth conversions.

To go one step further let's assume that upon inheritance of the remaining assets, Jeff draws $150,000 annually for care and other living expenses from the portfolio. If we run the projections out until Jeff is 83 years old (23 years later), assuming the same 6.5% rate of return on assets, the scenario containing the Roth conversion would show a larger value in net assets by a margin of just over $2.1 million in actual dollars and $430,000 in inflation adjusted dollars.

PART TWO

Tax Benefits for Parents of a Dependent Child with a Disability

The years where you incur one very large medical expense may be few and far between. It is more likely that you will incur smaller, more frequent medical expenses in connection with care for your child. Some common expenses that qualify as deductible medical expenses are listed below. Please note that this list is not all inclusive. Also note that this list includes a summary of some general type of expenses. In many cases there are nuances that need to be reviewed along with the facts and circumstances surrounding the expense to determine deductibility.

- Nursing services paid for in connection with providing care related to your child's condition. The services can be provided either at your home or at a designated facility. Expenses paid for this type of care that allows you to work may qualify for the child and dependent care credit (see more on this below). Expenses in this category cannot be used for both a medical expense deduction and the dependent care credit. (But nice try.)

- Expenditures for installing special equipment or improvements made to your home are deductible if the main purpose is for medical care or to accommodate your home for your dependent who has a disability. If the improvements made to your home increase the value of your property, then the cost of the improvement is reduced by the increase in the fair market value of your home to arrive at the deductible portion of the expenditure.

- Lodging in connection with medical care if certain criteria are met (subject to limitations).

- Expenses paid for special education. The special education has to be recommended by a doctor and the teacher must be specially trained in this area. The cost, including tuition, meals, and lodging at the school that provides special education to children with the intent of helping the children overcome learning disabilities can be covered. The main reason for attending the school must be to help the child overcome learning disabilities. Other ordinary education provided by the school must be incidental to the special education provided.

- Mileage to and from doctor's appointments and/or therapy sessions.

- Amounts paid in connection with attending medical conferences may be deductible as medical expenses if the conference is related to the chronic illness of your dependent, the medical conference is primarily for and necessary to the medical care of your dependent, and the majority of the time that you were at the conference was spent attending sessions on medical information. Expenses related to meals and lodging while attending the conference do not qualify for the medical expense deduction.

Child and Dependent Care Tax Credit

Another relevant tax incentive for working parents with dependent children is the child and dependent care tax credit. Expenses paid for the care of your dependent child that enable you (and your spouse if filing a joint tax return) to work could qualify for this tax credit. This benefit is a dollar-for-dollar credit against your tax liability for the year as opposed to a deduction against your income. This tax credit is limited to $3,000 (for one qualifying individual) or up to $6,000 (for two qualifying individuals) for 2023. Expenses paid for qualifying care for your dependent cannot be used for both the medical expense deduction and the child and dependent care credit. It is important to work with a qualified tax professional who can help you allocate the costs between medical care and dependent care to maximize the tax credit and the medical deduction, if applicable. To claim this tax credit, the care provider cannot be a spouse, parent, or another dependent child.

KEY IDEAS

- Consider making a large Roth conversion in the same year you are incurring significant medical expenses, including entrance fees to a residential care facility.

- Other medical expenses incurred by the parents (that otherwise may not be deductible because of the 7.5% of AGI limitation) could also be deductible, including prescription drugs, doctor and hospital co-payments, dental and eyecare expenses, Medicare premiums and Medicare supplemental premiums, qualified long-term care premiums, etc. as part of the medical deduction.

- Accelerating a Roth conversion in a year of significant medical expenses could be a game changer for a child with a disability.

- A combination of both Traditional IRA and Roth IRA money is often preferable when planning for your child with a disability.

- When both parents are working, the Child and Dependent Care credit is available up to $3,000 for one child and up to $6,000 for two children.

23

Family Gifting and Spending Strategies

"Life is Beautiful. It's about giving. It's about family."

—Walt Disney

Family Gifting: The Big Picture

Most of my current and prospective clients are looking for guidance on things like retirement plan distribution strategies, tax reduction, Roth IRA conversions, asset allocation, estate planning, saving and spending strategies so they never run out of money, appropriate wills and trusts, and other things covered in this book. Of course, our offices and the firms we work with try to do our best in these areas.[1] But sometimes, these areas incompletely reflect how we can provide the most value to clients and their families.

I can't tell you the number of people I consult with whose families could benefit from an aggressive gifting plan. Note, gifting and charitable donations are not the same things for tax purposes. You have likely heard stories of successful entrepreneurs who have given what the media refers to as "gifts" to a university, foundation, or charity. From a tax standpoint, that's not accurate. What they gave was a charitable donation. The gifting I am referring to now is transferring money or property to a person (likely a family member) rather than a charity.

When I meet with clients, I genuinely try to listen two-thirds of the time and talk one-third of the time. As you can imagine, that isn't always easy for me. I also try to address what the client says is their biggest concern. But of course, I eventually bring up something I think most clients should have as part of their plan, that is, a gifting plan.

---

1 Lange Accounting Group offers guidance on retirement plan distribution strategies, tax reduction, Roth IRA conversions, saving and spending strategies, optimized Social Security strategies and gifting plans. Although we bring our knowledge and expertise in estate planning, it will be conducted in our capacity as number-crunching CPAs. However, we will likely make recommendations that clients could have a licensed estate attorney implement. Life insurance can be offered by a member of Lange Life Care for those interested. Asset location, asset allocation and low-cost enhanced index funds are provided by the investment firms with whom Lange Financial Group is affiliated. This service would be offered in our role as an investment advisor representative. Please see the front of the book for disclaimers related to these services. In each of these instances, these services are provided by employees in their capacity as CPAs and are not legal services. The protection of the attorney-client relationship does not exist with respect to these accounting, insurance and asset management services. There is no solicitation being made for legal services by the author nor by Lange Legal Services, LLC. All investing involves risk, including the potential for loss of principal. There is never any guarantee extended that any investment plan or strategy will be successful. Please see the front of the book for full disclaimers.

I met a single older woman who had a $35 million estate. She was spending roughly $10,000/month and had children and grandchildren with significant financial needs. She was facing a massive federal estate tax liability if she didn't make any gifts or even if she did, for that matter. Aggressive gifting could have reduced her estate tax liability by millions and would also have had the benefit of helping her family when they were younger and needed the money most—before she died, rather than after.

I brought up the idea of giving some money to her family members now. I had significant (multi millions) gifting in mind but was hoping (and even expecting) to convince her to make at least some smaller gifts. Her response: "What if I get sick?"

Okay, so you are laughing. Are you sure you aren't at least a little bit guilty of the same type of thinking?

Of course, I will never advocate gifting to family members if it threatens your or your spouse's financial security or the financial security of your child with a disability. When estimating how much money you and your spouse will need, I always want to err on the high side. I also factor in provisions for long-term care and emergency buffers. I also factor in an unexpected market drop. I even add an optimistic if not realistic projection that I will convince you that you can start spending more than you currently spend and you actually do it.

But what if I do all that and there is *still a lot of excess money*. That's when I start thinking about gifting, even if it isn't on my client's radar.

The goal of life, and even good financial planning, is not to die with the most money.

I had an uncle who everyone claimed figured out a way to take his money with him after he died. That would be the only justification for having so much money and spending so little on both himself and his family.

Obviously, our explicit goal is to optimize the things we have been talking about, including the best distribution plan for your IRAs and other retirement plan assets, Roth IRA conversions, beneficiary designations, investments, asset allocation, etc.

I also understand being reluctant to gift in uncertain times. As we go into design, the market is down and inflation, while easing, has left us with higher prices on many necessities. The natural tendency is to wait until later to make gifts even if gifting is on your mind.

The truth is all times are uncertain and I do not see them becoming more certain as time goes on. I know you are going to say with Covid, global warming,

> **The goal of life, and even good financial planning,**
> **is not to die with the most money.**

the Russian invasion of Ukraine, problems with China and North Korea and the Middle East and most everywhere else for that matter, the extreme political divisiveness, etc. these aren't "normal times."

But really, when were times "normal"? If you talk to some of my older engineering clients, they will describe their lives in the early 60s. Many of them went to work and came home and worked on their bomb shelter in their back yards because they feared a Russian nuclear attack. So, I don't think "we aren't in normal times" is a great excuse.

But what if, based on current assets and income, even using the most conservative assumptions, our projections show that you have way more money than you will ever need?

Consider the Impact of Your Gift—and the Potential to Reduce Taxes

In a typical will or trust, without any lifetime gifting, all assets will be left to the surviving spouse at the first death. Ultimately, when the second spouse dies—often in their 80s or 90s and when the children are in their 60s—there will frequently be a massive income and potential estate or inheritance tax on a sizable estate.

Furthermore, without gifting, the children will not have benefitted from the family money when they were younger and had greater financial needs. All of this makes a compelling case for gifting while you are still alive.

Think about this. If you were given $100,000 today, would it make much of a difference in your life? Would you go on one more vacation or even go out to dinner one more time? What if you had inherited $50,000 thirty years ago (which is roughly $100,000 in today's dollars)? What kind of difference would it have made then?

I had another client with $3,000,000. He spent $7,500/month. It was reasonable to project that with his Social Security, he would die with a lot more money than he has now. He had never married and didn't have any kids. His sister, who he was close with, was too sick to work, had run up her credit cards, and was barely getting by with Social Security and a tiny pension. She lived in financial gloom. Her financial situation literally caused her to be sick. When he saw me for a review, and I learned of this situation, I suggested he give his sister $117,000. Much to my surprise, he did it.

That $117,000 gift truly did not have any significant impact on my client's finances. He didn't change his behavior one bit. The gift, however, made a life-changing difference for his sister. It was also life-changing for my client because he felt so good about the gift.

Gifting More than $17,000 (or $34,000, if Married) Per Year

You may wonder how my client made a $117,000 gift when the annual exclusion for 2023 is only $17,000 per beneficiary ($34,000 if you are married). Yes, theoretically, there would be a gift tax on the $100,000 remaining after the $17,000 exclusion. However, if you file the appropriate gift tax return, you can elect to have the $100,000 subtracted from your *lifetime gifting exemption*. (You should file a gift tax return, but you will not be taxed immediately if you do not.)

If you make a $117,000 gift, you simply subtract $17,000 that you are "allowed" to gift and deduct the $100,000 from your lifetime federal gifting exemption of $12.92 million (as of January 2023), leaving you with a federal gifting exemption of $12.82 million. As long as you don't die with more than $12,820,000, (and not taking subsequent legislative changes into account) there will not be any federal estate tax or transfer tax at your death.

If the sunset provisions of the 2017 Tax Cut and Jobs Act take effect as scheduled on January 1, 2026, your estate would still have to exceed the $5,000,000 (plus inflation) lifetime federal gifting exemption.

If you are married, double the exclusion to the current $25,840,000 exclusion or $10M (plus inflation) if the sunset provisions of the 2017 Tax Cut and Jobs Act kicks in in 2026.

A further benefit is that any of the appreciation that would have accrued on the gift from the time of the gift to your death is removed from your estate.

Don't get me wrong. The $17,000/year exclusion ($34,000/year if from a joint account or your spouse joins you in the gift) per beneficiary is a great starting point for a gifting program, especially if there are a lot of potential beneficiaries such as children and grandchildren.

If your child has an ABLE account, you can contribute up to the gift tax exclusion amount to it every year. As we discuss in detail in Chapter 14, ABLE accounts allow persons with disabilities to accumulate funds up to $100,000 without jeopardizing eligibility for SSI or Medicaid. Keep in mind that this annual contribution limit of $17,000 (for 2023) is *per beneficiary*, not *per donor*. Total contributions to an individual's ABLE account cannot exceed the current exclusion amount.

Another way you might be able to provide substantial financial support to family members is to pay their education or medical expenses. If you make payments directly to an educational institution or a medical provider on behalf of a loved one, those payments are not considered gifts and do not count towards the $17,000 annual exclusion. This is different from sending your grandchild money with the expectation that they will use the funds for college tuition or medical bills. Those payments count as gifts while payments made directly to the university or hospital do not.

I met with a married couple in their 70s who had much more money than they would ever need. They had an adult child who was basically broke. I told them if they gave their child $2 million dollars, it could potentially save many millions in taxes. Without the gift, in twenty years, the $2 million (assuming a 7% interest rate) would grow to $8 million which could trigger a federal estate tax of close to $3.2 million. True, by eating into their exclusion, they are only saving the estate tax on the growth, but that $6 million would be close to a $2.4 million savings for the family. Finally, even if there are no federal transfer tax savings, there could be substantial state inheritance tax savings with large gifts.

The fear of the child being inappropriate with the money or reducing the child's motivation to succeed still needed to be addressed. We solved that problem partially, though not 100%, by making a gift to a trust with the child as the primary beneficiary. A good source of information to address the issue of the psychological implications of gifting is a book called *Preparing Your Heirs* by Roy Williams.

Two other families come to mind. They are both wealthy, have one child, and can afford to make substantial gifts to their child. In both cases, their children are financially responsible and do extremely meaningful and fulfilling work for charitable organizations, and their parents approve of their children's careers. But (surprise, surprise) their children do not make a lot of money.

One father has been extremely generous to his child. His son was able to get married, he lives in a nice house, and the father contributed generously to a 529 plan for his grandchild's college education. It didn't reduce the motivation of the adult child who continues to have an extremely productive career working for the charitable organization.

The other father, in a comparable financial position, has a daughter, doing meaningful—but not well-paid—work, and she is essentially living barely above the poverty level. Despite my pleading, he has never made a large gift to her.

She is in her late fifties now. He will likely die owing massive taxes and she will inherit way more money than she will ever need when she is in her sixties or seventies. Which family do you think is making the best use of their roughly equal financial resources?

Another experience comes to mind about the challenges of persuading clients to spend more money and make gifts. I was always encouraging this client to spend more money on himself and his wife and give more money to his children. After a while, I gave up on trying to get him to spend more money on himself and his wife. I did, however, keep trying to get him to give more money to his children—I was not successful.

On one of the last times I saw him before he died, he said "I have considered what you have recommended about gifting money to family. Accordingly, I have decided I will happily accept any money my children wish to give to me."

So, if, after running a series of long-term financial projections using a series of very conservative assumptions, there is sufficient money to make gifts, I firmly believe you should strongly consider a formal gifting program. The combination of giving your family money when they need it most and dramatically cutting the family tax burden should be a major consideration in many parents' Financial Masterplans.

How a Gift Can Continue Giving

Another way to counter the problem of accelerated taxes on retirement plans and IRAs in the wake of the SECURE Act is to bestow gifts on family members via regular taxed withdrawals. Some readers would be better off if they cash in a portion of their IRA even before mandatory distributions. Then, pay the taxes and give the rest or a portion of the remaining funds to your heirs. Not indiscriminately, but with "leveraged gifting" techniques that provide tax advantages for both you and your beneficiary.

This strategy will slowly reduce the amount in your Traditional IRA, leaving less to face the "death tax" burden. Plus, it can confer significant advantages to your children while they are still young.

Different Forms of Gifting

Of course, gifting can take on many flavors. It could be a straightforward gift of cash. It could be a contribution to a 529 plan (a tax-free college funding mechanism typically for grandchildren). I love ABLE gifts for a child with a disability. For most older parents, these are two of my favorite ways to give away your money.

Read below about other things that 529 funds can be used for. I also like gifts that your beneficiary then uses to contribute to their own Roth IRAs or Roth 401(k)s.

If you can afford to make gifts to your family, I recommend six basic types of gifts.

1. A plain old, no-strings-attached gift.

2. A gift for a specific purpose, such as a down payment on a house. Technically, there should be no "strings" on a qualifying gift, but a strong hint is a viable option!

3. Help fund a Roth IRA for a child or grandchild or assist a child in maximizing their Roth 401(k) account at work. The money could also be used to pay the taxes on a Roth IRA conversion of the child's IRA.

4. The gift of education for grandchildren in the form of Section 529 plans or even direct tuition payments or health care payments (which aren't technically considered a gift).

5. A gift to an ABLE account. Please see chapter 14.

6. Permanent (not term) life insurance.

For some people, the source for the gift could be their retirement plan. The last four methods of gifting (assuming the source is the net proceeds after retirement plan withdrawals) are methods for transferring money from the taxable environment to the tax-free environment, all outside of your estate. That is like a Roth IRA conversion except the proceeds will be outside of your estate. All six gifting techniques could reduce the value of an Inherited Traditional IRA, thus reducing the tax liability on the inheritance.

Life insurance is free from income tax and, if set up properly, is also free from estate, inheritance, and transfer taxes. Because of the complexity of this type of gift, we discuss life insurance as a gifting option in Chapter 26.

Contributions to 529 Plans and ABLE Gifts Have Multiple Uses

- A recent change in tax law with the SECURE Act 2.0 allows beneficiaries of 529 plans to roll up to $35,000 from a 529 plan to a Roth IRA starting in 2024. This means that if a beneficiary doesn't spend all of their 529 plan funds on education, the tax-free growth of a 529 plan can continue in a different format. However, this change comes with limitations:

- The beneficiary has a lifetime limit of $35,000 that can be rolled from a 529 plan to a Roth account.

- The 529 account must have been open for at least 15 years.

- No contributions or earnings on contributions made in the last five years can be transferred.

- Transfers are subject to annual Roth IRA contribution limits.

- The beneficiary needs to have earned income equal to the amount of the rollover, subject to the amount of the annual contribution limit.

- However, if your child is receiving governmental support such as SSI, rolling the funds from a 529 plan to a Roth IRA could jeopardize that support. Funds in 529 plans are not considered "countable resources" by SSI while Roth IRAs are. Any distribution from a 529 plan for any purpose other than educational purposes will be considered a "countable resource" and may result in a reduction of governmental benefits. A better use for unused 529 funds in this situation is to roll them over to an ABLE account, as explained in Chapter 14. Briefly, on an annual basis, you can roll up to the gift tax exclusion amount ($17,000 for 2023) from a 529 plan into an ABLE account for your child. The original beneficiary of the 529 plan does not need to be the same person who is the beneficiary of the ABLE account. See Chapter 14 for a full explanation.

The Exception to the Rule as it Relates to Gifting

Earlier I said, "Don't Pay Taxes Now, Pay Taxes Later, Except the Roth." Taking money from your IRA, paying the taxes, and then using that money to buy life insurance or contribute to an ABLE account, a 529 plan, or even a Roth IRA for your children is conceptually similar to making a Roth IRA conversion. Taking money from your IRA and using the proceeds for these purposes is likely an excellent strategy. In all instances, you are paying income taxes now in return for tax-free growth in the future. In the last three instances above, the added bonus is that, if handled correctly, they can avoid all transfer and estate taxes. That said, Roth IRA conversions, life insurance, 529 plans, and other gifting techniques should be complementary rather than competing strategies.

I have done a series of webinars for CPAs called Transferring Money from the Taxable World to the Tax-Free World. Of course, Roth IRA conversions were one focus. Withdrawing money from a retirement account, paying tax on it, and gifting it to family members who then use it for tax-free investments was the other focus.

Annuities and Gifting

As I'm sure you can tell, I'm not a big fan of commercial annuities. I have never sold one nor recommended a client buy one. They typically have high internal hidden costs. In addition, assuming they were purchased with after-tax dollars, all the appreciation will eventually be subject to ordinary income, not capital gains tax treatment. There is no step up in basis with commercial annuities. But, even after all these disadvantages, I often recommend clients keep the commercial annuities they have already purchased.

Many of these contracts have penalties for cashing them in early. In addition, since many of these products have guarantees and owners have already incurred the high costs, it is often best to keep what you have. The other factor is if they were purchased many years ago when interest rates were higher than today, it might be a reasonable investment to hang on to.

But even though I don't recommend purchasing them, many of my professor clients, especially those who work for state schools, own them.

One thing to keep in mind is if they have a guaranteed return (and be careful because some of the guarantees that you may assume are a living benefit turn out to be only a death benefit.) If there is a true living guarantee, then consider investing in the riskiest asset class the annuity company offers. Notwithstanding you are investing in something aggressive, you can treat it as a fixed income investment for the purposes of asset allocation because of the guarantee.

But it can also be used as a source of income for you and/or your heirs. Most owners keep them until death, but then all the appreciation is subject to ordinary income taxes for the heirs. You might consider annuitizing early, and if you do not need the money, give the income to your children. If you have come to the point where you will be required to annuitize, it may make sense for you to elect an option that will provide a guaranteed income over your own lifetime as well as that of a younger survivor. The annuity income will stop as soon as your survivor dies. On the other hand, if the survivor has a long life, it could work out quite well financially and your survivor will be reminded of your gift every year for the rest of their lives, many years after you have passed. But, before you select this option, you should take into account not only your own life expectancy, but also the life expectancy of your heirs.

In addition to the types of gifts mentioned above, here is one more idea to protect yourself and your heirs from the death of the stretch IRA.

Spend More Money

Spend more money! To be honest, I have been only moderately successful in my efforts to convince clients to spend more money, even when they can easily afford it. Even if they intellectually understand the math and calculations behind the recommendations we make, few of my clients who are age 65 or older are great spenders relative to their income and net worth. I know it isn't easy to get a leopard to change its spots, but I will aim for some change in the spending area.

One couple I worked with was drastically underspending. During our review, the man said that he had changed, and he wanted recognition for changing his spending. He said he was spending money on things he would not have purchased in the past. He wanted me to congratulate him for paying $12/month for no ads or commercials on YouTube! My suggestion had been to spend money of a different magnitude.

Specifically, I suggested they rent or buy a place in the city where their daughter, who is having a baby, lives. Mom instantly liked that idea and to be fair, so did Dad.

Suggestions for Spending More Money

Practically all my clients err on not spending enough. Even my clients who have children with a disability, and who have more than enough funds for both their lives and to support their child after they are gone struggle with this. Even my wife and I at times need to be reminded that we need not be completely frugal. When I show them they can afford to spend a lot more money than they are spending, they have often said, "I have everything I want, what else could I spend money on?"

You might be saying the same thing to yourself right now. As I mentioned earlier, most conversations where I encourage clients who can afford to spend more money to do so usually lead to a simple and relatively unequivocal response: "No." So, I will take the liberty of giving you some suggestions. Some of these ideas are/were particularly helpful during the Covid-19 crisis, but many can improve the quality of your lives post-Covid or at least as "post" as we are.

For many clients, adopting even just a few of these quality-of-life enhancers over many years might mean the difference between dying with $3 million instead of $3.3 million, but the added enjoyment and gained quality-of-life will be well worth it. It is worth thinking about. Many times, people deprive themselves of certain luxuries because they want to pass more money to their children.

I often ask clients if we were to ask their children if they would prefer that their parents spend more money that would give their parents more pleasure or save that money for a larger inheritance for the children, the clients without exception say their kids would encourage them to spend more money on themselves.

I have always encouraged clients to spend more money on taking care of themselves. I believe all these things will bring you a higher return than the market, even in good times. Well, here are a few ideas.

Ideas for Spending Money That I Embrace

Consider:

- A housekeeping service.
- Hire someone to do things you don't like to do.
- Travel or go someplace warm for a month or longer during the winter.
- Of course, I have long been a fan of your taking your entire family on an annual vacation with you footing the bill.
- Support a good cause. I purchased and distributed 50,000 KN-95 masks, mainly to charities and non-profits, but also to my family and clients. Ultimately, I consider the mask distribution campaign a health protection campaign. It may have been the best six-figure investment I ever made.

After spending money on experiences, my next priority is health—for my immediate family, my extended family, and my clients and their families, and for the world at large.

Consider:

- Buy high quality organic food.
- Make use of a food service or a private chef.
- Hire a nutritionist who would design an individual meal plan that would incorporate what is best for you, keeping in mind what you like to eat.
- Join a concierge medical practice.
- Hire a personal trainer. (I find the discipline of having a regular appointed time for exercise and having a built-in accountability coach keeps my workouts regular.)
- Invest in treatments that may not be covered by insurance. I receive mesenchymal stem cell treatments every year for psoriatic arthritis (they have really helped me, and I recommend them for people who suffer from an autoimmune disease).

A Few More Thoughts About Spending

Please note that a discussion of the safe withdrawal rate, sequence of returns, and other issues regarding how much you can safely spend is beyond the scope of this book.

We like to calculate how much money clients can afford to spend without ever running out of money. Depending on your situation and how much you want or need to leave behind, chances are good that you can spend more than you are spending right now.

I am not suggesting you spend frivolously. You would not be where you are today if you did. As an example, though I am extravagant in many areas, I have never paid to fly first class. My wife and I used to drive 11 and 13-year-old Subarus until we gave one to my daughter. My wife, who has a master's degree in electrical engineering from Carnegie Mellon University, and my daughter, also a STEM kid, are both much thriftier than I.

True, I work long hours, and I am in the prime of my career in terms of productivity and earning capacity. One rationalization for what some may think is a lavish lifestyle is that I am buying time; I can make much more money per hour working than I spend paying for many of the things on this list like shopping, cooking, or cleaning. That said, I am also buying health. To be fair, I have only spent like this in recent years and only after I thought I could afford it, and after my wife and I had reassured ourselves that our daughter Erica will have plenty of money to keep herself comfortable after we are gone.

The point of this chapter, however, is to show that additional spending and making gifts to your family can increase the quality of your and your family's lives and be a great hedge against future taxes. The next chapter extends this idea addressing the intersection of money, spending, and happiness. If that seems off-topic for a financial book, just keep an open mind!

KEY IDEAS

- Consider if you can afford more gifts for your family.
- Buying experiences, particularly with family and friends, is likely the best way to spend your money.
- There are many ways to spend your money to enhance the quality of your health and your life.
- Gifting is the most tax- and cost-efficient method of transferring wealth to your heirs.

24

Money Can Buy Happiness

"There is a puritanical streak that runs through all aspects of money in America…And most of the conversations about spending more money start with no."

—Ramit Sethi

Fortunately, for most of my readers, money does buy happiness in that it protects from hardship. Being able to count on access to good medical care, care for your children, a general sense of wellbeing, a cadre of good friends and family, shelter, and food goes a long way to fostering happiness. But if we are in the position to be able to afford more, can we be happier spending more?

I am not advocating for spending carelessly. But, when the resources are there, if there is enough money to care for your child who has a disability, are there ways to make your money "work for you" outside the investment realm?

The authors Elizabeth Dunn and Michael Norton published a book called ***Happy Money: The Science of Smarter Spending***. They espouse five principles for ways to spend money to increase your happiness.

1. **Buy experiences.** I would add, buy things that allow you to do what you want to do. (For example, my e-bikes and house in Tucson allow me to significantly enhance my bicycling experience and that makes me happy.)

2. **Make it a treat.** Don't indulge in your favorite ice cream every day—it stops being a treat. (This is the hard one for me to get.)

3. **Buy time.** Pay people to do what you do not like doing. Or don't buy the cheapest airline ticket if it results in an endless layover where you do not want to be.

4. **Pay now, consume later.** That paid-for vacation seems "free" by the time you take it.

5. **Invest in others.**

Perhaps what gives the authors of this advice additional credibility is that they are both full time professors at the University of British Columbia and Harvard, respectively. A simple Google search about "spending money and happiness" leads to countless other sources of inspiration but they pretty much have the bases covered. As peer-reviewed authors, I would say those five criteria, make a pretty good start.

Host a Family Vacation—Two Birds with One Stone—Experiences and Investing in Others

My favorite way to spend your money is for you to sponsor a family vacation. My 99-year-old father-in-law hosts a family vacation every year, picking up the tab for the entire family. He has been doing this for more than 25 years (though we obviously skipped during the worst years of the pandemic). For a four-day weekend, the entire family drives, or flies into a resort called Woodloch in the Poconos (a recreational area in the mountains of Pennsylvania). All of the children, grandchildren, and now great-grandchildren come and hang out together to play games, swim in the pool, go to the "beach," kayak in the lake, play golf and tennis, laugh at the comedy show, and enjoy family activities. We eat all of our meals together in the walled off semi-private dining room.

My daughter, Erica, our only child who is now 28 years old, knows all her cousins well, despite living in different states, and they are in frequent contact. She would not have this sense of being part of a bigger family were it not for these annual family gatherings. During the pandemic isolation, my daughter had a blast chatting online with her cousins.

When my father-in-law passes, he will leave less money to his family, but he will have provided the priceless legacy of strengthened family bonds and a sense of "clan," even though we live all over the country.

This advice, incidentally, is consistent with multiple other authors who say, "buy experiences, not things." Imagine how much your loved ones would appreciate such an experience after being unable to go anywhere or do anything during the pandemic. Better yet, make it an annual event.

A secondary benefit is that experiences tend to get better with memory. Remember that wonderful vacation you took…the minor inconveniences you experienced generally fade into the background and the good times grow even rosier. And then you can also relive the best parts with the people you shared the time with.

I have encouraged clients to spend more money for years and usually without a lot of success. Taking their family on a vacation, however, is one area that many clients have changed and now it is a regular event for many of my client's families.

Usually, the hardest part is working around everyone's busy schedule. My answer to that is to consider everyone's needs, and then pick a date. Mention that

you are updating your wills and trusts and you sure hope that they will be able to make the annual family gathering.

Beware of False Economy—Treats are OK

Towards the end of her life, I took my mom on mini vacations to New York City, Washington D.C., and Cleveland. Can you think of a better way for me to spend my time and money?

She was in her mid-nineties when my wife, Cindy, my daughter, Erica, and I took her on the mini vacation to New York City. A retired professor, my mom was basically as sharp as ever. This mini vacation in New York City was a real treat for all of us, but one of the top attractions for my mom was to buy a silk scarf at Bloomingdales. She anticipated the purchase and spoke of it many times—we were very aware that it was a priority for her!

While there, we did the normal touristy things like going to museums, visiting Central Park, eating at wonderful restaurants, and seeing a Broadway show. On the last day, I misjudged the time it would take to get to Bloomingdales. We arrived before closing but without much time to spare.

Mom picked out a beautiful silk scarf. I was so happy because this was the crown jewel of the trip for her. I told the salesclerk we would take it.

Then, Mom asked the salesclerk for the price. Frantically shaking my head, I tried to alert the salesperson that she shouldn't tell my mom the price. I would buy it as a gift, my mom didn't need to know the price, but my timing was too late. The salesperson told Mom the scarf cost $100. Instantly my mom said that that was much too expensive. They didn't have a less expensive alternative that she liked. I pleaded with my mom to let me buy her the $100 scarf. She would have none of it.

As we were leaving, I tried to slip back and buy the scarf, but my mother knew me too well. She said, "I know you're going back there to buy that scarf, and you may *not* buy that scarf for me." She was my mother, I had to listen and be respectful, but it made me a little sad. The $100 would have meant nothing to me. My mother could have had the pleasure of receiving a gift and owning the scarf and wearing it even if only a few times. After her death, it could have gone to my daughter, Erica, and that would have triggered a fond memory of that trip we all took to New York. But no, my mother could not accept my paying $100 for a scarf.

I see this type of thinking all the time with many of my clients.

Both my daughter, Erica, and my wife are not great spenders. Erica made fun of me for buying a karaoke machine that adjusted the pitch of your voice, so it sounded like you sang in tune. (I have a good ear and a bad voice.) It was featured on Shark Tank where I often buy the product the entrepreneurs are pitching. Erica accurately predicted I would spend hundreds of dollars on this machine, use it once, and it would accumulate dust in our basement, which is exactly what happened. So, I also suggest that you give yourself permission to forgive yourself if you make a mistake!

How do you balance desires with practicalities? On the scale of the trip, buying the scarf was inconsequential. But for my mother, the financial outlay for a personal indulgence crossed the line—too expensive. But, while I spend money on things that I think are important, I am a little bit the same way with things that I feel are just too expensive.

I was away from home recently and felt like watching television for a little while. (I needed a break from writing this book.) Like most of us in this "cord-cutting" era, I hate all the commercials on the regular channels, and, thanks to streaming service subscriptions, I've become accustomed to life without them. But the only alternative at this hotel for movies without commercials was to pay $19.95. I couldn't do it. So, I just watched the regular lousy television with the commercials!

So, how do you come to terms with what you can or cannot afford? When is an indulgence perfectly acceptable? When can you turn a dream into a reality? The decisions are ultimately personal but thinking about your choices and knowing how much you can really afford (which, of course, is part of our Financial Masterplan service[1]) is important.

---

1   Please see the end of the book for more information about the Financial Masterplan and the related disclaimers.

Donate to Charity—Spend Money on Others

Dunn and Norton make some great observations about charity. In their research (you can listen to a short TED talk by Michael Norton on this topic at **https://www.ted.com/speakers/michael_norton**), they found that the amount of money you spend doesn't actually matter that much. What's most important is that you spend it on somebody else. They found a universal positive correlation between giving and happiness. So, focus a bit more on pro-social activities.

Purchasing and distributing 50,000 KN-95 masks to charities, family, friends, and clients was "worth" many times what I paid for them.

This increased happiness can be achieved by supporting your favorite charities on a large or small scale, but it can also mean investing in your friendships or building some camaraderie with your neighbors. Throw a party for your friends. Make a lunch date—your treat.

Buy Time

I belong to a business coaching group called Strategic Coach and we did an interesting exercise. Dan Sullivan, the coach, told everyone to write down what they would do if they had an extra 1,000 hours of time per year. Answers included spend more time with family, expand their business, play more golf, write a book, join a gym, eat better, etc.

Then, he said, OK, now figure out a way to free up those thousand hours. At least in my case, the way I free up time is to pay others to do stuff that I don't want to do. Hint: delegating chores to our spouse is not what Dan or I have in mind.

Dan thinks we often ask ourselves the wrong question in attempting to solve a difficult, unpleasant time-consuming problem. Our natural inclination is to question "how" as in "How can I deal with this problem?" While many things cannot be appropriately delegated, many can. If so, the right question might be "Who can do this for me?" not "How can I do this?" Hence the name of his recommendation and the name of one of his books, *Who, Not How*.

I dove headfirst into this discussion in the previous chapter. You can always review my list. But I encourage you to sit down and make your own list of stuff you do that you would rather not do. Then, think about ways to free up your time to do the stuff you want to do.

A Personal Note On Avoiding Taxes

Your happiness is more important than your money.

Your happiness is more important than your money.

I have a lot of snowbird clients who spend several months a year in the south every winter. I go to Tucson myself and think avoiding the Northeast winters is a fine idea. Neither Texas nor Florida has a state income tax or an inheritance tax so there is certainly tax-reduction motivation in having either state as your primary residence.

If you were planning on living in a tax-favored state five months and 29 days, (not that time spent in the state is the sole residency test), fine. Spend a few more days there, become a resident and save money on taxes while you are alive and after you are gone. What if you only want to spend three months a year there? Should you spend three more months in a state where you don't want to live just so you can save money in taxes?

I would say no.

I have a client who has homes in Florida and California and way more money than he will ever spend. He would like to spend about 9 months a year in California and 3 months in Florida. But he spends more than 6 months in Florida to save on taxes. Does that really make sense?

It's the same thing when it comes to saving inheritance taxes. Do you want to spend your last years in a state where you don't want to live so you can save taxes for your heirs?

The purpose of saving taxes, though it varies from reader to reader, is to have a more financially secure life, be able to do whatever it is that you want to do, and to optimally pass money to your family. You could ask any one of your kids point blank- "What do you prefer, that I live in a place where I don't want to be so I can save taxes when I die so you can receive a bigger inheritance, or would you prefer that I live where I want?"

If any of your children were to say they would prefer you try to save money on their taxes regardless of where you live, you have a bigger problem than a tax problem. In reality, I hope every child would say "your happiness comes first." In my experience, every client that I have would say that is what their children would say.

Don't let the tail wag the dog. Live where you want to live.

KEY IDEAS

- Most discussions of spending start with "No." If there is enough money to care for your child who has a disability, please try to keep an open mind about spending, because the right type of spending can buy you happiness.

- Think about delegating things you do not want to do and that somoone else could do for you, even if you have to pay them.

- Happiness is more important than saving taxes. Even if an option such as living in a state with no state income tax or inheritance tax could save you a bundle on taxes, don't choose that option if it won't also make you happy.

25

Get Married for The Money

"I can handle being married for my money; it's being married for my life insurance that gives me pause."

—Jacob M. Appel

This chapter is for people in a long-term committed relationship who aren't legally married. There are significant financial and tax implications of getting married. With appropriate planning, getting married will likely be extremely beneficial for the couple as well as their heirs from a financial standpoint.

First, let me address a common objection. You want to keep finances separate and want to control how much you want to leave your partner, if anything, and how much you want to leave others. I get it. Though it isn't a perfect answer, the obvious answer is to have a prenuptial agreement, which I almost always recommend for even a first marriage.[1] This is especially important if you are trying to protect assets that you want to leave to your child with a disability.

The agreement can be as simple as what's mine is mine, what's yours is yours, what's ours is ours. If we ever split, I keep mine, you keep yours, and we split ours. We each retain the right to leave as much or as little as we want to anyone we want in our wills, trusts, beneficiary designations, etc.

In reality, especially as you are married for more years and your commitment and love grow and mature, you can be much more generous than the prenuptial agreement indicates. But having a solid prenuptial agreement is a great start.

I have known many people in committed relationships when the partner with significant financial resources didn't want to get married, despite my best efforts at financial persuasion. Now if you don't want to get married because you don't want to get married for non-financial reasons, that is another story.

But, if you don't want to get married for financial reasons, the prenuptial agreement should be able to protect you. In addition, you could be adding enormous financial benefits for your partner, even if you don't leave your partner one red cent. (See the section on Social Security below.)

---

1 There is no solicitation for legal services being made by me, James Lange, nor by Lange Legal Group, LLC.

I have long known about the financial benefits of getting married. Back in 2014, I saw a "loophole" for same-sex couples to enjoy the financial advantages of marriage even if they lived in states that didn't recognize in-state marriages.

So, to help same-sex couples enjoy the same financial benefits as married couples, I wrote the book *Retire Secure! For Same-Sex Couples*, with testimonials from a lot of financial experts. The fun testimonials were from Billie Jean King and Martin Sheen. Evan Wolfson, founder of Freedom to Marry, wrote the foreword.

The emphasis of that book was on the financial advantages and disadvantages of getting married, all of which are summarized in this chapter. At that time, for federal income tax, federal estate tax, and Social Security benefits, the federal government and the Social Security Administration recognized same-sex marriages that were performed in a state where same-sex marriage was legal (the state of celebration) even if the couple resided in a non-recognition state. So, the thrust of the book was that same-sex couples living in non-recognition states travel to recognition states and get married there so they could return and enjoy the tax and Social Security benefits of being married.

Now, of course, same-sex couples can be married in all 50 states, so that recommendation is no longer relevant, but the advantages of getting married for the money are even more relevant today than they were then.

As an aside, though the book was favorably mentioned on wsj.com and Bloomberg and many other sources, I never got a lot of business from it. Potentially, the problem in hindsight was that I didn't have a personal affinity with the audience because I am not gay. I should have written *Retire Secure for Parents of a Child with a Disability* first because I have affinity with these parents since I am one also.

When I was promoting *Retire Secure! For Same-Sex Couples*, it was natural for me to partner with somebody who was well known in the same-sex marriage world. And fortunately, I had a personal connection with Evan Wolfson, the founder of Freedom to Marry. Evan was the attorney in many of the cases, including the first case that allowed same-sex couples to be married in Hawaii.

Evan also appeared on my radio show. Evan is quick to admit that he doesn't have any special insights about finance, money, and taxes. That radio show with Evan was the only one I ever did that had nothing to do with money and everything to do with love.

That message of love is core to his book, *Why Marriage Matters: America, Equality, and Gay People's Right to Marry*. If you read Evan's book or listen to him speak, he doesn't sound like a Harvard lawyer, even though Evan is a Harvard lawyer. In that book and when he speaks, he discusses the advantages of lifelong partnership in marriage.

This is a money book. I'm not here to provide relationship advice, but I have encouraged couples to marry for financial reasons. Universally, the couples who followed my advice and got married said it did change things in their relationship, and that change was for the better. So, in addition to the financial justifications for marriage, a better relationship is a definite plus for getting married. Of course, though, with any decision that has financial implications, it's essential to take precautions with iron-clad prenuptial agreements and to have open and candid discussions about all financial matters.

I understand that some couples, whether same-sex or not, feel that they don't need a piece of paper to validate their relationship. But I would be remiss in my desire to help partners create a financially secure retirement if I omitted the financial benefits that come from marriage. So, this chapter is about how unmarried couples can significantly increase their financial security by getting married and making specific decisions that are available to them under the law only if they are legally married. The difference can be so significant, in fact, that I will say that most committed but unmarried couples (where at least one member is age 60 or older) should, either on their own or with an advisor, evaluate whether it makes financial sense for them to marry.

Many of the strategies in *Retire Secure! For Same-Sex Couples* were based on finding ways to optimize dollars in retirement for couples who back then could not or did not want to get married.

For couples with a net worth of less than $1,000,000, the tax savings will not be as great. Getting married for couples with less than $1,000,000, however, could mean the difference between the surviving partner/spouse being financially secure and living comfortably, versus the survivor living out his or her retirement years in relative poverty.

I want to make sure that, no matter what happens to the stock market, and no matter what happens to their partners or spouses—my clients and readers and hopefully their partners will always have food on the table, shelter over their heads, gas in the car, and a little bit of money for Saturday night. Getting married and taking the appropriate steps can, in many instances, make the difference between the financially dependent partner/spouse being secure and not having those basic necessities.

Let's assume you are in a committed relationship but not married. Let's further assume you are in a much stronger financial position than your partner. (Your partner likely doesn't read these types of books.) If you get married and if you predecease your partner and you leave your partner some of your assets, there will be substantial income tax advantages as well as estate and inheritance tax advantages. The advantages are even more profound if you have a large retirement plan because of the miserable law known as the SECURE Act, which is extremely unfavorable for unmarried couples, but extremely favorable for married couples. Presumably, you could leave more money to your spouse and less to Uncle Sam by getting married. But to be fair, I will also cover some of the financial downsides of getting married—or, at least, the downsides of getting married in the short term.

Stretch IRA for Unmarried Partners

Chapters 9 and 10 detail the changes to the timing of distributions from Inherited IRAs and retirement plans under the SECURE Act. If you inherit an IRA or a Roth IRA from your partner, you will be able to take advantage of the ability to stretch or defer taxable payments over your life but only if you meet one of the exceptions to the ten-year rule. One important exception related to this chapter is leaving your IRA or retirement plan to your spouse as opposed to your unmarried partner. Another relevant exception is a beneficiary who is not more than ten years younger than the IRA owner. The two most likely beneficiaries that aren't more than ten years younger than you are unmarried partners and siblings. For parents of a child with a disability who qualifies as an eligible designated beneficiary, another exception is leaving your IRA to that child or to a special needs trust for that child, as we discuss in Chapters 10 and 11. If your unmarried partner is more than ten years younger than you, there is an even stronger financial incentive to get married.

Let's assume you are planning to leave at least a portion of your IRA or retirement plan to your unmarried partner who is not more than 10 years younger than you. The good news is that as long as your partner is no more than ten years younger than you, your partner will be able to use their life expectancy factor under the single life expectancy tables as the divisor to determine the RMD for the Inherited IRA. This is consistent with the old (pre-2020) law. This is more favorable than if your partner is more than ten years younger than you, in which case they would be able to "stretch" the Inherited IRA or Roth IRA for only ten years. But in both cases, it is still much worse than leaving your IRA or Roth IRA to a married partner who can use a far more favorable (lower) distribution rate.

If you marry and then die, your spouse could roll the IRA into their IRA (I prefer trustee-to-trustee transfer, please see Chapter 7) and have a much slower distribution schedule. If your spouse isn't 73 yet at your death, they could do a trustee-to-trustee transfer and not take any RMDs until they turn 73 and even then, take much smaller distributions, or the age when RMDs need to start for them, which may be as late as 75.

A new provision in the SECURE Act 2.0 will allow surviving spouses to elect to be treated as if they were the deceased spouse for the purpose of the timing of RMDs from Inherited IRAs. This is most beneficial if the surviving spouse is older because that means that RMDs can be postponed until the decedent would have been required to start taking them. RMDs will also be smaller in this case, because they will be based on the younger decedent's age and longer life expectancy.

Federal and State Gift, Estate, and Inheritance Taxes

For federal tax purposes, every legally married U.S. citizen is entitled to an unlimited marital deduction for receiving gifts or money transferred at the death of their spouse. That means you could give or leave your spouse a billion dollars, and there would not be one cent of gift or estate tax at your death. Beyond that, there is a $12.92 million exemption from gift and/or estate taxes for individuals who die in 2023. With savvy planning, a married couple could gift and/or bequeath double that amount, or $25.84 million without paying any estate tax. However, unless Congress makes changes, in 2026 those generous levels could plunge by nearly half to an estimated $7 million ($5 million plus inflation since 2017) under the sunset provisions of the Tax Cuts and Jobs Act.

But, even forgetting the exemption for married couples, very few people will have federal gift or estate tax worries because most people will have less than $12.92 million, or even $7 million when the generous estate and gift tax exemption expires in 2026. But, for those of you who might have a federal estate and/or gift tax problem, getting married grants you and your spouse an unlimited marital deduction.

Save State Inheritance Taxes by Getting Married

At the state level, multiple states impose their own estate tax or inheritance tax which can inflict significant financial burdens on unmarried couples. However, married couples who leave or give their property and money to each other don't face similar problems because all states that assess a transfer tax also have an unlimited marital deduction. As of the writing of this book in 2023, 17 states plus D.C., including Hawaii, Illinois, Massachusetts, New York, and Pennsylvania, still have either an estate tax or an inheritance tax or both but have unlimited marital deductions.

Social Security Benefits for Married Couples Can Be More Now, and Much More After the First Death

Even if you don't plan on leaving your partner any of your money, without any cost to you, you could significantly protect your partner's income with your Social Security benefits, as explained below. So, even if you want to leave most or all of your money to your biological family or someone else or even your favorite charities, you would likely be able to get a prenuptial agreement that would protect your biological family and other heirs and help your partner out financially without costing you a nickel.

Social Security Survivor Benefits

One of the great advantages of getting married is the death benefits rules for married couples. Typically, the surviving spouse is going to receive benefits based on the higher of the two earnings records. So, by holding off until age 66, 67 or 70, as opposed to collecting at age 62 or 65, you are not only creating a higher benefit for the rest of your life, but you're also protecting your lower-earning surviving spouse in the event you predecease them. This is an extremely important area and may even be seen by some as so critical for protecting the lower-earning spouse, that this fact alone may justify getting married. If the objective is to have enough money to live comfortably for the rest of both of your lives, then the person with the stronger earnings record will usually be well advised to get married and wait until age 70 to collect. Providing for the lower-earning spouse, in my opinion, should weigh heavily in the decision of when the spouse with the stronger earnings record should begin collecting Social Security benefits. It is not just an individual issue—it is a family issue.

Scenario 1: Married, Surviving Spouse Collects Survivor Benefit

Let's assume that the spouse with the stronger earnings record waits until age 70 to collect benefits, and their benefit grows to $4,000/month (close to the maximum in 2023). Let's assume the lower earning spouse has a benefit on their own lower earnings record of $1,000/month. The spouse with the stronger earnings record then dies. The surviving spouse, even though their benefit is only $1,000/month, can claim the full amount (which would be the $4,000/month), provided that the surviving spouse has reached full retirement age of 66 or 67, depending upon when they were born. Calculating the survivor benefit can be more complicated if the survivor hasn't reached full retirement age. There is a phaseout from the years 1955 through 1959 adding additional month(s) to reach your full retirement age. For those born in 1960 and later, the full retirement age is age 67. It is also more complicated if the deceased spouse claimed benefits before full retirement age.

The important thing to remember is that the spouse with the weaker earnings record, who is also likely the spouse that needs financial protection, will get at least a large portion of their spouse's Social Security if their spouse predeceases them, but not if they are not married.

Scenario 2: Unmarried, No Survivor Benefit for Surviving Partner

Same fact pattern as Scenario 1 but the couple in question is not married. Let's assume the same benefits: thelower-earner's benefit is $1,000/month and the higher-earning partner's is $4,000/month. Then the higher-earning partner dies. The surviving partner will continue to receive $1,000/month. The other partner's benefits stop when they die. No survivor benefit is paid to the surviving unmarried partner.

The potential for the lower earner to take a survivor benefit if the stronger earner dies first could mean the difference between being broke and being marginally okay (the difference between $1,000/month and $4,000/month), assuming that there are no other resources. This is especially true if there is a big difference between the higher earner's benefit and the lower earner's benefit. The issue of providing for the partner with the lower earnings record is critical. (

Living Spousal Benefits

A spousal benefit is a Social Security benefit paid to someone based upon their spouse's earning history while you are both alive. You can receive Social Security based upon your own earning history, or, if your spouse has a much higher earnings record than you do, you can choose to receive a spousal benefit (50% of your spouse's Primary Insurance amount) ÷ the amount they would be entitled to at full retirement age, which, for people born before 1954, is 66, if it is claimed at full retirement age. As stated above, there is a phaseout from years 1955 through 1959 adding additional month(s) to reach your full retirement age. For those born in 1960 and later, the full retirement age is age 67.

The important thing to remember is that the spouse with the weaker earnings record, who is also likely the spouse that needs financial protection, will get at least a large portion of their spouse's Social Security if their spouse predeceases them, but not if they are not married.

Thus, the lower wage earner can often collect a higher Social Security benefit based upon their spouse's benefit. The higher wage earner's monthly benefit is not affected in any way. The lower wage earner is eligible to collect more, simply because they are married. Generally, spousal benefits are available during a couple's joint lifetimes, and you have to have been married for at least one continuous year.

Consider an example. Sue and Mary are the same age (born before 1954) and they got married. Sue has a $4,000/month benefit at age 66 and she decides to take it then. Mary, her spouse, on her own earnings record, has a $1,500/month benefit at age 66. At age 66, Mary can collect a $2,000 ($4,000 times 50%) spousal benefit, instead of the $1,500/month benefit due Mary based on her own earnings record. In order to receive the spousal add-on, the spouse needs to have claimed their Social Security benefit. If Sue was deferring claiming her Social Security benefit until age 70, Mary would not be eligible to receive the spousal add-on until then.

Another way you can get your full spouse's benefit—even if you are under full retirement age— is if you care for your child who has a disability and if that child is entitled to receive benefits on your spouse's record.

I've mentioned elsewhere in this book that coordinating the timing of when you claim Social Security with Roth conversions can make a big difference in your long-term financial situation. For more about the various Social Security strategies, please download our best-selling Social Security book, *The $214,000 Mistake: How to Double Your Social Security & Maximize Your IRAs*, for free by going to **https://PayTaxesLater.com/Books/**.

In addition, since there is likely a child with a disability involved if you are reading this book, saving taxes and increasing Social Security benefits (which could impact the SSDI benefits) is even more important for your family.

Marriage May Be a Good Idea if You are Selling Your House

Another reason to get married and file jointly is if you are planning to sell your house for a significant gain. If you are married, you get a $500,000 exemption from your capital gain, but if you are single, the exemption is only $250,000. If you're going to sell your house and make a lot of money on the sale of the house, which would incur a higher capital gain, you are financially better off getting married. You must meet ownership and use tests and must not have excluded gain from another home in the past two years.

Tying the Knot or Not: Financial Considerations for Unmarried Couples

So, if financial considerations weigh into your decision to get married, does it make sense to get married? Now, don't get all excited about the federal estate tax because if you don't have more than seven million dollars, and are not likely to grow your estate to seven million dollars, the unlimited marital deduction for your estate may not be relevant for federal transfer tax purposes, but could be for state transfers tax or inheritance tax purposes.

For IRA and retirement plan owners, the financial implications of getting married are enormous. The ability to enjoy survivor and spousal benefits for Social Security can also make a big difference for couples where one member has a much higher monthly benefit than the other.

The Financial Downside of Getting Married

It sounds like I am pitching getting married for the money, and I am. But there are also financial reasons why you might NOT want to get married. The Tax Cuts and Jobs Act of 2017 attempted to adjust the tax brackets, deductions, and credits to eliminate any 'marriage penalty.' But they didn't fully eliminate the so-called marriage penalty.

If you and your spouse are both high-income earners, your income taxes could actually increase if you get married. The marriage penalty means that if you get married, you could end up paying more income taxes than both of you would have paid if you had both filed single, which is bad. On the flip side, there is also a marriage bonus, which could mean that you will pay less in taxes, which is good. This is most often the case when one member has a substantially higher income than the other one.

Besides the potential marriage penalty, there are potential financial disadvantages of getting married. I counseled one couple that is choosing not to get married now because the financially dependent partner can get cheap health insurance through the Affordable Health Care Act, (Obamacare) but would lose that opportunity if they got married. Their plan is to wait until the financially weaker spouse qualifies for Medicare and then get married. That might work out well, or it could be disastrous if the financially stronger spouse dies before they get married. Only time will tell if it was a "penny wise and pound foolish" decision.

For the purposes of this book and for what our CPAs do in our accounting practice, it is best to "run the numbers" to get a more accurate picture of the advantages and disadvantages of getting married.

After (or Before) You Say I Do, Do These Things

If you decide that the financial reasons—as well as the intangible relationship reasons—are on the side of marriage, here are some things you need to be sure to take care of.

1. Strongly consider getting a prenuptial agreement. Legal documents such as prenuptial agreements and other property agreements may be unpleasant, but are often necessary, particularly if you are marrying later in life. Besides setting out the division of property in the unhappy circumstance of a divorce, these agreements can also go a long way in easing fears for your children and grandchildren who may be concerned that the other spouse's family will inherit everything, leaving them high and dry.

   The psychological and financial misery of going through a drawn-out financial divorce settlement can make both of you miserable. Billy Crystal sums up the potential damage in the movie *When Harry Met Sally*:

   > *But you gotta know that sooner or later you're gonna be screaming at each other about who's gonna get this dish. This eight-dollar dish will cost you a thousand dollars in phone calls to the legal firm of That's Mine, This Is Yours.*

2. Update your wills, trusts, and beneficiary designations for IRAs and other retirement plans. Remember that the beneficiary designations on your IRAs and retirement plans—not the language of any trust or will—will govern who and how those plan assets will be disbursed at your death. Also, keep in mind *who gets what?* Usually, it will make more sense to leave the IRA to the dependent spouse or the child with a disability (if the child is qualified as an EDB) and the after-tax money to the heirs in a higher tax bracket. Running the numbers for your situation will help determine the best strategy.

3. Apply for spousal and survivor Social Security benefits when, after reviewing the entire picture, you and/or your trusted advisor feel it is appropriate.

Remember, this is a book about money, so this chapter has focused on the financial benefits of marriage. And these may be good enough reasons to tilt the scale in favor of marriage. But I implore you to consider choosing love above all as the real reason to marry.

KEY IDEAS

- Spouses (and children with disabilities who have qualified as EDBs) have more favorable laws to defer payments from an Inherited retirement plan (IRA, Roth IRA, etc.) than unmarried couples.

- Married couples can take advantage of the unlimited marital deduction for both federal and state estate, inheritance, and transfer taxes. Marriage also allows a couple to utilize both of their estate and gift tax exemptions.

- Spousal benefits for Social Security can be higher while both members are still living and for the survivor but only if the couple is married.

- Married couples can double the capital gains deduction on the sale of a house, from $250,000 to $500,000.

- That said, you should still check to see if there is a marriage penalty or marriage bonus for federal income tax purposes.

- It might not be prudent to get married if the dependent spouse is currently using Obamacare for their health insurance.

- Since there is likely a child with a disability involved, saving taxes and increasing Social Security benefits (which could impact the SSDI benefits for the child) is even more important for your family.

26

Life Insurance as an Estate Planning Tool

*"You can't put a value on a human life, but my wife's life
insurance company made a pretty fair offer."*

—Unknown Author

*For the purposes of this chapter, I am not writing about life insurance for a surviving
spouse or for minor children who will need support should a wage earner die
prematurely. In this chapter, we are talking about permanent life insurance that
guarantees a death benefit.*

*If you need to protect the income of one or two wage earners, the best way to do
this is usually with laddered term insurance, which I discuss in Chapter 2, **The
Accumulation Years: Fund Retirement Plans to the Maximum.***

Most of my clients would rather get a root canal than either talk about
life insurance or pay for life insurance premiums. I urge you to keep an open
data-driven mind for this chapter.

Life insurance in the context of this chapter is about preserving and transferring
wealth to the next two generations in the most tax-efficient manner possible. It
is really a variation of a gift. If you can't afford or are not willing to make a gift
to your children or grandchildren, you should skip this chapter.

If, on the other hand, there is sufficient money to make gifts, the gift of life
insurance should be considered for a portion of the total amount of gifts you
want to provide for your family.

Buying life insurance where you give up ownership of the policy is one of the
most tax- and cost-efficient methods of transferring wealth to your heirs.

Options for Buying Life Insurance

One way to buy a life insurance policy for you and your spouse is using a
classic technique known as a *pension rescue*. With a pension rescue, you cash in
a portion of your IRA, often one or two percent of the balance of the IRA, pay
the taxes on the distribution, and use the remainder to buy a life insurance policy.
Perhaps a Second-to-Die policy, or a policy with a long-term care or chronic
illness rider. I'll discuss both of these options below.

Many professionals have a lot of money in Traditional rather than Roth retirement plans. If this is also true for you, adding life insurance to your estate plan can get your beneficiaries more money and provide them with additional liquidity. Because life insurance proceeds are tax-free, a policy can provide much-needed cash not only to settle the estate but also to pay income taxes that will be due on accelerated Inherited Traditional IRA withdrawals. Without life insurance, your heirs may have to withdraw more money than required from the Inherited Traditional IRA just to pay the tax due on the transfer and withdrawals—leading to yet more taxes and forcing more and more money out of the tax-deferred environment. Life insurance could be a great solution. In addition, if you are paying the premiums from the proceeds of cashing in part of your IRA or retirement assets, you are reducing the amount of the Inherited IRA that is subject to the accelerated income tax.

We recommend combining life insurance and other techniques, like Roth IRA conversions and a variety of charitable giving techniques, including giving IRA and retirement plan money to charity at your death in the strategy known as *Who Gets What?* which is discussed in Chapter 19.

For now, however, I am talking about life insurance as a type of gift to your children. As I said at the beginning, if you don't think that you can afford to give your heirs a gift of any kind, you should not give them gifts, and you should not consider buying life insurance to make their situation easier.

How the SECURE Act Has Altered My Thinking on Life Insurance

Considering that several of the members of our accounting firm are licensed to sell life insurance, you may find it surprising that we have sold an incredibly small number of life insurance policies over the years.[1] One reason is that most clients, if they make gifts at all, prefer to take advantage of the first five gifting strategies mentioned in Chapter 23—an outright gift, a gift for a specific purpose, a gift to fund a retirement plan, a gift to fund an education, and/or a gift to an ABLE account. I was not opposed to life insurance, but I wasn't passionate about it.

I did recognize the value when we "ran the numbers" under the old law, but it wasn't one of the first things I would think about when optimizing a client's estate plan.

Since the passage of the SECURE Act, however, my thinking has shifted significantly in favor of life insurance. It isn't because life insurance is a much better

---

1 Life insurance can be offered by a member of Lange Life Care, LLC for those interested. These are not legal services. The protection of an attorney-client relationship does not exist with respect to insurance services.

deal than before the SECURE Act. It is because the stretch IRA was a reasonable choice. Now that the stretch IRA is mainly gone—for your children who do not qualify as EDBs—life insurance is a great partial solution, because dying with a large IRA is so unappealing. Even if your child has a disability and is able to qualify for the stretch IRA as an EDB, life insurance can also play an important role in your estate planning. It is a guaranteed investment that could at least partially fund financial security for your child. See Chapter 13, where we discuss the strategy of making a special needs trust for your child as the beneficiary of life insurance.

Be Conservative with the Amount of Insurance You Buy

If you decide an insurance solution should be part of your overall plan, I recommend that you be somewhat conservative in the amount of coverage you purchase so that you and your spouse will always be comfortable with the premium. As always, different situations require different solutions. In addition, life insurance isn't always a pure numbers decision.

Sometimes life insurance can be looked upon as a guaranteed investment that, given a normal or even long life, offers a great income-tax-free return on your investment. It is especially appropriate if you have a child with a disability who needs to receive a certain amount of money no matter what happens to the stock market.

You Can Often Feel You Can Afford to Spend More Money if You Have Life Insurance

One interesting aspect of purchasing life insurance is that for some clients, it frees up what they can spend. If you want your children to receive a certain minimal amount of money at your and/or your spouse's death, and you get life insurance for at least part of that need, it frees you up to spend more money now.

Since we have a daughter with a disability, my wife and I want to leave her enough money so that upon our deaths, she can maintain her standard of living and afford to pay the high costs she is either incurring now or can reasonably be anticipated to need for the rest of her life. In terms of investments, if you don't count the value of my business, we haven't hit that number. With the life insurance we have purchased, we can come a lot closer. My daughter's future insurance proceeds after our deaths gives us "permission" to spend more now.

As you would expect, we have a lot of life insurance, which alleviates our worries about our daughter's financial future, and allows us to enjoy a better lifestyle ourselves.

> Now that the stretch IRA is mainly gone—for your children who do not qualify as EDBs—life insurance is a great partial solution, because dying with a large IRA is so unappealing.

Nitty Gritty of the Insurance Cindy and I Have

Personally, I have a term policy on my life because my wife and daughter would need to replace my income if I died prematurely. I also have a combination life and Long-Term Care policy, as does my wife. (See below why I like that product and don't like traditional long-term care policies.) We have a Second-to-Die life insurance policy, as well. We have also converted most of our Traditional retirement plans to Roth IRAs or Roth 401(k)s and have most of our money invested in Dimensional Fund Advisors (DFA) enhanced index funds.

In addition, we have appropriate business, liability, car, and homeowner's insurance. Of course, we also have an umbrella policy.

Umbrella Policies

We have a $5,000,000 umbrella policy and I recommend you rethink your umbrella coverage. Assuming you have one, which you probably do, there is an excellent chance you are under-insured. The higher your net worth, the more umbrella insurance coverage is needed. The reason for this is that the world we live in is much more litigious than the world in which our parents lived. If you or a member of your household were to be involved in an at-fault automobile accident or if someone gets injured while on your property, the injured party could potentially see big dollar signs at your expense. The additional protection provided by a personal umbrella policy would cover not only the claim costs but any legal costs to defend the allegations, whether they are warranted or not. Purchasing your umbrella insurance coverage through either your automobile or homeowner's insurance company will often provide you with a policy discount. Even if you double the coverage—which I urge you to consider doing—the additional premiums will likely be just in the hundreds, not thousands of dollars per year.

Quick Get Enough Insurance Story

I met with an insurance guy regarding my business in 1995. He made a recommendation for fire, business interruption, flood, etc. Not giving it more than ten seconds thought, I said "Double it," meaning I wanted to double the coverage he was recommending.

We had a fire in our business on February 16, 1998. Doubling the coverage from the amount the insurance professionals recommended saved my you-know-what.

So, for what it is worth, I practice what I preach!

Life Insurance as Part of the Masterplan

Life insurance is no better now than it was before the SECURE Act. But it is an option to consider if the alternative is leaving your children a lot of money in a Traditional IRA, which will suffer massive income tax acceleration under the SECURE Act. The exception to this income tax acceleration is if the IRA money were to go to a child who is an eligible designated beneficiary because of their disability or a trust for the benefit for that child. Even in the circumstances of this exception, a life insurance gift is an option to consider in your Financial Masterplan.

Another important thing to consider is that different policies work better in different situations, even if the life insurance proceeds are identical.   Personal preferences for how and when you want your money distributed will also come into play.

In most cases you are the owner of your life insurance policy. You can use Lange's 'Cascading Beneficiary Plan' for the beneficiary of your life insurance policy, wherein you name a primary beneficiary of the life insurance, for example, your spouse, and then your child with a disability and/or other children as the secondary beneficiaries. If your spouse does not need the insurance proceeds, they can 'disclaim' the life insurance proceeds to the contingent beneficiaries.

Depending upon the size of your estate, you may want to make the owner and the beneficiary of the life insurance policy be an Irrevocable Life Insurance Trust (ILIT). This will remove the insurance proceeds from your estate for federal estate tax purposes. As always, we recommend consulting with a competent estate attorney before completing the decision of who owns the policy as well as completing the appropriate beneficiary designation forms.[2]

Second-to-Die Life Insurance

In the past, when recommending life insurance to help preserve an estate, we typically recommended a Second-to-Die policy for owners of large IRAs who could afford the premium.[3]

---

2   There is no solicitation being made for legal services by James Lange nor by Lange Legal Group, LLC.
3   Life insurance can be offered by a member of Lange Life Care, LLC for those interested. These are not legal services. The protection of an attorney-client relationship does not exist with respect to insurance services.

A Second-to-Die policy "matures" as the insurance people say, upon the death of the second spouse. The premiums are substantially lower than individual policies on one or both spouses because the life insurance company won't have to pay the proceeds until both spouses are deceased.

In the case of a married couple, the likelihood is that one spouse will outlive their life expectancy. Therefore, when determining the appropriate mortality cost assumptions, this likelihood is baked into the cost structure and reduces the overall premiums required.

Also, with the advent of Covid and the prolonged lowered interest rate trends, the premiums have been increasing. Quite a few insurance companies have reduced the attractiveness of the 100% guaranteed product or reduced the product contractual guarantees. We will see where premiums go now that interest rates, at least as we go to press, have risen considerably.

Most people who are considering this type of product are over age 55, and often age 70 or older. Obviously your and your spouse's overall health can affect how the policy is rated from a pricing standpoint. Having the ability to go to multiple insurance companies to obtain the best possible rates has the potential to save thousands of premium dollars.

Many life insurance agents are not fans of Second-to-Die policies and recommend other wealth transfer insurance policies such as a whole life insurance policy from which you can borrow. I won't say some of the other life insurance strategies aren't sound. I will say I prefer Second-to-Die permanent policies because it is often the best deal in terms of the amount of premiums paid, over time, compared to the death benefit received. Also, these policies are pretty simple.

Another reason I like Second-to-Die is because it is a very common type of policy and virtually every major insurance carrier offers it, so it is easy to obtain meaningful competitive quotes. We will cover the best way to receive a competitive quote near the end of this chapter.

I usually like insurance for the death benefit, not to be used as your personal bank which I know is another popular insurance strategy. If you are going to use a policy for a death benefit and want to keep your premiums as low as possible and the death benefit as high as possible, a Second-to-Die policy is often the best solution.

If there is concern about the surviving spouse paying future premiums after one of the spouses dies, a popular design has been to pay the premiums over a limited number of years, such as 15 or 20 years. By doing so, the future pressure of making premium payments in the latter years is eliminated. This is especially important if there is concern about the mental deterioration of either of the spouses, as the premiums are paid up on the policy, and the policy remains in force. The other advantage of using this paid-up premium strategy is that the total premiums paid in your lifetime are fixed, as ongoing premium payments are eliminated. With a traditional full-pay policy, the longer you live, the more premiums you pay.

That said, I am generally a cheapskate and usually prefer the smallest premium with the biggest death benefit, even though that usually means paying a premium for the rest of your and your spouse's lives.

Quantifying the Benefits of Life Insurance

After running the numbers using current tax laws, the results of buying a Second-to-Die policy are impressive.

If income tax rates go up in the future, buying life insurance will work out even better for your children. The reason is the children will be getting a tax-free inheritance, rather than inheriting a bigger Traditional IRA, which will be subject to the ten-year rule for income tax acceleration and, potentially, to inheritance taxes. Of course, if the beneficiary is a child who qualifies as an EDB due to their disability or chronic illness or SNT for the benefit of that child, the traditional retirement plan could be stretched over their lifetime.

Another major advantage is the life insurance proceeds are guaranteed. They are not subject to market fluctuations or interest rates.

Here's an example. Let's say that you buy a $1 million Second-to-Die life insurance policy, and the premiums are $20,000 every year. Fifteen years later, both you and your spouse have passed. You've paid $300,000 in premiums, but your children are going to get a check from your insurance company for $1 million. That's a $700,000 difference—that is income, inheritance, and capital gain tax-free.

Since the SECURE Act, we are also examining policies on the life of one spouse. In some cases, it can be beneficial to make a Roth IRA conversion with the insurance payout after the first spouse dies. Depending on the situation, this may be better than doing Roth IRA conversions now and buying a Second-to-Die life insurance policy.

A key consideration is that you may file a joint tax return for the year that the first spouse dies. So, you could take advantage of the lower married rates on just the year of death of the first spouse. Following that year, unless you qualify for another type of filing status, the survivor will have to file as a single taxpayer which have much higher tax rates.

However, a Second-to-Die policy is usually my starting point, assuming both spouses are insurable and want to pass tax-free money to their heirs.

Let's Look at an Example

Let's go back to our bread-and-butter example, Second-to-Die. We will compare two families with identical finances, interest rates, taxes, etc. The only difference is one buys a million dollar Second-to-Die policy, and the other does not. Using the reasonable assumptions detailed in the Appendix, the children of the couple with insurance will have $2,000,000 more over their lifetime than the children of the couple who didn't buy life insurance.

Why the big difference? If you don't buy life insurance, your beneficiaries are forced to pay taxes on an Inherited Traditional IRA within ten years after the

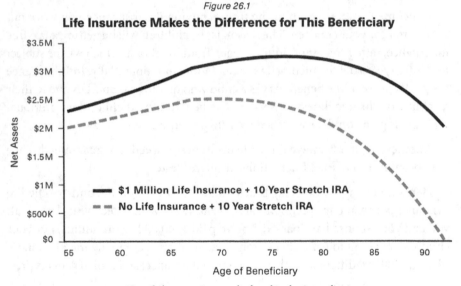

Figure 26.1

Life Insurance Makes the Difference for This Beneficiary

Detailed assumptions can be found in the Appendix.

second death, a devastating effect. Figure 26.1 shows that buying life insurance can go a long way toward minimizing those effects and preserving your wealth for future generations. Of course, in the scenario where you don't buy the insurance and the beneficiary is an EDB who can stretch the Inherited IRA over their lifetime, then not buying the insurance would be more favorable than in this example.

When is the best time to buy? A Chinese proverb says the best time to plant a tree is twenty years ago. The second-best time is now.

If you think buying life insurance might make sense for you, you should look into it as soon as possible. The generally accepted rule for life insurance is to buy it while you are still insurable. Future health problems may cause insurance companies to reject you or rate your health so badly that the premium will be too expensive to consider. I had a client who really wanted to buy a second-to-die policy but decided to wait until he lost some weight to try to get a better rate. He never lost the weight, and he developed cancer and became uninsurable.

An Alternative to Long-Term Care Insurance (LTC)

As long as we are talking about insurance, I would like to share my thoughts on long-term care (LTC) insurance. Simply put, I am not generally a fan of LTC. I am licensed to sell LTC but haven't sold a traditional LTC insurance policy for probably 20 years or more.

A significant problem I see with LTC is that the premiums are not guaranteed, and buyers often suffer huge increases after the purchase. After the inevitable price increase, you face the option of dropping the policy in which case all the previous premiums paid go out the window, or you agree to the higher rates and end up with a higher premium.

Another problem is that if you die in your boots without the need for long-term care, you have paid all those premiums and received no benefit other than peace of mind.

An effective alternative to a traditional LTC policy is a combination LTC and life insurance policy. This type of product is typically called a "linked benefit plan." Technically, this is a life insurance policy with an LTC or Chronic Illness rider.

Here's an example scenario subject to exclusions. Suppose you purchase a $500,000 combination LTC and life insurance policy. If you are fortunate enough not to require long-term care, your heirs will receive the full $500,000 death benefit when you die. If, on the other hand, you need $250,000 of care, the policy will cover your care, and your heirs will be paid the remaining $250,000 upon your death. Finally, let's say you need $600,000 worth of care. In this case, the insurance company would pay the first $500,000, and you would be responsible for the other $100,000.

Another nice feature of this combination policy is that LTC disbursements are tax-free under current law. And since it is a life insurance policy with an LTC rider, it will likely be much easier for you to qualify for coverage at a more favorable rating than a traditional LTC policy.

Another important consideration is that many carriers offer complete waiver of premiums for all premiums due after an LTC claim is approved. This obviously will have a dramatic effect on the long-term cost of the product. I believe this is one of the most important product features required when choosing a product. A more detailed discussion of the combination LTC and life insurance policy is a different topic for a different day, but it is something I prefer for most clients over a traditional LTC policy.

A favorable provision included in SECURE Act 2.0 was to permit retirement plan owners (401(k) plans, IRAs, etc.) to withdraw penalty-free 10% of their account balance up to $2,500 annually beginning in 2026, adjusted for inflation, towards the payment of a traditional quality long-term care policy. The provision does not apply to a life insurance policy with a chronic care rider.

You can do what you were planning to do anyway which is not get life insurance because you don't like life insurance or the insurance industry. You can feel that way and be a very nice person and you are actually in the majority. I get it. Life insurance is only one of many tax reducing strategies. So, if you don't like insurance, fine, but then it is even more imperative to consider and implement other tax reduction strategies.

Getting the Best Deal on Life Insurance

Let's assume for discussion's sake you have decided on a Second-to-Die policy and the amount of insurance you want. The amount you choose might vary depending on the premium but assume you have at least a range in mind. Let's also assume that the primary goal is a low premium and a high death benefit. How can you get the best deal?

Since this is a competitive and fluid marketplace, it is essential when looking to purchase this product that you use a broker who represents a wide variety of insurance companies and is unbiased about the selected product. The most efficient way to do this is to work with an ethical insurance broker who has access to many insurance company products.

Yes, there may be some differences in premiums with different companies at different times. The biggest difference in the premium is likely going to be determined by the insurance company's analysis of your life expectancy based on an application you must fill out, a paramedical examination, and their review of your medical records. Since most people who are considering this type of product are over age 55, overall health can affect how the policy is rated from a pricing standpoint.

You would think in this day and age there would be whiz bang computer programs that all the big life insurance companies would use—pop in your stats and out comes their assessment of your life expectancy. That isn't the case at all. In reality, your information will be given to one of the underwriters who work for the company. The underwriter then consults with medical experts and actuaries. Obviously, opinions will vary greatly among insurance companies.

To oversimplify, you could be rated as uninsurable, standard, preferred, or super-preferred. Obviously, the better the rating, the lower the premium. In a Second-to-Die policy, it is usually the woman's health that is more important because she typically has a longer life expectancy simply because she is a woman.

But here is the kicker. Even with identical applications and health records, you could receive significantly different quotes from different companies. Since it is in effect a generic product, usually assuming the company is rated at least AA or better by Standard and Poor's, if you get one company that offers a substantially lower premium, that company is the obvious choice. Comparing multiple insurance companies to find the best possible rates has the potential to save thousands of dollars on your premium payments.

I have witnessed enormous disparities in quotes, and the insurance broker we work with usually recommends the company with the lowest premium.

In one case, a couple who both had health issues— the husband had a heart condition and the wife had several health problems—applied for a $1M Second-to-Die policy. The rating came back as standard for him and preferred for her. The premium was much lower than I expected.

After being presented with the information, the clients said they wanted to get a $2M policy instead. I hesitated. I feared that if they didn't take the $1M and asked for $2M, the insurance company would take a closer look, realize they made a mistake, and give them a much higher premium per million. I recommended the client take the $1M policy and apply for another million. That is what they did, and the second quote came in much higher, so the client just kept the one policy.

As mentioned earlier, the best way to buy life insurance is by using a knowledgeable and ethical broker who has the ability to shop the policy to a number of potential insurance companies. At this point, there is no such thing as "no-load life insurance." It would be extremely time-consuming for you to try to do this on your own and, in the end, you wouldn't save any money.[4]

4   Life insurance can be offered by a member of Lange Life Care, LLC for those interested. These are not legal services. The protection of an attorney-client relationship does not exist with respect to insurance services. There is no solicitation being made for legal services by James Lange nor by Lange Legal Group, LLC.

Finally, one more tip. The most important factor in the premiums is obviously the type of insurance and the age of the insured. But the medical records and the physical are also critical. Here is what I would recommend for your physical. For most policies, a nurse will come to your house or office, ask some questions, draw blood, do a few other non-invasive tests and report back to the company. It is obviously in your interest to look as healthy as possible to the insurance company. I recommend you schedule your physical first thing in the morning. After your evening meal the night before the exam, don't eat anything or drink anything except water. Without getting into the science behind this recommendation, it could potentially result in a lower quote.

Also, we have found many people automatically assume they cannot obtain life insurance because of a pre-existing medical condition. This may or may not be the case. We have found that often we can informally underwrite without an exam to determine your insurability on a confidential basis. Since this is an 'informal' process, any underwriting results will not become public record and will be held in strict confidence. This will keep your information from being reported to the Medical Information Bureau (MIB) which could possibly negatively impact your insurability in the future. MIB is a membership group owned by insurance companies designed to protect the insurance companies, policyholders, and applicants from attempts to conceal or omit information material to underwriting life and health insurance. Once you receive an informal offer from an insurance company, the majority of the time the offer is honored even after you take the physical exam so long as there is not a material change in your health.

Policy Exit Strategies

In the event you cannot afford your life insurance coverage or decide your life insurance needs have changed, it is important to understand you have options to receive some value out of your policy versus just cancelling your policy. Below is a list of these options:

- **Reduce the Face Amount of the Policy**—Depending upon the type of policy you purchased, you have the option to reduce the coverage and pay less in premiums.

- **Purchase Paid-Up Insurance**—If your policy has cash surrender value, which some do and some don't, you may have the option of reducing the death benefit and using policy values to maintain a reduced amount of coverage for the rest of your life.

- **Sell the Policy to a Third-Party Institutional Investor** (Life Settlement Viatical)—There are institutional investors willing to purchase your policy at older ages depending upon your determined life expectancy at the time of purchase. This has become an increasingly popular option and is deserving of exploration in the event you want to terminate your policy in the future. Again, we recommend using an unbiased, ethical insurance broker to analyze this option for you.

- **Tax-Free Exchange for a Longevity Annuity** –This is often my favorite, but it is a rarely used solution. You may be able to exchange the cash value of a life insurance policy you no longer want for a longevity annuity.

KEY IDEAS

- Life insurance offers a tax- and cost-efficient method of transferring wealth to your heirs.

- Depending upon the circumstances, you may want a term policy, and/or combination life and LTC policy, and/or a Second-to-Die life insurance policy.

- By using a guaranteed death-benefit policy, you will have a guaranteed rate of return and assets leverage versus equities which will fluctuate with the market.

- Using a linked benefit policy to pay for LTC and chronic care expenses on a tax-free basis is much more tax-efficient than using other types of assets.

- Be conservative in the amount of life insurance that you buy so that you and your spouse will always be comfortable with the premium.

- Life insurance can be a great hedge against future tax increases on IRAs, especially in light of the elimination of the Stretch IRA under the SECURE Act.

- An informal underwriting process is worth pursuing when medical conditions exist.

Key Ideas continue on the following page.

KEY IDEAS
(continued)

- Consider policy exit strategies before cancelling your life insurance policy.

- You can do what you were planning to do anyway which is not get insurance because you don't like life insurance or the insurance industry. But in this case, you need to implement other tax-saving strategies, so your heirs are not hit with huge—and largely avoidable—tax bills.

27

More is Better:
The Benefits of Combined Strategies

"The whole is greater than the sum of its parts."

—Aristotle

We have presented a myriad of strategies for savvy retirement and estate planning, tax savings, and investing. Rarely will one strategy address all the issues. And despite what some advisors might tell you, there is no one-size-fits-all solution.

We have found that the key to truly successful comprehensive planning only surfaces when we combine strategies that we customize to each client.

The United States has enacted laws that provide enormous rewards for implementing tax-savvy strategies. Let's look at one dramatic combination: Roth conversions and life insurance.

Combine Roth IRA Conversions and Life Insurance

This figure compares two families with identical resources. One family makes a series of Roth IRA conversions and buys life insurance. The other family makes neither any Roth IRA conversions nor buys life insurance. The figure shows the trajectory of wealth over the life of the child. The child of the family who made the optimal series of Roth IRA conversions and bought life insurance has $7 million when the child beneficiary is in his eighties, and the child of the family that bought neither life insurance nor did Roth IRA conversions is broke at the same point in time.

Figure 29.1 literally blew me away when I saw it. It seemed too good to be true. It categorically quantifies the benefits of combining Roth IRA conversions (done over several years) and life insurance. Please note in this example we are assuming only a 10-year stretch of the Inherited IRA. (If you leave your retirement plan to a child who is an EDB due to their disability or chronic illness, they would be able to stretch the retirement plan over their lifetime. For this case the results of the analysis would be different.)

Combining multiple strategies allows you to create even greater wealth to enhance the financial security of your entire family. The stakes are especially high

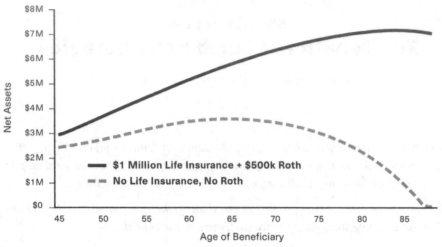

Figure 27.1

Combine Life Insurance and Roth Conversions to Protect Heirs from The SECURE Act Taxes*

Detailed assumptions can be found in the Appendix.

when you have a child with a disability, especially when that disability makes it difficult or impossible for your child to work and support themselves.

Roth IRA conversions, Lange's Cascading Beneficiary Plan (LCBP), life insurance, low-cost enhanced index funds, asset location, and other strategies can be used individually in your retirement and estate plan to benefit you and your heirs. We don't stop there. We combine Roth IRA conversions, optimized Social Security strategies, enhanced low-cost index fund investing, gifting, "who gets what" analysis, and our favorite estate plan, Lange's Cascading Beneficiary Plan. This has been very successful for most married couples who have children only from that marriage (we have other solutions for blended families and unmarried couples).

The Challenge of Running the Numbers

In this example, we combined life insurance and Roth IRA conversions. We usually arrive at the best solution, however, by combining a number of different strategies after "running the numbers."[1] One of the reasons that running the

1   Please note that if you engage Lange Accounting Group, LLC for our Financial Masterplan service or receive Financial Masterplan services as part of our assets-under-management arrangement with Lange Financial Group, LLC, these services are provided by employees in their capacity as CPAs and are not legal services. The protection of the attorney-client relationship does not exist with respect to these accounting and asset management services. There is no solicitation for legal services being made by me, James Lange, nor by Lange Legal Group, LLC.

numbers is so hard is that the person running the numbers must decide, in consultation with the client, which strategies to run and how to combine different strategies. Then even if you know which strategies you are going to combine, the next questions are, "How much of each? How big of a Roth IRA conversion should you make and when?" How much life insurance, if any, should you buy? And many of these calculations are synergistic, meaning that what you do with one variable will have an impact on a different variable, but potentially using both strategies in concert will confer more advantages than using both strategies separately. The matrix is very complicated.

Any examples are meant only to illustrate the potential value of combining multiple strategies.

We could present an array of successful strategy combination plans—but as mentioned earlier—each person's circumstances are unique, so we cannot say any one particular combination will work for everyone. But Figure 27.1 makes abundantly clear that there is an enormous difference between optimal and mediocre planning.

The overarching message of this book is that *doing nothing*—when you know there are so many great strategies to protect and secure your financial future and the future of your heirs, especially if one of the heirs is a child with a disability or chronic illness—*shouldn't be an option*. Please consider combining strategies to have the biggest impact for yourself and your family. We offer these roadmaps to our clients, and many are hundreds of thousands of dollars better off because they listened, learned, and acted.

Please see the section titled "*When your Child has a Disability…Save More, Have More, and Leave More to Your Child in a Tax-Advantaged Manner that Preserves Government Benefits! The Lange Edge: A Truly Integrated Long-Term Financial Masterplan for Parents Who Want to Ensure That Their Child Is Financially Secure for Life --- Even After Mom and Dad Are Gone*" at the end of the book to see how you could work with me and my team to get the most out of your retirement assets.

KEY IDEAS

- Roth IRA conversions, **Lange's Cascading Beneficiary Plan (LCBP)**, charitable remainder trusts, gifting, optimized Social Security strategies, "who gets what" analysis, low-cost enhanced index funds and life insurance can be used individually in your estate plan to benefit you and your heirs. By combining two or more of these strategies, you can create even greater financial security that will benefit you and your heirs for generations to come.

- There is a phenomenal difference between optimal and mediocre planning. Strive for optimal planning.

Glossary

Individual Retirement Accounts (IRAs): I recognize that IRAs are only one type of retirement account that generally consists of funds that have not yet been subject to income taxes but will eventually. Of course, there are many other types of retirement plans such as 403(b)s, 401(k)s, 401(a)s, 457(b)s, etc. that in many ways are quite similar to IRAs, at least for tax purposes. For convenience, though I will sometimes distinguish between the different type of retirement plans, I will refer to all these plans as IRAs or IRAs and retirement plans.

401(k)/Roth 401(k) Plan: A tax advantaged defined contribution retirement plan offered by many employers, typically in the private sector. Depending on the rules established by the employer, employees can add to their account by making Traditional or Roth contributions.

403(b)/Roth 403(b) Plan: Also called a tax-sheltered annuity or TSA plan, a 403(b) is a type of defined contribution plan offered by public schools and certain tax-exempt organizations. Depending on the rules established by the employer, employees can add to their account by making Traditional or Roth contributions.

After-Tax Contribution: Money paid into a retirement account after income tax has already been deducted.

Annuitization: The process of converting an annuity investment into a series of periodic income payments.

Annuitization [method]: An annuity distribution structure that defines the periodic income payments that will be paid over the life of the annuitant (or annuitants), or for a specified period of time.

Annuity: A contract offered by a life insurance company that requires the insurer to make payments to you, either immediately or at some point in the future.

Annuity, fixed: A contract issued by a life insurance company that pays a guaranteed rate of interest on the owner's contributions.

Annuity, immediate: A contract between an individual and an insurance company that, in exchange for an up-front premium, pays the owner a guaranteed income immediately.

Annuity, joint life: An annuity payment agreement that guarantees an income for the life of the annuity owner and a survivor, generally their spouse.

Annuity, nonqualified: A contract issued by an insurance company that is purchased with contributions made on an after-tax and non-Roth basis.

Nonqualified annuities can be used when a participant in a qualified retirement plan has contributed the maximum amount to the plan that is permitted by the IRS. Contributions are not tax-deductible, and annuitized payments are partially taxable.

Annuity, single life: An annuity payment agreement that guarantees an income for the life of the annuity owner only.

Annuity, variable: A type of annuity that can rise or fall in value depending on the performance of its underlying investment portfolio.

Defined Benefit Plan: Commonly called a "pension plan," this is a type of retirement plan in which the employer contributes money according to a formula described in the plan documents that will allow them to provide a promised monthly benefit to the employee at retirement. The amount of the benefit is determined by a formula that considers the number of years of service, salary and age, and the employer is responsible for paying the benefit regardless of the performance of the investments in the plan.

Defined Contribution Plan: A type of retirement plan that allows the employee or employer to contribute to an account on the employee's behalf. Depending on the plan rules, employee contributions can be made on a Traditional or Roth basis. As of this writing, all employer matching contributions must be made on a Traditional basis.

Direct Rollover: A method of transferring a retirement account from one custodian to another, during which the account owner takes possession of the money. The account owner is responsible for depositing the funds into a new retirement account within 60 days. In general, there is only one direct rollover permitted every 365 days from the same IRA and the IRA to which the distribution was rolled over regardless of the number of IRAs you own. The limit will apply by aggregating all of your individual IRAs, including SEP and SIMPLE IRAs as well as Traditional and Roth IRAs. This means all of your IRAs are treated as one IRA for purposes of the limit.

Guarantee Period: An annuitization option that allows the contract owner to receive income over a specific period of time, such as ten years or over a lifetime.

Mutual Fund: An investment vehicle that consists of a portfolio of stocks, bonds, or other securities. It allows small investors access to diversified, professionally managed portfolios at a low cost.

Non-qualified Retirement Plan: A retirement plan that falls outside of the Employee Retirement Income Security Act (ERISA) guidelines, such as a deferred-compensation plan offered to executives.

Qualified Retirement Plan: A retirement plan that meets the requirements of IRS Code Section 401(a) and is therefore eligible to receive certain tax benefits, such as a 403(b) or 401(k) plan.

Roth Contribution: A contribution made to a retirement plan that is not tax-deductible but is generally tax-free when withdrawn if certain conditions are met.

SERS (State Employees Retirement System): A defined benefit pension plan that covers employees of many state-owned universities.

Subaccounts: Investment options that are available within variable annuities, including CREF, that are similar to mutual funds, in that they have specific investment objectives and may result in a higher rate of return than fixed annuities.

Traditional Contribution: A contribution that can be made to a retirement plan before federal and municipal taxes are deducted, assuming certain rules are met. Withdrawals are taxable, and plan owners are generally required to start withdrawing money at age 72, 73 or 75 depending upon your year of birth

Trustee-to-Trustee Transfer: Our preferred method for transferring a retirement account from one trustee to another. The financial institution holding your IRA makes the payment directly to another IRA or retirement plan. The account owner never takes possession of the money.

Appendix

The assumptions used in the Figures presented in this book are as follows:

Figure 1.1: Tax-Deferred Savings Build Wealth

1. 7% rate of return.
2. Annual salary to age 67 was $100,000.
3. Social Security at age 67 was $30,000 + spousal of $15,000.
4. Annual contributions to retirement plans were $12,000.
5. Annual spending was $80,000; $70,000 after retirement.

Figure 1.2: Spend the Right Money First

1. Investor retires at age 65 with $1.1 million in qualified retirement accounts.
2. Assumes annual Social Security income of $25,000 + spousal of $12,500.
3. 24% ordinary tax rates.
4. Beginning annual spending of $84,000; adjusted for inflation annually by 3.5%.
5. 6.5% rate of return.
6. Actual dollars.
7. No state or inheritance tax is factored into analysis.

Figure 2.1: Retirement Plans and Tax-Deferred Savings vs. After-Tax Accumulations

1. Investment rate of return is 6% including 30% ordinary income and 70% capital appreciation with a 15% portfolio turnover rate.
2. Mr. Pay Taxes Later contributes $8,000 per year to his pre-tax retirement savings plan. Mr. Pay Taxes Now invests $6,080 per year (24% less due to income taxes). Both amounts are indexed for 3% annual raises, starting at age 30 until age 70.
3. Starting at age 72, spending from both investors' accounts is equal to the RMDs from Mr. Pay Taxes Later's retirement plan, less related income taxes.
4. Mr. Pay Taxes Later withdraws only the RMD, pays the 24% income tax due on his distribution, and spends the rest. Mr. Pay Taxes Now

spends the same amount plus he pays income taxes due on his interest, dividends, and realized capital gains.

5. This figure does not take into account the additional monies earned if Mr. Pay Taxes Later invested the 24% tax savings into an investment account.

6. Ordinary income tax rates are 24%.

7. Capital gains tax rates are 15%.

8. Dividends are taxed as qualified dividends at the capital gains tax rate.

9. AGI is assumed to be less than $340,000 and there is no state income tax.

Figure 2.2: **Retirement Assets Plus an Employer Match vs. After-Tax Accumulations**

1. Investment rate of return is 6% including 30% ordinary income and 70% capital appreciation with 15% portfolio turnover rate.

2. Retirement savings of $8,000 per year.

3. After-tax savings of $7,000 per year.

4. Both amounts are indexed for 3% annual raises, starting at age 30 until age 70.

5. RMDs from retirement accounts start at age 72.

6. After-tax funds fully depleted at age 84 when retirement accounts still have $5,446,284 remaining.

7. After-tax accumulation withdrawals reduced by tax = 74% of retirement distributions.

8. Ordinary income tax rates are 24%.

9. Capital gains tax rates are 15%.

10. Employer match is 100%.

Figure 3.5: **Roth IRA Savings vs. Traditional IRA Savings**

1. Contributions to a Roth IRA are made in the amount of $7,000 per year, beginning in 2022, for a 55-year-old investor, for 11 years until he reaches age 65.

2. Contributions to a regular deductible IRA are made in the amount of $7,000 per year by a different 55-year-old investor, for 11 years until he reaches age 65. This investor's IRA contribution creates an income tax deduction for him of 24 %, or $1,680.

I will give the best-case scenario and say that this investor did not spend his tax savings. Instead, he invested his tax savings into his after-tax investment account and did not spend it.

3. The investment rates of return on the Traditional IRA, the Roth IRA and the after-tax investment accounts are all 6% per year.

4. For the after-tax monies, the rate of return includes 70% capital appreciation, a 15% portfolio turnover rate (such that much of the appreciation is not immediately taxed), 15% dividends, and 15% ordinary interest income.

5. Ordinary income tax rates are 24% for all years.

6. Tax rates on realized capital gains are 15%.

7. Beginning at age 72, the RMDs from the traditional IRA are reinvested into the after-tax savings account.

8. The balances reflected in the graphs reflect spending power, which is net of an income tax allowance of 24% on the remaining Traditional IRA balance. If the full amount was actually withdrawn in one year, however, the tax bracket may be even higher and make the Roth IRA appear more favorable.

Figure 4.1: Roth 401(k) Savings vs. Traditional 401(k) Savings – RMD is Spent Annually-Lower Income Taxpayer

1. Contributions to a Roth 401(k) and Traditional 401(k) are $27,000 for 11 years from age 55 to age 65, until he retires at age 66. This investor's IRA contribution creates an income tax deduction for him of 24%, or $6,480.

2. I will give the best-case scenario and say that this investor did not spend his tax savings. Instead, he invested his tax savings into his after-tax investment account and did not spend it.

3. The investment rates of return on the Traditional 401(k), the Roth 401(k) and the after-tax investment accounts are all 6% per year.

4. 24% ordinary incremental tax rate during his working years.

5. 24% ordinary incremental tax rate during his retirement years.

6. Capital gains tax rates are 18%.

Figure 4.2: Roth 401(k) Savings vs. Traditional 401(k) Savings –
RMD is Spent Annually-Higher Income Tax Bracket

1. Contributions to a Roth 401(k) and Traditional 401(k) are $27,000 for 11 years from age 55 to age 65, until he retires at age 66. This investor's IRA contribution creates an income tax deduction for him of 37%, or $9,990.

2. I will give the best-case scenario and say that this investor did not spend his tax savings. Instead, he invested his tax savings into his after-tax investment account and did not spend it.

3. The investment rates of return on the Traditional 401(k), the Roth 401(k) and the after-tax investment accounts are all 6% per year.

4. 37% ordinary incremental tax rate during his working years.

5. 37% ordinary incremental tax rate during his retirement years.

6. Capital gains tax rates are 18.8%.

Figure 5.1: Benefits of Spending After-Tax Savings Before
Traditional Retirement Plans

1. Both Mr. Pay Taxes Now and Mr. Pay Taxes Later start from an identical position in 2022. They are both 65 years old and both have $300,000 in after-tax funds and $1,100,000 in pre-tax retirement funds.

2. Both Mr. Pay Taxes Now and Mr. Pay Taxes Later receive $25,000 per year in Social Security income.

3. The investment rates of return on all investment accounts are 6.5% per year.

4. Spending is $86,000 annually, after paying income taxes.

5. Income tax assumptions include ordinary income and capital gains tax rates established by the Tax Cuts and Jobs Act of 2017 and subsequent tax laws. State income taxes are ignored.

6. Capital gains tax rates are 15%.

7. Actual dollars.

8. No state or inheritance tax is factored into this analysis.

Figure 9.1: Old Law for IRA Distributions: Old Law – Inherited IRA
Distributed Over Lifetime

1. $1,000,000 inherited at age 45.

2. 7% rate of return.

3. 3.5% rate of inflation.

Figure 9.2: IRA Distributed Under the SECURE Act: SECURE Act - Inherited IRA Distributed Over 10 Years

1. $1,000,000 inherited at age 45.

2. 7% rate of return.

3. Annual distributions of $142,500 with balance fully distributed within 10 years.

Figure 10.1: Impact of The SECURE Act – Ten Year Distribution

1. Child inherits $1 million IRA (adjusted to purchasing power) at age 45 and earns salary of $100,000 annually increasing at 3.5%.

2. Child retires at age 67 and receives $40,000 in Social Security income annually.

3. 7% rate of return.

4. Expenses are $90,000 and increase by 3.5% annually.

5. Inherited IRA annual distributions of $147,000.

Figure 10.2: Grandchild Inherits the IRA

1. Grandchild inherits the IRA at age 11 and pays college tuition of $60,000 for four years from proceeds of IRA.

2. During his/her working years, he/she earns $80,000 increased annually at 3.5%.

3. The grandchild retires at age 67 and receives $40,000 in Social Security income annually.

4. Expenses are $80,000 and are adjusted by 3.5% annually.

5. Rate of return is 7%.

Figure 11.1: Benefit for an Eligible Designated Beneficiary Inheriting a Roth IRA with Lifetime Stretch vs. Inheriting a Traditional IRA with 10-Year Stretch

1. Starting balances: $65,000 after-tax investments; $250,000 Traditional IRA in 1998.

2. 28% income tax rate on distributions for parent; 15% for disabled child.

3. 28% Roth conversion tax rate (1998) - $249,000 Roth conversion done in 1998.

4. 15% tax on growth of after-tax investments.

5. Distributions are not spent by parent.

6. 6.5% rate of return (3.5% inflation).

7. Parent converts Traditional to Roth in 1998 - $249,000 (parent age 41; child age 2).

8. Parent dies at 85 in year 2041 when disabled child is age 46.

9. Figure shows child stretches retirement plan for 40 years when child is age 86.

10. Annual expenses for child after parent dies = $275,000, indexed by 3.5% annually for inflation.

11. Maximum 401(k) contributions by parent in years 1998 – 2026 (age 70).

12. Maximum IRA contributions by parent and spouse in years 1998 – 2026 (age 70).

13. We do not include any government benefits the child has received already or may receive in the future.

14. In year 2042, when the child is age 46, the child will pay his/her expenses using inheritance.

15. Since this is 20 years from now, we used $275,000 in annual expenses for the disabled child which equates to $138,200 in today's dollars or $11,500/month.

16. Inheritance taxes, estate taxes, and any state income tax on a Roth conversion have not been included in the analysis as Pennsylvania does not tax retirement distributions.

Figure 11.2: **EDB Child with An Inherited Stretch Roth IRA vs. Traditional IRA**

1. 6.5% rate of return.

2. Traditional IRA assets = $500,000 + $152,000 after-tax dollars at death.

3. Roth IRA assets = $557,000 + $0 in after-tax dollars at death.

4. Owner dies age 85.

5. Child inherits at age 54.

6. In *"inflation-adjusted"* dollars.

7. Tax rates = per AGI.

8. Child Social Security = $25,000 (plus 3% inflation).

9. Expenses = $103,000 [18 years from now (plus 3.5% inflation) which is less than $4,650/month in today's dollars].

10. Child with Traditional IRA runs out of money when he is age 88.

11. Child with Roth IRA has money through age 100.

Figure 16.1: Original IRA Owner after Roth Conversions

1. 7.5% rate of return.

2. 2.5% rate of inflation.

3. Inflation-adjusted dollars.

4. At age 65, IRA value is $1 million.

5. At age 65, other assets are $500,000.

6. Roth Case: Annual $175,000 Roth conversions for 5 years.

7. Each spouse earns Social Security income of $37,356.

8. Two-life pension of $50,000.

9. Annual living expenses are $125,000.

10. First spouse dies at age 80.

11. Second spouse dies at age 90.

Figure 16.2: Child Inherits Roth IRA vs. Traditional IRA after The SECURE Act

1. 7.5% rate of return.

2. 2.5% rate of inflation

3. Inflation-adjusted dollars.

4. Child's Social Security income is $25000.

5. Child's annual living expenses are $150,000.

6. Bump is end of 10 years when Inherited IRA must be closed.

Figure 26.1: Life Insurance Makes the Difference for This Beneficiary

1. 7% rate of return.

2. 3.5% rate of inflation.

3. $1 million life insurance policy.

4. Parents pay $22,000 annual premium on second-to-die policy at age 62 forward.

5. At age 66, parents have IRA balance of $1.5 million and after-tax savings of $500,000.

6. Parent's combined Social Security at FRA is $52,500.
7. Parent's annual living expenses are $90,000.
8. Parents die at age 85.
9. Child's wages are $60,000 annually.
10. Child retires at age 60.
11. Child's Social Security at age 62 is $15,000.
12. Child's spending is $120,000 annually.
13. Reported in actual dollars.

Figure 27.1: **Combine Life Insurance and Roth Conversions to Protect Heirs from the SECURE Act Taxes**

1. Planning parents do five $100,000 Roth conversions.
2. Both parents die at age 85.
3. Child inherits balance of all accounts at age 45.
4. Child lost his savings and retirement plan in divorce.
5. Unmarried child retires at age 60.
6. Unmarried child collects $15,000 in Social Security at age 62, COLAs at 3.0%.
7. Unmarried child spends $120,000 annually.
8. Numbers are in actual dollars.
9. 7% rate of return.
10. 3.5% rate of inflation.

Please note, rates of return are not representative of any particular investment or portfolio of investments and cannot be guaranteed. Portfolios holding securities are subject to risk, including the potential for loss of principal. Actual returns will fluctuate.

Table I: Single Life Expectancy

(For use by beneficiaries)

Age	Life Expectancy	Age	Life Expectancy
0	84.6	31	54.4
1	83.7	32	53.4
2	82.8	33	52.5
3	81.8	34	51.5
4	80.8	35	50.5
5	79.8	36	49.6
6	78.8	37	48.6
7	77.9	38	47.7
8	76.9	39	46.7
9	75.9	40	45.7
10	74.9	41	44.8
11	73.9	42	43.8
12	72.9	43	42.9
13	71.9	44	41.9
14	70.9	45	41.0
15	69.9	46	40.0
16	69.0	47	39.0
17	68.0	48	38.1
18	67.0	49	37.1
19	66.0	50	36.2
20	65.0	51	35.3
21	64.1	52	34.3
22	63.1	53	33.4
23	62.1	54	32.5
24	61.1	55	31.6
25	60.2	56	30.6
26	59.2	57	29.8
27	58.2	58	28.9
28	57.3	59	28.0
29	56.3	60	27.1
30	55.3	61	26.2

Table I: Single Life Expectancy

(For use by beneficiaries—continued)

Age	Life Expectancy	Age	Life Expectancy
62	25.4	92	4.9
63	24.5	93	4.6
64	23.7	94	4.3
65	22.9	95	4.0
66	22.0	96	3.7
67	21.2	97	3.4
68	20.4	98	3.2
69	19.6	99	3.0
70	18.8	100	2.8
71	18.0	101	2.6
72	17.2	102	2.5
73	16.4	103	2.3
74	15.6	104	2.2
75	14.8	105	2.1
76	14.1	106	2.1
77	13.3	107	2.1
78	12.6	108	2.0
79	11.9	109	2.0
80	11.2	110	2.0
81	10.5	111	2.0
82	9.9	112	2.0
83	9.3	113	1.9
84	8.7	114	1.9
85	8.1	115	1.8
86	7.6	116	1.8
87	7.1	117	1.6
88	6.6	118	1.4
89	6.1	119	1.1
90	5.7	120+	1.0
91	5.3		

Table III: Uniform Lifetime

Age	Distribution Period	Age	Distribution Period
72	27.4	97	7.8
73	26.5	98	7.3
74	25.5	99	6.8
75	24.6	100	6.4
76	23.7	101	6.0
77	22.9	102	5.6
78	22.0	103	5.2
79	21.1	104	4.9
80	20.2	105	4.6
81	19.4	106	4.3
82	18.5	107	4.1
83	17.7	108	3.9
84	16.8	109	3.7
85	16.0	110	3.5
86	15.2	111	3.4
87	14.4	112	3.3
88	13.7	113	3.1
89	12.9	114	3.0
90	12.2	115	2.9
91	11.5	116	2.8
92	10.8	117	2.7
93	10.1	118	2.5
94	9.5	119	2.3
95	8.9	120+	2.0
96	8.4		

Table III is for use by:

Unmarried owners.
Married owners whose spouses aren't more than 10 years younger.
Married owners whose spouses aren't the sole beneficiaries of their IRAs.

When your Child has a Disability...
Save More, Have More, and Leave More to Your Child in a Tax-Advantaged Manner that Preserves Government Benefits!

The Lange Edge:
A Truly Integrated Long-Term Financial Masterplan for Parents Who Want to Ensure That Their Child Is Financially Secure for Life— Even After Mom and Dad Are Gone

What if you could embrace the future with confidence knowing you were taking all the right steps to provide for yourself, your partner, your child with a disability, and the rest of your family? It has made a world of difference for me and my wife, Cindy, and our daughter, Erica.

From the time it became clear that our daughter Erica's health problems were a sign of something more serious, we embarked on a crusade. First, to find a diagnosis and any treatment that would help. Then, when it became evident that her health issues were so severe that it was unlikely she would ever be able to work to support herself, we temporarily shifted our focus from taking care of her immediate needs to ensuring she would be safe and financially secure long after we were gone.

Despite our relative financial comfort, our anxiety was *through the roof* worrying about how Erica would manage her life and health when we were no longer around to directly facilitate and finance her daily life. How would she support herself, especially when she got older? These thoughts consumed us.

But we were lucky. In this battle with financial anxieties and fear, we had a big advantage: For the last 39 years I have made my living as a retirement and estate planning CPA/Attorney and financial advisor helping couples plan so they—and their heirs—never run out of money. My specific area of expertise in Roth IRA conversions and minimizing taxes to maximize inherited IRAs and retirement plans after death gave me the perfect background to devise the best plan to provide for Erica.

With the help of a talented team of number crunching CPAs and estate attorneys who practice in this area—plus a lot of grit and determination—we put together a plan for Erica that would provide the relief, money, security, and peace of mind that Cindy and I desperately needed. After Erica was approved for SSDI, and the rest of the plan was put in place, we felt enormous relief. So did Erica. Like many people with a disability, she is prone to anxiety. She confided to me and Cindy that she was also enormously relieved to know she was going to be financially secure for the rest of her life.

And for Cindy and me, having this plan has freed up mental and emotional energy that we can now redirect toward improving the non-financial aspects of Erica's health and well-being.

The difference between being proactive in our planning vs. maintaining the status quo will provide Erica with $1.9 million (in today's dollars) over her lifetime, not including government assistance. (See p. 441 Figure 11.1 for assumptions.)

And especially now that you may have read at least a few portions of the book that are most relevant to your family's particular situation and goals, you might be eager to take the next steps towards securing your and your child's future by incorporating some of the strategies we recommend into your financial planning.

What are The Next Steps?

Some readers will assume they have the capacity and time to implement the strategies they learn from this book by themselves. And to those dyed-in-the-wool do-it-yourselfers, I truly hope you find value in this book and success in implementing some of the recommended strategies. But I'll also urge you to take action now. Don't just read it and think, "That was great information; maybe I'll do something about it later." Because for so many of us, me included, "later" often ends up being "never."

Take action now. A happier, less stressful, and more abundant life awaits.

Other readers may already have an appropriate team of advisors who give you confidence that you are doing all you can. Hopefully, they may have helped you execute many of the strategies we've recommended in the book. But maybe now that you have been presented with so many new strategies that make a lot of sense, you may have some doubts. For example, did your team provide you with a complete analysis of Roth IRA conversion options with recommendations of how much and when to convert? Detailed Roth IRA conversion planning accounted for over a million dollars of additional support for Erica. True, that is more additional benefit than is typical, but large savings are quite common with the right Roth IRA conversion plan. As I mention in the book, we believe that optimizing Roth IRA conversions is a matter of math, not opinion.

If, however, you are not a dyed-in-the-wool do-it-yourselfer and/or you do not have an appropriate team of advisors who have your full confidence, read on to learn how our team can help you implement the long-term financial planning ideas and strategies that have brought my family the relief, money, security, and peace of mind that all parents want, crave, desire, and deserve.

An Easy Path to Financial Success for Parents of a Child with a Disability

Using our expertise and experience, my team and I developed a Financial Masterplan for our family that has ensured that Erica will have an additional $1,890,544 (measured in today's dollars) to support her over her lifetime, and $1,297,500 of that savings came from optimizing our family's Roth IRA conversion strategy.

Our talented team of CPAs and estate planners can provide your family with your own comprehensive individualized Financial Masterplan that can help your family get the most out of what you've got. The Financial Masterplan includes a review of your estate plan and your IRA and retirement plan beneficiary designations. It also includes a detailed "running the numbers" analysis to help optimize the steps you can take now and in the future. Included in the analysis are projections for how much and when to convert an IRA to a Roth IRA, but that is only one of the many strategies we analyze. Legacy planning to minimize taxes over your child's life is mission critical.

We have taken all that we have learned over the years and applied it to the particular circumstances facing parents of children with disabilities. I know firsthand how important it is to get the planning right. It is up to us to safeguard our children's futures.

If you are interested in getting help on the financial strategies including ideal long-term Roth IRA conversion and estate planning strategies and the best use of ABLE accounts, I encourage you to read on and explore whether our firm is the right fit to work with you.

It All Starts with a Meeting with Me

Please note that we operate a boutique office, and there are constraints on both my availability and that of our diligent CPAs. While we aspire to maintain our current process of initial consultations directly with me, our growing workload may limit our ability to do so in the near future.

The details of our consultation are below, but under current circumstances all qualified prospective clients who are parents of a child with a disability will have an *Initial Consultation* (without charge) with me, Jim Lange.

To be clear, you must qualify for an appointment with me. Our office will ask you to complete a questionnaire and provide a list of your assets, and wills, trusts, and beneficiary designations of your IRAs and retirement plans. If you are married, subject to rare exceptions, both spouses must agree to attend the meeting. Your child need not attend but may if you like.

After a preliminary review of your completed questionnaire and a review of your estate plan, if we don't think we can provide enormous value for you and your family, we will not meet. But we WILL send you some extremely useful resources free of charge.

Naturally, as the parent of a child with a disability, I have a strong sense of empathy for the challenges and worries facing other moms and dads of children with disabilities. So if I think we can genuinely help you, we will bend over backwards to do so.

If, after reviewing your family's financial situation and goals, I think you are a good candidate to benefit from our services, our office will coordinate with you to schedule your *Initial Consultation* meeting. To that meeting, I will bring my expertise as a CPA and my knowledge of estate planning as a nearly 39-year veteran CPA, estate attorney, and strategist for IRA and retirement plan owners. One of our "number crunching" CPAs will also attend the meeting.

I have held a countless number of these free consultations over the years, including many with people who flew in from distant parts of the country to meet in our Pittsburgh offices. No one has ever said or even hinted that it wasn't worth their time. That said, as a courtesy to me, our team, and other parents who know they want our help, if you know in advance of scheduling a meeting with me that you are not really interested in working with us, we respectfully request that you do not sign up for a consultation.

At the end of our meeting, I will summarize our discussion and make valuable suggestions. If I don't think we can provide enormous value—certainly worth many times your investment for our services—I will tell you and still provide you with the written summary. This summary in and of itself can provide enormous value.

If I think we would be a good fit to work together, and you would like to work with us, towards the end of the consultation, I will propose a plan of action.

I would like to emphasize that, at least at this point in time, your Initial Consultation is with me. You would literally be meeting with the guy who wrote the book on helping families of children with disabilities maximize their retirement and estate plan. (I have also written eight other best-selling financial books for IRA owners). You would also be meeting with one of our experienced CPAs who also worked on this book with me. That number-crunching CPA will be the person who does most of the work on your Financial Masterplan if we all agree this would be a valuable engagement for you and your family.

There are Two Paths to Developing a Financial Masterplan

PATH 1: Working with Lange Accounting Group, LLC[1] to Develop a Financial Masterplan Without Assets-Under-Management

We offer a pure fee-for-service Financial Masterplan without a money management component. For a one-time professional services fee between $12,500 and $25,000 (most often around $20,000), depending on the level of complexity and time required. For that fee, I and one of our CPAs can help you develop a Financial Masterplan without entering into an assets-under-management (AUM) arrangement. It is also likely we will make significant recommendations regarding your estate plan. In this model, you implement our recommendations and handle the investments without our ongoing support and continuing services.[2]

How We Work with You

First and foremost, we make sure your long-term financial, retirement, and legacy planning are totally on track. You will be working with a caring, smart, tax-savvy CPA, who works in this area and will be very proactive in their advice; all our CPAs are fiduciaries *who are required to act in your best interest.* We will make sure you're not going to make costly tax mistakes. And we will provide you with tax-saving strategies and ideas you might never have considered.

----

1 Lange Accounting Group, LLC, offers guidance on retirement plan distribution strategies, tax reduction, Roth IRA conversions, saving and spending strategies, optimized Social Security strategies, and gifting plans. Although we bring our knowledge and expertise in estate planning into our recommendations, they are only offered in our capacity as financial planning professionals and not as attorneys. We will likely make recommendations, however, that clients could have a licensed estate attorney implement.

2   Please note that if you engage Lange Accounting Group for our Financial Masterplan development services, you are not engaging us to be your attorney, nor do we act as your attorney, and the protection of the attorney/client relationship does not exist in this advisory context. If we make estate planning recommendations, we give you the option of sharing our recommendations with either your existing estate attorney, a different estate attorney, or one that we might recommend.

"Running The Numbers" Provides Invaluable Information and Direction

One critical component of developing a Financial Masterplan is *running the numbers*. "Running the numbers" is our shorthand for testing a variety of strategies to see which will work best for you and your family. For example, we may test many Roth IRA conversion options, ABLE options, "Who Gets What" strategies (see p. 335), some variation of Lange's Cascading Beneficiary Plan (see p. 285), different accumulation and distribution strategies, and gifting options. Of course we also test different Social Security, and Medicare strategies too, as well as many more estate planning strategies covered in the book, and some that are not mentioned in the book, because they are very specific to particular circumstances. Of course, your hopes and dreams for your own retirement and your legacy planning are critical components. Most likely the best solution will be some combination of a number of these and other strategies.

We use a variety of specialized software programs, as well as our in-house tax preparation software, and our special applications in Excel˚ to aid us in this analysis. But it is my expertise plus the expertise of our highly qualified number-crunching CPAs that really makes the difference.

My assessments and recommendations, based on your goals and circumstances, serve as the starting point, and then the ideas are tested and, frankly, challenged by our top-level CPAs who do the actual analysis. You are very much a part of the process, and you will give input, and get personalized guidance, from our CPAs who are analyzing and calculating the outcomes of different financial scenarios.

Our process is unique and performed by the Lange team of highly skilled CPAs, the same CPAs who helped with the quantitative analysis in this book.

This process usually takes several meetings and much back-and-forth analysis.

While this may seem like a lot of information, be assured our initial discussion is followed by a summary memo from me to you, our number crunching CPA, and possibly your attorney.

"What If" Scenarios

When we run the numbers, a major component involves projecting scenarios for your financial future—and your child's. During these sessions our experienced CPA, in conjunction with you and your spouse, quantify *what you have, what you and your family will have given the status quo using reasonable assumptions,* and *what you and your family could have* with different strategic steps that you could take under our guidance.

Since you are in the room—in person or virtually—when we do at least part of the work, you will know how and why we arrive at the recommendations we make for you. We typically start broadly, but eventually narrow the possibilities to a few choices. Typically, we identify our preferred solution, and provide you with our recommendations, calculations, and reasoning. Once we agree on a preferred course of action, we double check our work and recreate your tax return. By plugging in our best solutions, we can identify potential tax conflicts—perhaps due to Medicare Income-Related Monthly Adjustment (IRRMA) amounts—to give us additional information to make the wisest plan. Of course, the plan will reflect your goals and desires. Ultimately, the decision of what to do is yours.

How We Summarize Our Analysis for You

What we don't give you is 70 pages of computer-generated mumbo jumbo.

Our projections are clearly summarized. We outline which scenarios seem best for your situation and why. We also give you the spreadsheets to see how we arrived at our conclusions. Ultimately, you get to choose your path, but we are guiding you through the entire process and empower you to make great decisions.

As part of the Financial Masterplan development process, we will also review your estate plan and, when appropriate, make recommendations regarding updates or changes that could be made to optimize your plan.[3] Now we may find that the plans you already have in place do the job. But frankly, that is rare. More often, they require vetting, changes, and updates. Our goal is to make sure your estate plan is optimized for your situation and consistent with the Financial Masterplan we develop.

If you are interested in working with us to develop your family's Personalized Financial Masterplan on a fee-for-services basis there are four easy ways to request your complementary *Initial Consultation* with me.

By Phone: Call toll-free **1-800-387-1129**.

Online: Visit **https://PayTaxesLater.com/NextSteps** and complete the form.

By Mail: Erin Einwag, Client Services Coordinator
Lange Accounting Group, LLC
2200 Murray Avenue
Pittsburgh, PA 15217

By Fax: Complete the form on page 458 and fax to **412-521-2285**

---

3 Although we will bring our knowledge and expertise in estate planning to that review, it will be conducted in our capacity as your financial planning professionals. We will not be acting as your attorneys and there will not be the protection of an attorney/client relationship with respect to these services. However, we will likely make recommendations that you could have a licensed estate attorney implement. There is no solicitation for legal services being made by me, James Lange, nor by Lange Legal Group, LLC.

PATH 2: Put Your Financial Success on Autopilot as an Assets-Under-Management Client

If, after our first meeting, you are interested in an assets-under-management (AUM) arrangement, you will have a second meeting with the number-crunching CPA who was in the first meeting, and our recommended affiliated money manager. Lange Financial Group does not manage money. We leave the money management to our strategic partners so they can do what they do best. But collectively, we need to agree that the working relationship is a good fit.

Becoming an assets-under-management client is often the best choice. Currently, the Financial Masterplan as described above is just one component of a package of services that recur annually.[1] The Financial Masterplan is included as part of the service our CPAs provide at no additional cost to you. You pay the money manager their standard fee which starts at 1% of the assets under management, but the percentage may decrease depending on how much money is invested. They pay us a portion of the fee you pay them. We consider this a win/win/win arrangement. That is, the money management firm gets a client they would otherwise never have met. We get paid for the value we add and our time. You get an excellent money management team as well as ongoing reviews of your Financial Masterplan for the same price as paying a money manager without our additional value.

With annual reviews, our CPAs can work with you to adjust your Financial Masterplan to account for any of your financial and life changes as well as any tax law changes that may have an impact on your plan.

By becoming an AUM client, you get the Financial Masterplan described above as the starting point. Then, at a minimum, our office, typically the CPA who did the work on the Masterplan, provides an annual review; you will potentially have more frequent reviews with the money management firm.

We work closely with an elite group of top investment advisory firms that bring the same kind of dedication and concentration to their field as we do to ours. Our strategic partners follow a core investment philosophy rooted in the findings of Modern Portfolio Theory. That theory says that the best way to manage risk in an investment portfolio is through proper diversification within a broad asset allocation strategy. Our partners follow an academic approach to money management that is rooted in the best academic thinking, and they will work

---

1   Financial Masterplans prepared by Lange Accounting Group, LLC for assets-under-management clients are completed in consideration for the portion of the client's account management fee that Lange Financial Group receives from the investment advisor and at no additional charge to the client.

closely with you to understand your financial goals and risk tolerance which will be used to develop an asset allocation designed to generate long-term returns that allow you to achieve your financial goals. As mentioned above, we leave the money management to our strategic partners so they can do what they do best.

As part of our AUM service, we help get the different components of your plan in order, and your assets are continually evaluated for asset allocation and asset location by the investment advisory firm.

You'll meet, usually virtually, with the money management firm's team, usually more often than once a year. At those meetings, you and your money manager will review portfolio asset allocation and investment strategies and track whether you are still on course to meet your financial goals.

Importantly, our investment partners do much more than simply manage the money. They have their own processes that support effective planning to help you reach your financial, retirement, and life goals. Yes, there is some redundancy between what they do and what we do, but, again, that is a good thing—a valuable "second opinion."

---

1 Asset location, asset allocation and low-cost enhanced index funds are provided by the Lange Financial Group, LLC's affiliated investment firms. All services are offered in our role as an investment advisor representative and not as an attorney. The protection of the attorney/client relationship does not exist with respect to these services. There is no solicitation for legal services being made by me, James Lange, nor by Lange Legal Group, LLC.

Lange Financial Group, LLC is a registered investment advisory firm registered with the Commonwealth of Pennsylvania Department of Banking, Harrisburg, Pennsylvania. In addition, the firm is registered as a registered investment advisory firm in the states of Arizona, Florida, New York, Ohio, Texas, and Virginia. Registration does not imply a certain level of skill or training. Lange Financial Group may not provide investment advisory services to any residents of states in which the firm does not maintain an investment advisory registration. This does not in any way imply that Lange Financial Group is failing to preserve its rights under the respective states' de minimis rule. The presence of this book shall not in any direct or indirect fashion, be construed or interpreted to suggest that the firm is offering to sell or soliciting to provide investment advisory services to residents of any state or states in which the firm is not maintaining an investment advisory registration. Again, Lange Financial Group preserves all rights under each state's de minimis rule but wishes to emphasize that it is not directly or indirectly soliciting investment advisory clients in states where it has no legal right to do so.

All investing involves risk, including the potential for loss of principal. There is never any guarantee extended that any investment plan or strategy will be successful.

☑ ***Yes****, **Jim***, I want to provide lifetime financial security for me, my partner, and especially for our child with a disability for the rest of their life.

In particular, I'm interested in (check all that apply):

☐ Initial Consultation that includes assets-under-management.

☐ Initial Consultation for a Personalized Financial Masterplan that doesn't include assets-under-management.

Name _____

Address _____

City _____ State _____ Zip _____

Phone _____ Email _____

4 Easy Ways to Respond:

By Phone:	Call toll-free **1-800-387-1129**.
By Fax:	Fax this completed form to **412-521-2285**
Online:	Visit **https://PayTaxesLater.com/NextSteps**
By Mail:	Erin Einwag
	Lange Accounting Group, LLC
	2200 Murray Avenue
	Pittsburgh, PA 15217

Please read all disclaimers in the footnotes for this section of the book.

Protect Your Legacy from Taxes While Still Preserving Government Benefits

By Julieanne E. Steinbacher, Esq.

Deborah wrote about how critical it is to have your child approved for SSI or SSDI and how important it is to maintain that status even after you die. Jim wrote about how critical it is (though not in every case) to make a series of Roth IRA conversions and have your inherited Roth IRA or even traditional IRA or retirement plan be "stretched" over your child's life expectancy. He also wrote that the difference between doing this right and not getting it right could be hundreds of thousands of dollars or more for your child with a disability.

But, if you don't have the right language in your special needs trusts, which is one of the common solutions we recommend, two terrible things could happen:

1. **Your child could lose their government benefits or worse, the government goes into your legacy for money they already paid.**

2. **Your child loses the "Inherited stretch Roth or Traditional IRA" status causing immediate distribution and in the case of the traditional IRA massive acceleration of income taxes.**

Did you know that special needs trusts must meet four technical conditions to qualify for the "stretch" treatment?

Thus, the attorney drafting these documents must know the right language to protect the stretch and comply with the four conditions, as well as, getting the language right to protect government programs.

Not only that, but the attorney must know how to fill out the beneficiary form for the IRA and Roth IRA, with precision or bad things could happen after you are gone.

It would be a tragedy (this is not an exaggeration) if your child ran out of money after you were gone because the attorney didn't use the exact right language.

In addition to getting the mechanics and the language right, this is an area that requires a lot of judgment. You want the attorney to have years of experience in this field and be used to getting involved in nitty gritty judgment issues.

For example, I often hear:

"Don't give any inheritance to your child with special needs."

"Give money for your child with special needs to their sibling to hold for them and use for them."

This is advice that is given by attorneys and other professionals to parents who have children who have special needs. I find it frustrating. In my opinion, it's the worst advice that can be given to the parents who are trying to plan for their child who has special needs. What if the sibling gets divorced? What if the sibling passes away or becomes sick themselves? What if while on benefits, the child with a special need requires money for something? The fact is that the child who has a special need may need the money more than any other child. They certainly deserve a better plan than solely relying on changing governmental benefits that are subject to political change.

A child who has special needs deserves their parents to have a conversation with a special needs planning attorney about what is necessary, what the care needs look like in the future, and what is really fair for that child and the whole family. For me being an attorney who helps families plan for children who have special needs is a privilege that allows me to help them design a successful way forward. This plan includes good estate planning documents such as powers of attorneys, last will and testaments, guardianships, and special needs trust. But more important than those documents are the conversations and plan for a way forward. Helping the family construct a "Summary of Our Wishes" that directs the care and future needs of the child who has special needs is important to help after the parent is no longer able to advocate and direct the care.

At our firm, we have served families with special needs children in all stages of life, from those who are still children and those who are adults, whether dependent, independent or interdependent. We are able to maximize benefits, reduce overall taxes and provide a plan for the best transition. We help make sure that families get all the benefits that they are able to use. For those who have applied for SSI or SSDI or Veterans Benefits for those with dependent children, and have been denied, our law firm does appeals and often are able to successfully obtain these benefits.

We offer counseling on first party special needs trust, third party special needs trusts, powers of attorney, and guardianships. We also work with the family one on one to understand the diagnosis, the needs of those who have special needs and what the family support options are at the time. We evaluate what any future costs of care can include to get good care. Parents with children with special needs should work with a law firm who understands this highly complex area of law while also using the support of social workers to make a plan forward for care that is individualized to the needs of the child with special needs and the goals of the family. An important planning consideration for anyone with a child who has a special needs is understanding that in most areas of the country assets can be transferred to a child with special needs or to a trust for their benefit even after their parent goes into a nursing home. The law is written to support the child with special needs and not subject the parent to the 5-year look back period that many are aware of and concerned about.

As part of our planning, we always include the child with special needs, and evaluate the use of guardianship or power of attorney for the child who has special needs. We utilize mental health powers of attorney, living wills, health care powers of attorney and financial powers of attorney. Often with some other law firms focusing on estate planning, the planning of the child themselves is not addressed or one of these documents is missing.

Investing the time to build a plan is essential for the best financial outcome and the best transition for the child with special needs. Having conversations about what will happen when the parent becomes ill or passes away makes the transition easier because there is a plan in place with options that have been thought through and communicated. For the child with special needs and the whole family, it is important to start the planning process now. At the cornerstone of our plan is solid legal documents to protect your goals and your loved ones needs. We look forward to helping you or those you know get the best plan in place for their loved one.

Please note our legal services are limited to residents of Pennsylvania.

Additional Related Services—SSI and SSDI Appeals (not limited to Residents of Pennsylvania)

I agree with my co-author Deborah McFadden. It is best to qualify on the first application for SSI or SSDI. But, that usually doesn't happen. Then what? You can appeal. Jim Lange's wife Cindy was the main person who literally spent thousands of hours appealing the initial rejection for their daughter. The first attorney they hired made a mess. If you have applied for SSI or SSDI for your child and been rejected, you can appeal that decision. Although that process is not covered in this book, it is something we do as part of our law practice.

Additional Related Services—Social Worker (not limited to residents of Pennsylvania)

We have social workers on staff because our clients don't just need legal services, they also often require the services of a social worker that works closely with their estate attorney. I was a social worker before I became a lawyer. That experience helped me understand clients much better and allowed me to hire the most appropriate social workers that are often needed. For example, we helped Jim Lange's daughter get approved for benefits in Massachusetts due to our social workers' expertise in getting insurance applications approved.

Contact Information for

Julieanne E. Steinbacher, Esq., CELA*

STEINBACHER, GOODALL & YURCHAK
Your elder care and special needs law firm
Quality representation in litigation

- Legal Planning
- Estate Planning
- Long-Term Care Pre-Planning
- Guardianship
- Nursing Home Medicaid Planning
- Veterans Benefits Planning

- Special Needs Planning
- Wealth Protection & Tax Planning
- Dementia & Alzheimer's Planning
- Business Succession Planning
- Estate Administration & Probate

More information for legal services can be found at https://www.paeldercounsel.com/. Relevant information that is not limited to PA residents can be found at https://www.planningandprotecting.com/.

Fellow, American College of Trust and Estate Counsel
Fellow, National Academy of Elder Law Attorneys

Our commitment to clients is realized through our Core Values of Quality, Service, Integrity, and Empathy provided in a relationship that values mutual trust.

6 locations across Central, PA

Williamsport, PA
413 Washington Blvd
Williamsport, PA 17701
570-322-2077

Wyalusing, PA
243 Second St., P.O. Box 114,
Wyalusing, PA 18853
570-746-3844

State College, PA
328 S Atherton St
State College, PA 16801
814-237-4100

Wysox, PA
1864 Golden Mile Rd.
Wysox, PA 18854
570-265-1800

Altoona, PA
1913 East Pleasant Valley Blvd.
Altoona, PA 16602
814-900-7613

Wilkes-Barre, PA
273 East Northampton St.
Wilkes-Barre, PA 18702
570-266-7034

Special Section for Parents of a Child with a Disability Who Has Not Yet Qualified for SSI/SSDI or Vocational Rehabilitation

By Deborah L. McFadden

The first step of virtually all the planning recommended in this book is getting your child approved for SSI or SSDI.

The Social Security Administration states that 65% of people applying for the first time were denied in 2022. After a denial, the appeals process is long and difficult and potentially very expensive. It is much better to get approval on the first application. The vast majority of the parents (95%) who hire me to get their child on SSI/SSDI and Vocational Rehabilitation (VR) are approved on their initial applications.

Not only is qualifying for SSI/SSDI a critical prerequisite for virtually all of the strategic planning recommendations that my co-authors and I have made in this book. The value your child could derive from SSI/SSDI and Vocational Rehabilitation alone is significant.

So, for a moment, let's set aside the hundreds of thousands of dollars (or more) in financial benefits that a child with a disability could receive over their lifetime if you incorporate some combination of the tax and estate planning strategies that Jim and Julie have shared in this book, and just focus on the potential value of SSI/SSDI and VR benefits.

Here's a conservative hypothetical example of the monetary value of the benefits my clients have received from SSI/SSDI and VR programs:

This example assumes that the hypothetical client is attending college[1] during the period of time that these benefit calculations cover.

----

1   According to the most recent data on undergraduate retention and graduation rates published by the National Center for Education Statistics (NCES), in the US the average student takes 6 years to earn a 4-year undergraduate degree. For the summary of benefits below I've assumed client spends 5 years pursuing postsecondary education.

$11,316[2] per year in SSI benefits
- SSI 5-year Total: = $56,580

Between $10,000 and $40,000[3] per year in VR benefits
- VR 5-year Total: Between $50,000 and $200,000

Student Loan Forgiveness on **$5,500** per year in subsidized and unsubsidized Federal Student Loans
- **Student Loan Forgiveness 5-year Total: = $27,500**

Total 5-year Value of SSI/SSDI & VR Benefits Received: Between $134,080 and $284,080

I also routinely help clients find and secure additional funding for college from scholarship programs, which has led to clients receiving more than **$434,080** in **total assistance.**

The totals in this example also do not include any estimation of the benefits a client could receive from other governmental programs that their SSI/SSDI status could qualify them for, namely Medicaid and Supplemental Nutrition Assistance Program (SNAP).

The Vocational Rehabilitation benefits and supports are available to help your child get a job which includes training through technical programs as well.

Generally, your child can stay on SSI until there is a major life event change such as getting a job. But if they will never work taking today's dollars from the age of 18 to 65 this has a cash value of more than $531,382.

I help parents from across the United States. If your child with a disability has not yet

qualified for SSI/SSDI or Vocational Rehabilitation and you are interested in learning more about my services, I encourage you to read the summary below that describes who can benefit most from those services.

....

2   Determined using current, 2024, SSI Federal Benefit Rate of $943 per month.
3   Maximum annual VR benefits vary by state, with $40,000 being the highest and $10,000 the lowest.

Here is a description of the parents I can help the most:

- Your child is at least 18 years old.

- Your child is a US citizen.

- Your child has a permanent disability that is expected to last a lifetime.

- Your child is not able to work or only is able to earn a small amount below what Social Security **calls a Substantial Gainful Activity (SGA). In 2023 the monthly earnings are limited to $1,470.**

- You are willing to put in the time and effort required to get letters from your child's doctors. *(I can give you guidance on what they should be writing, but I can't contact your doctors, teachers at school, etc., so you must be willing and able to put in that time and effort.)*

Contact Information for
Deborah L. McFadden
Former U.S. Commissioner of Disabilities

If you would like to learn more about me, my services, and how you could work with me you can:

Visit **https://AbilitiesCount.com**

Email me at **info@AbilitiesCount.com**

Or call me at **301-495-9710**

About the Authors

About James Lange, CPA/Attorney

Jim is the author of nine financial books that help IRA and retirement plan owners make the most of what they have. The *Wall Street Journal* has endorsed his tax and estate planning strategies on 36 different occasions.

His most recent book *Retire Secure for Professors and TIAA Participants* was published in October 2023.

Jim has an undeniable investment in the financial planning recommendations he and his coauthors endorse. Jim and his wife, Cindy Lange, have a young adult daughter, Erica Lange. Erica has dysautonomia which makes it impossible for her to earn an independent living. Structuring a plan for her long-term financial security became a priority as soon as the diagnosis was confirmed. Before they had a plan, worry and sleepless nights consumed their lives. Their first resolve—which turned into a monumental effort—was to get Erica qualified for SSDI. The next step was to get the estate planning right. Then, given Jim's extensive background in Roth IRA conversions and the negative impact of the SECURE Act on retirement assets, he devised a solution to ensure her continued financial security long after they were gone. In his daughter's case, given certain reasonable assumptions, after Jim and Cindy die, she will be better off by $1.9 million in today's dollars (not including government benefits) than if Jim and Cindy had not been proactive in their planning.

When he realized how critical—potentially life changing—his solution could be for other parents of a child with a disability, his drive to write yet one more book became a mission. It was the best way he knew to get the information to the millions of parents who could benefit. He partnered with his two co-authors to create what all three of them think is the best resource for a parent or parents who want to ensure the long-term financial security of their child with a disability.

Jim's most recent book, **Retire Secure for Professors and TIAA Participants**, features a glowing foreword written by the distinguished economist, Burton Malkiel, most noted for his classic finance book *A Random Walk Down Wall Street*, which sold more than a million copies. His book has also received endorsements from other top financial experts including Bob Keebler, Jim Dahle, Steve Leimberg, Larry Swedroe, and many more. Other books have received endorsements from Charles Schwab, Larry King (who wrote the foreword for the third edition of **Retire Secure!**), Ed Slott, Jane Bryant Quinn, Roger Ibbotson, and Jonathan Clements and more than fifty other financial luminaries.

Jim lives in Pittsburgh in his family home with his wife of 30 years, Cindy. Cindy has a master's degree in electrical engineering from Carnegie Mellon University. When Jim is not devising strategies for clients and readers to save taxes, preserve wealth, and protect their families' financial security (which is most of the time) he enjoys bicycling, hiking, and traveling with family and friends. He also plays chess and bridge both online and with friends.

About Julieanne E. Steinbacher, Esq., CELA, LLM in Estate and Elder Law

Julieanne E. Steinbacher, Esq., CELA, is the founding shareholder of Steinbacher, Goodall & Yurchak, an elder care and special needs planning law firm, with offices in Williamsport, State College, Wyalusing and Wysox, Wilkes-Barre, and Altoona PA.

As a former social worker, she has seen the devastating effects the lack of planning for long-term care can have on a family. As an attorney, her goal is to educate the community and empower them to make planning decisions. Each of her law offices has social workers on staff to help families coordinate care and benefits. She can represent people appealing SSI or SSDI rejections in 50 states. She has over 20 years of experience drafting special needs planning documents for families and administering estates.

Prior to becoming an attorney, Julieanne was employed by AARP and as a geriatric social worker at Valley View Nursing Facility. As an attorney, her goal is to provide a bridge between legal services and the aging network. Julieanne is Certified as an Elder Law Attorney (CELA) by the National Elder Law Foundation. In 2008, she developed The Elder & Special Needs Resource Center in Williamsport, which hosts frequent public seminars to educate the public. She has co-authored The Pennsylvania Trust Guide (Editions I and II), The Pennsylvania Special Needs Planning Guide, as well as several books in a Protect Your Family series that inform people about planning for the second half of life. Julieanne is founder and president of Estate & Long-Term Care Planning, an organization that educates estate attorneys from across the nation in areas of law and best practices.

About Deborah L. McFadden

As a person with a disability, Deborah McFadden has been a tireless advocate for disabled individuals and their families for her entire career, working to improve the lives of people with physical and cognitive challenges. She is founder and President of Abilities Count, an organization dedicated to increasing the "competitive edge" of people with disabilities in public recognition, access to higher education, equitable pay, sponsorships, and full inclusion.

She was one of the original 12 authors of the Americans with Disabilities Act and was appointed by President George H.W. Bush as U.S. Commissioner of Disabilities, a position she held from 1989-1993. At the time, she was the highest-ranking female Presidential Appointee with a disability in government service. For years, she has been working with individuals with disabilities to help them secure SSI, SSDI, and other crucial resources they are entitled to and is a nationally recognized spokesperson for these programs.

She is the mother of two USA Paralympic athletes. Her daughter Hannah is ranked third in the world in rock climbing and participated alongside her sister Tatyana as a wheelchair racer at the London Paralympics in 2012. Tatyana is the most honored and recognized athlete with a disability in the world. In high school, Tatyana, with her mother's support, filed a lawsuit against Howard County Public Schools and forced the high school to treat her as an equal member of the track team. This led to passage of the Fitness and Equity Act in Maryland, which became a federal mandate during the Obama Administration, forever changing the face of middle and high school sports.

She has worked nationally and internationally as a consultant and advisor to create policies and strategies to achieve full integration into society for people with disabilities. She has also worked to raise funds to support orphaned and abandoned children, including placement of more than 2,000 children with families throughout the United States.

Deborah McFadden holds a Bachelor of Science degree in Special Education from the University of Maryland with additional studies at the London School of Economics, Gallaudet University Graduate School, and Bucknell University. She is fluent in sign language.